Takane & Hana

10

STORY AND ART BY

Yuki Shiwasu

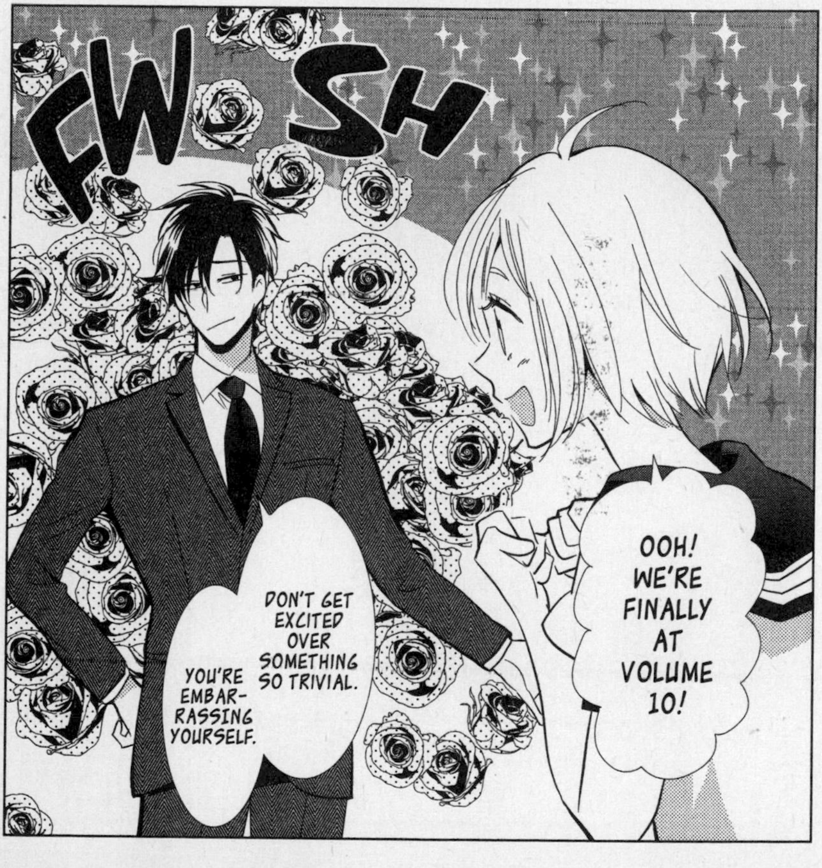
FWSH
OOH! WE'RE FINALLY AT VOLUME 10!
DON'T GET EXCITED OVER SOMETHING SO TRIVIAL.
YOU'RE EMBAR-RASSING YOURSELF.

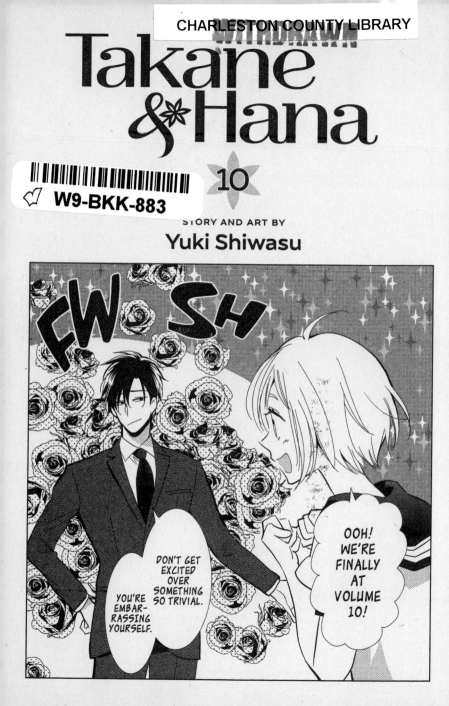

Takane &✳Hana

10

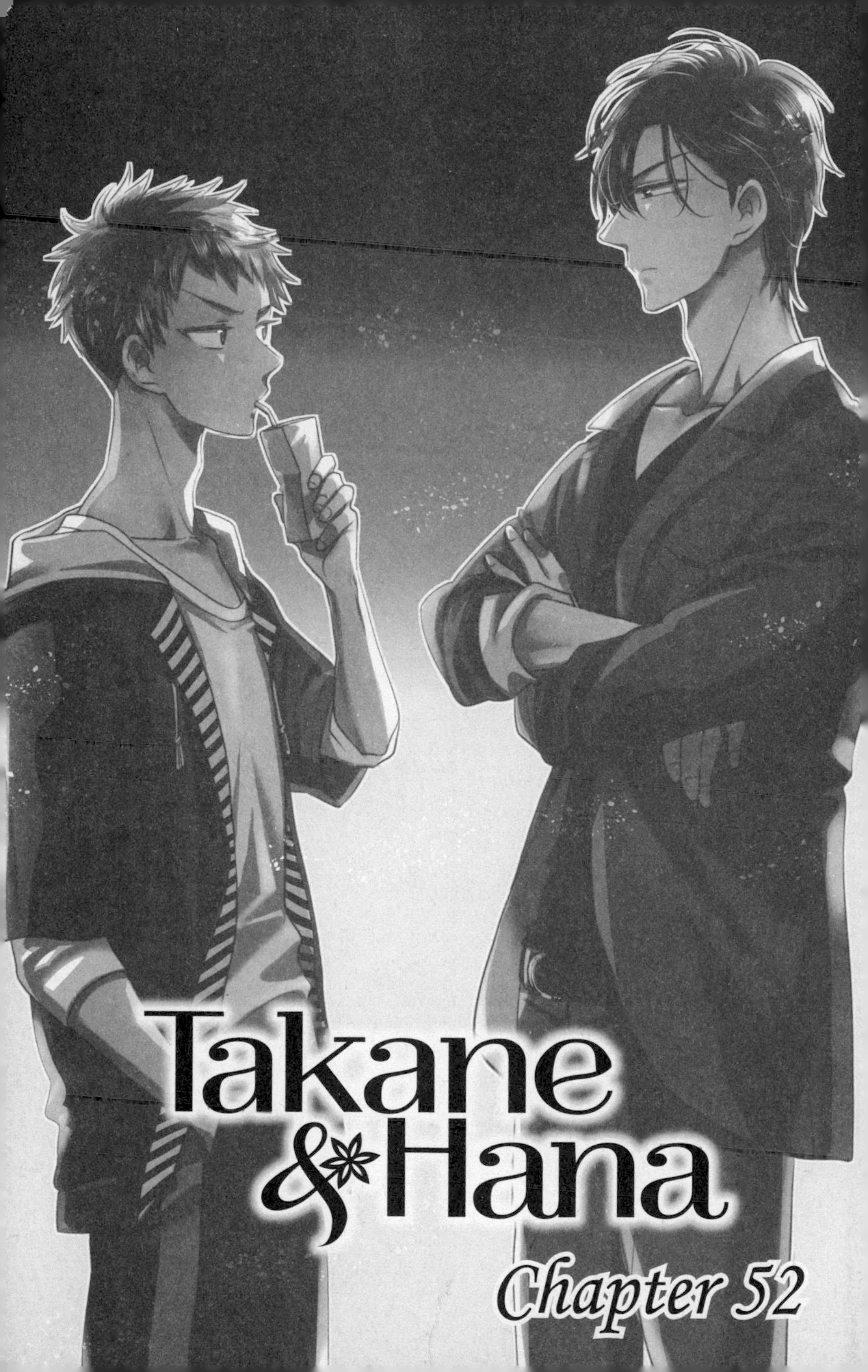
Takane & Hana
Chapter 52

Eiji Kirigasaki's Job Responsibilities

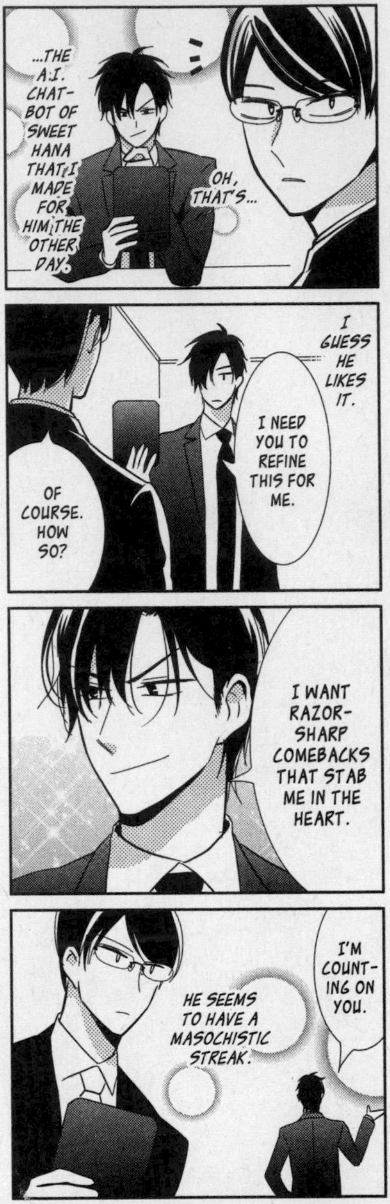
OH, THAT'S...
...THE A.I. CHATBOT OF SWEET HANA THAT I MADE FOR HIM THE OTHER DAY.
I GUESS HE LIKES IT.
I NEED YOU TO REFINE THIS FOR ME.
OF COURSE. HOW SO?
I WANT RAZOR-SHARP COMEBACKS THAT STAB ME IN THE HEART.
I'M COUNTING ON YOU.
HE SEEMS TO HAVE A MASOCHISTIC STREAK.

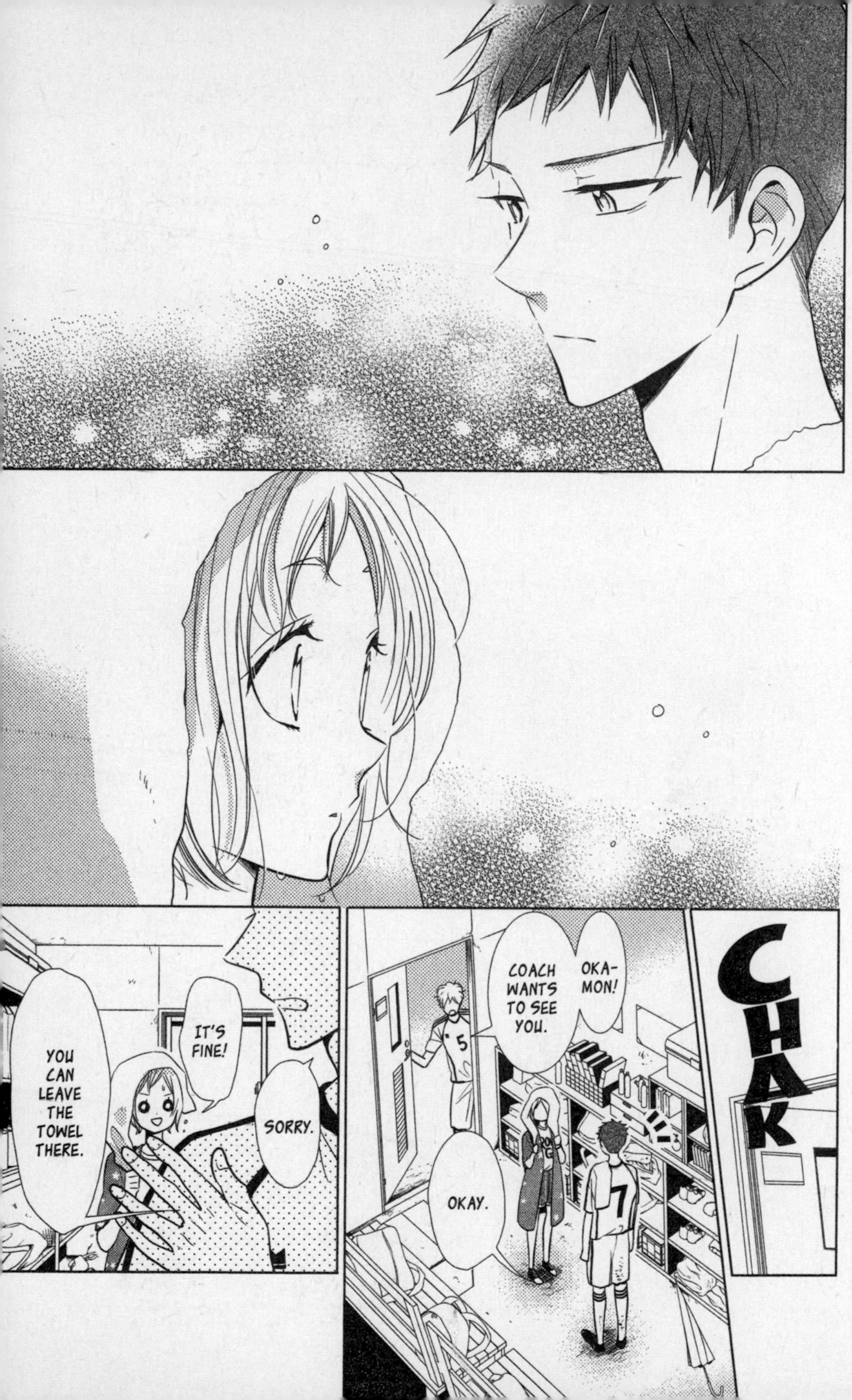
CHAK
OKA-MON!
COACH WANTS TO SEE YOU.
OKAY.
IT'S FINE!
SORRY.
YOU CAN LEAVE THE TOWEL THERE.

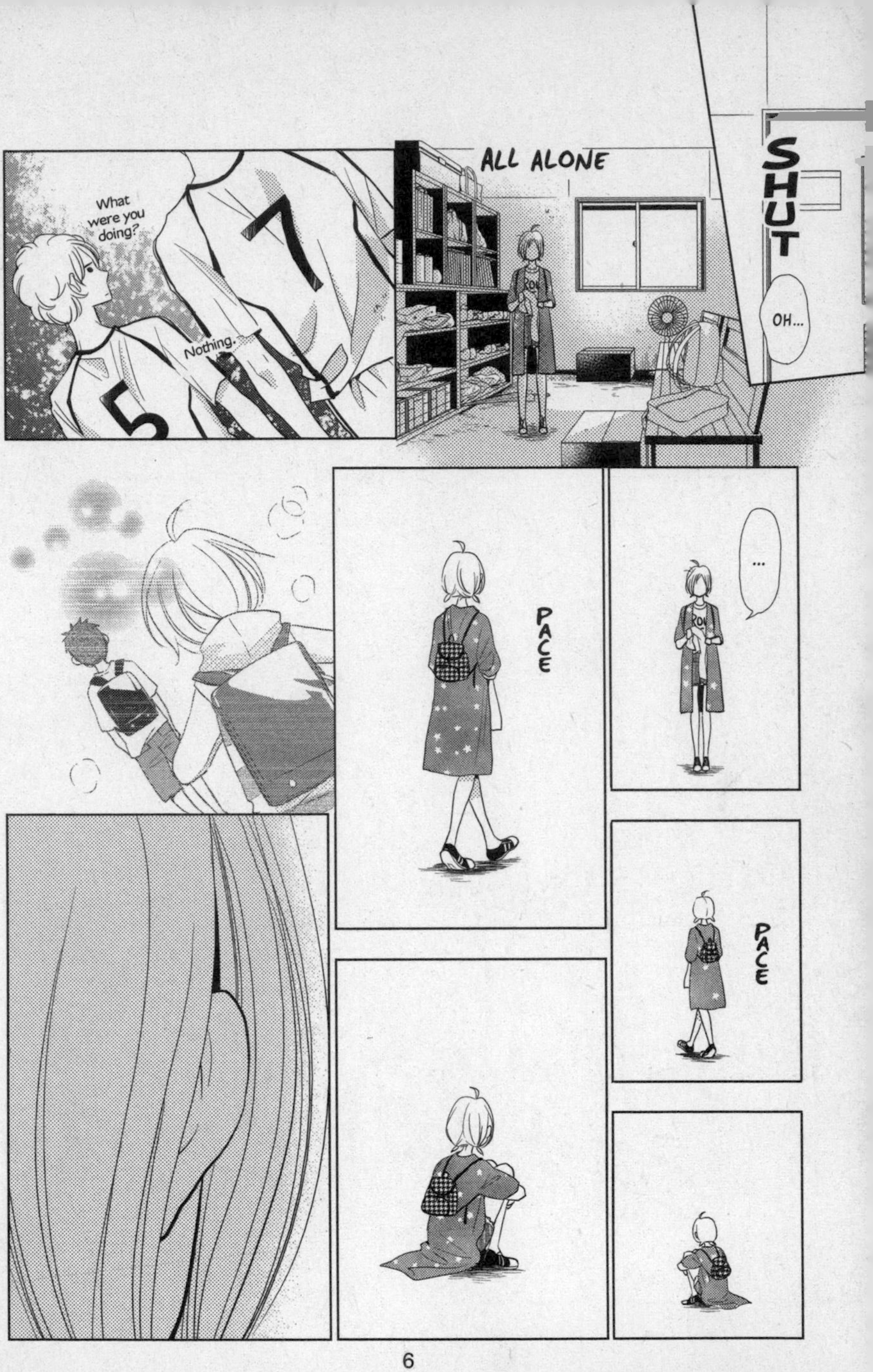
SHUT
OH...
ALL ALONE
What were you doing?
Nothing.
...
PACE
PACE

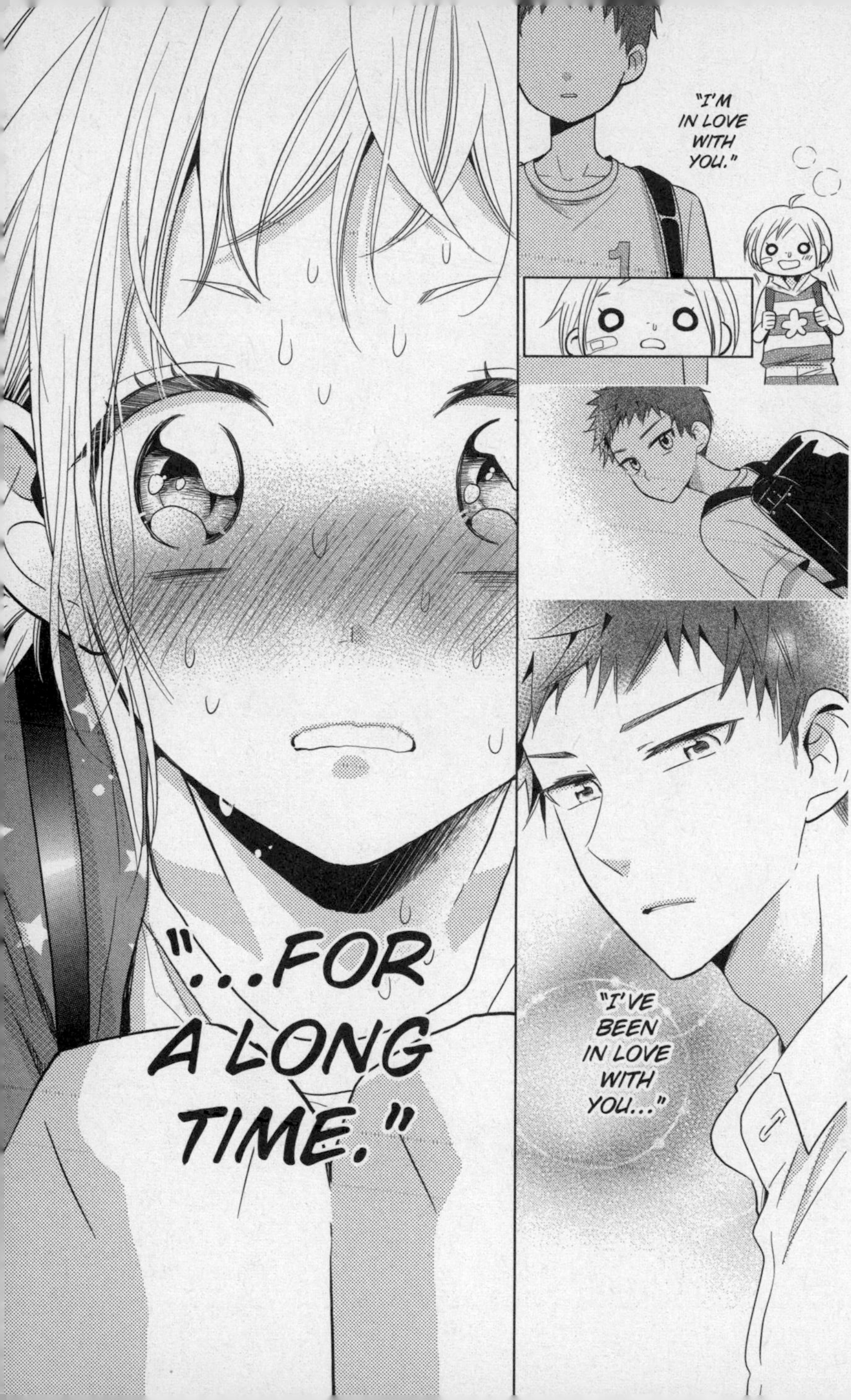
"I'M IN LOVE WITH YOU."
"I'VE BEEN IN LOVE WITH YOU..."
"...FOR A LONG TIME."

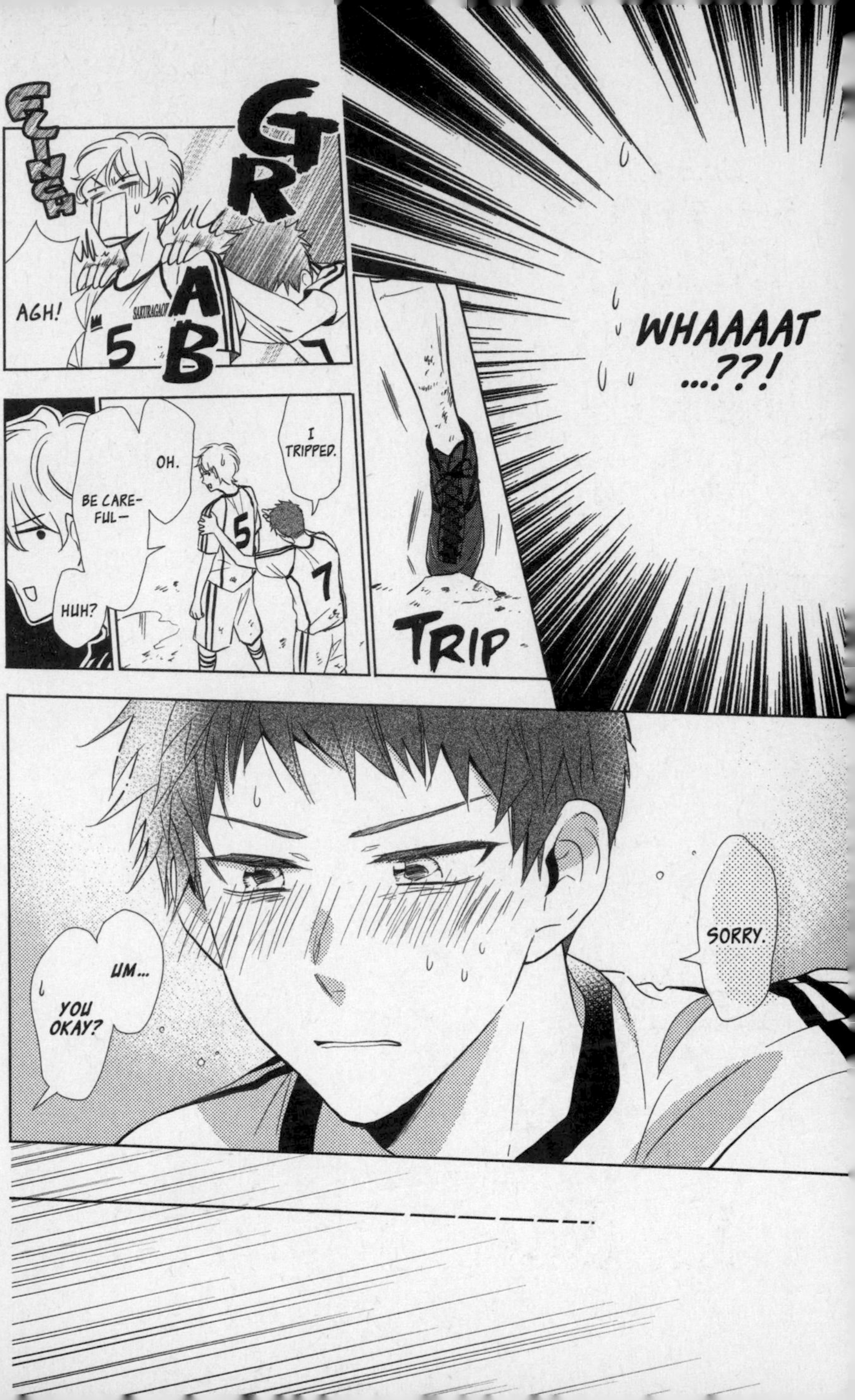
TRIP
FLINCH
GRAB
AGH!
I TRIPPED.
OH.
BE CARE-FUL—
HUH?
WHAAAAT ...??!
SORRY.
UM... YOU OKAY?

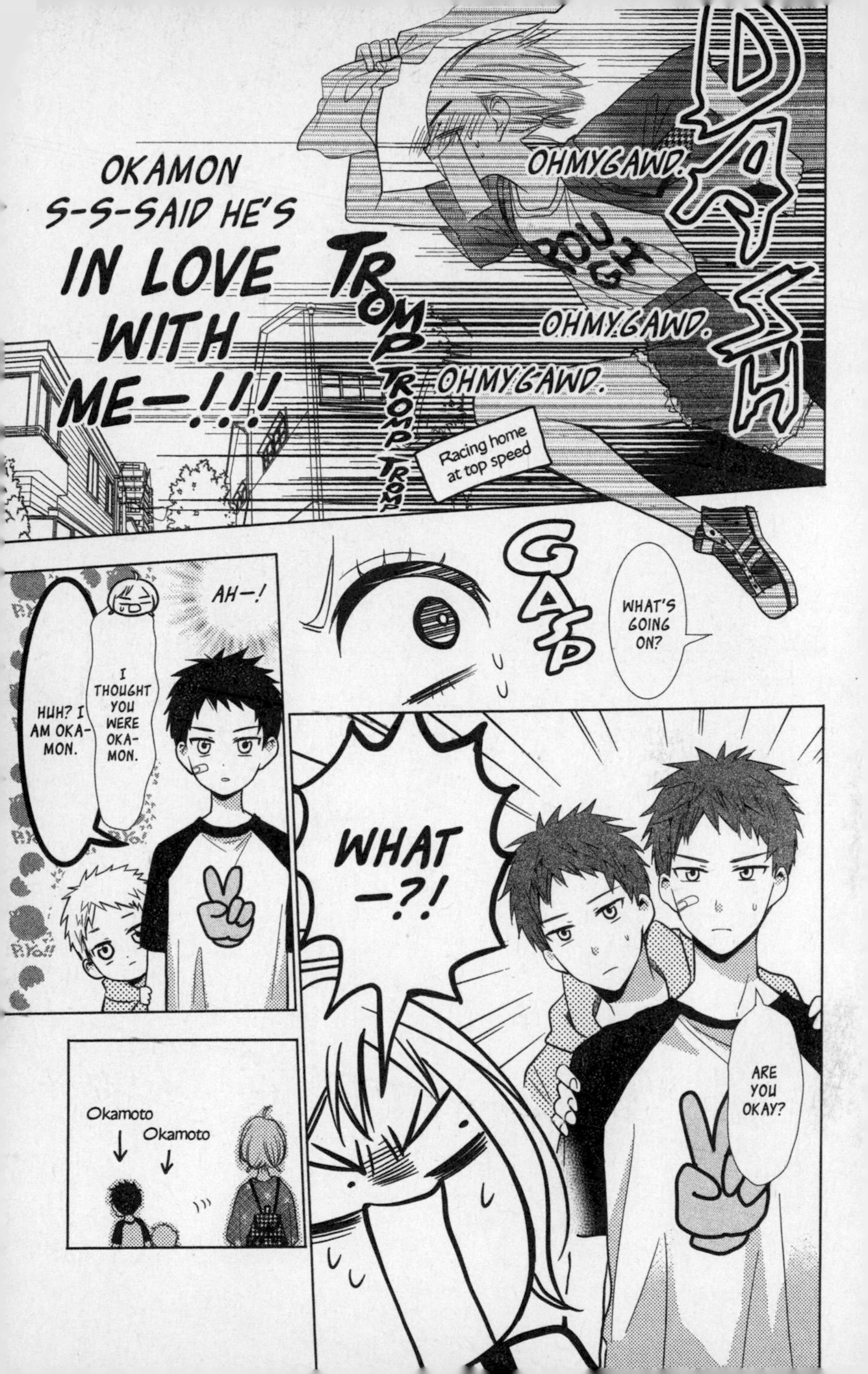
DASH
OHMYGAWD.
ROUGH
OHMYGAWD.
OHMYGAWD.
TROMP TROMP TROMP TROMP
Racing home at top speed
OKAMON S-S-SAID HE'S IN LOVE WITH ME—!!!
GASP
WHAT'S GOING ON?
ARE YOU OKAY?
WHAT—?!
AH—!
I THOUGHT YOU WERE OKA-MON.
HUH? I AM OKA-MON.
Okamoto
Okamoto

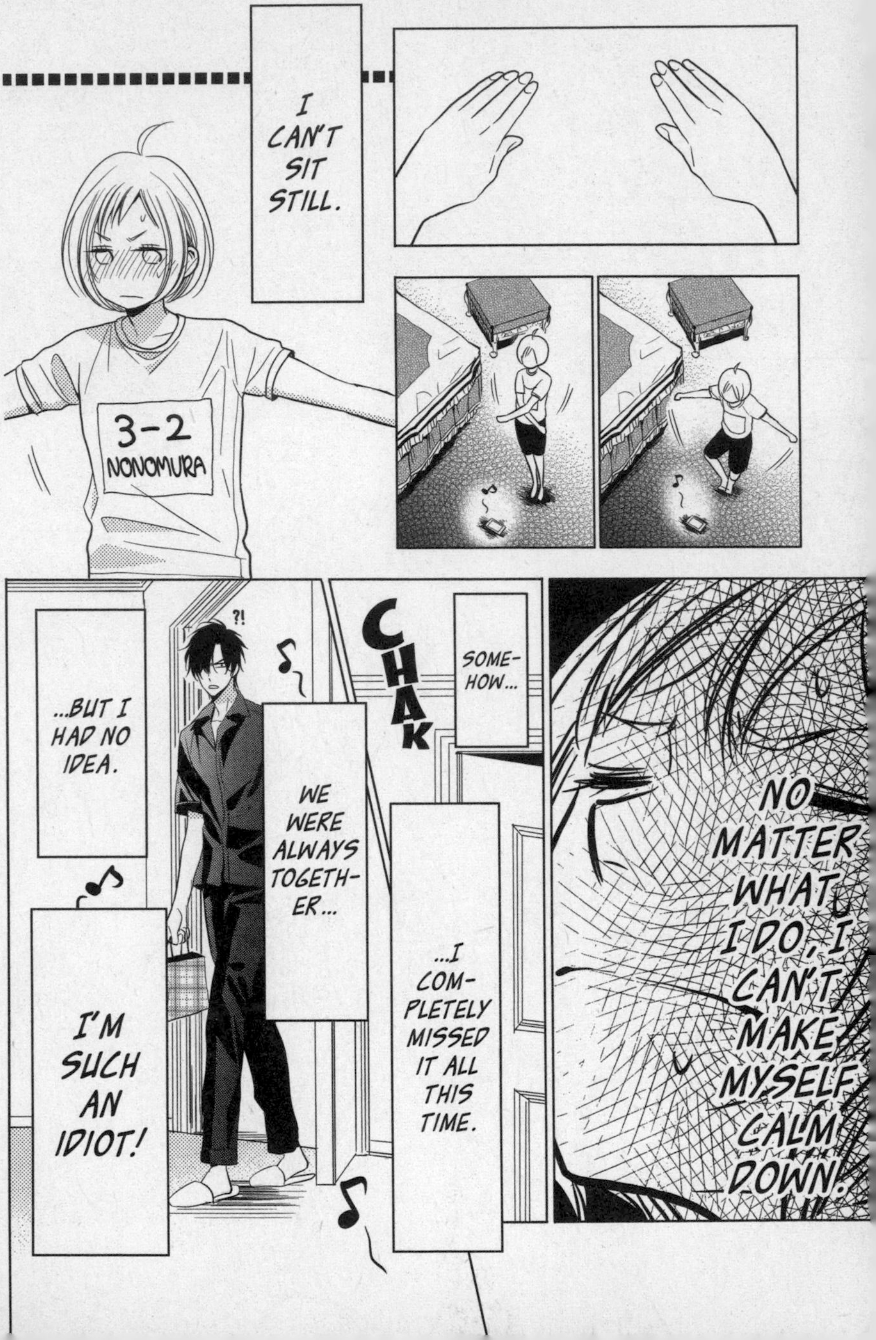
I CAN'T SIT STILL.
3-2 NONOMURA
NO MATTER WHAT I DO, I CAN'T MAKE MYSELF CALM DOWN.
CHAK
SOMEHOW...
WE WERE ALWAYS TOGETHER...
...I COMPLETELY MISSED IT ALL THIS TIME.
?!
...BUT I HAD NO IDEA.
I'M SUCH AN IDIOT!

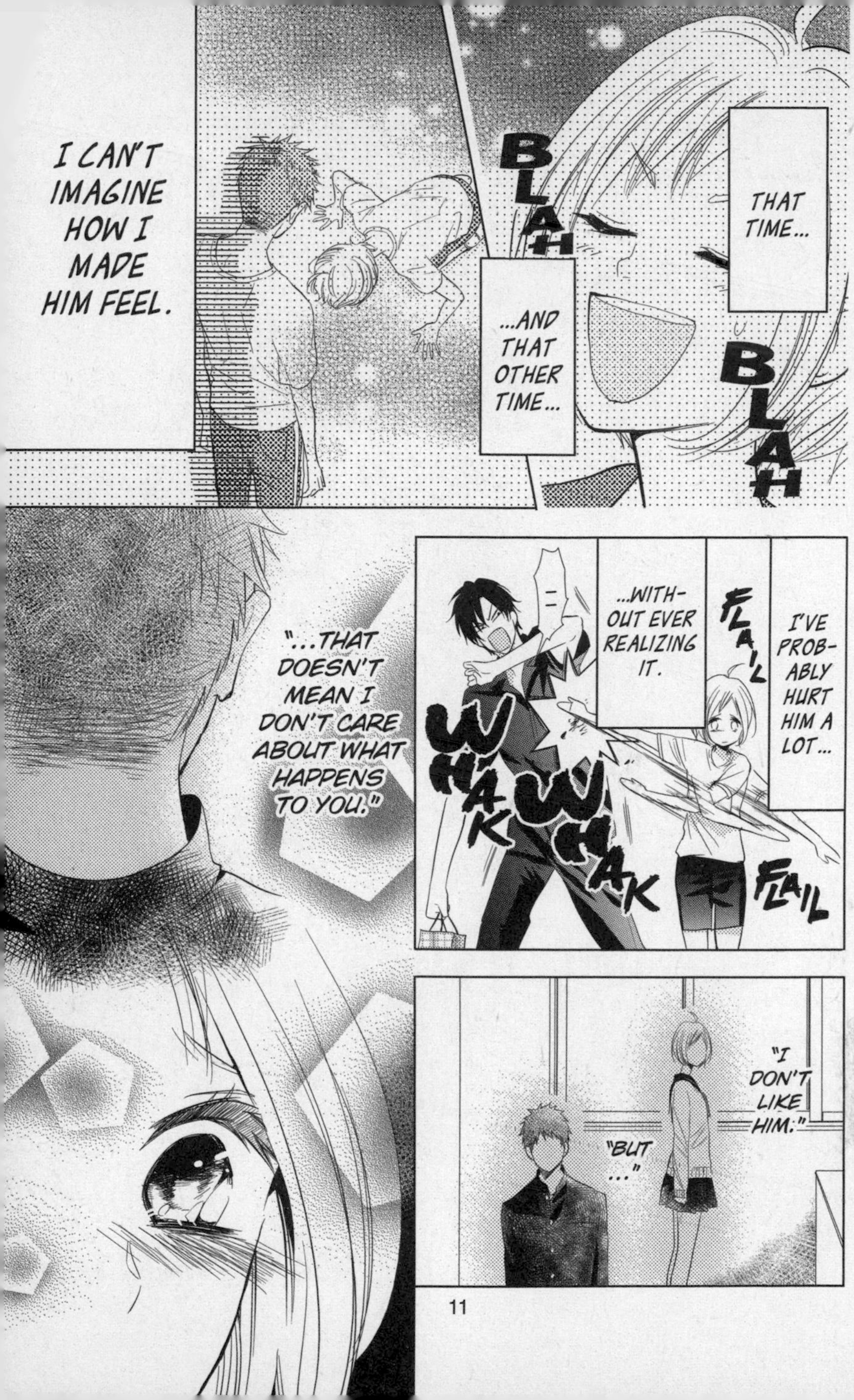
THAT TIME...
BLAH
...AND THAT OTHER TIME...
BLAH
I CAN'T IMAGINE HOW I MADE HIM FEEL.
I'VE PROBABLY HURT HIM A LOT...
FLAIL
...WITHOUT EVER REALIZING IT.
WHAK
WHAK
FLAIL
"I DON'T LIKE HIM."
"BUT..."
"...THAT DOESN'T MEAN I DON'T CARE ABOUT WHAT HAPPENS TO YOU."

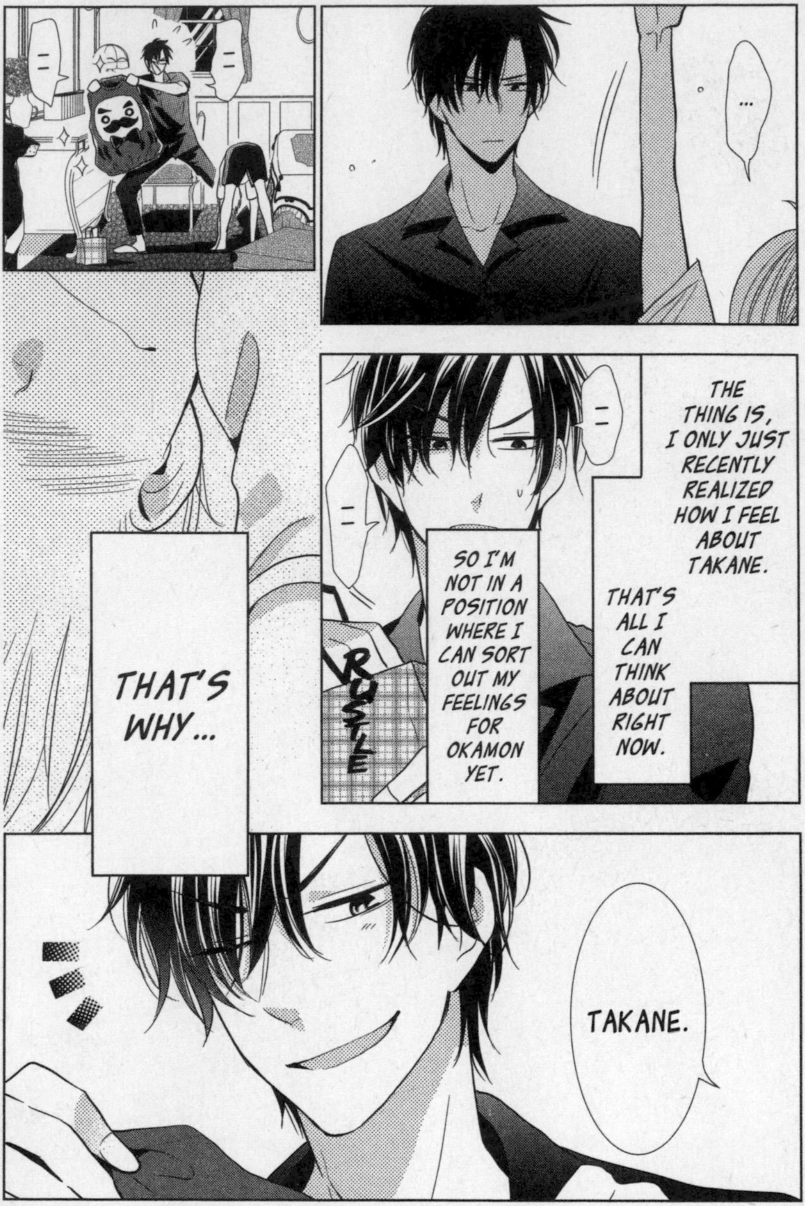
...
THE THING IS, I ONLY JUST RECENTLY REALIZED HOW I FEEL ABOUT TAKANE.
THAT'S ALL I CAN THINK ABOUT RIGHT NOW.
SO I'M NOT IN A POSITION WHERE I CAN SORT OUT MY FEELINGS FOR OKAMON YET.
RUSTLE
THAT'S WHY...
TAKANE.

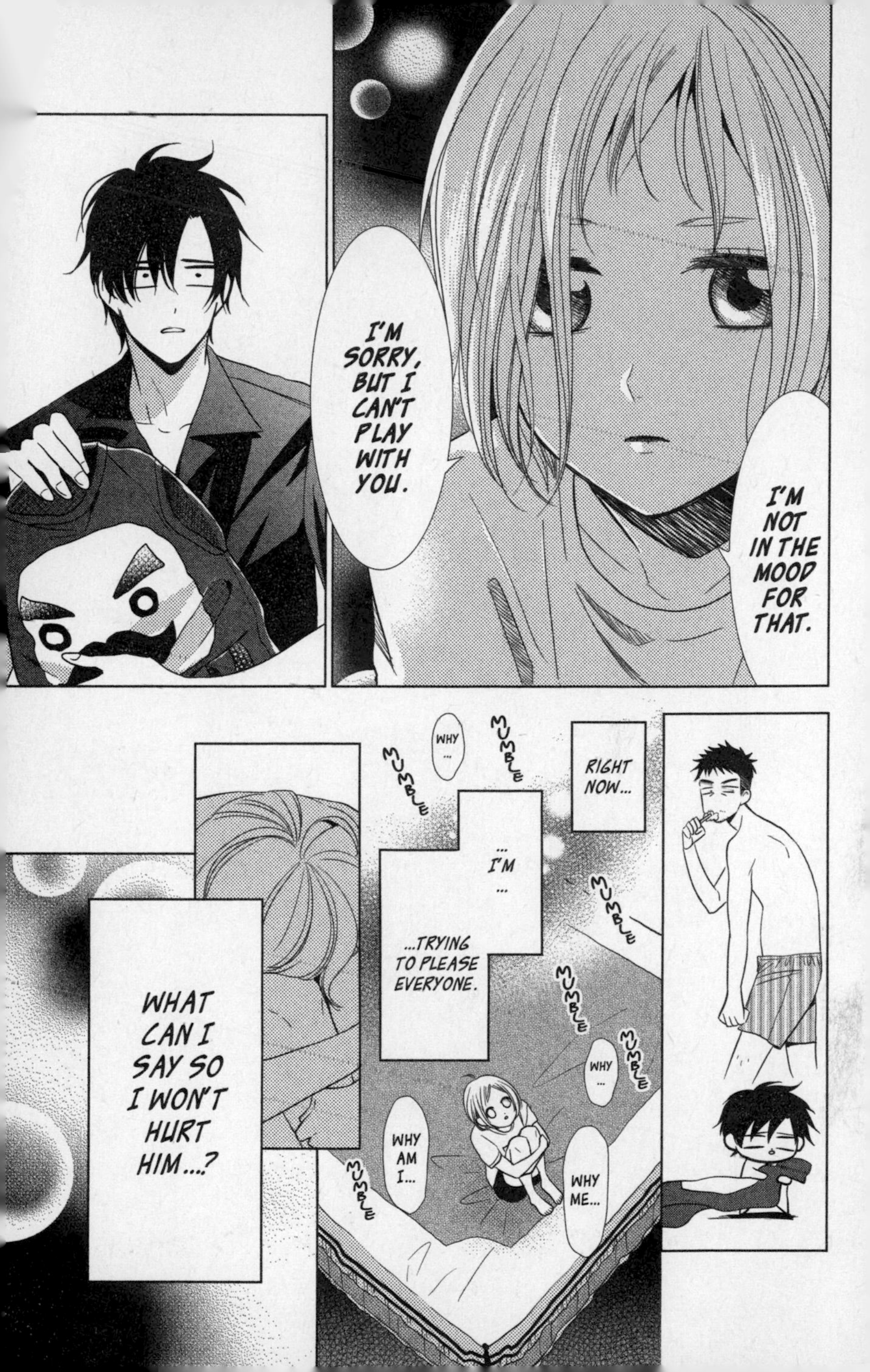
I'M SORRY, BUT I CAN'T PLAY WITH YOU.
I'M NOT IN THE MOOD FOR THAT.
RIGHT NOW...
MUMBLE
WHY ...
MUMBLE
...I'M...
...TRYING TO PLEASE EVERYONE.
MUMBLE
MUMBLE
MUMBLE
WHY ...
WHY ME...
WHY AM I...
MUMBLE
WHAT CAN I SAY SO I WON'T HURT HIM...?

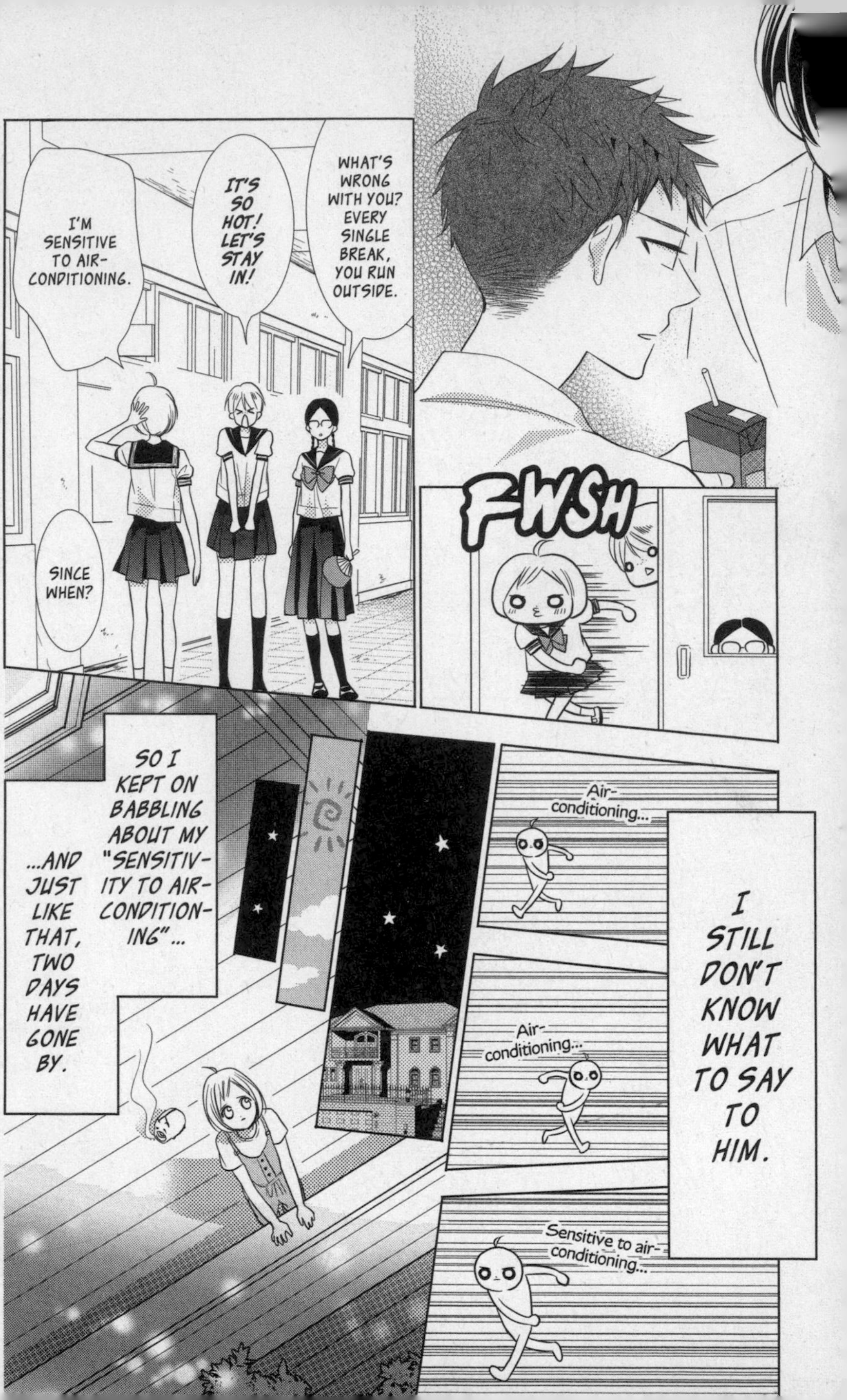
F-WSH
WHAT'S WRONG WITH YOU? EVERY SINGLE BREAK, YOU RUN OUTSIDE.
IT'S SO HOT! LET'S STAY IN!
I'M SENSITIVE TO AIR-CONDITIONING.
SINCE WHEN?
Air-conditioning...
I STILL DON'T KNOW WHAT TO SAY TO HIM.
Air-conditioning...
Sensitive to air-conditioning...
SO I KEPT ON BABBLING ABOUT MY "SENSITIVITY TO AIR-CONDITIONING"...
...AND JUST LIKE THAT, TWO DAYS HAVE GONE BY.

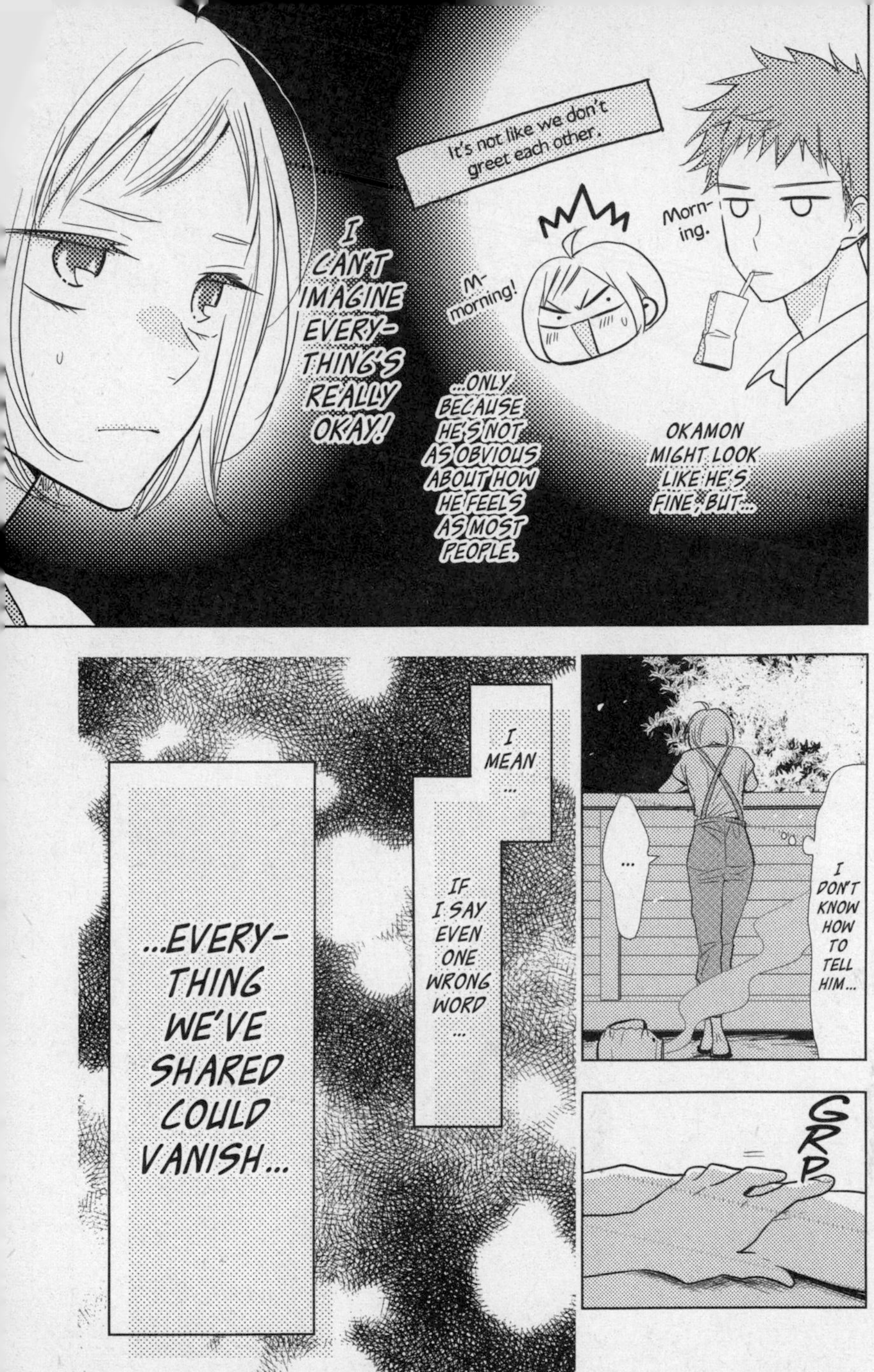
Morn-ing.
M-morning!
It's not like we don't greet each other.
OKAMON MIGHT LOOK LIKE HE'S FINE, BUT...
...ONLY BECAUSE HE'S NOT AS OBVIOUS ABOUT HOW HE FEELS AS MOST PEOPLE.
I CAN'T IMAGINE EVERY-THING'S REALLY OKAY!
I DON'T KNOW HOW TO TELL HIM...
...
GRP
I MEAN...
IF I SAY EVEN ONE WRONG WORD...
...EVERY-THING WE'VE SHARED COULD VANISH...

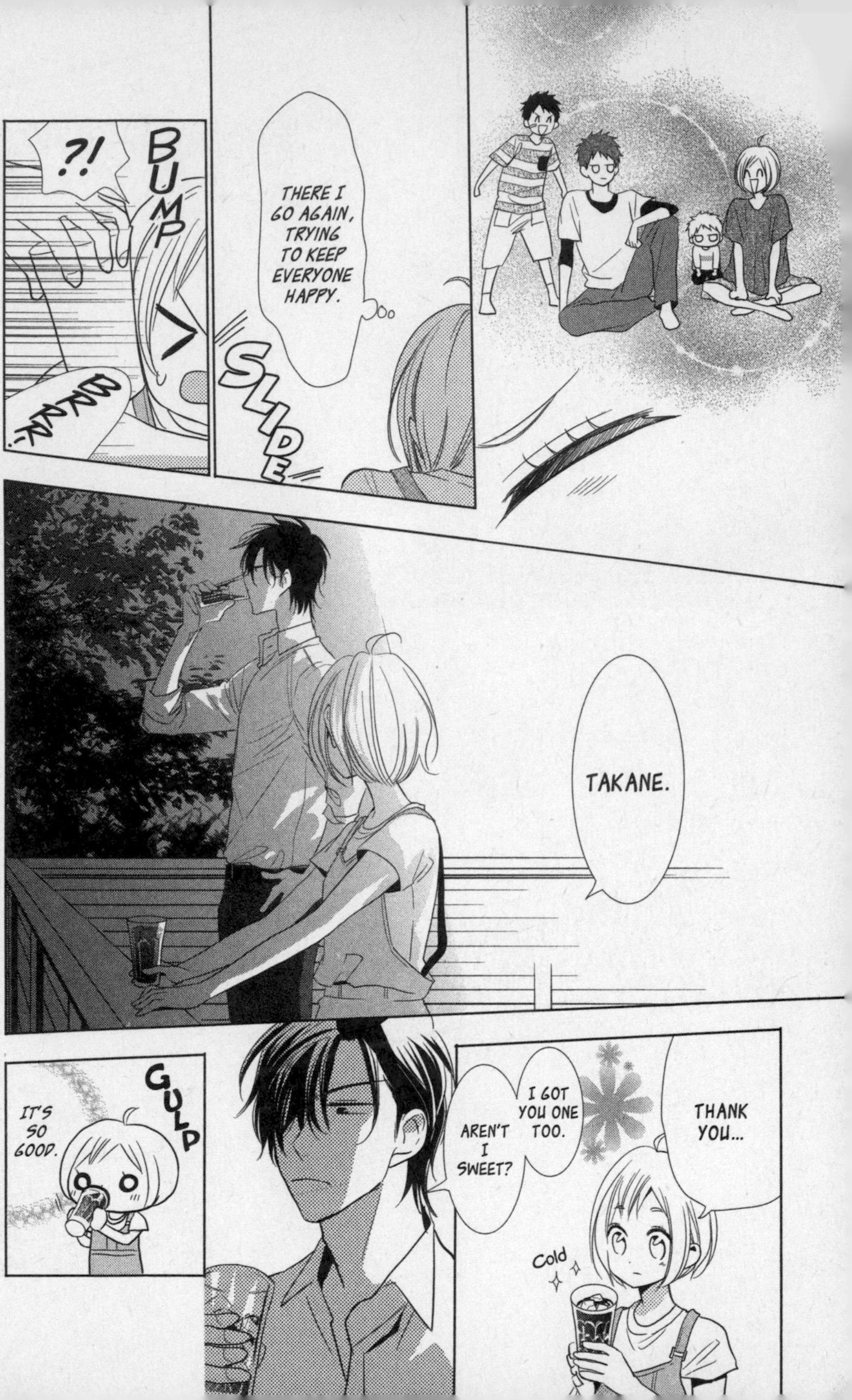
THERE I GO AGAIN, TRYING TO KEEP EVERYONE HAPPY.
SLIDE
?!
BUMP
BRRR...
TAKANE.
THANK YOU...
Cold
I GOT YOU ONE TOO.
AREN'T I SWEET?
GULP
IT'S SO GOOD.

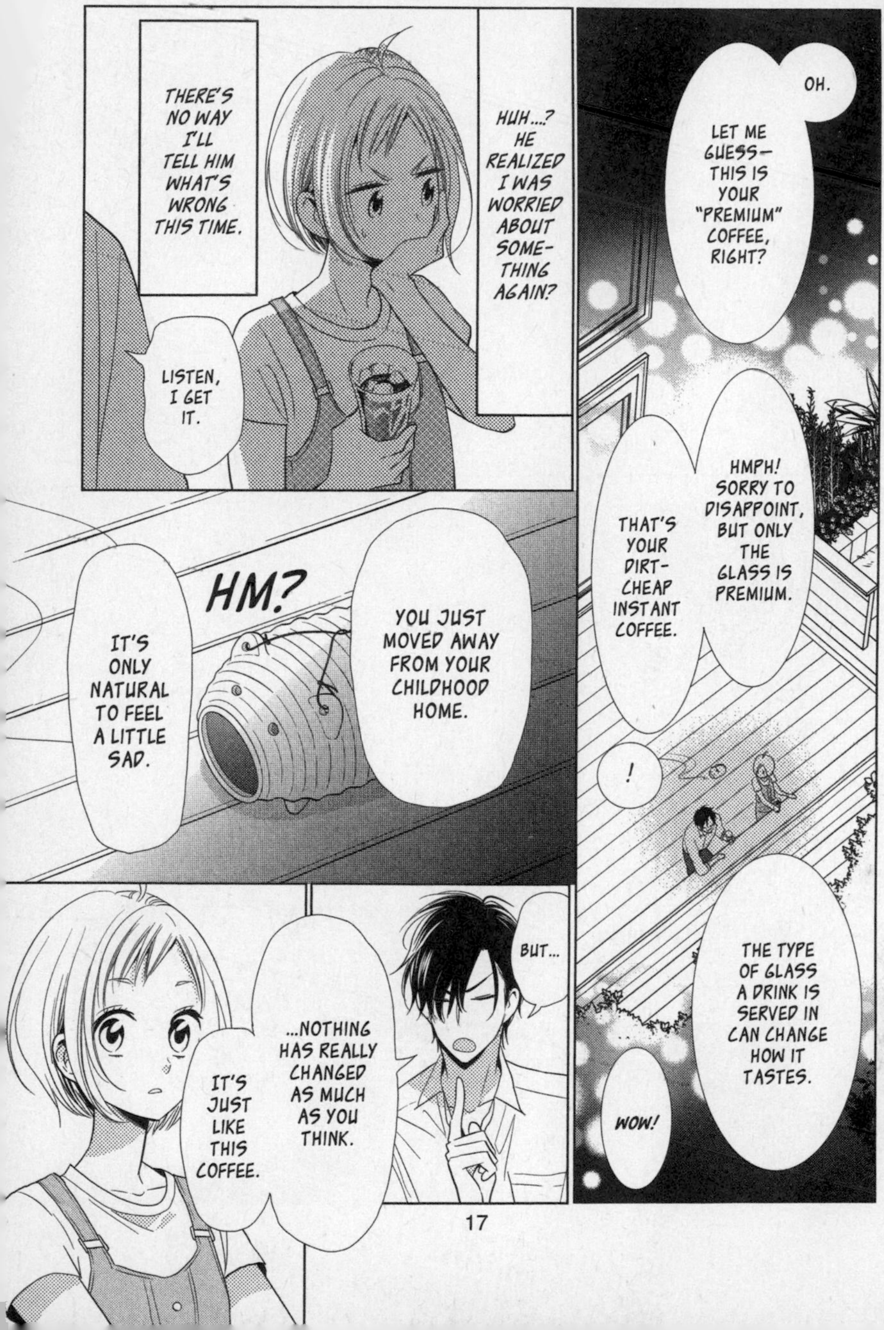
OH.
LET ME GUESS—THIS IS YOUR "PREMIUM" COFFEE, RIGHT?
HMPH! SORRY TO DISAPPOINT, BUT ONLY THE GLASS IS PREMIUM.
THAT'S YOUR DIRT-CHEAP INSTANT COFFEE.
!
THE TYPE OF GLASS A DRINK IS SERVED IN CAN CHANGE HOW IT TASTES.
WOW!
HUH...? HE REALIZED I WAS WORRIED ABOUT SOMETHING AGAIN?
THERE'S NO WAY I'LL TELL HIM WHAT'S WRONG THIS TIME.
LISTEN, I GET IT.
HM?
YOU JUST MOVED AWAY FROM YOUR CHILDHOOD HOME.
IT'S ONLY NATURAL TO FEEL A LITTLE SAD.
BUT...
...NOTHING HAS REALLY CHANGED AS MUCH AS YOU THINK.
IT'S JUST LIKE THIS COFFEE.

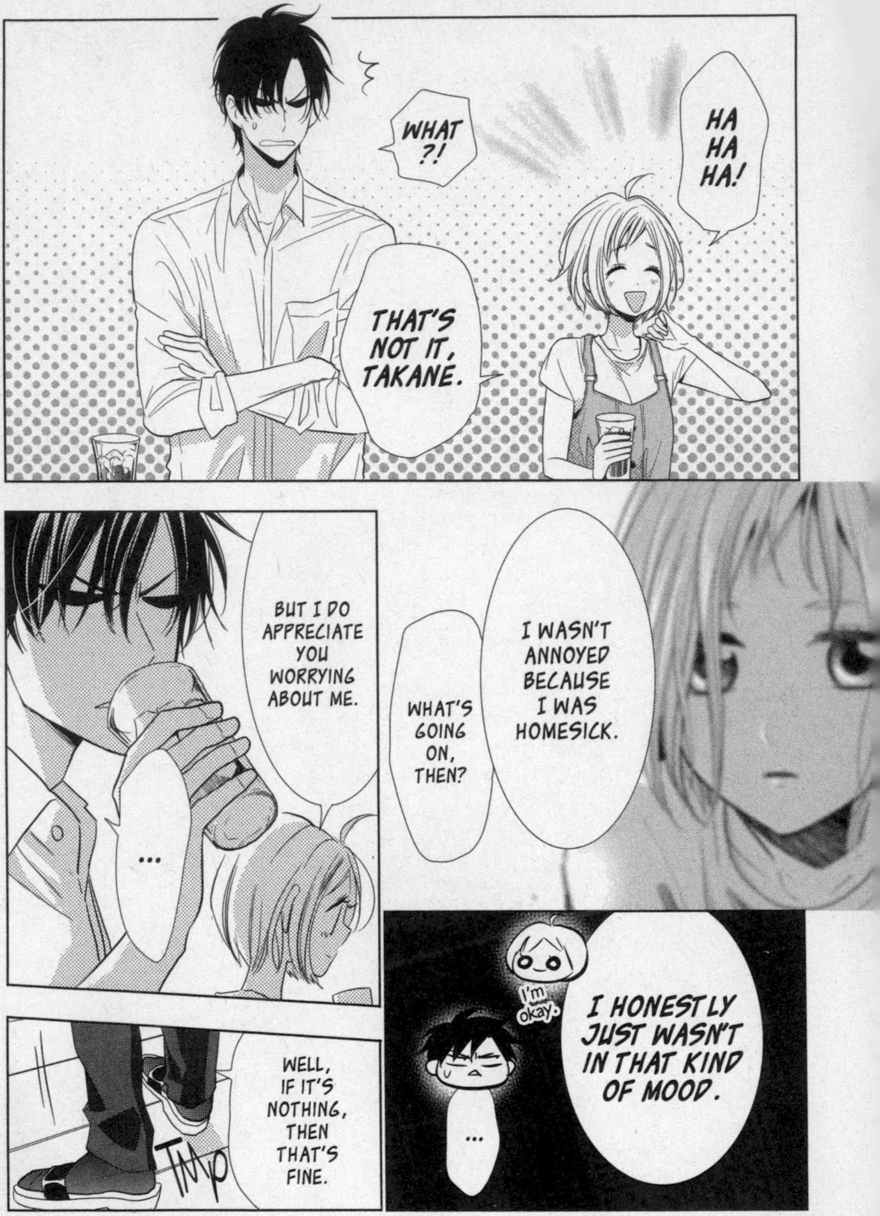
HA HA HA!
WHAT?!
THAT'S NOT IT, TAKANE.
I WASN'T ANNOYED BECAUSE I WAS HOMESICK.
WHAT'S GOING ON, THEN?
BUT I DO APPRECIATE YOU WORRYING ABOUT ME.
...
I HONESTLY JUST WASN'T IN THAT KIND OF MOOD.
I'm okay.
...
WELL, IF IT'S NOTHING, THEN THAT'S FINE.
TMP

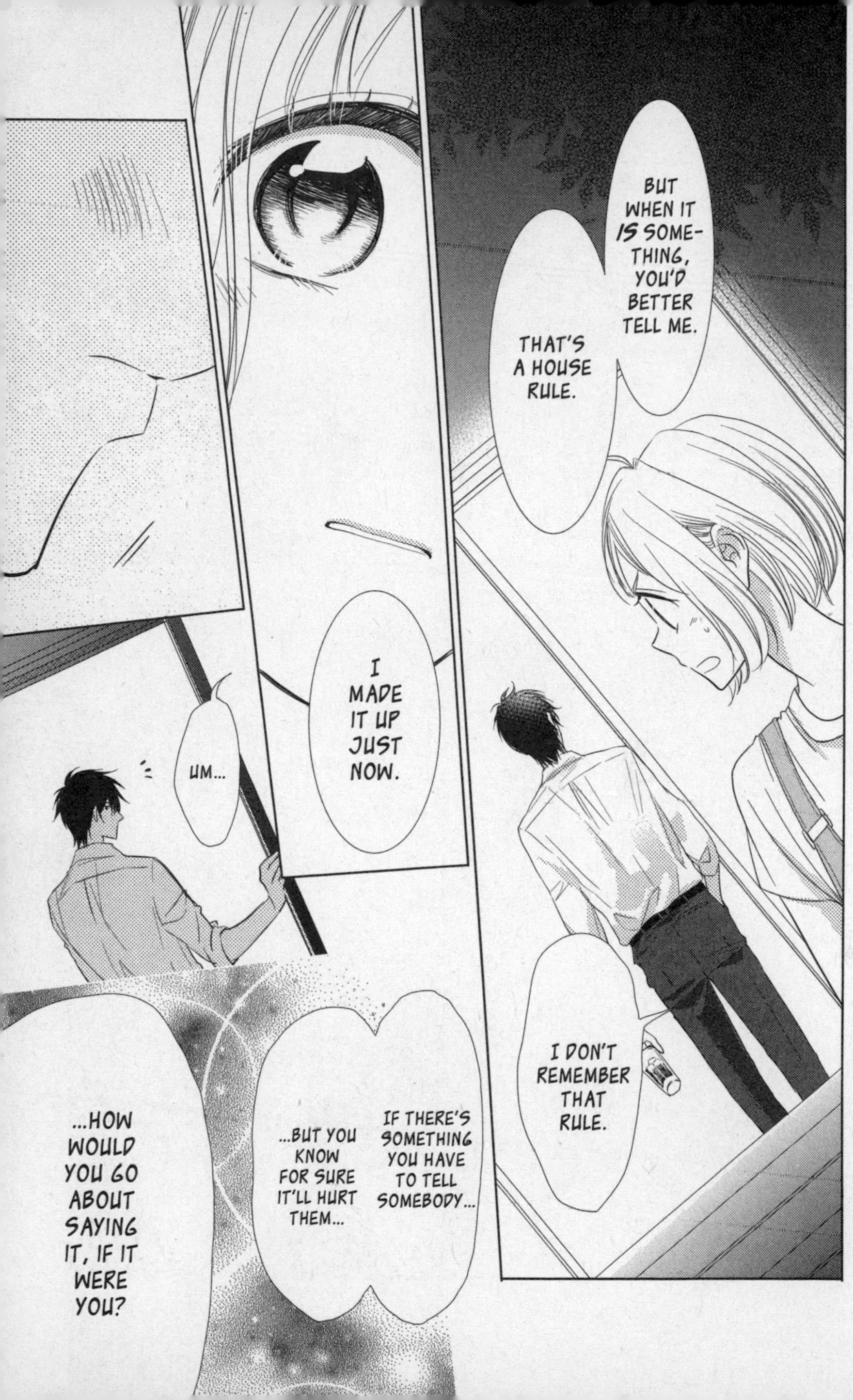
BUT WHEN IT IS SOMETHING, YOU'D BETTER TELL ME.
THAT'S A HOUSE RULE.
I DON'T REMEMBER THAT RULE.
I MADE IT UP JUST NOW.
UM...
IF THERE'S SOMETHING YOU HAVE TO TELL SOMEBODY...
...BUT YOU KNOW FOR SURE IT'LL HURT THEM...
...HOW WOULD YOU GO ABOUT SAYING IT, IF IT WERE YOU?

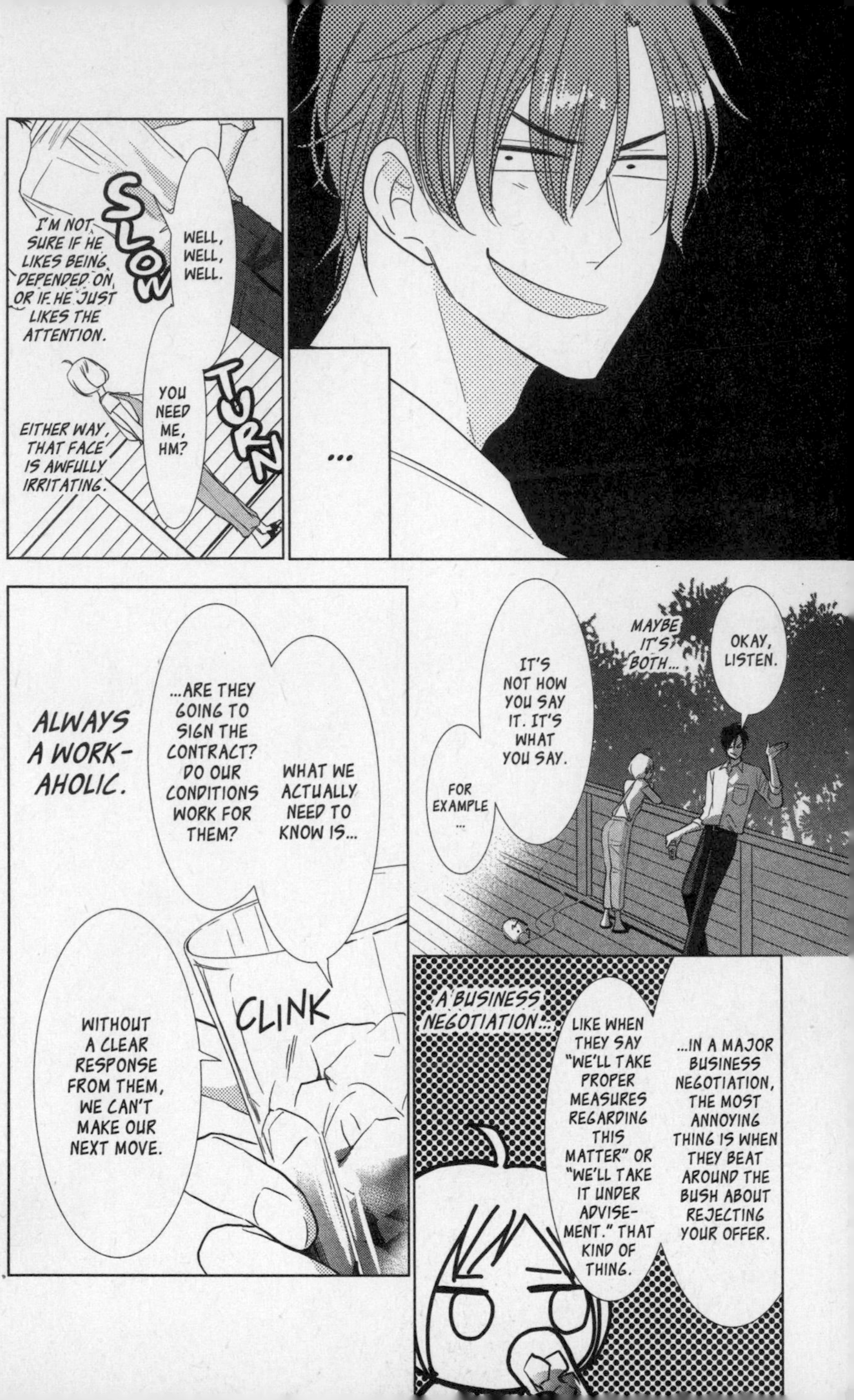
...
WELL, WELL, WELL.
SLOW
I'M NOT SURE IF HE LIKES BEING DEPENDED ON, OR IF HE JUST LIKES THE ATTENTION.
YOU NEED ME, HM?
TURN
EITHER WAY, THAT FACE IS AWFULLY IRRITATING.
OKAY, LISTEN.
MAYBE IT'S BOTH...
IT'S NOT HOW YOU SAY IT. IT'S WHAT YOU SAY.
FOR EXAMPLE...
...IN A MAJOR BUSINESS NEGOTIATION, THE MOST ANNOYING THING IS WHEN THEY BEAT AROUND THE BUSH ABOUT REJECTING YOUR OFFER.
LIKE WHEN THEY SAY "WE'LL TAKE PROPER MEASURES REGARDING THIS MATTER" OR "WE'LL TAKE IT UNDER ADVISE-MENT." THAT KIND OF THING.
A BUSINESS NEGOTIATION...
WHAT WE ACTUALLY NEED TO KNOW IS...
...ARE THEY GOING TO SIGN THE CONTRACT? DO OUR CONDITIONS WORK FOR THEM?
ALWAYS A WORK-AHOLIC.
CLINK
WITHOUT A CLEAR RESPONSE FROM THEM, WE CAN'T MAKE OUR NEXT MOVE.

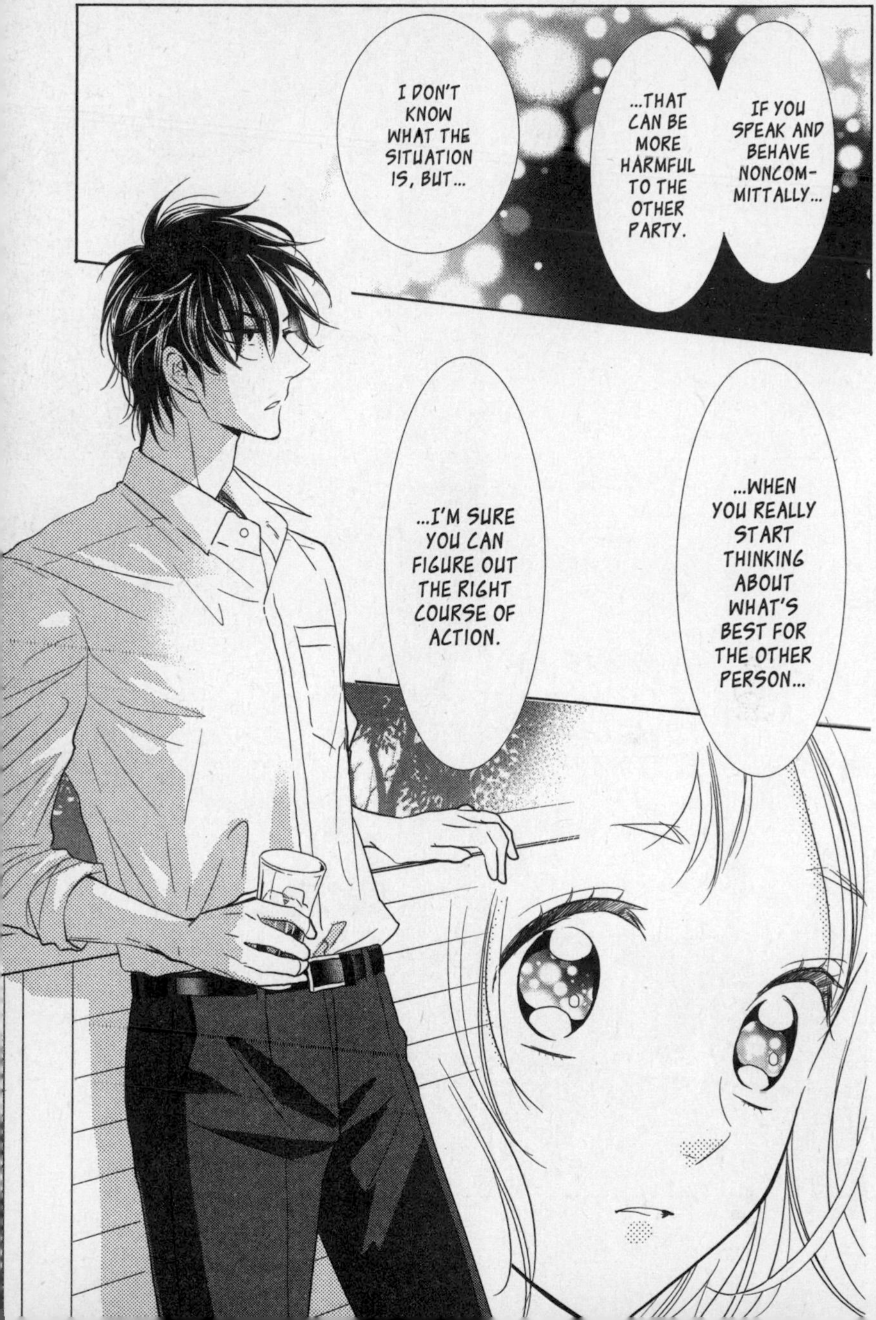
IF YOU SPEAK AND BEHAVE NONCOM-MITTALLY...
...THAT CAN BE MORE HARMFUL TO THE OTHER PARTY.
I DON'T KNOW WHAT THE SITUATION IS, BUT...
...WHEN YOU REALLY START THINKING ABOUT WHAT'S BEST FOR THE OTHER PERSON...
...I'M SURE YOU CAN FIGURE OUT THE RIGHT COURSE OF ACTION.

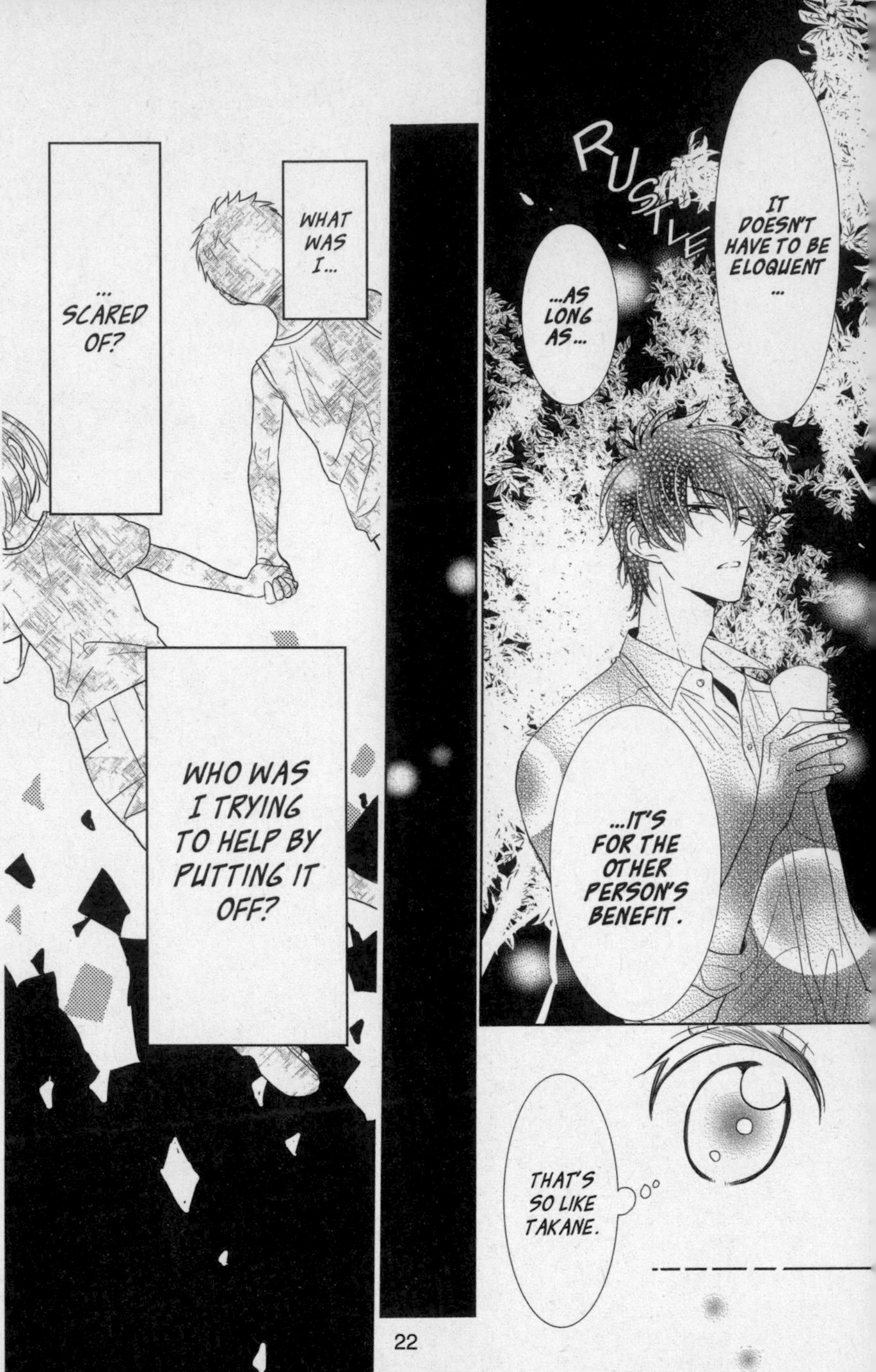
IT DOESN'T HAVE TO BE ELOQUENT ...
RUSTLE
...AS LONG AS...
...IT'S FOR THE OTHER PERSON'S BENEFIT.
THAT'S SO LIKE TAKANE.
WHAT WAS I...
... SCARED OF?
WHO WAS I TRYING TO HELP BY PUTTING IT OFF?

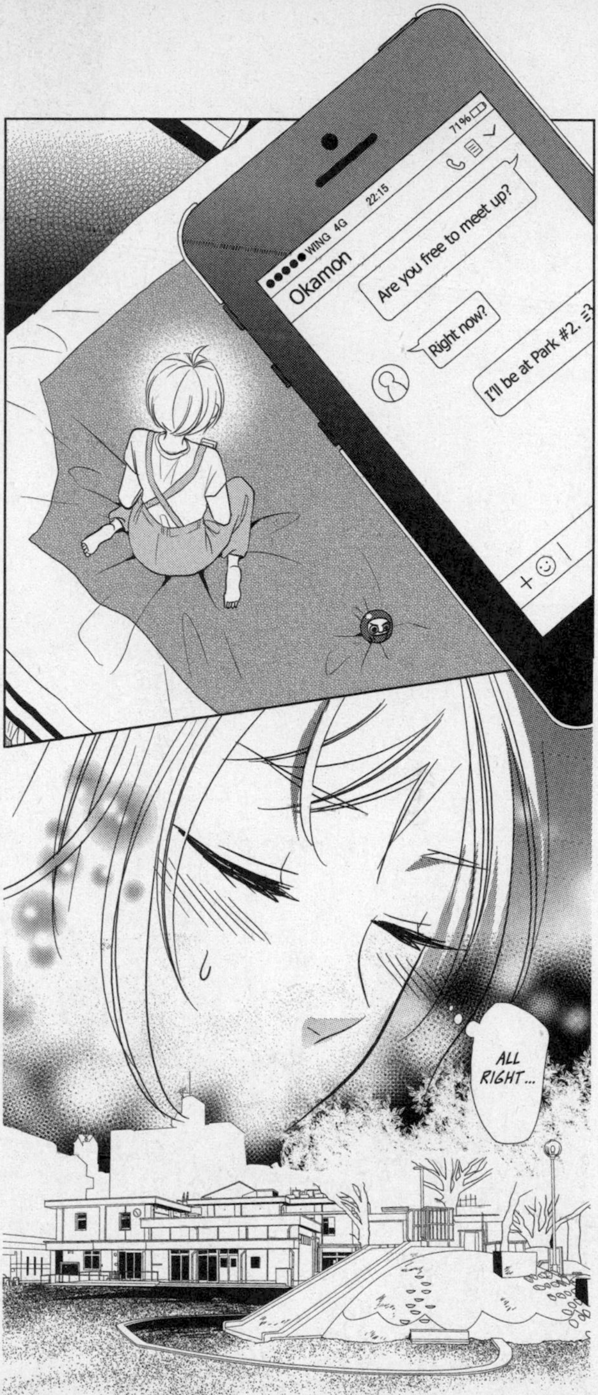
WING 4G
22:15
71%
Okamon
Are you free to meet up?
Right now?
I'll be at Park #2.
ALL RIGHT...

• Volume 10! •

We're now in double digits, and yet there're still no signs of them getting together!

In other romantic comedies, what would the relationship be like by volume 10?

I've always wanted to draw an extreme close-up of just one character for the cover, but seeing as this is the tenth volume, I decided to include both leads.

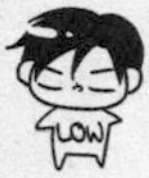
LOW

• The Bonus Story •

The bonus story at the end is newly written for this volume.

Since I had seven pages left, I put a lot of thought into what I wanted to draw.

Let's say I drew four-panel comic strips for all seven pages—that would mean I'd draw a maximum of 14 four-panel comics! But that would be...

IMPOSSIBLE!

I'm not a four-panel artist, so I can't come up with that many ideas!

And that's why I decided on a short manga installment! Chronologically, it takes place before chapter 57.

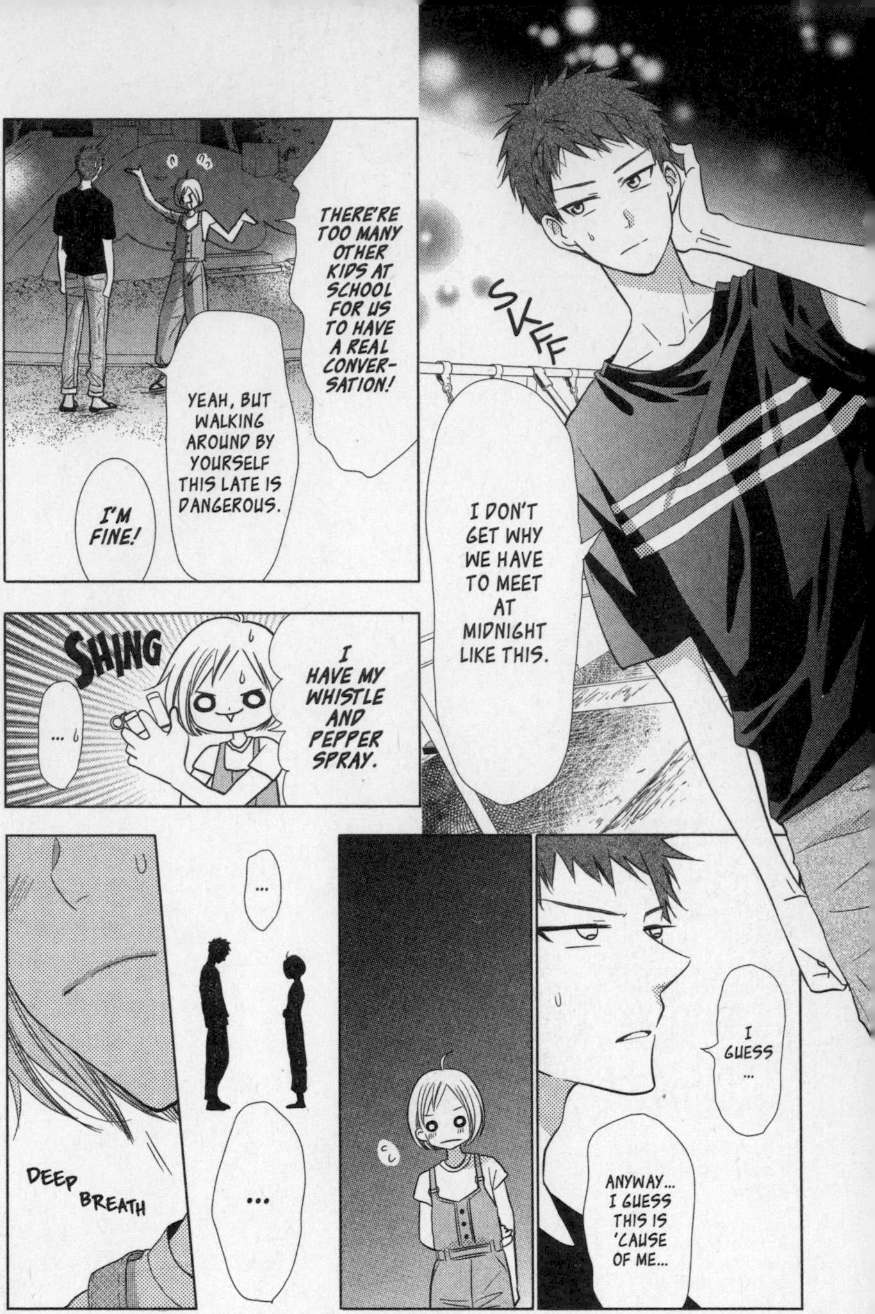
SKFF
I DON'T GET WHY WE HAVE TO MEET AT MIDNIGHT LIKE THIS.
THERE'RE TOO MANY OTHER KIDS AT SCHOOL FOR US TO HAVE A REAL CONVER-SATION!
YEAH, BUT WALKING AROUND BY YOURSELF THIS LATE IS DANGEROUS.
I'M FINE!
I HAVE MY WHISTLE AND PEPPER SPRAY.
SHING
...
I GUESS ...
ANYWAY... I GUESS THIS IS 'CAUSE OF ME...
...
...
DEEP BREATH

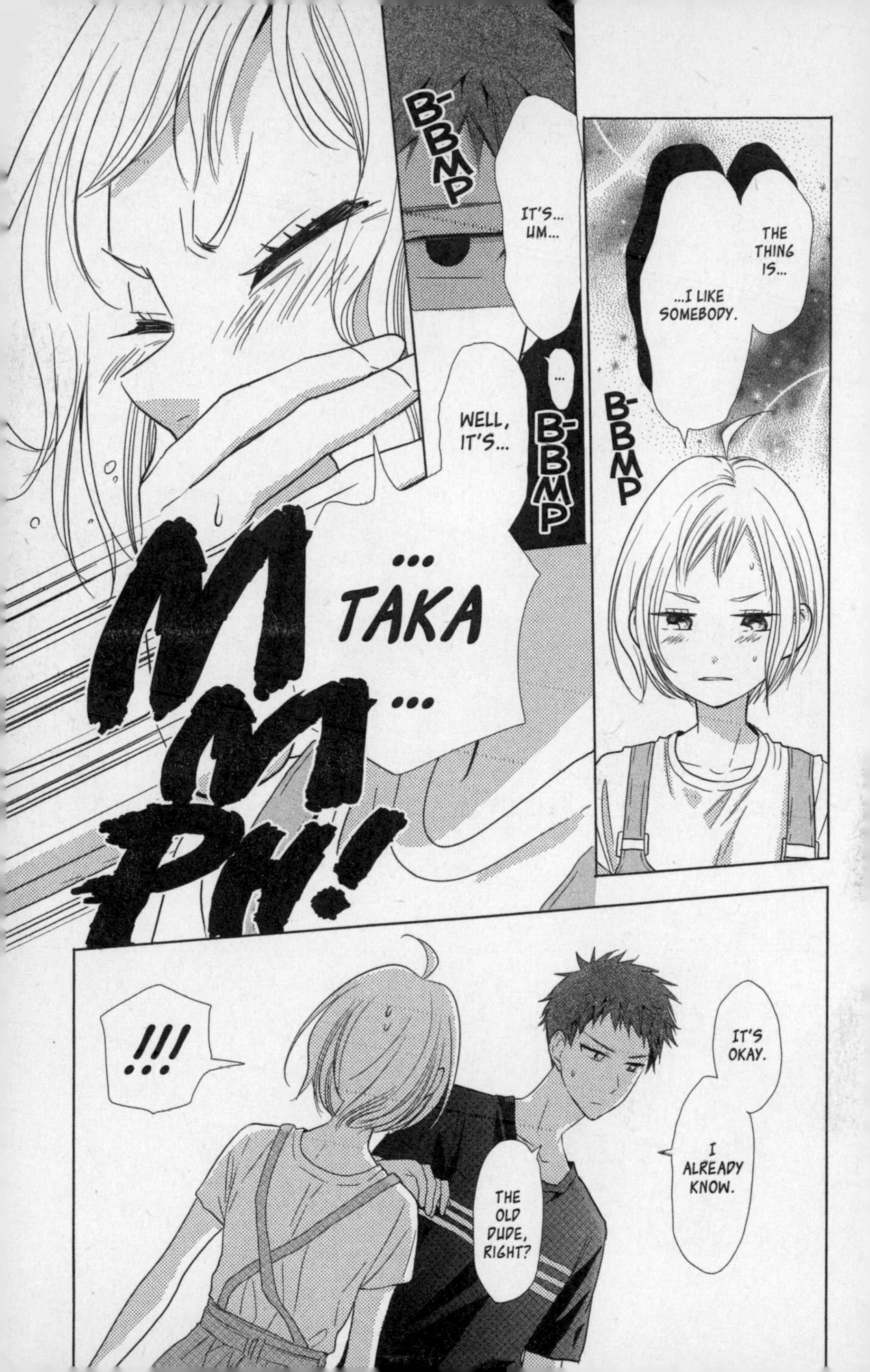

THE THING IS...
...I LIKE SOMEBODY.
B-BBMP
B-BBMP
IT'S... UM...
...
B-BBMP
WELL, IT'S...
...TAKA...
MMPH!
IT'S OKAY.
I ALREADY KNOW.
THE OLD DUDE, RIGHT?
!!!

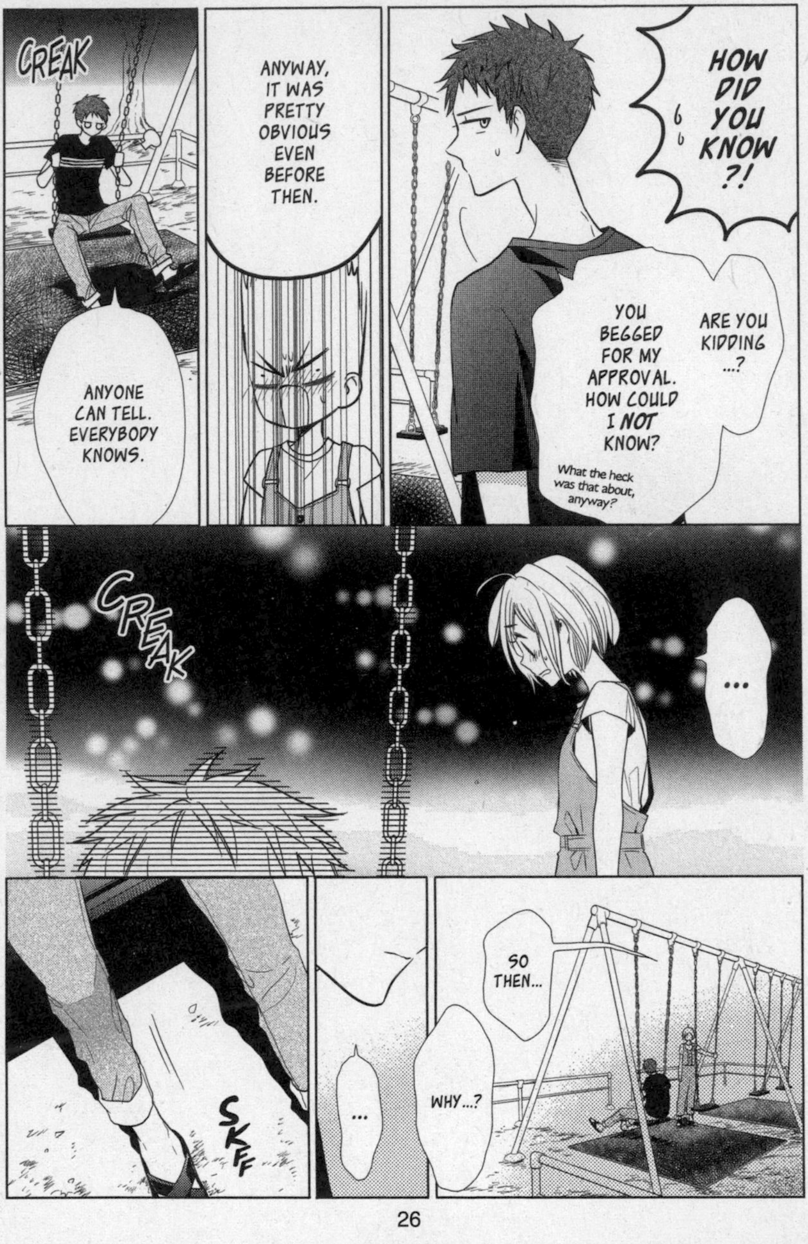
HOW DID YOU KNOW?!
ARE YOU KIDDING...?
YOU BEGGED FOR MY APPROVAL. HOW COULD I NOT KNOW?
What the heck was that about, anyway?
ANYWAY, IT WAS PRETTY OBVIOUS EVEN BEFORE THEN.
CREAK
ANYONE CAN TELL. EVERYBODY KNOWS.
...
CREAK
SO THEN...
WHY...?
...
SKFF

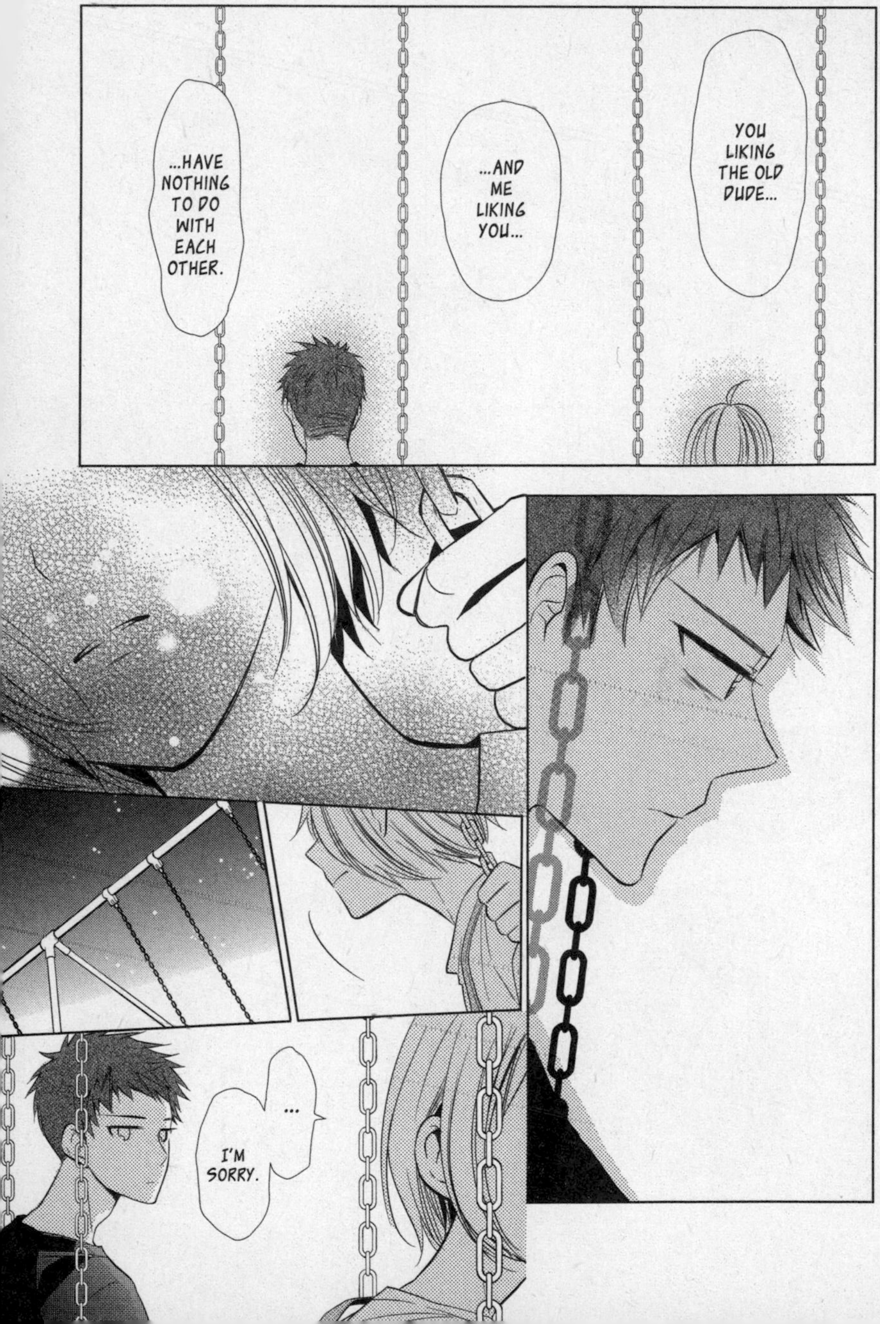
YOU LIKING THE OLD DUDE...
...AND ME LIKING YOU...
...HAVE NOTHING TO DO WITH EACH OTHER.
...
I'M SORRY.

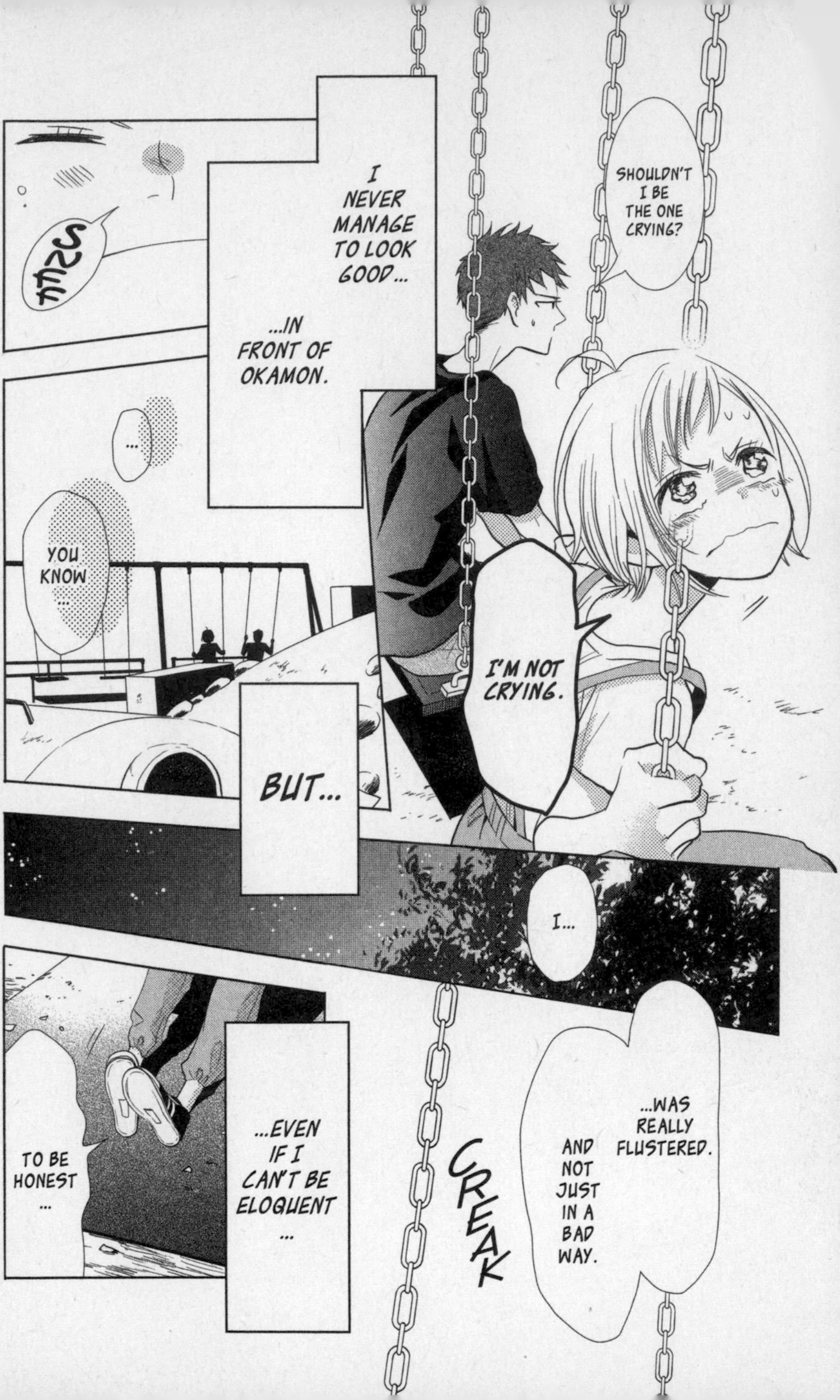
SHOULDN'T I BE THE ONE CRYING?
I NEVER MANAGE TO LOOK GOOD...
...IN FRONT OF OKAMON.
SNFF
I'M NOT CRYING.
...
YOU KNOW...
BUT...
I...
...WAS REALLY FLUSTERED.
AND NOT JUST IN A BAD WAY.
CREAK
...EVEN IF I CAN'T BE ELOQUENT...
TO BE HONEST...

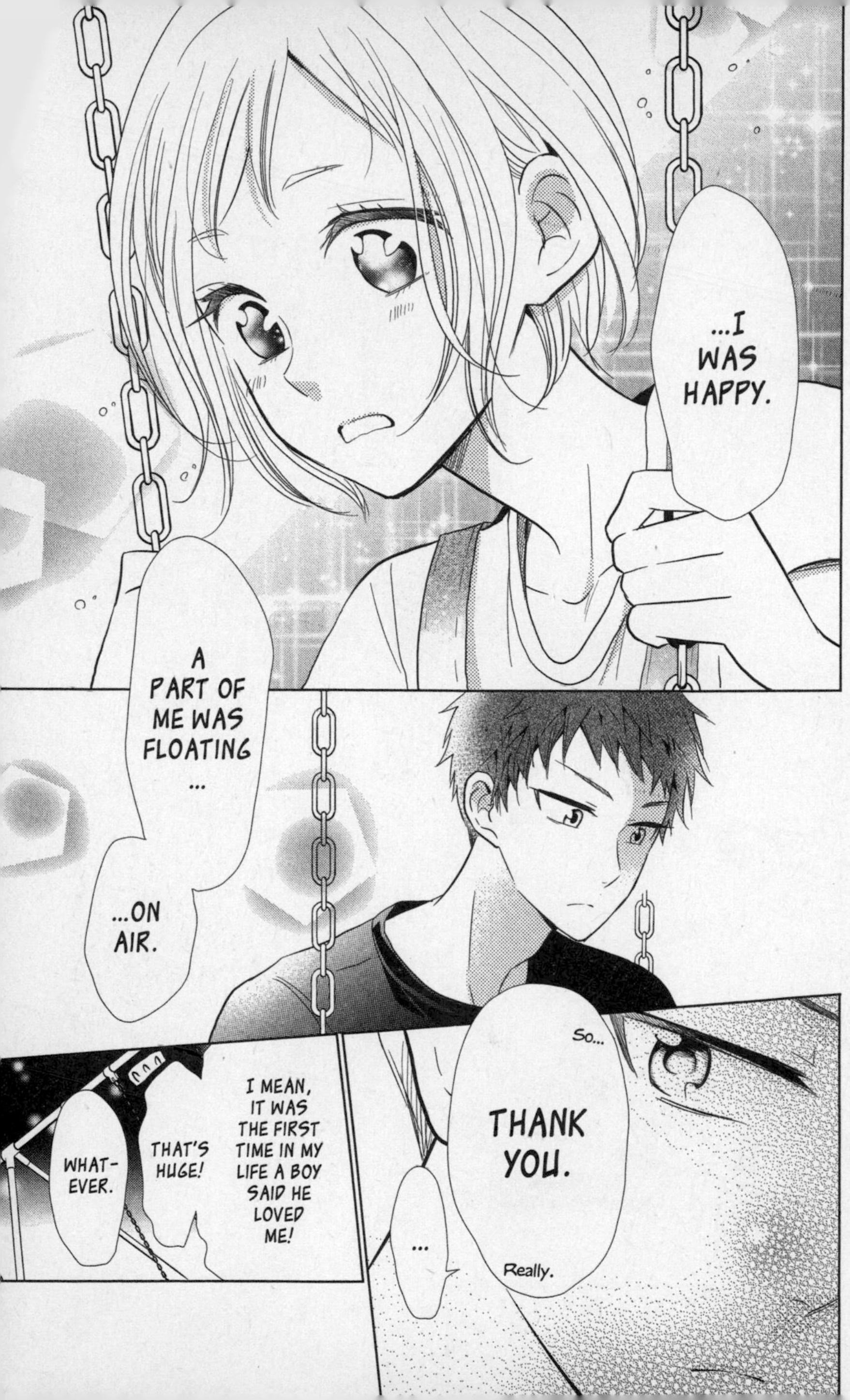
...I WAS HAPPY.
A PART OF ME WAS FLOATING ...
...ON AIR.
So...
THANK YOU.
Really.
...
I MEAN, IT WAS THE FIRST TIME IN MY LIFE A BOY SAID HE LOVED ME!
THAT'S HUGE!
WHAT-EVER.

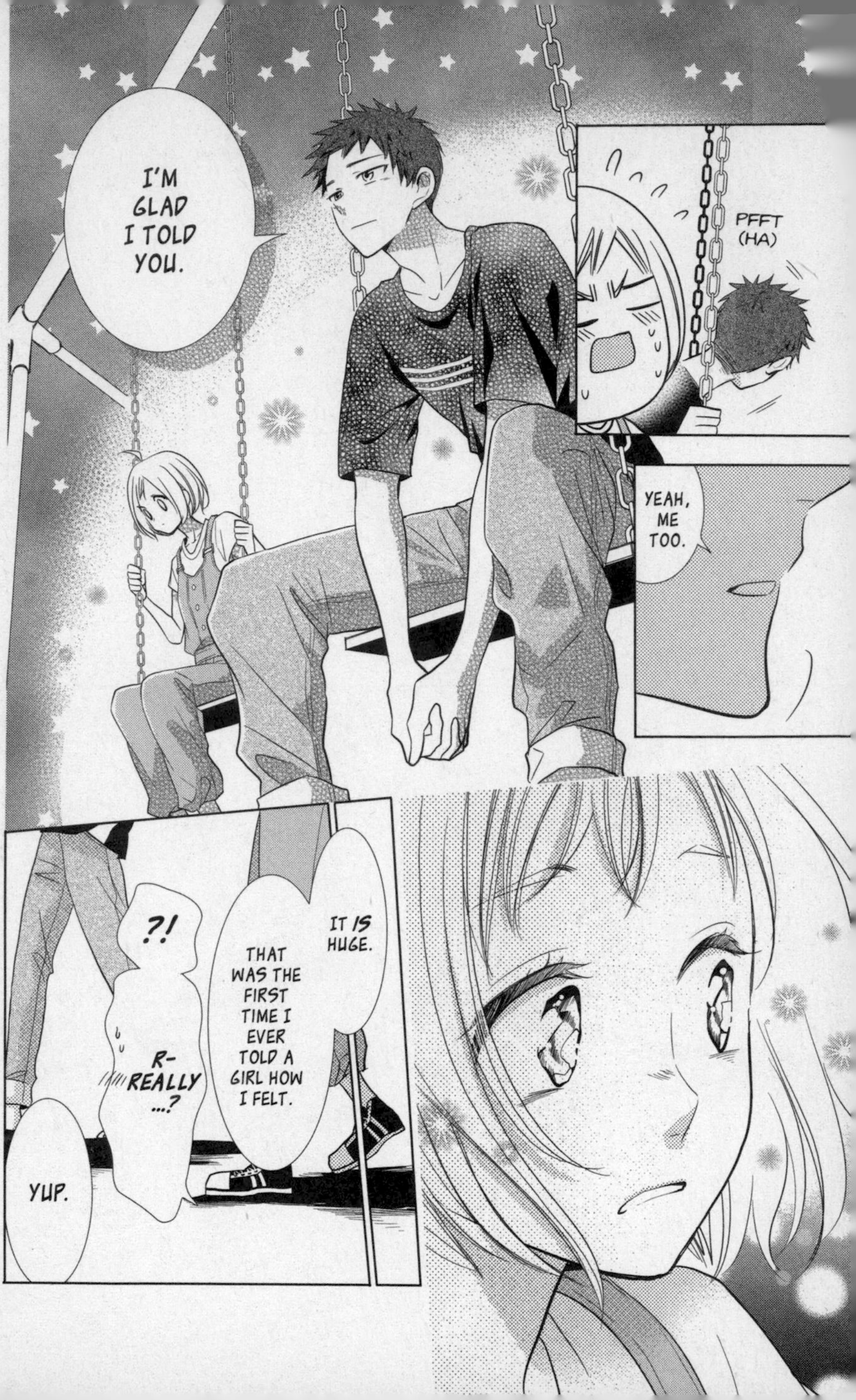
PFFT (HA)
YEAH, ME TOO.
I'M GLAD I TOLD YOU.
IT IS HUGE.
THAT WAS THE FIRST TIME I EVER TOLD A GIRL HOW I FELT.
?!
R-REALLY ...?
YUP.

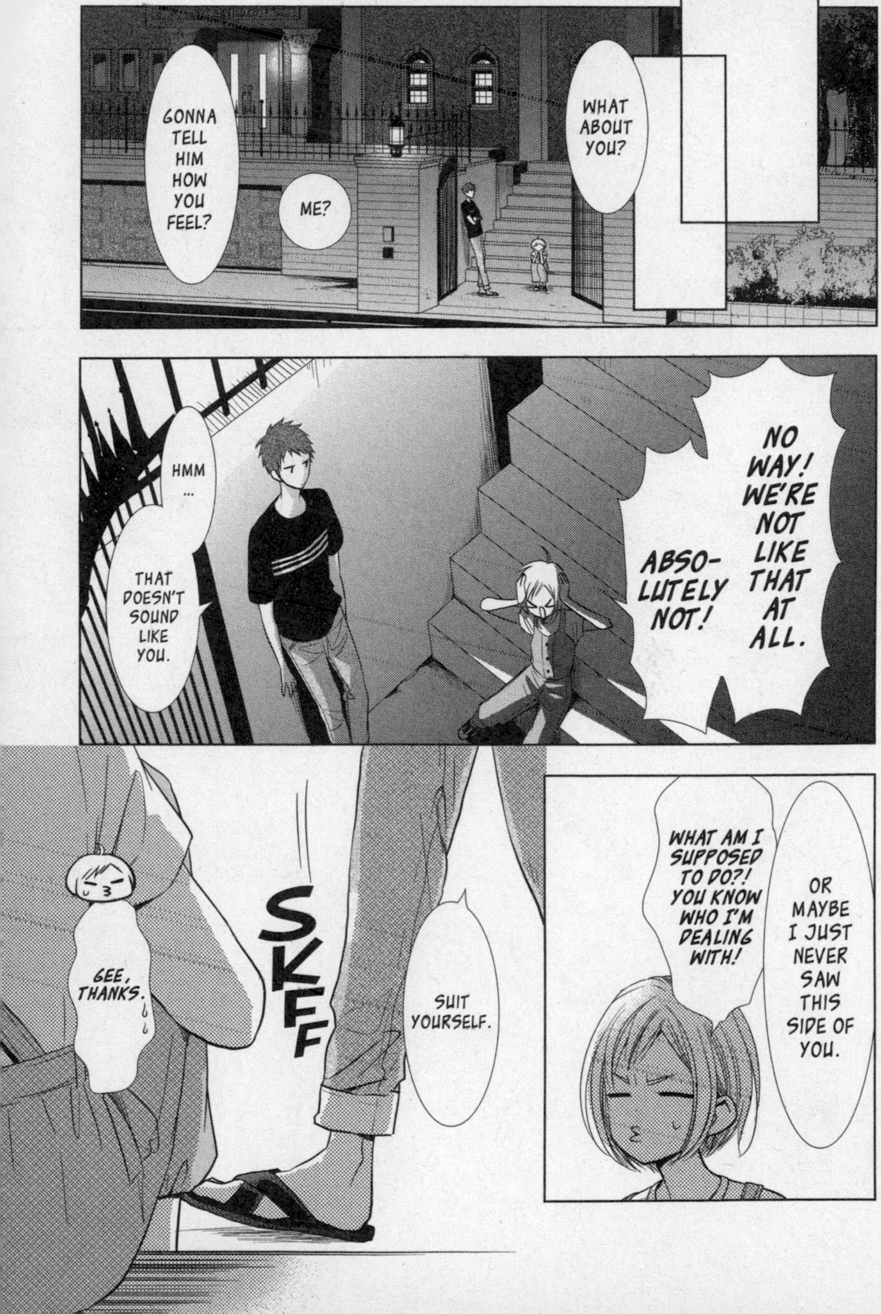
WHAT ABOUT YOU?
ME?
GONNA TELL HIM HOW YOU FEEL?
NO WAY! WE'RE NOT LIKE THAT AT ALL.
ABSO-LUTELY NOT!
HMM ...
THAT DOESN'T SOUND LIKE YOU.
OR MAYBE I JUST NEVER SAW THIS SIDE OF YOU.
WHAT AM I SUPPOSED TO DO?! YOU KNOW WHO I'M DEALING WITH!
SUIT YOURSELF.
SKFF
GEE, THANKS.

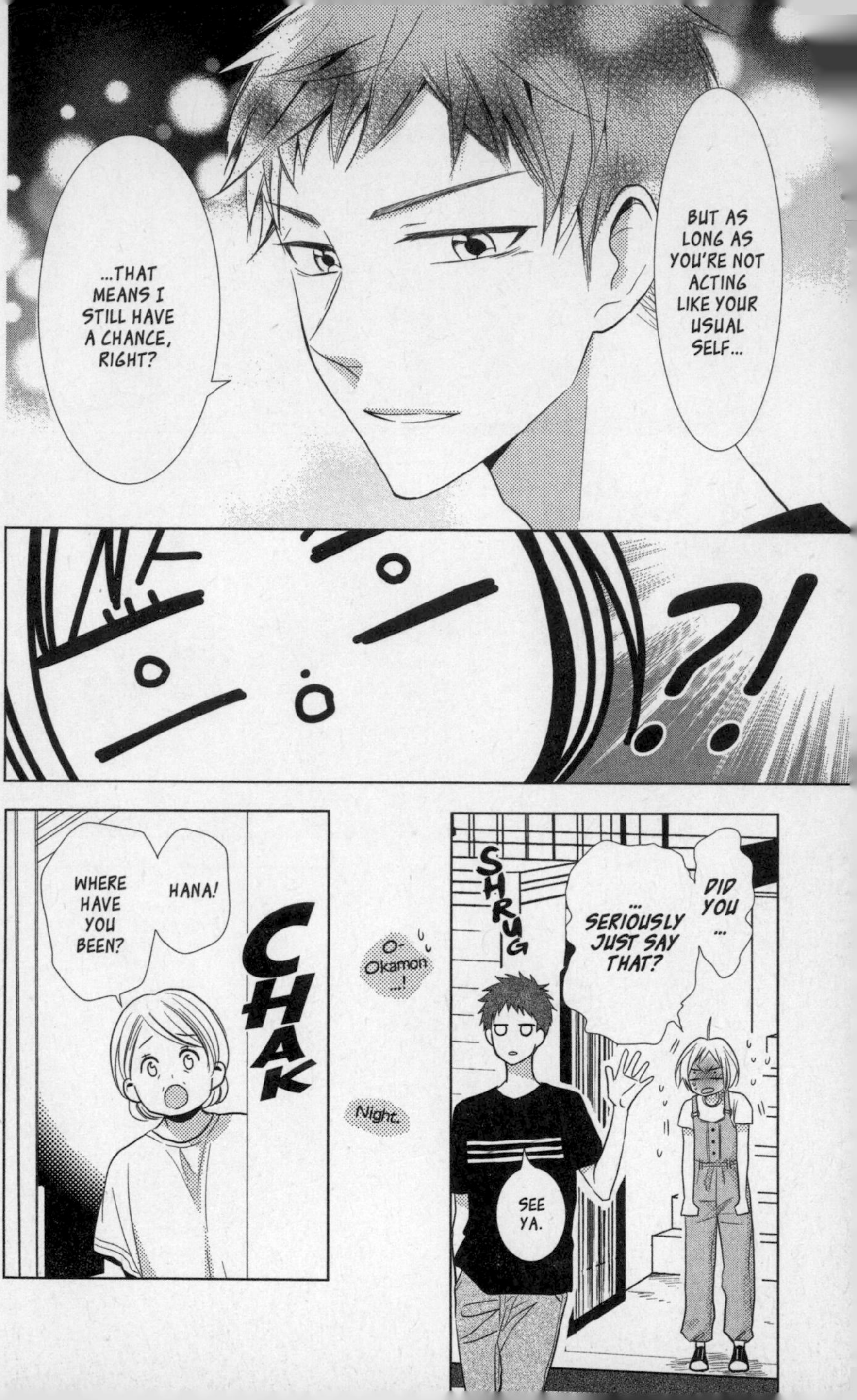
BUT AS LONG AS YOU'RE NOT ACTING LIKE YOUR USUAL SELF...
...THAT MEANS I STILL HAVE A CHANCE, RIGHT?
?!
DID YOU ...
... SERIOUSLY JUST SAY THAT?
SHRUG
SEE YA.
O-Okamon...!
Night.
HANA!
WHERE HAVE YOU BEEN?
CHAK

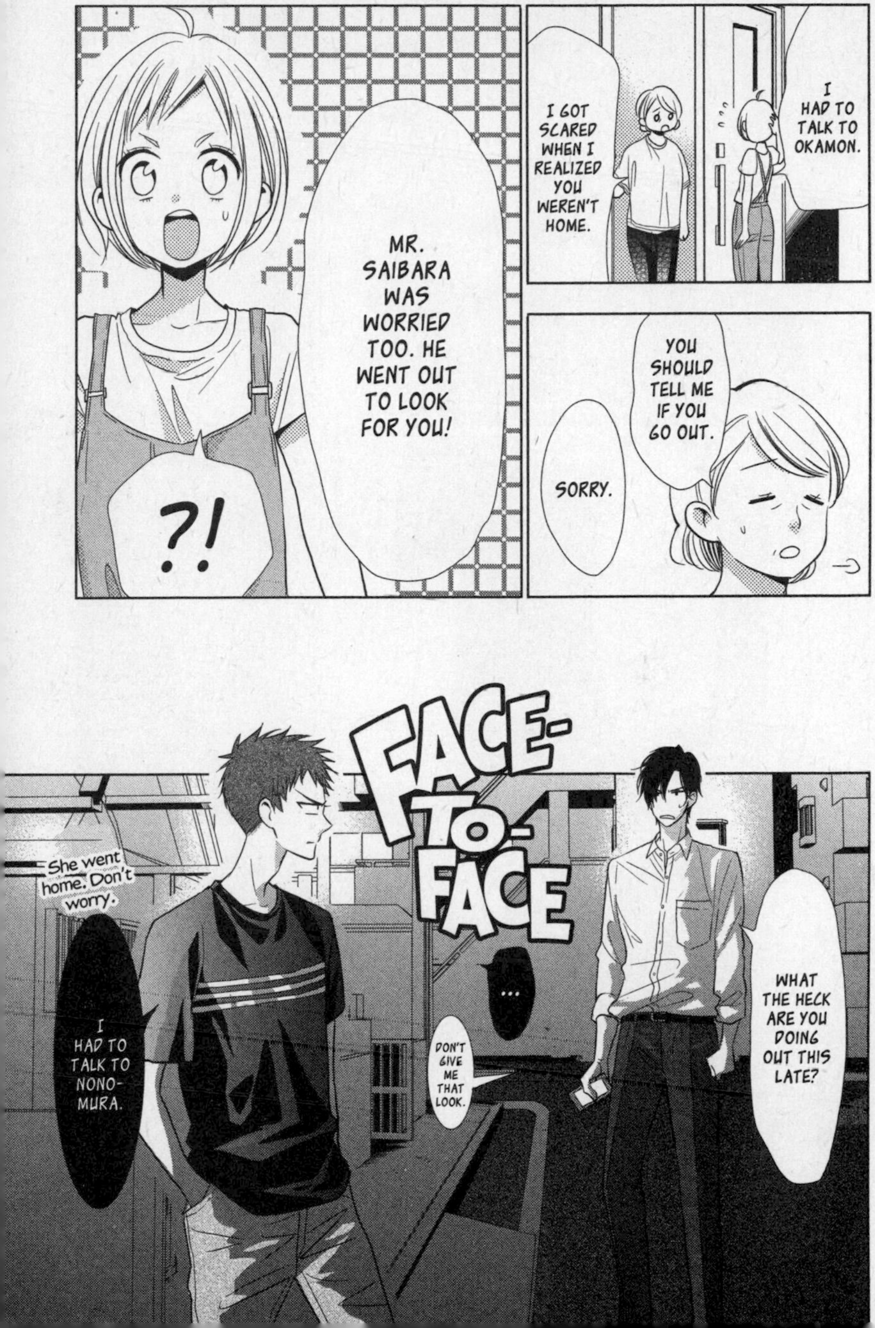
I HAD TO TALK TO OKAMON.
I GOT SCARED WHEN I REALIZED YOU WEREN'T HOME.
YOU SHOULD TELL ME IF YOU GO OUT.
SORRY.
MR. SAIBARA WAS WORRIED TOO. HE WENT OUT TO LOOK FOR YOU!
?!
FACE-TO-FACE
WHAT THE HECK ARE YOU DOING OUT THIS LATE?
...
DON'T GIVE ME THAT LOOK.
I HAD TO TALK TO NONOMURA.
She went home. Don't worry.

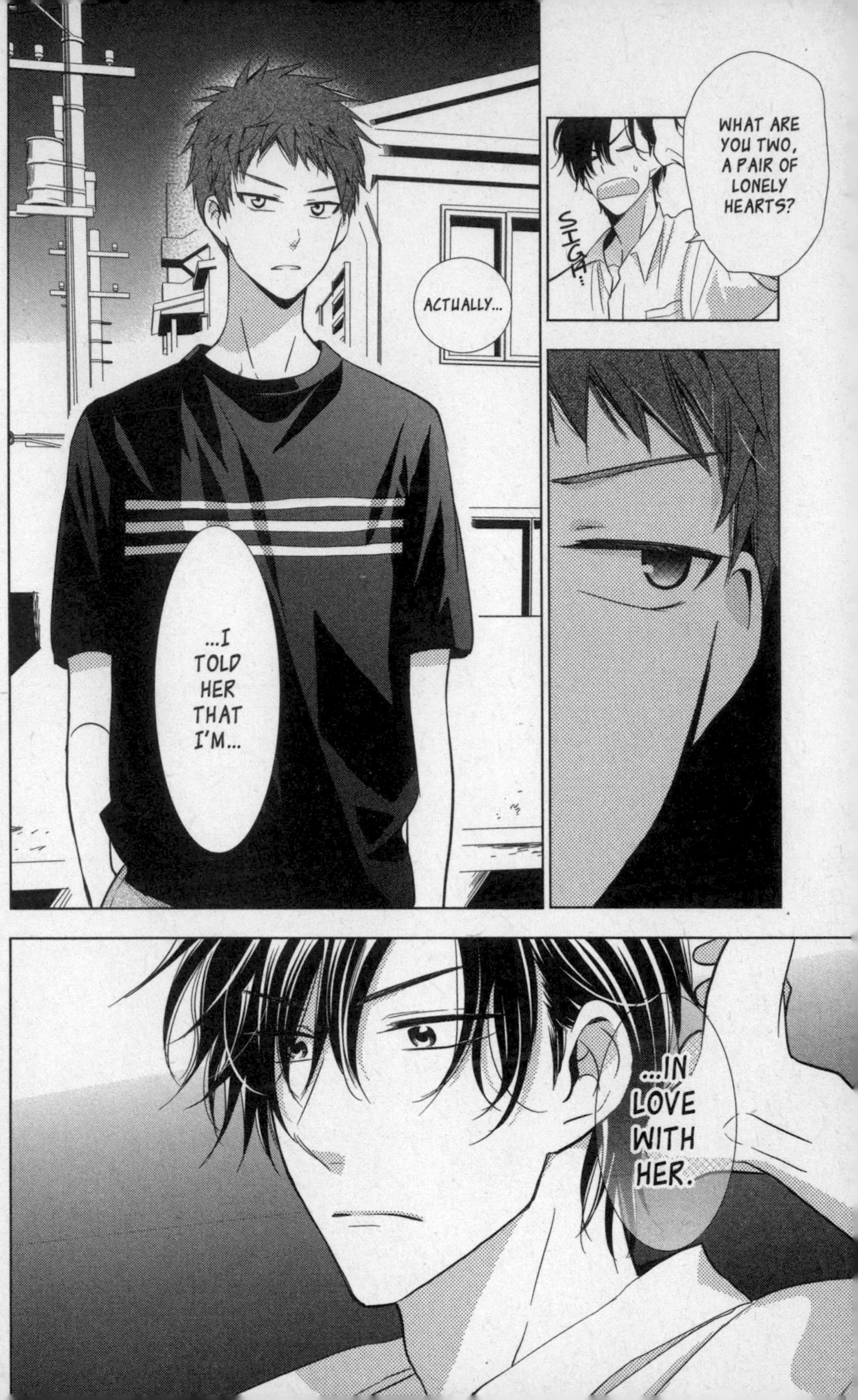
WHAT ARE YOU TWO, A PAIR OF LONELY HEARTS?
SIGH...
ACTUALLY...
...I TOLD HER THAT I'M...
...IN LOVE WITH HER.

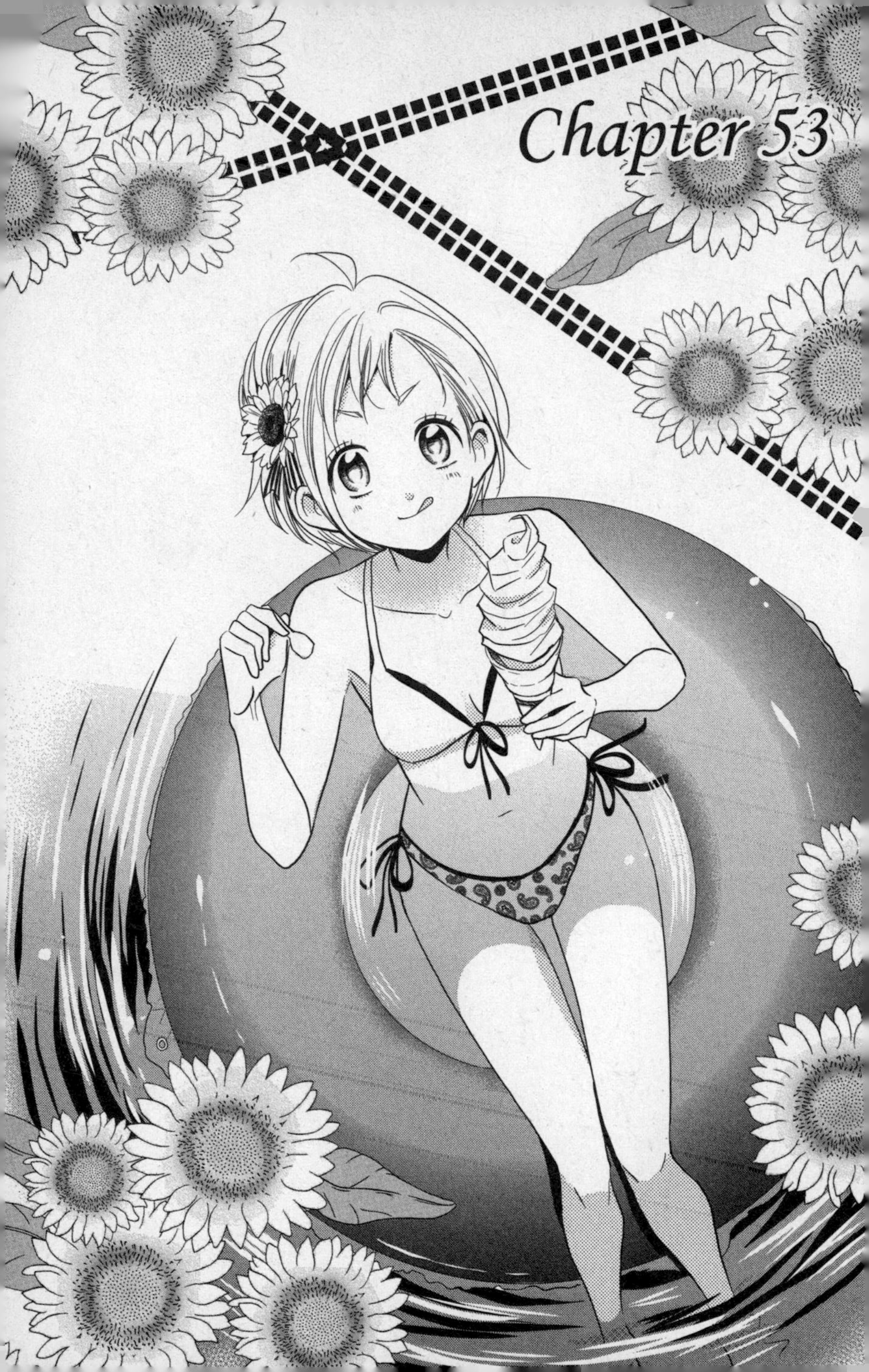
Chapter 53

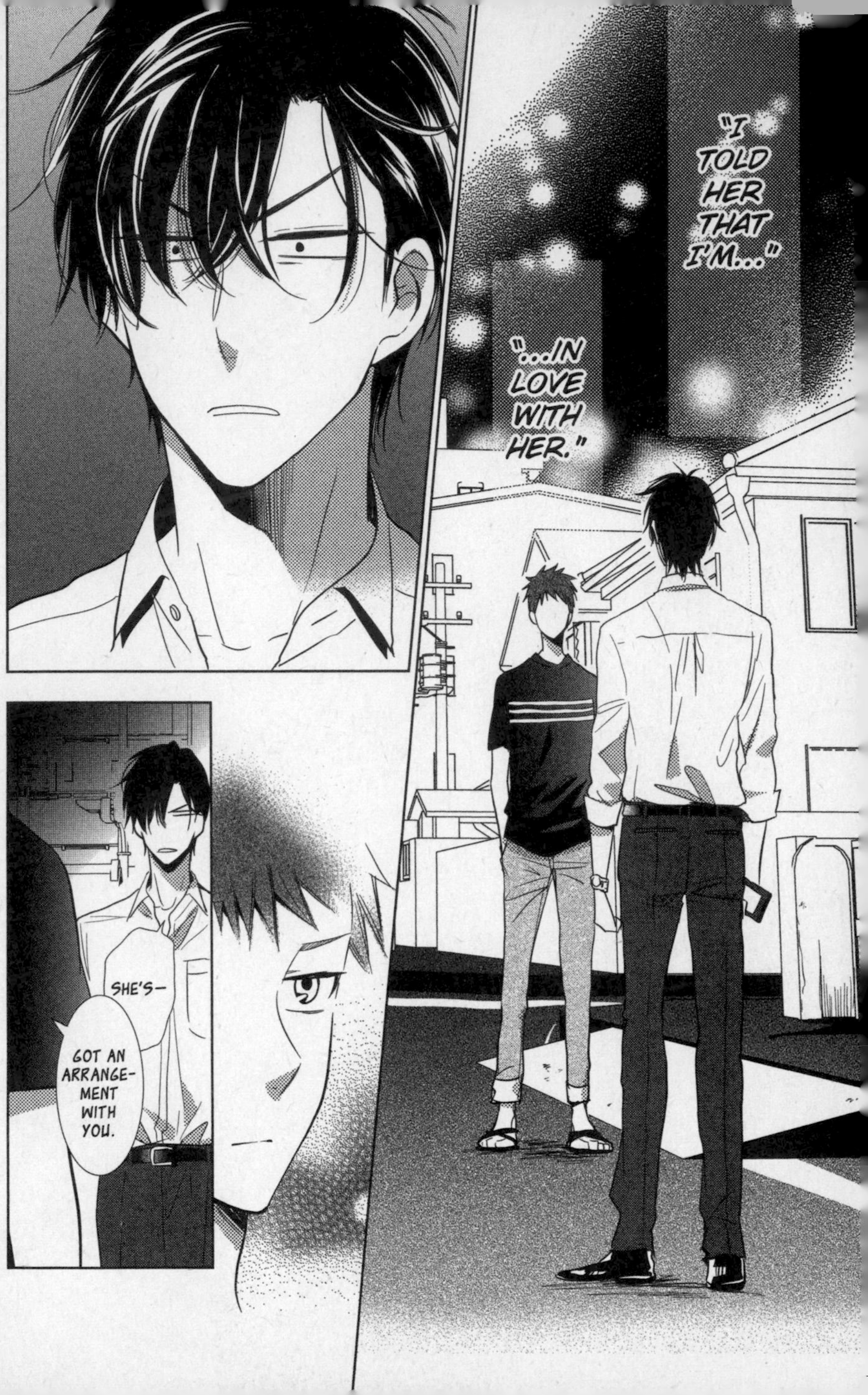
"I TOLD HER THAT I'M..."
"...IN LOVE WITH HER."
SHE'S—
GOT AN ARRANGE-MENT WITH YOU.

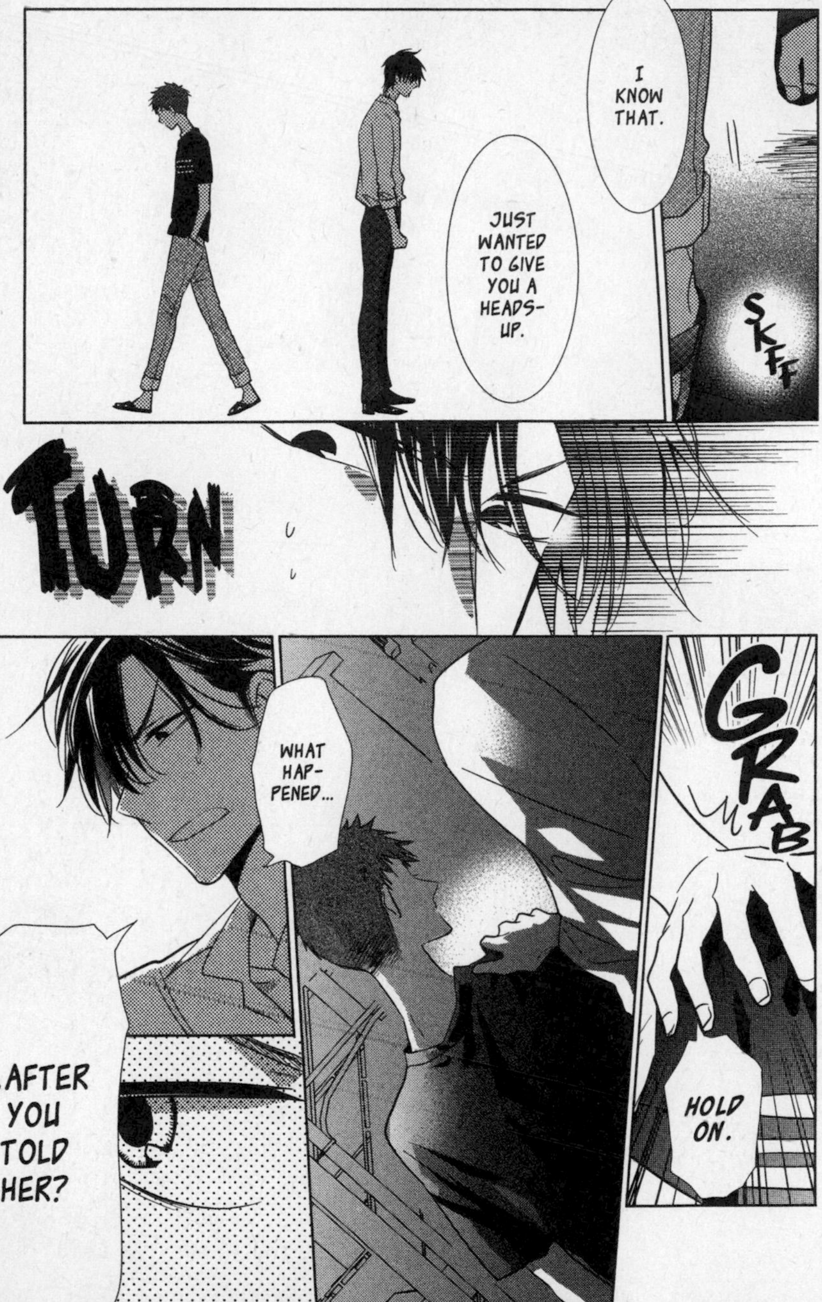
SKFF
I KNOW THAT.
JUST WANTED TO GIVE YOU A HEADS-UP.
TURN
GRAB
HOLD ON.
WHAT HAPPENED...
...AFTER YOU TOLD HER?

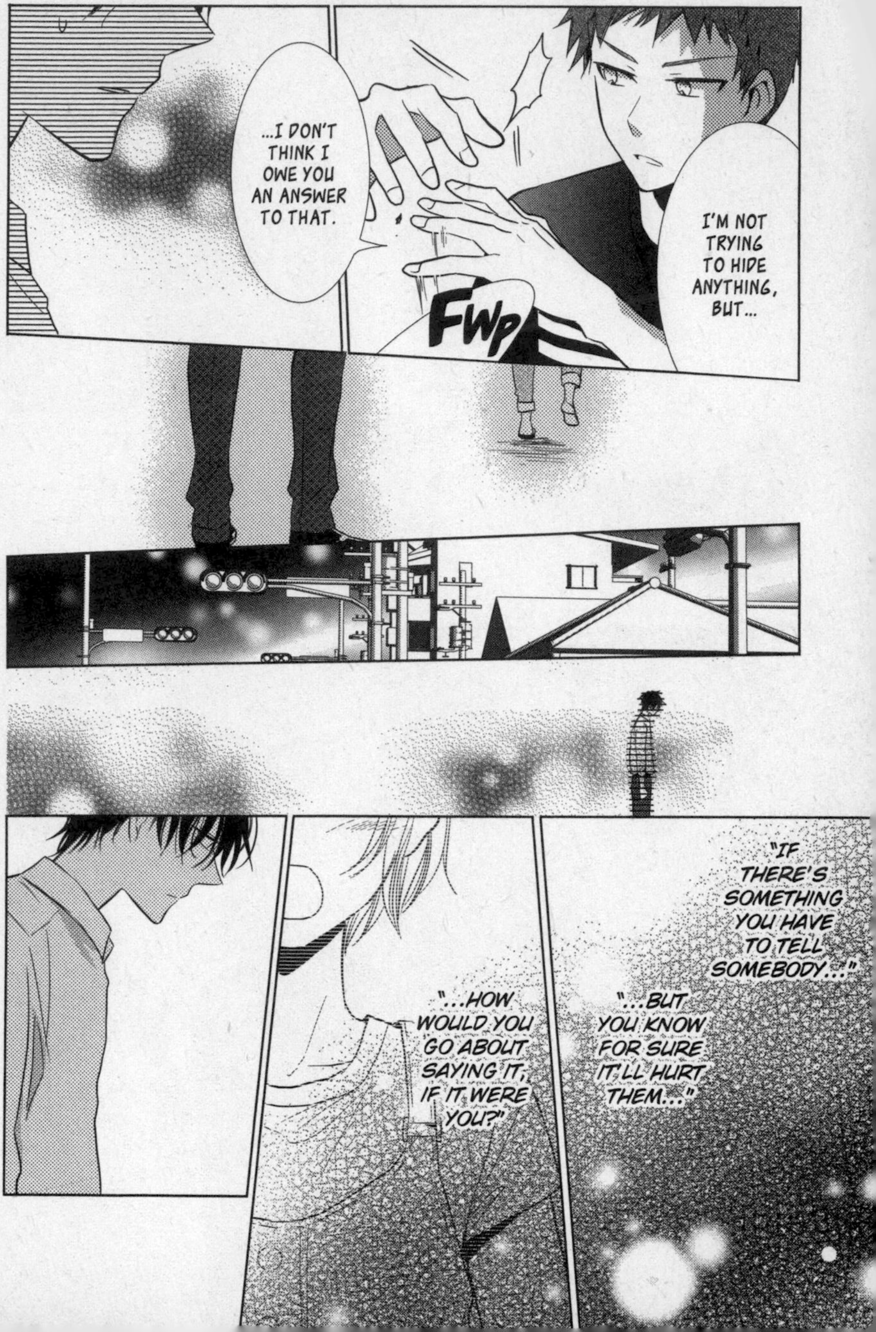
I'M NOT TRYING TO HIDE ANYTHING, BUT...
FWP
...I DON'T THINK I OWE YOU AN ANSWER TO THAT.
"IF THERE'S SOMETHING YOU HAVE TO TELL SOMEBODY..."
"...BUT YOU KNOW FOR SURE IT'LL HURT THEM..."
"...HOW WOULD YOU GO ABOUT SAYING IT, IF IT WERE YOU?"

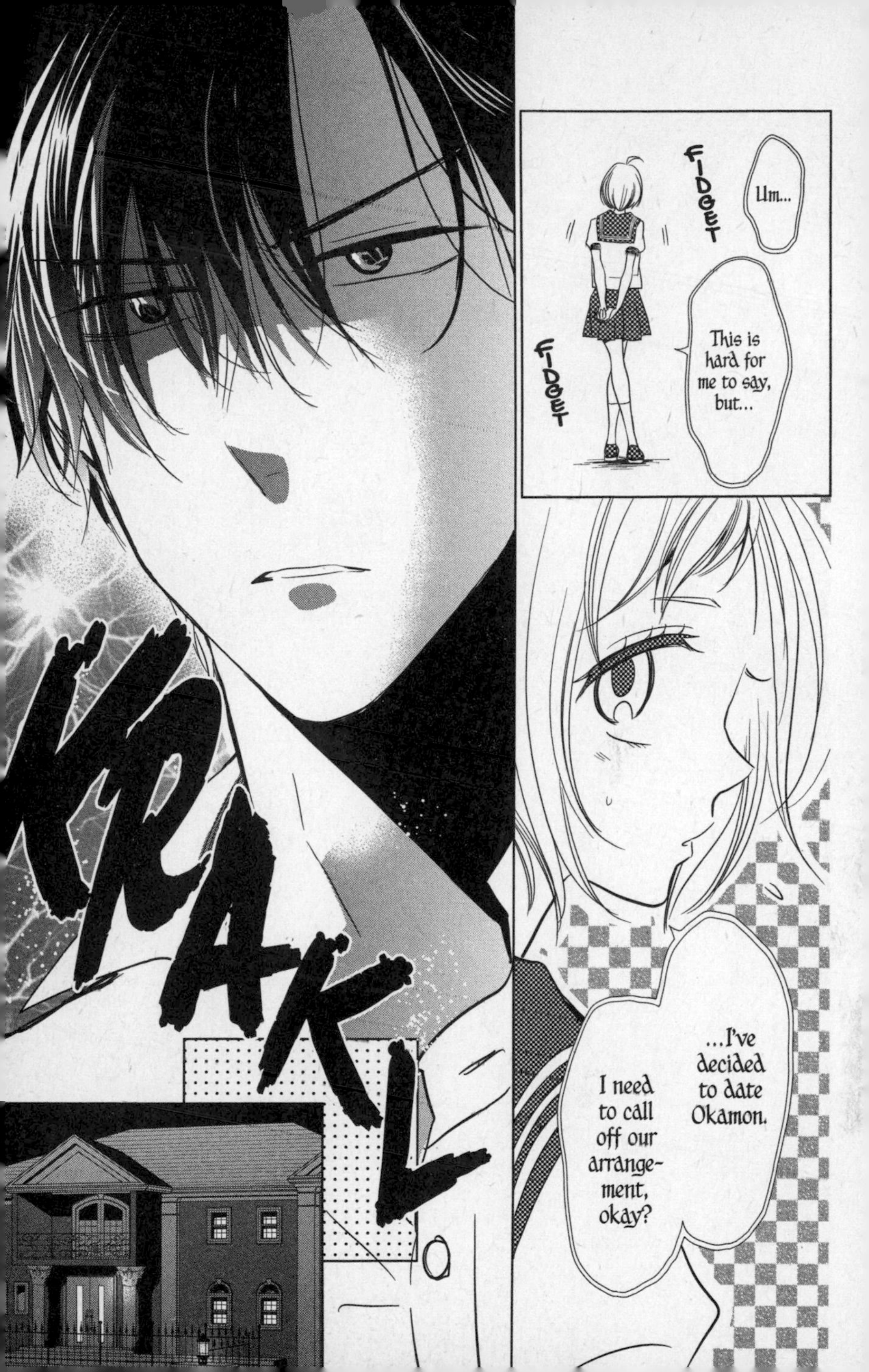
Um...
FIDGET
This is hard for me to say, but...
FIDGET
...I've decided to date Okamon.
I need to call off our arrangement, okay?

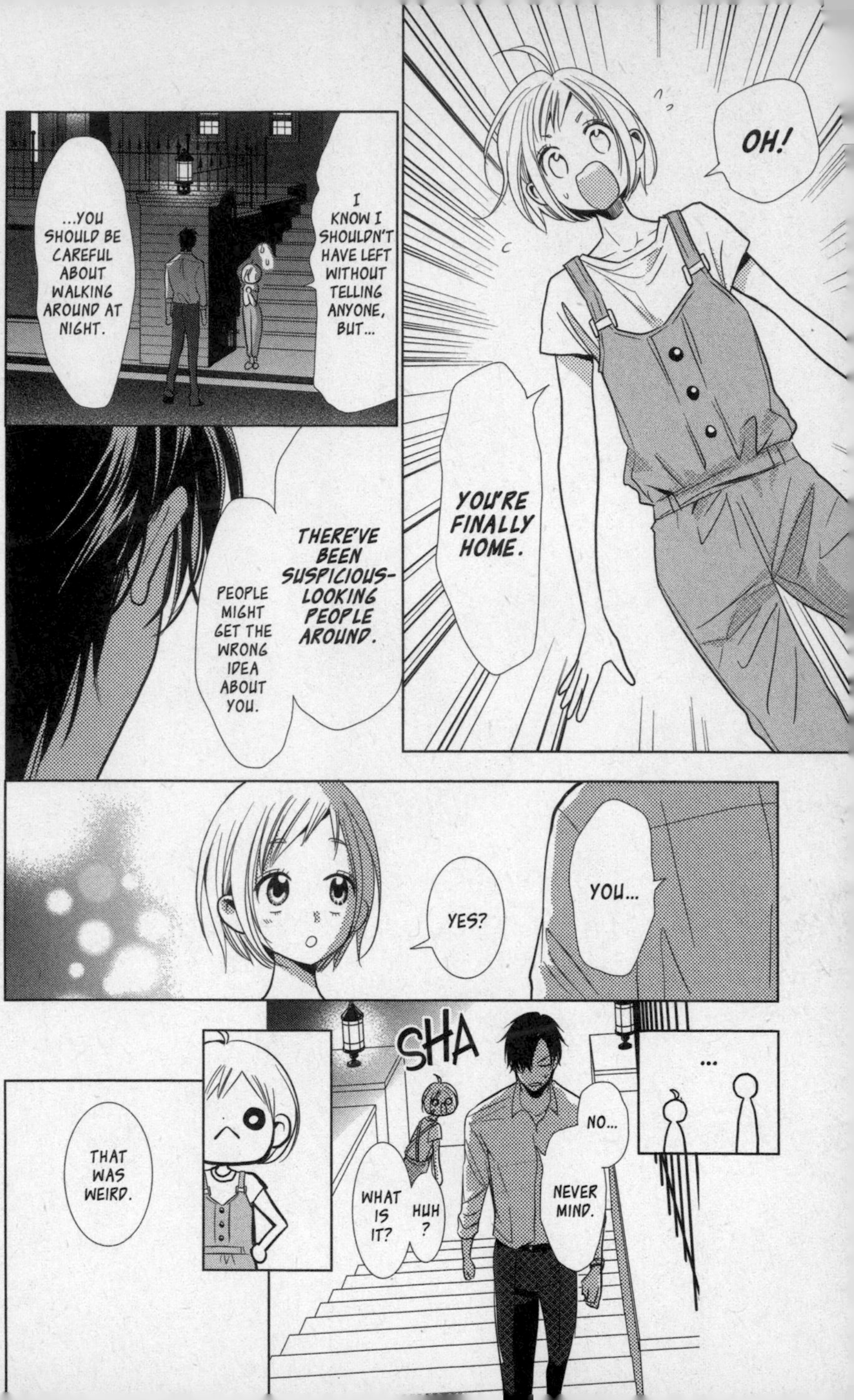
OH!
YOU'RE FINALLY HOME.
I KNOW I SHOULDN'T HAVE LEFT WITHOUT TELLING ANYONE, BUT...
...YOU SHOULD BE CAREFUL ABOUT WALKING AROUND AT NIGHT.
THERE'VE BEEN SUSPICIOUS-LOOKING PEOPLE AROUND.
PEOPLE MIGHT GET THE WRONG IDEA ABOUT YOU.
YOU...
YES?
...
SHA
NO...
NEVER MIND.
HUH?
WHAT IS IT?
THAT WAS WEIRD.

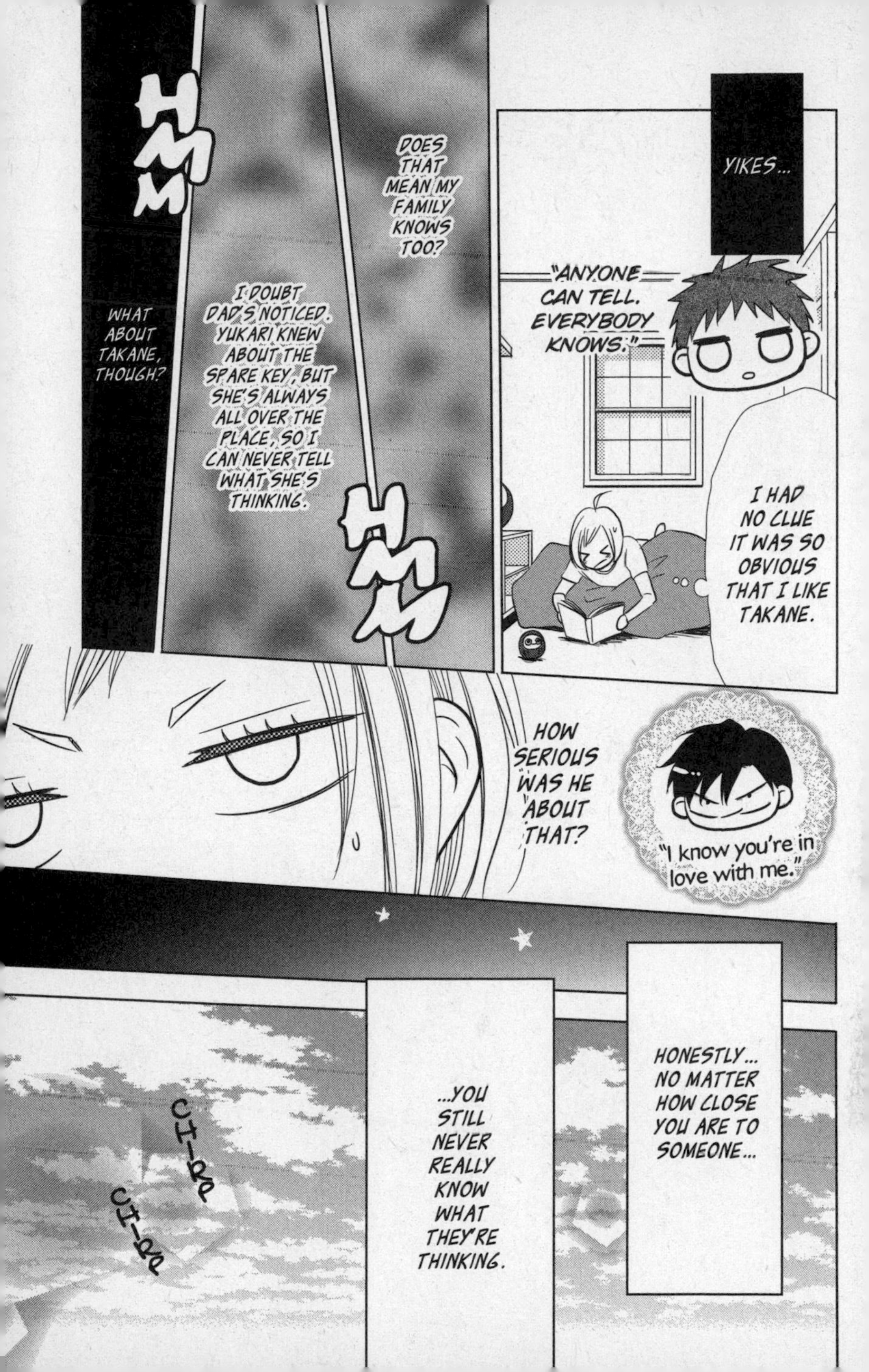
YIKES...
"ANYONE CAN TELL. EVERYBODY KNOWS."
I HAD NO CLUE IT WAS SO OBVIOUS THAT I LIKE TAKANE.
DOES THAT MEAN MY FAMILY KNOWS TOO?
I DOUBT DAD'S NOTICED. YUKARI KNEW ABOUT THE SPARE KEY, BUT SHE'S ALWAYS ALL OVER THE PLACE, SO I CAN NEVER TELL WHAT SHE'S THINKING.
HMM
HMM
WHAT ABOUT TAKANE, THOUGH?
"I know you're in love with me."
HOW SERIOUS WAS HE ABOUT THAT?
HONESTLY... NO MATTER HOW CLOSE YOU ARE TO SOMEONE...
...YOU STILL NEVER REALLY KNOW WHAT THEY'RE THINKING.
CHIRP
CHIRP

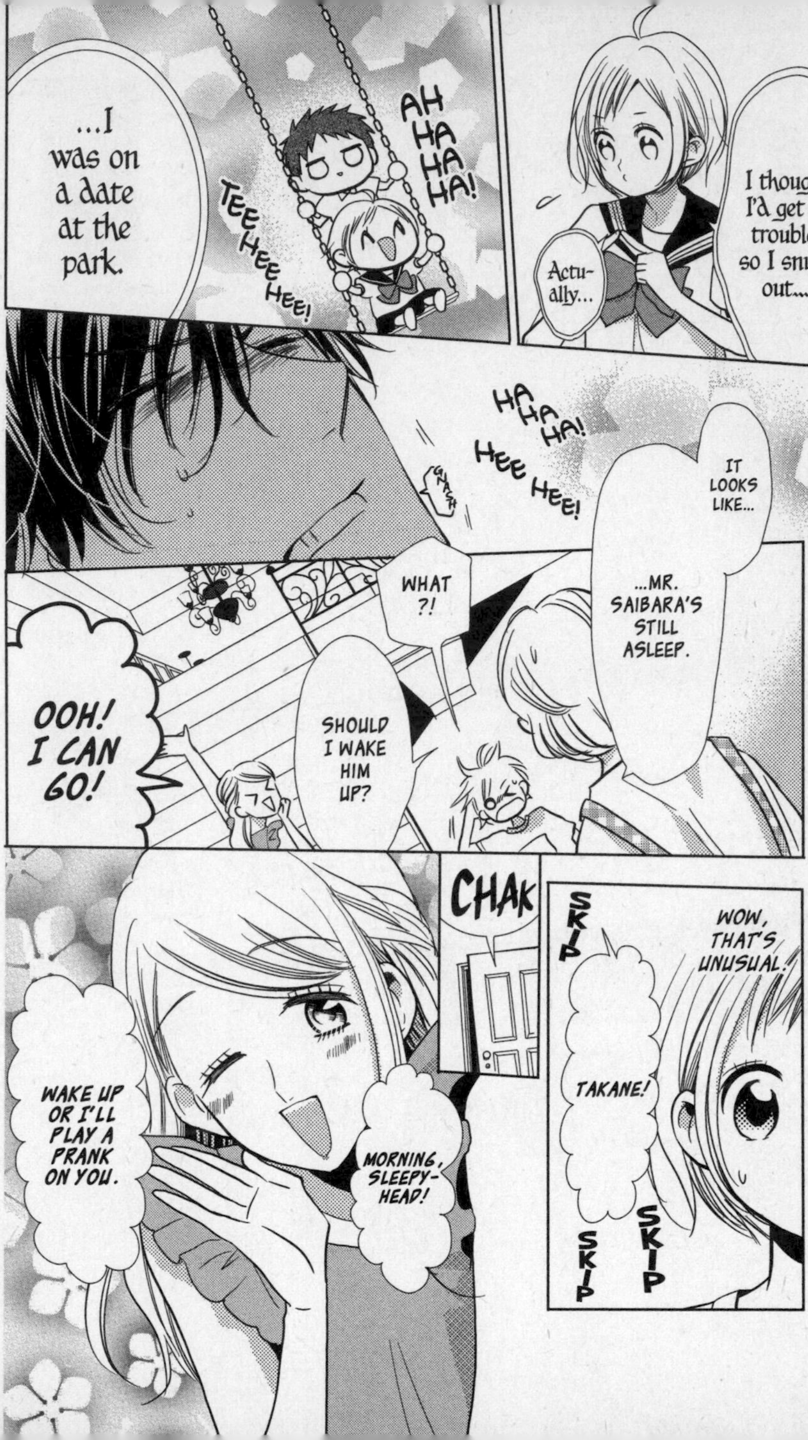
Actually...
I thought I'd get in trouble, so I snuck out...
...I was on a date at the park.
AH HA HA HA!
TEE HEE HEE!
HA HA HA!
HEE HEE!
GNASH
IT LOOKS LIKE...
...MR. SAIBARA'S STILL ASLEEP.
WHAT?!
SHOULD I WAKE HIM UP?
OOH! I CAN GO!
WOW, THAT'S UNUSUAL.
SKIP
TAKANE!
SKIP
SKIP
CHAK
MORNING, SLEEPYHEAD!
WAKE UP OR I'LL PLAY A PRANK ON YOU.

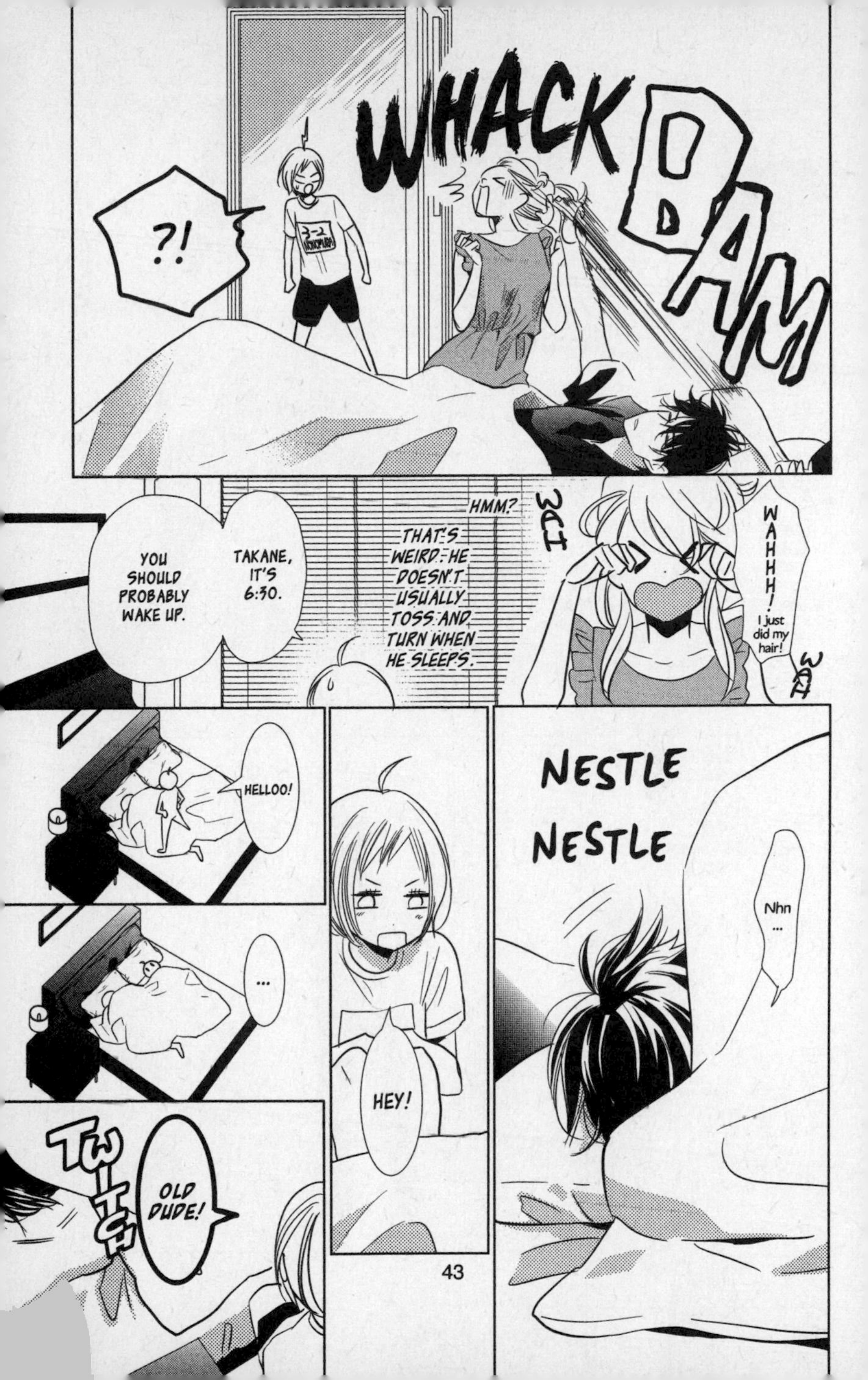
WHACK
DAM
?!
WAH
WAHHH! I just did my hair!
WAH
HMM?
THAT'S WEIRD. HE DOESN'T USUALLY TOSS AND TURN WHEN HE SLEEPS.
TAKANE, IT'S 6:30.
YOU SHOULD PROBABLY WAKE UP.
NESTLE
NESTLE
Nhn ...
HEY!
HELLOO!
...
TWITCH
OLD DUDE!

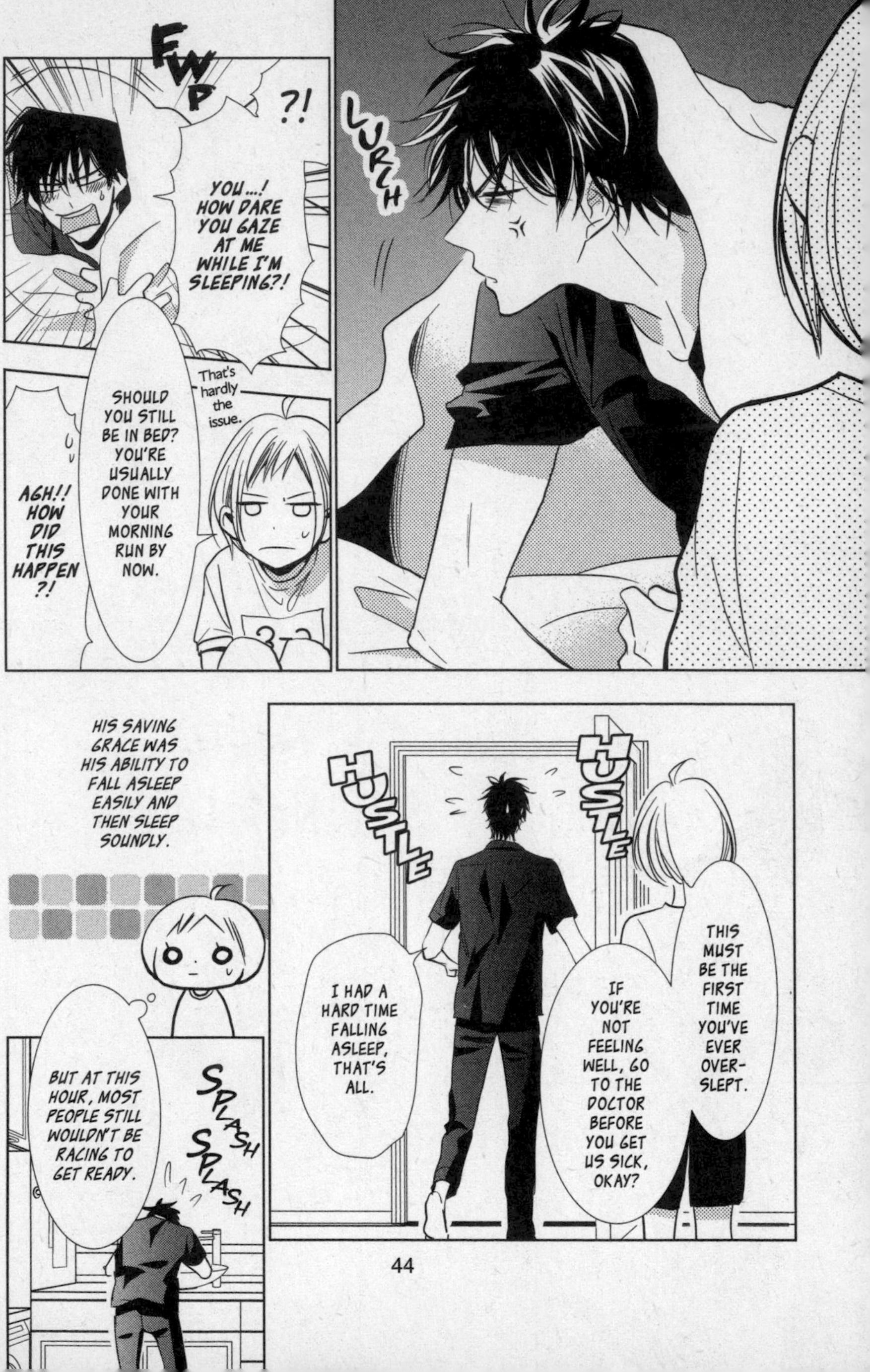
LURCH
?!
FWP
YOU...! HOW DARE YOU GAZE AT ME WHILE I'M SLEEPING?!
That's hardly the issue.
SHOULD YOU STILL BE IN BED? YOU'RE USUALLY DONE WITH YOUR MORNING RUN BY NOW.
AGH!! HOW DID THIS HAPPEN?!
HUSTLE
HUSTLE
THIS MUST BE THE FIRST TIME YOU'VE EVER OVER-SLEPT.
IF YOU'RE NOT FEELING WELL, GO TO THE DOCTOR BEFORE YOU GET US SICK, OKAY?
I HAD A HARD TIME FALLING ASLEEP, THAT'S ALL.
HIS SAVING GRACE WAS HIS ABILITY TO FALL ASLEEP EASILY AND THEN SLEEP SOUNDLY.
BUT AT THIS HOUR, MOST PEOPLE STILL WOULDN'T BE RACING TO GET READY.
SPLASH
SPLASH

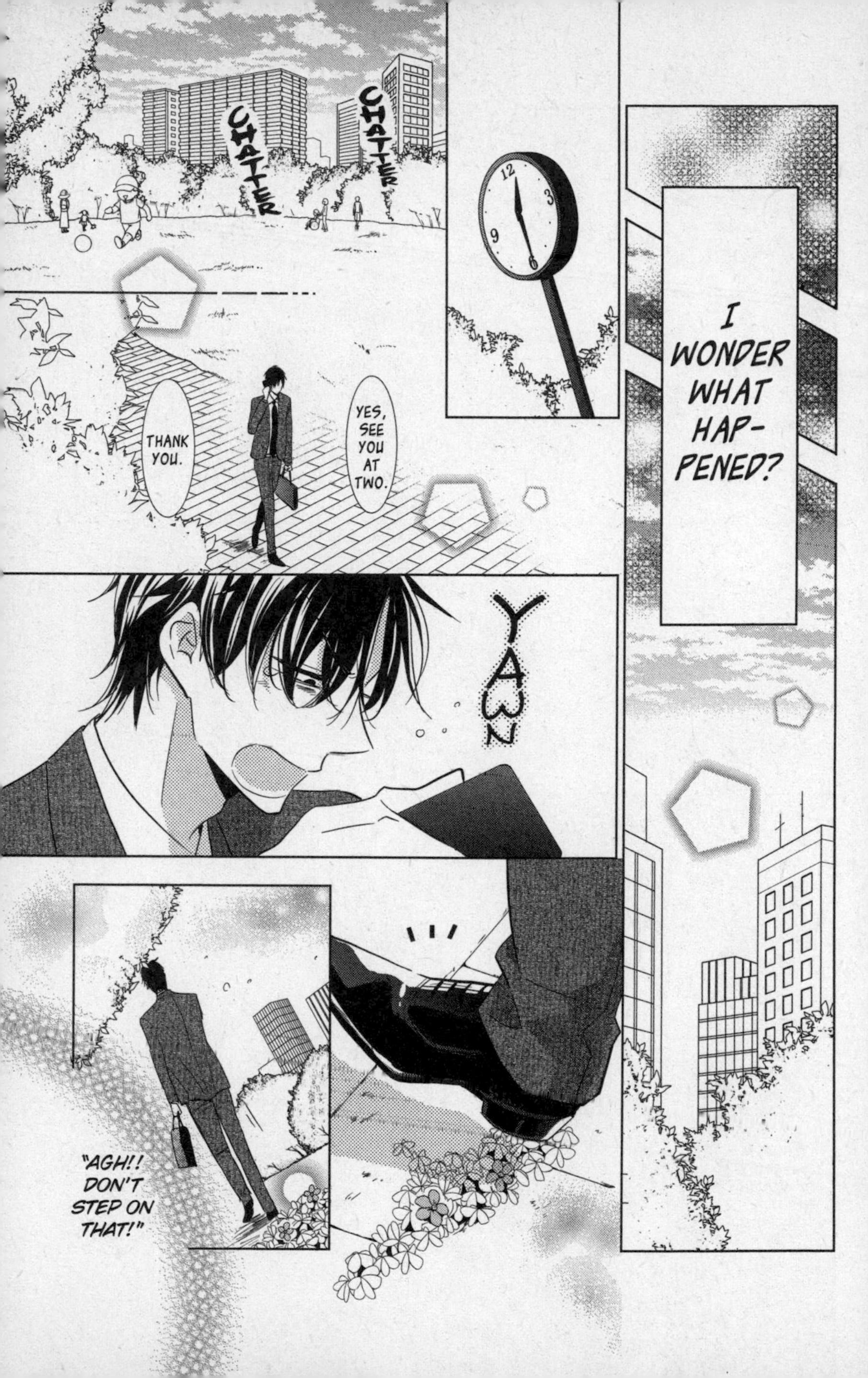
I WONDER WHAT HAP-PENED?
CHATTER
CHATTER
YES, SEE YOU AT TWO.
THANK YOU.
YAWN
"AGH!! DON'T STEP ON THAT!"

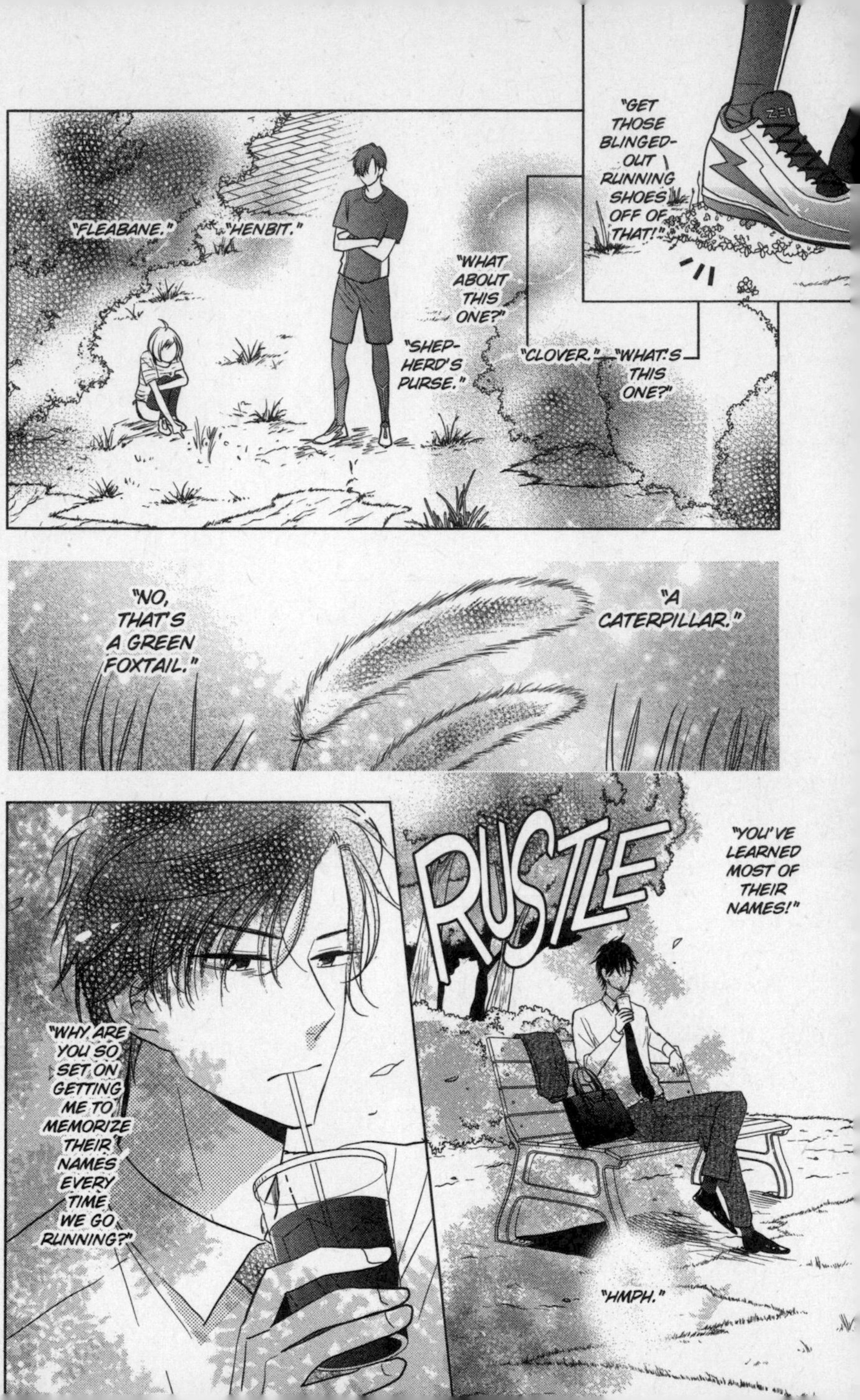
"GET THOSE BLINGED-OUT RUNNING SHOES OFF OF THAT!"
"WHAT'S THIS ONE?"
"CLOVER."
"WHAT ABOUT THIS ONE?"
"SHEP-HERD'S PURSE."
"HENBIT."
"FLEABANE."
"A CATERPILLAR."
"NO, THAT'S A GREEN FOXTAIL."
"YOU'VE LEARNED MOST OF THEIR NAMES!"
RUSTLE
"HMPH."
"WHY ARE YOU SO SET ON GETTING ME TO MEMORIZE THEIR NAMES EVERY TIME WE GO RUNNING?"

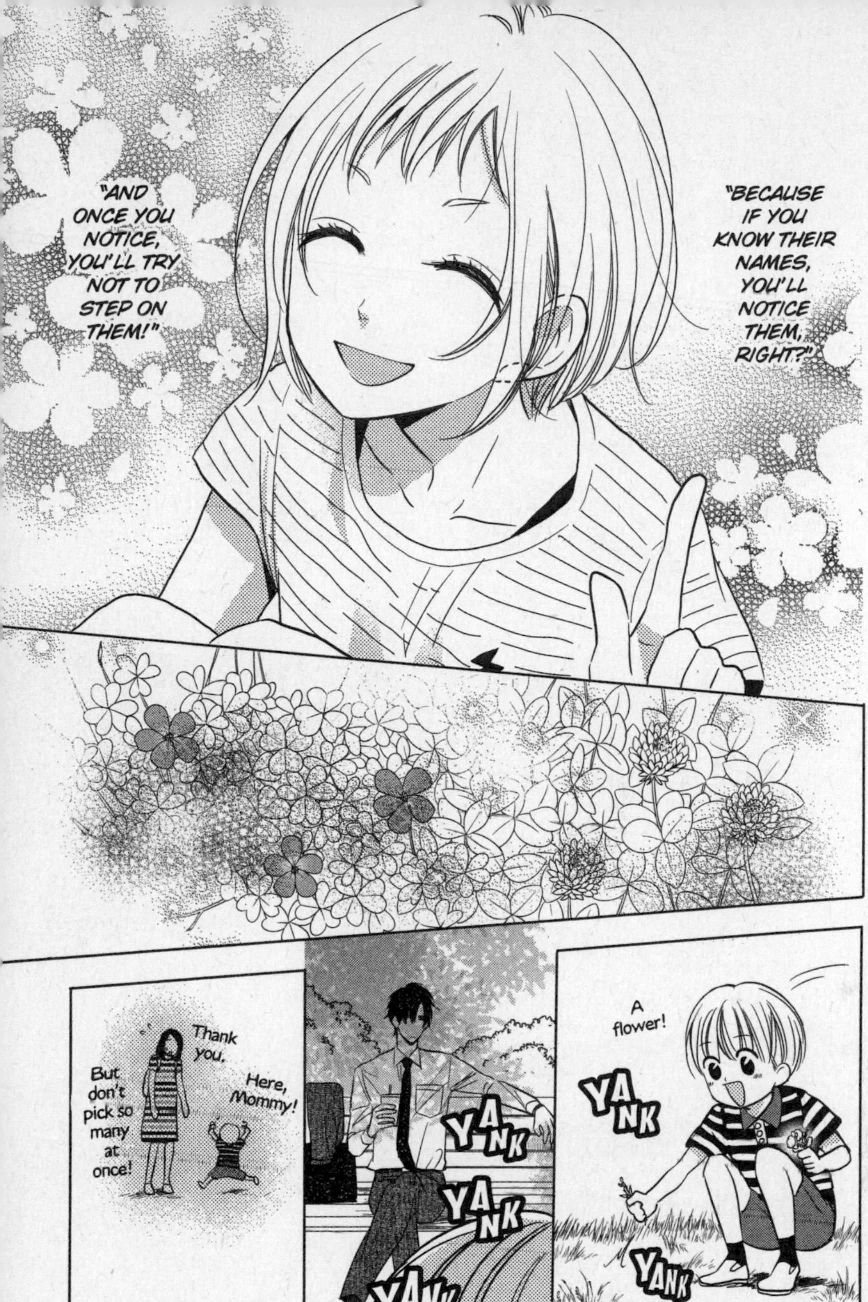
"BECAUSE IF YOU KNOW THEIR NAMES, YOU'LL NOTICE THEM, RIGHT?"
"AND ONCE YOU NOTICE, YOU'LL TRY NOT TO STEP ON THEM!"
A flower!
YANK
YANK
YANK
YANK
YANK
Here, Mommy!
Thank you.
But don't pick so many at once!

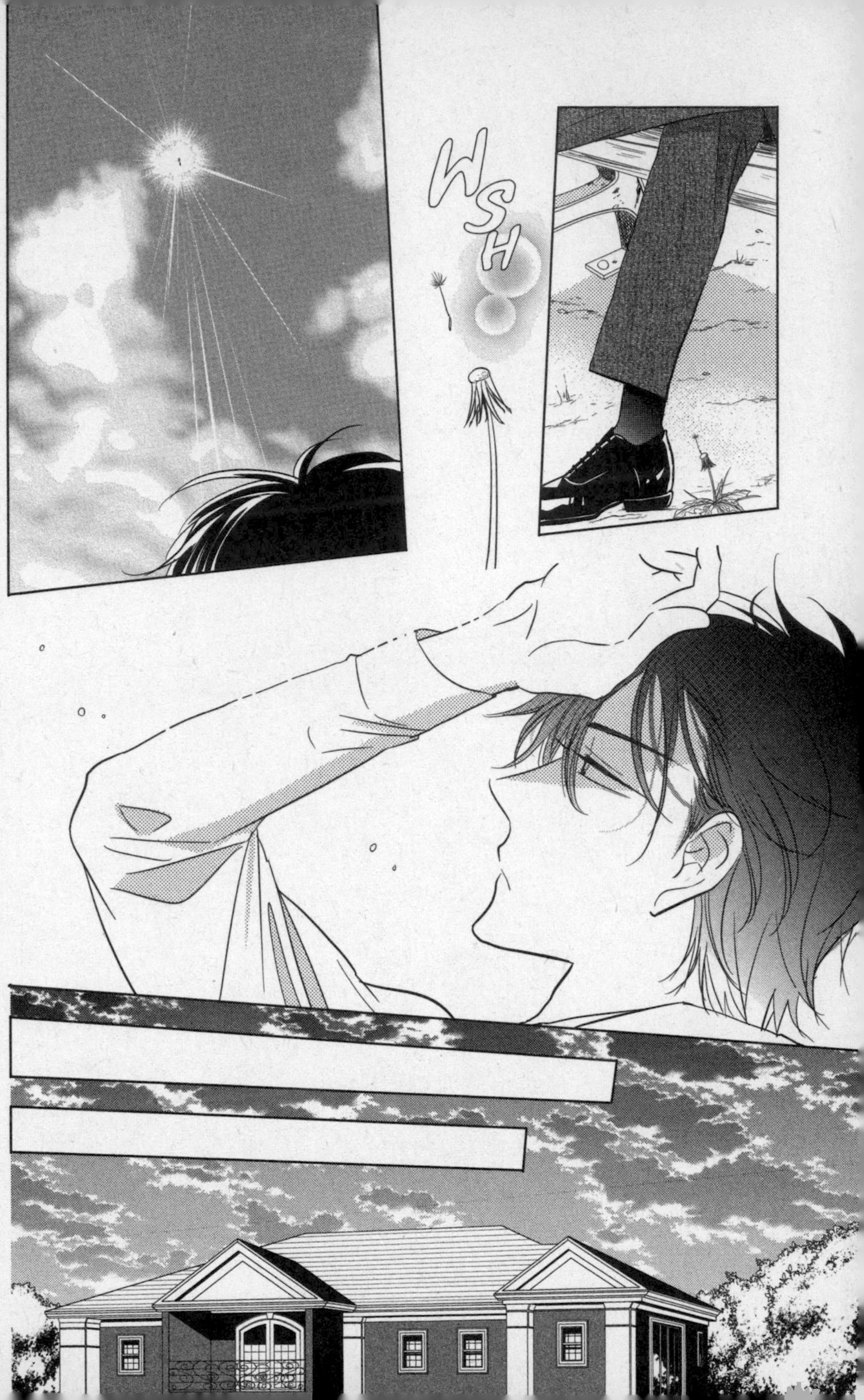
WSH

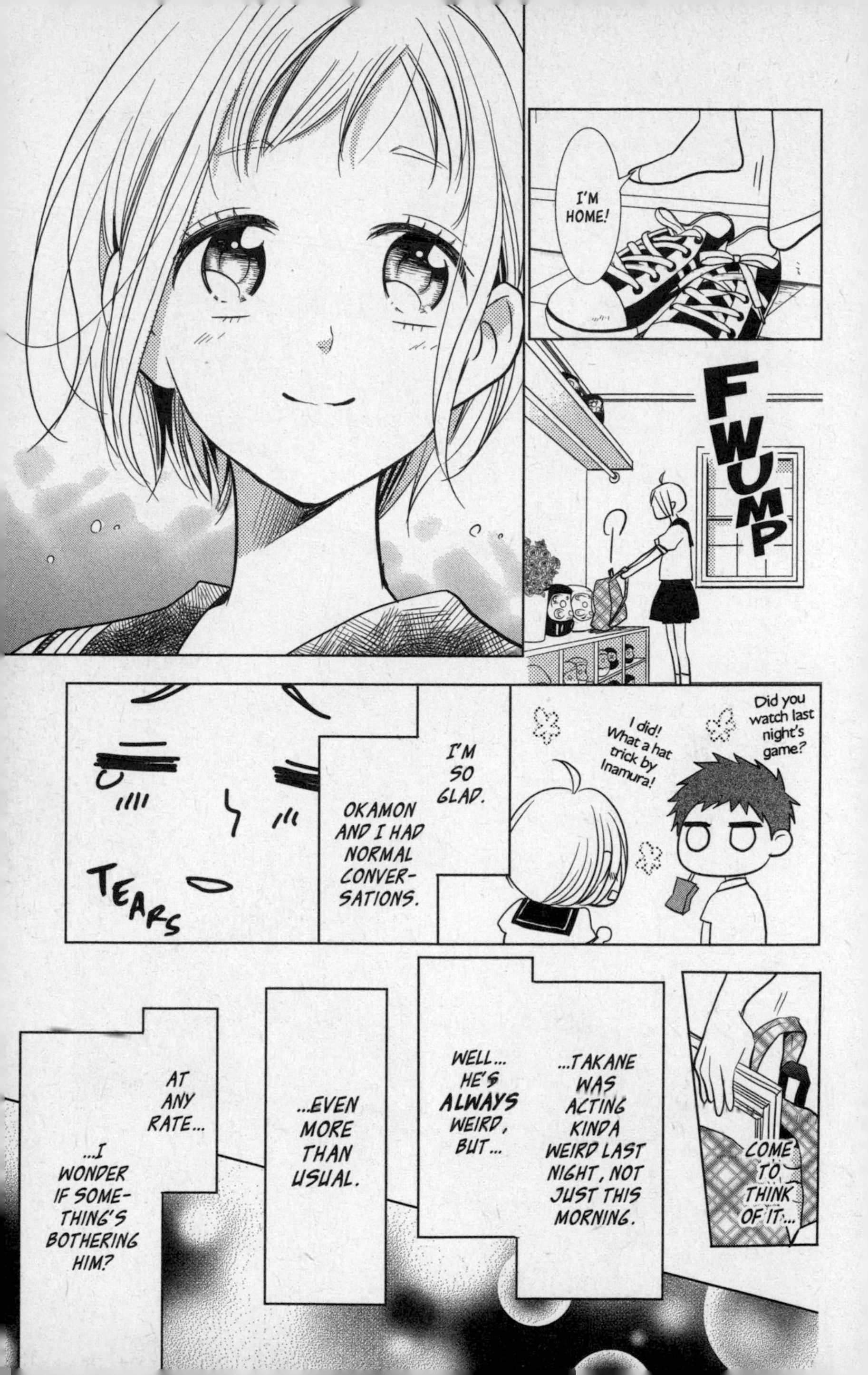
I'M HOME!
FWUMP
Did you watch last night's game?
I did! What a hat trick by Inamura!
I'M SO GLAD.
OKAMON AND I HAD NORMAL CONVER-SATIONS.
TEARS
COME TO THINK OF IT...
...TAKANE WAS ACTING KINDA WEIRD LAST NIGHT, NOT JUST THIS MORNING.
WELL... HE'S ALWAYS WEIRD, BUT...
...EVEN MORE THAN USUAL.
AT ANY RATE...
...I WONDER IF SOME-THING'S BOTHERING HIM?

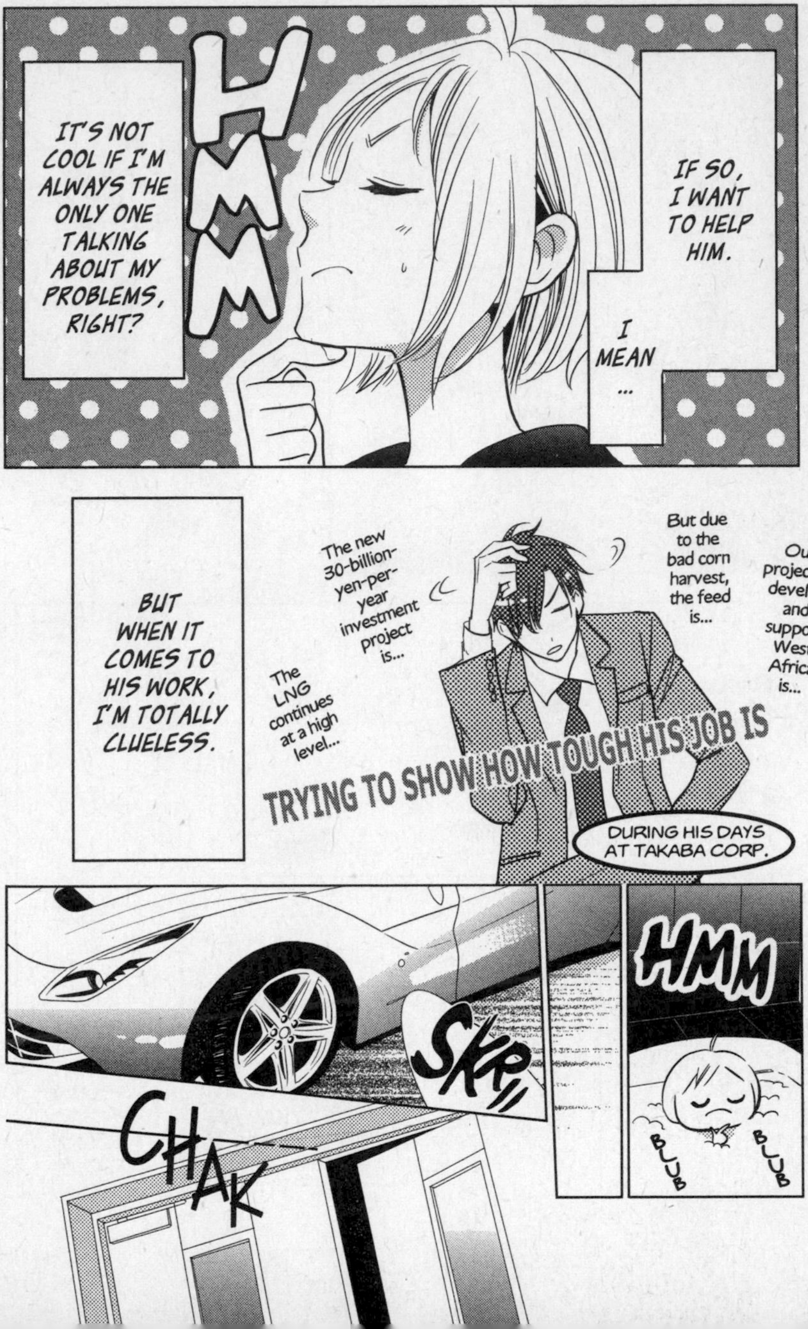
IF SO, I WANT TO HELP HIM.
I MEAN...
HMMM
IT'S NOT COOL IF I'M ALWAYS THE ONLY ONE TALKING ABOUT MY PROBLEMS, RIGHT?
Our project to develop and support West Africa is...
But due to the bad corn harvest, the feed is...
The new 30-billion-yen-per-year investment project is...
The LNG continues at a high level...
TRYING TO SHOW HOW TOUGH HIS JOB IS
DURING HIS DAYS AT TAKABA CORP.
BUT WHEN IT COMES TO HIS WORK, I'M TOTALLY CLUELESS.
HMM
BLUB
BLUB
SKR
CHAK

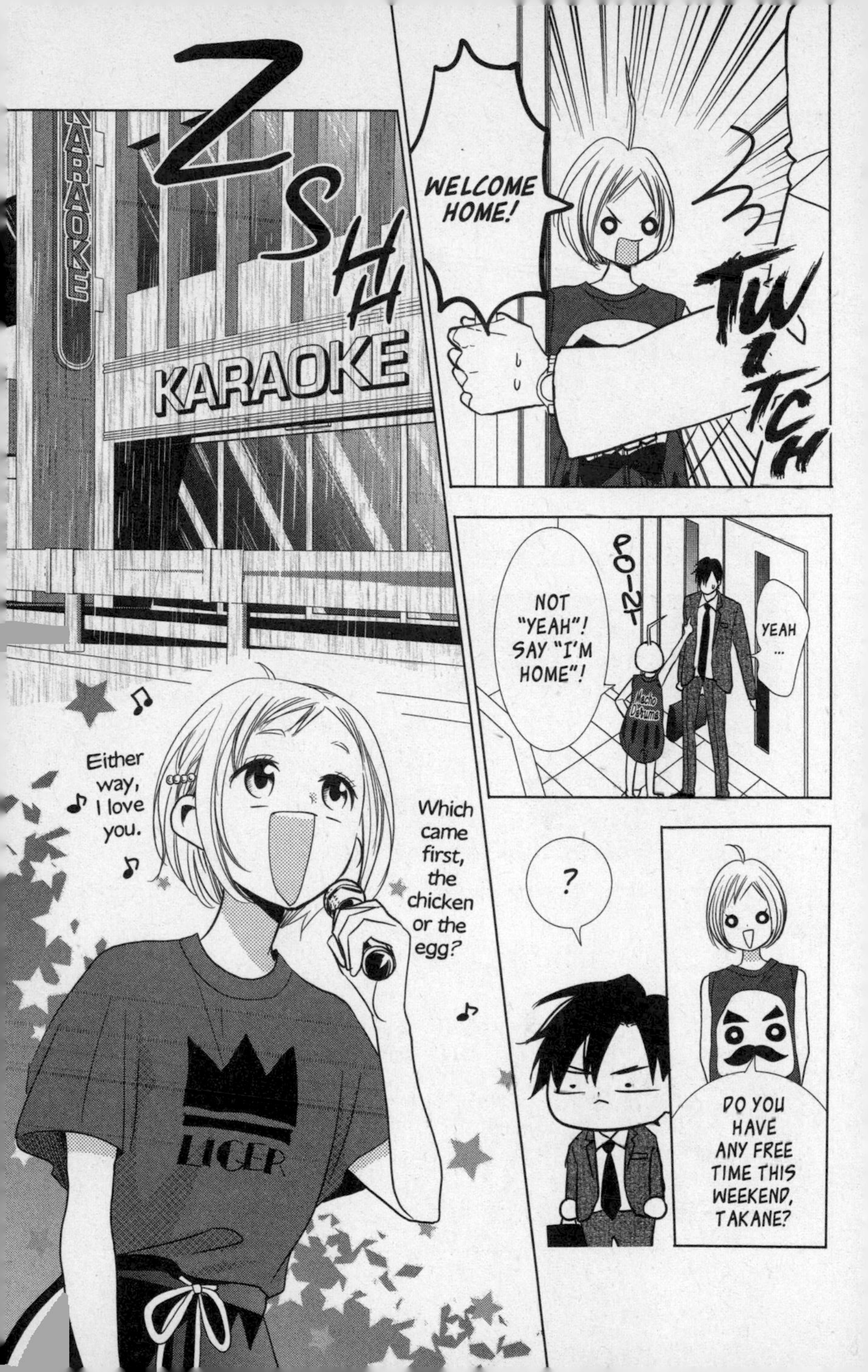
WELCOME HOME!
TWITCH
YEAH ...
PO-INT
NOT "YEAH"! SAY "I'M HOME"!
Macho Daruma
DO YOU HAVE ANY FREE TIME THIS WEEKEND, TAKANE?
?
ZSHH
KARAOKE
KARAOKE
Which came first, the chicken or the egg?
Either way, I love you.
LIGER

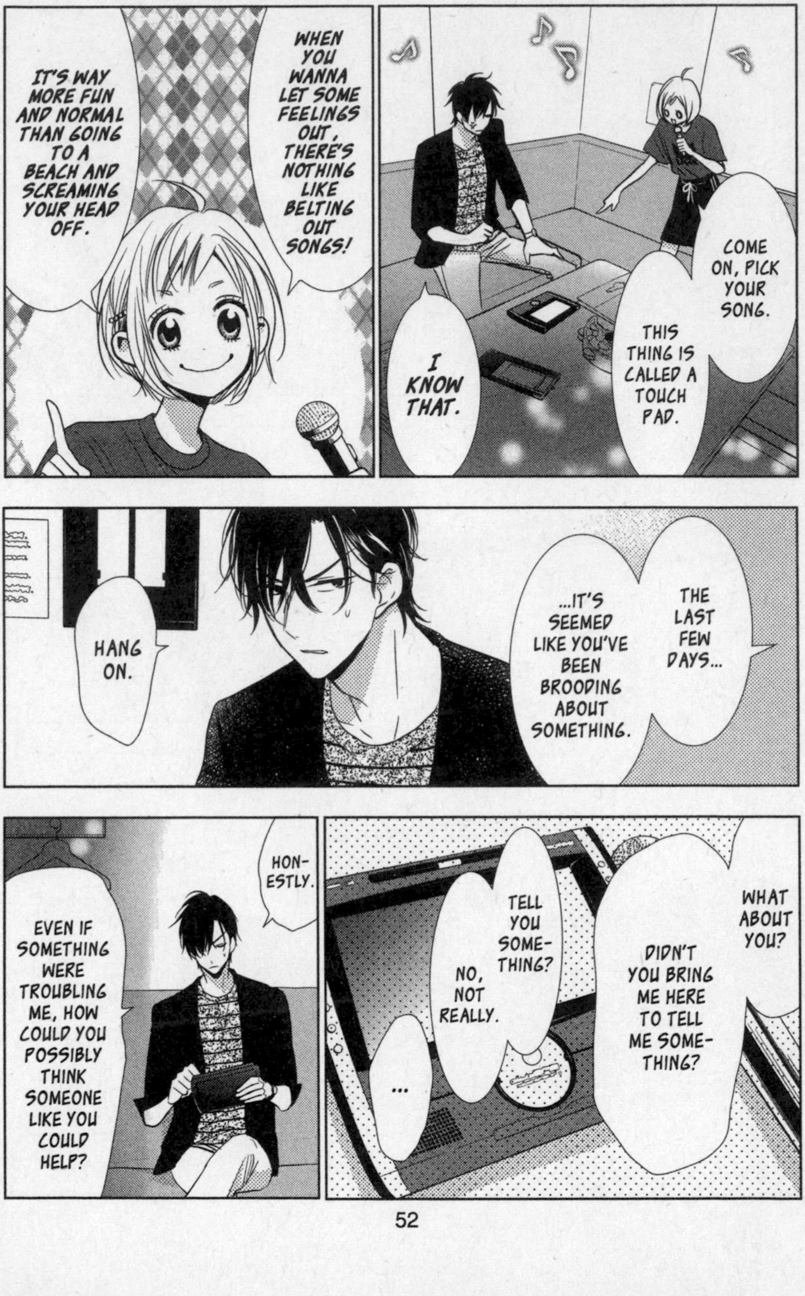
COME ON, PICK YOUR SONG.
THIS THING IS CALLED A TOUCH PAD.
I KNOW THAT.
WHEN YOU WANNA LET SOME FEELINGS OUT, THERE'S NOTHING LIKE BELTING OUT SONGS!
IT'S WAY MORE FUN AND NORMAL THAN GOING TO A BEACH AND SCREAMING YOUR HEAD OFF.
THE LAST FEW DAYS...
...IT'S SEEMED LIKE YOU'VE BEEN BROODING ABOUT SOMETHING.
HANG ON.
WHAT ABOUT YOU?
DIDN'T YOU BRING ME HERE TO TELL ME SOME-THING?
TELL YOU SOME-THING?
NO, NOT REALLY.
...
HON-ESTLY.
EVEN IF SOMETHING WERE TROUBLING ME, HOW COULD YOU POSSIBLY THINK SOMEONE LIKE YOU COULD HELP?

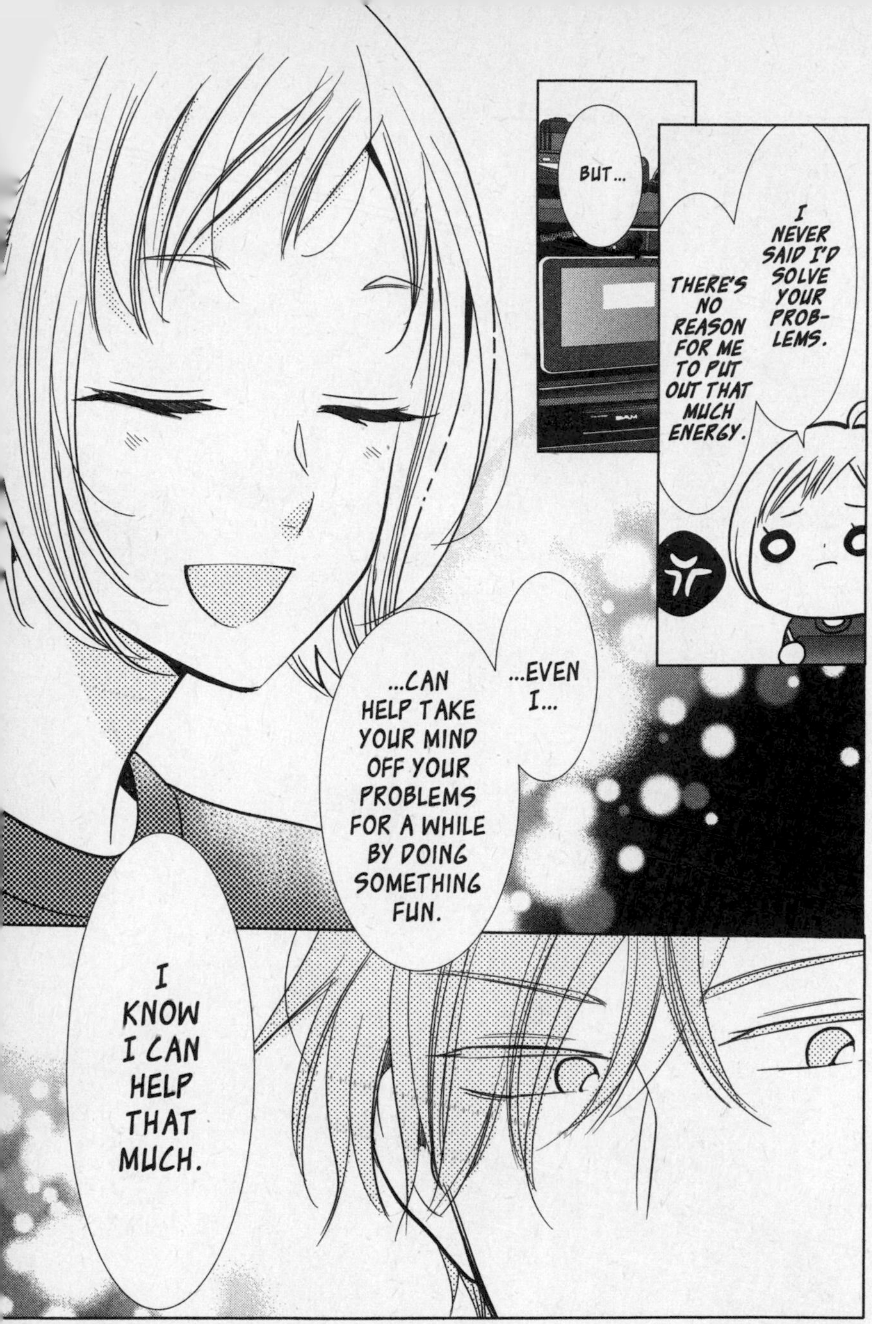
I NEVER SAID I'D SOLVE YOUR PROBLEMS.
THERE'S NO REASON FOR ME TO PUT OUT THAT MUCH ENERGY.
BUT...
...EVEN I...
...CAN HELP TAKE YOUR MIND OFF YOUR PROBLEMS FOR A WHILE BY DOING SOMETHING FUN.
I KNOW I CAN HELP THAT MUCH.

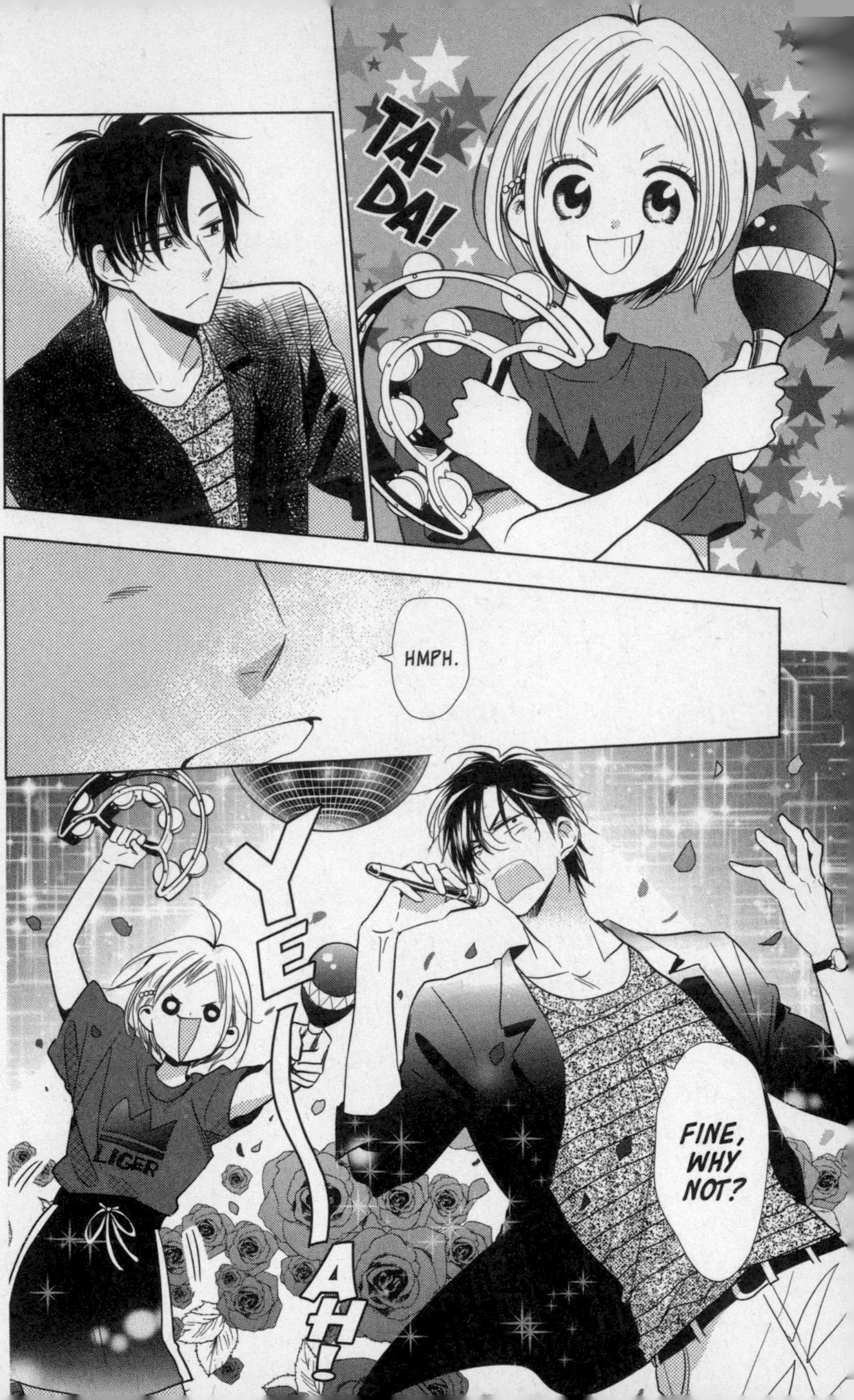
TA-DA!
HMPH.
FINE, WHY NOT?
YEAH!
LIGER

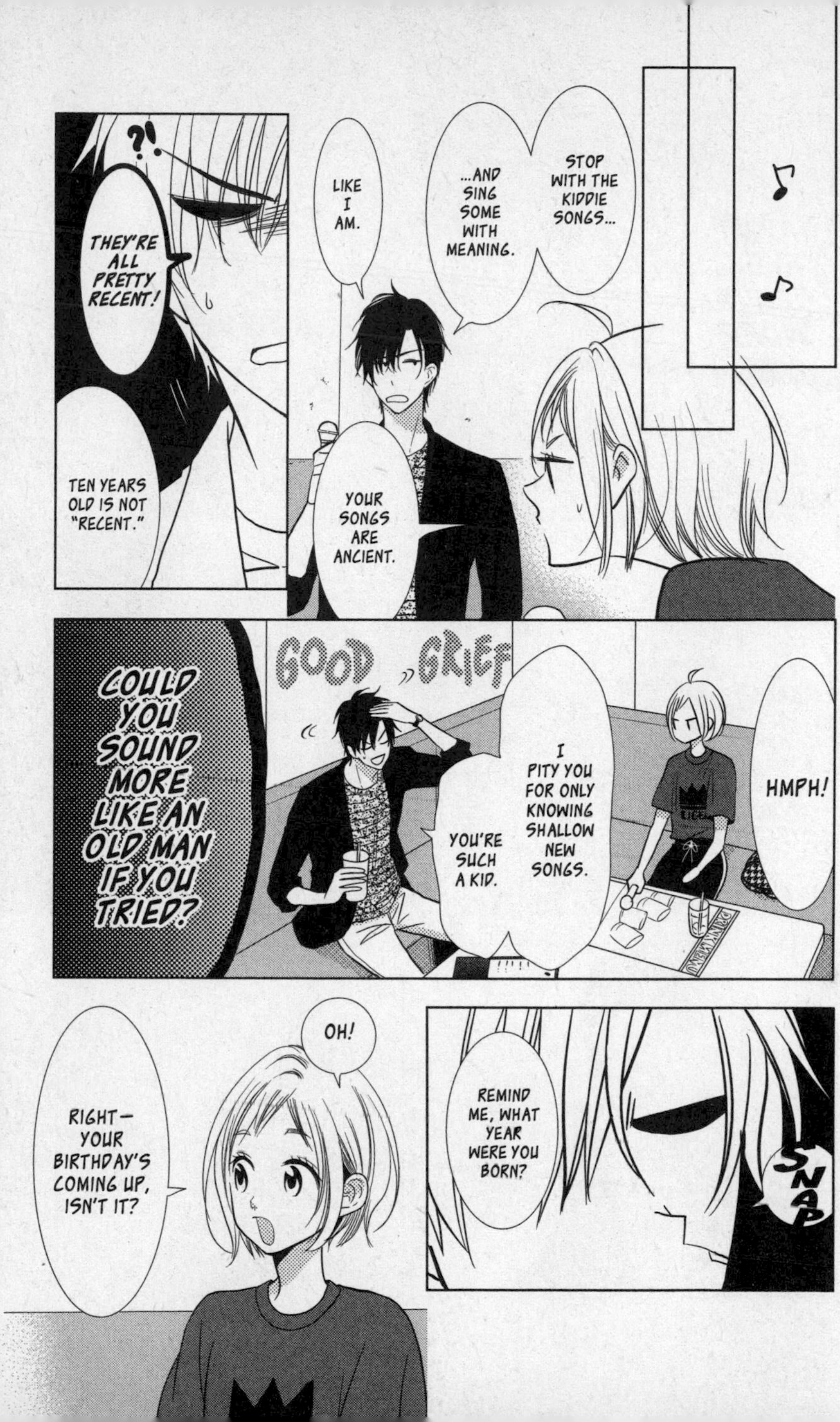

STOP WITH THE KIDDIE SONGS...
...AND SING SOME WITH MEANING.
LIKE I AM.
YOUR SONGS ARE ANCIENT.
?!
THEY'RE ALL PRETTY RECENT!
TEN YEARS OLD IS NOT "RECENT."
HMPH!
I PITY YOU FOR ONLY KNOWING SHALLOW NEW SONGS.
YOU'RE SUCH A KID.
GOOD GRIEF
COULD YOU SOUND MORE LIKE AN OLD MAN IF YOU TRIED?
REMIND ME, WHAT YEAR WERE YOU BORN?
SNAP
OH!
RIGHT— YOUR BIRTHDAY'S COMING UP, ISN'T IT?

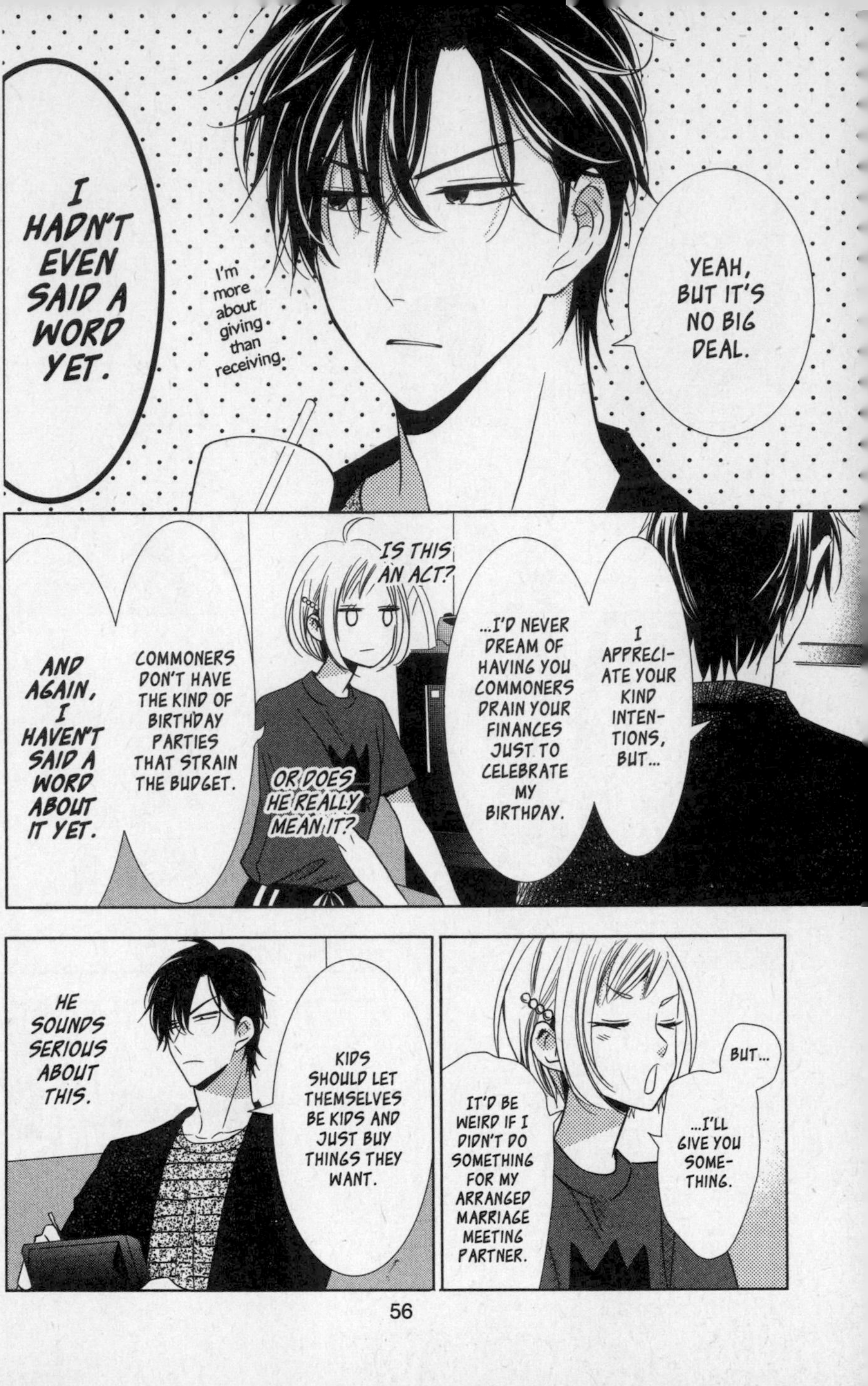
YEAH, BUT IT'S NO BIG DEAL.
I'm more about giving than receiving.
I HADN'T EVEN SAID A WORD YET.
I APPRECIATE YOUR KIND INTENTIONS, BUT...
...I'D NEVER DREAM OF HAVING YOU COMMONERS DRAIN YOUR FINANCES JUST TO CELEBRATE MY BIRTHDAY.
IS THIS AN ACT?
OR DOES HE REALLY MEAN IT?
COMMONERS DON'T HAVE THE KIND OF BIRTHDAY PARTIES THAT STRAIN THE BUDGET.
AND AGAIN, I HAVEN'T SAID A WORD ABOUT IT YET.
BUT...
...I'LL GIVE YOU SOMETHING.
IT'D BE WEIRD IF I DIDN'T DO SOMETHING FOR MY ARRANGED MARRIAGE MEETING PARTNER.
KIDS SHOULD LET THEMSELVES BE KIDS AND JUST BUY THINGS THEY WANT.
HE SOUNDS SERIOUS ABOUT THIS.

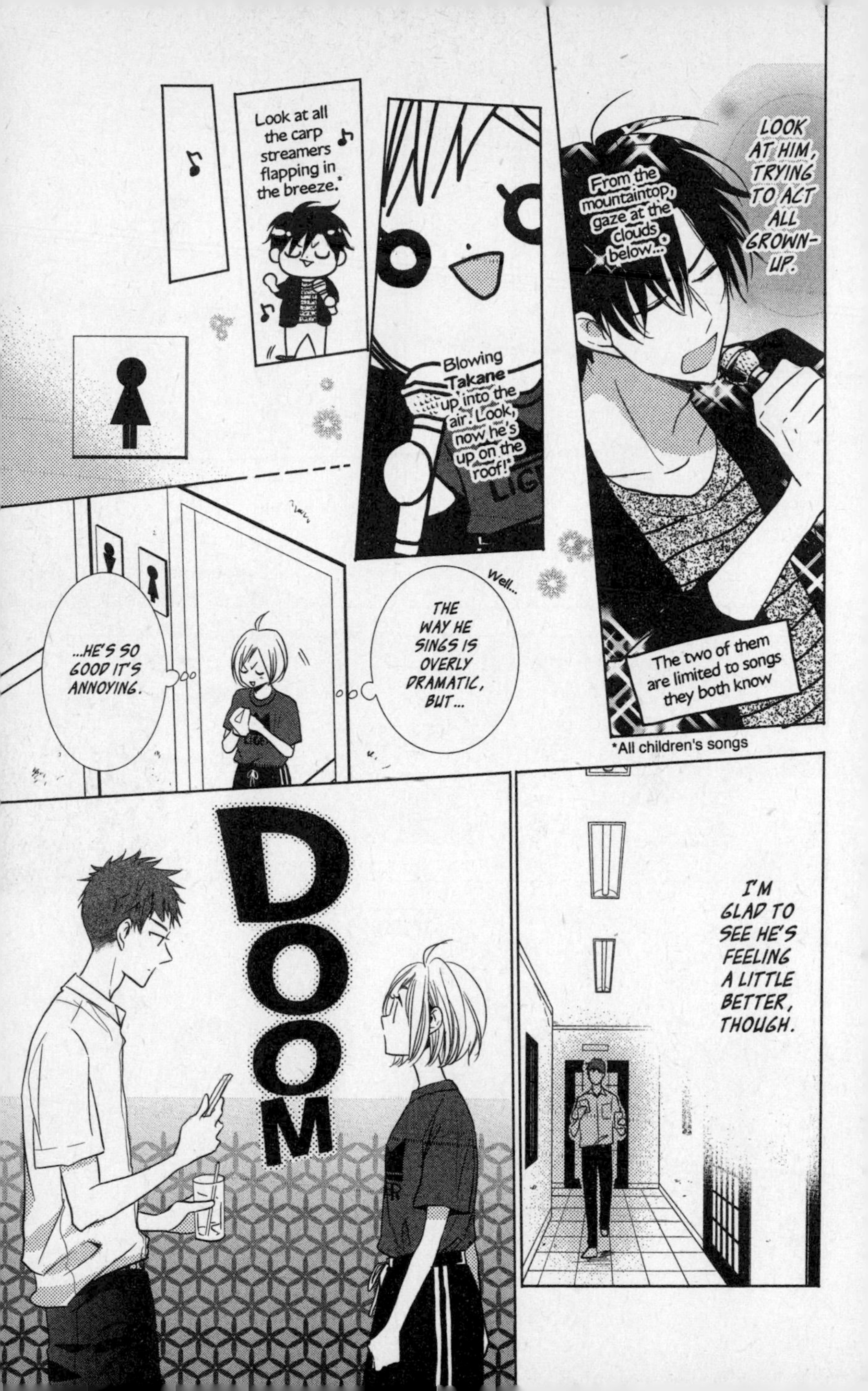
LOOK AT HIM, TRYING TO ACT ALL GROWN-UP.
From the mountaintop, gaze at the clouds below...*
The two of them are limited to songs they both know
Blowing Takane up into the air. Look, now he's up on the roof!*
Look at all the carp streamers flapping in the breeze.*
Well...
THE WAY HE SINGS IS OVERLY DRAMATIC, BUT...
...HE'S SO GOOD IT'S ANNOYING.
I'M GLAD TO SEE HE'S FEELING A LITTLE BETTER, THOUGH.
DOOM

*All children's songs

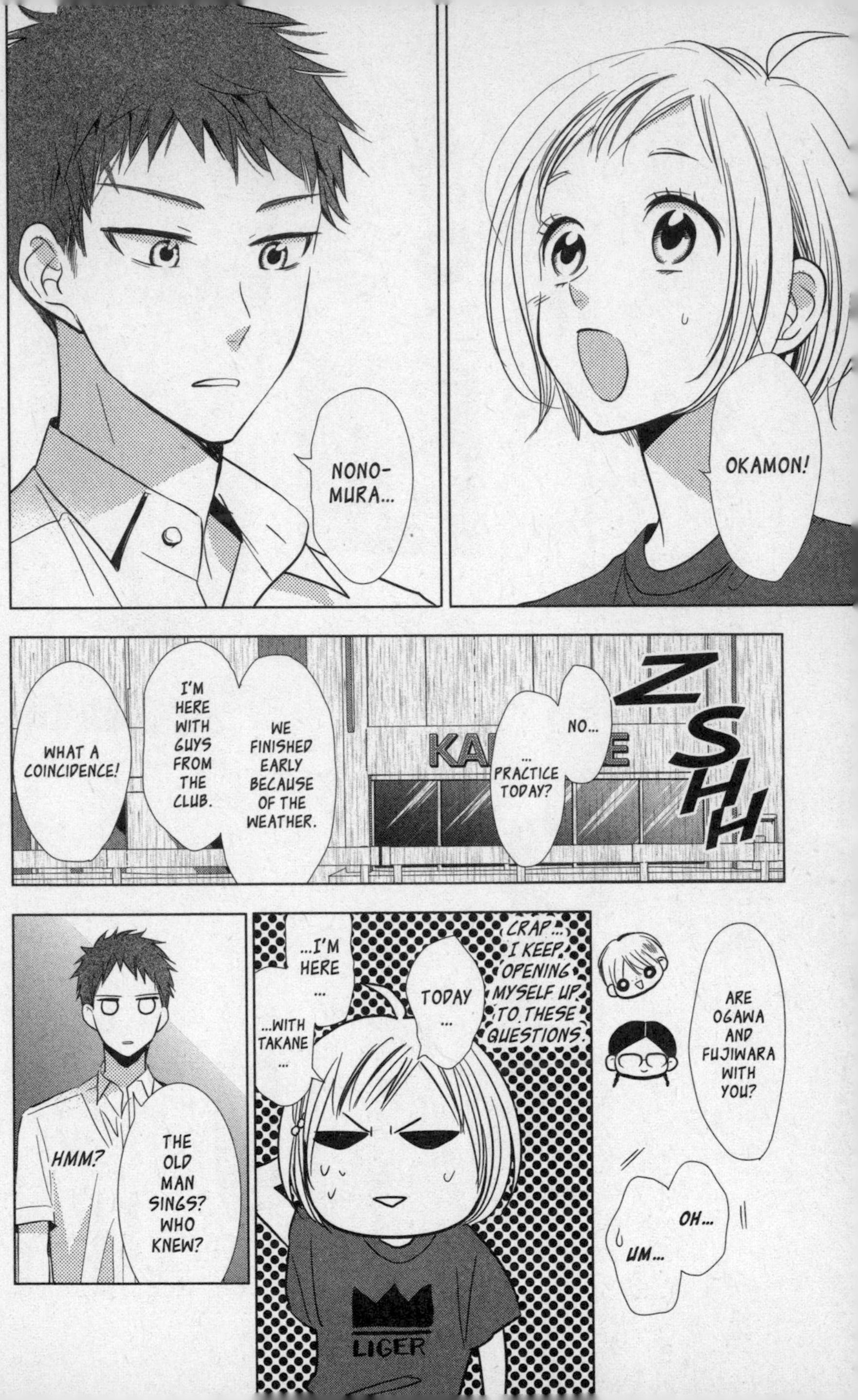
OKAMON!
NONO-MURA...
ZSHH
NO... ... PRACTICE TODAY?
WE FINISHED EARLY BECAUSE OF THE WEATHER.
I'M HERE WITH GUYS FROM THE CLUB.
WHAT A COINCIDENCE!
ARE OGAWA AND FUJIWARA WITH YOU?
OH... UM...
CRAP... I KEEP OPENING MYSELF UP TO THESE QUESTIONS.
TODAY ...
...I'M HERE ... ...WITH TAKANE ...
LIGER
HMM?
THE OLD MAN SINGS? WHO KNEW?

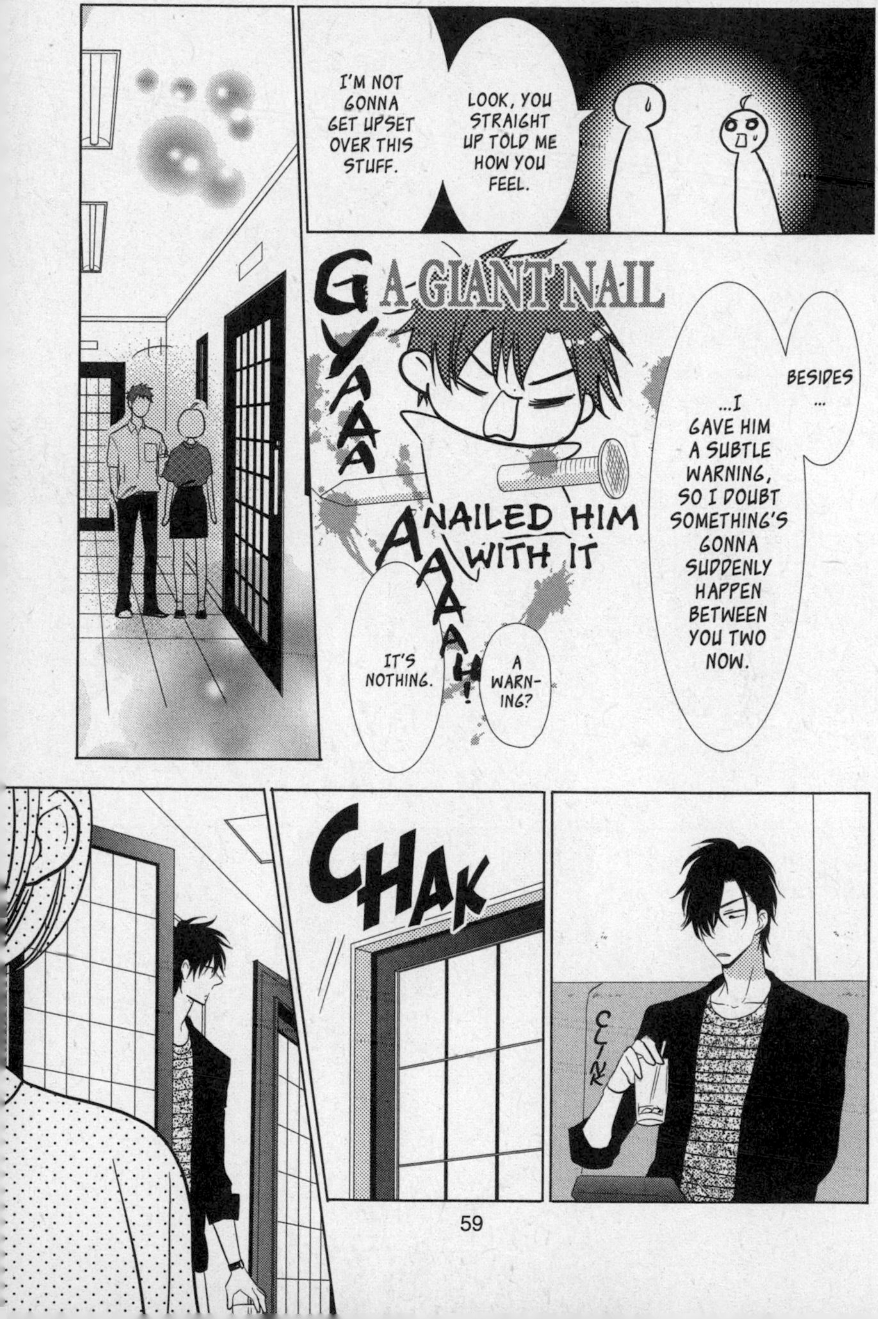
LOOK, YOU STRAIGHT UP TOLD ME HOW YOU FEEL.
I'M NOT GONNA GET UPSET OVER THIS STUFF.
BESIDES ...
...I GAVE HIM A SUBTLE WARNING, SO I DOUBT SOMETHING'S GONNA SUDDENLY HAPPEN BETWEEN YOU TWO NOW.
A GIANT NAIL
GYAAA
NAILED HIM WITH IT
AAAAH!
A WARNING?
IT'S NOTHING.
CLINK
CHAK

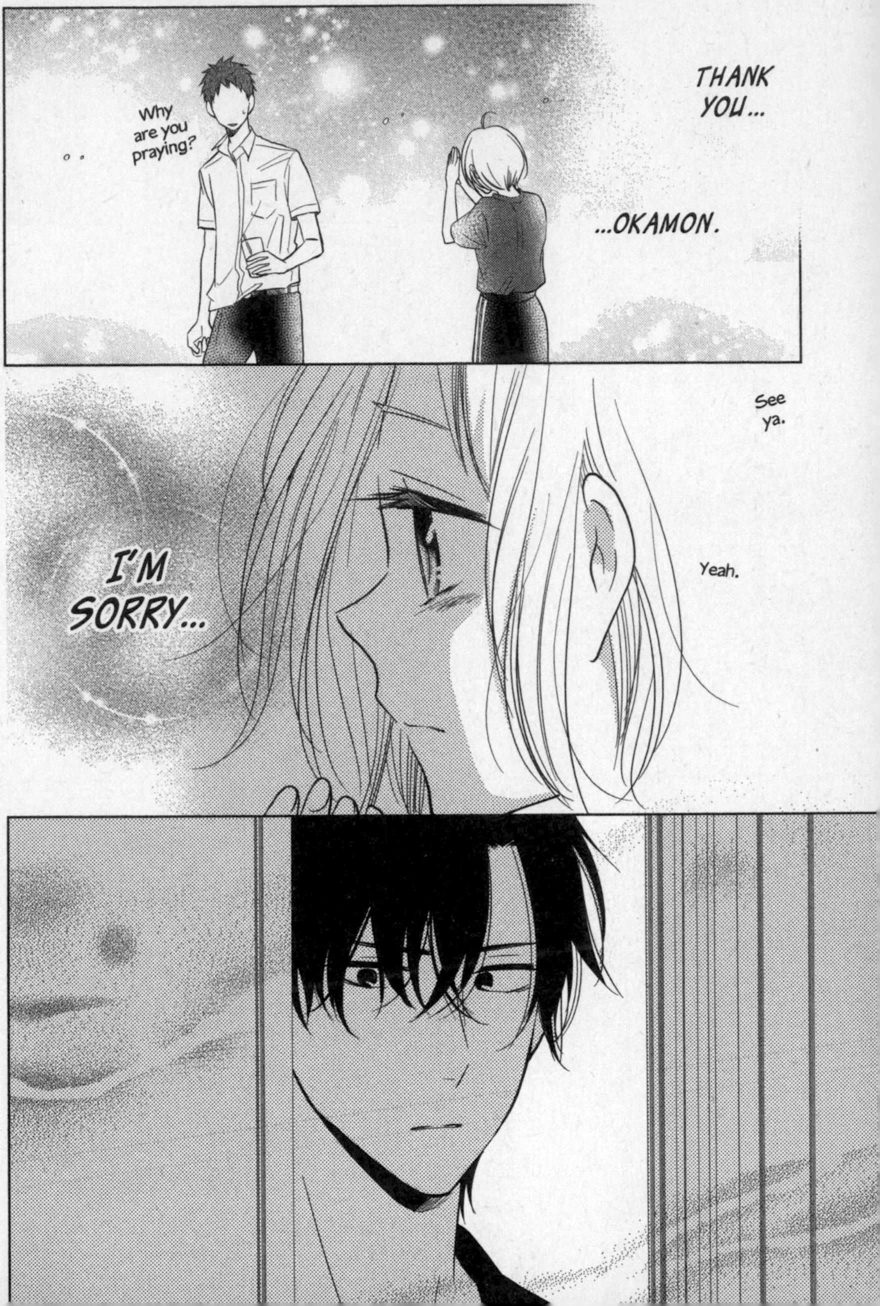
THANK YOU...
...OKAMON.
Why are you praying?
See ya.
Yeah.
I'M SORRY...

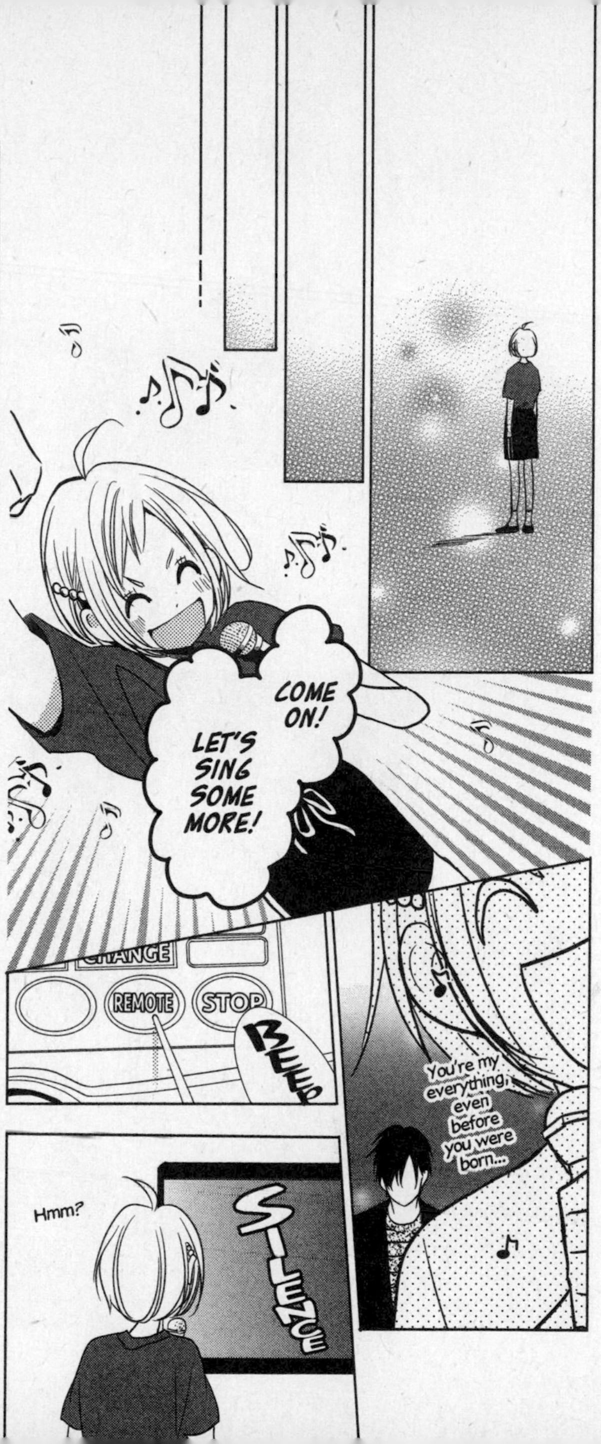
COME ON!
LET'S SING SOME MORE!
You're my everything, even before you were born...
CHANGE
REMOTE
STOP
BEEP
Hmm?
SILENCE

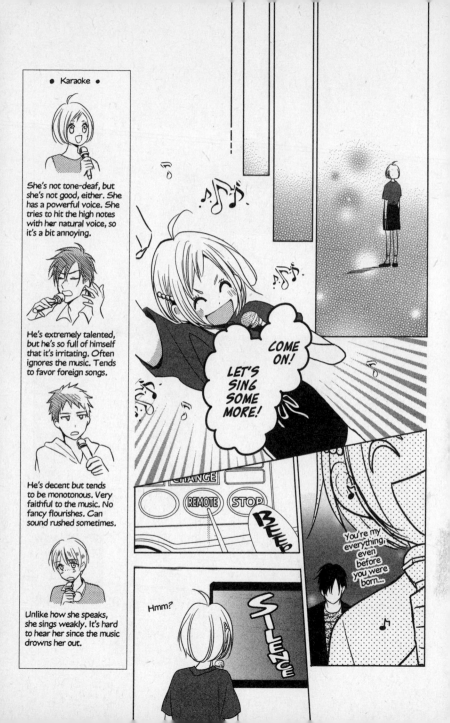

• Karaoke •

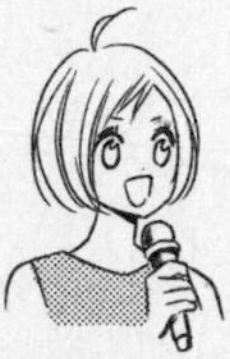

She's not tone-deaf, but she's not good, either. She has a powerful voice. She tries to hit the high notes with her natural voice, so it's a bit annoying.

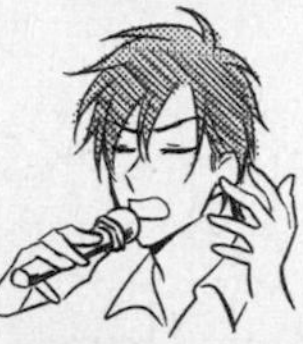

He's extremely talented, but he's so full of himself that it's irritating. Often ignores the music. Tends to favor foreign songs.

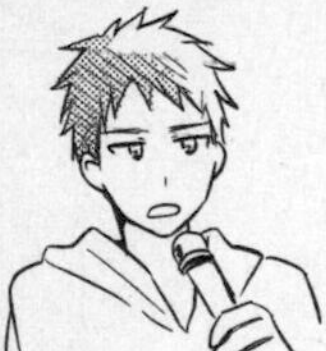

He's decent but tends to be monotonous. Very faithful to the music. No fancy flourishes. Can sound rushed sometimes.

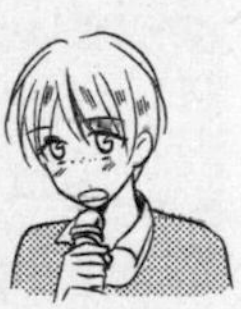

Unlike how she speaks, she sings weakly. It's hard to hear her since the music drowns her out.

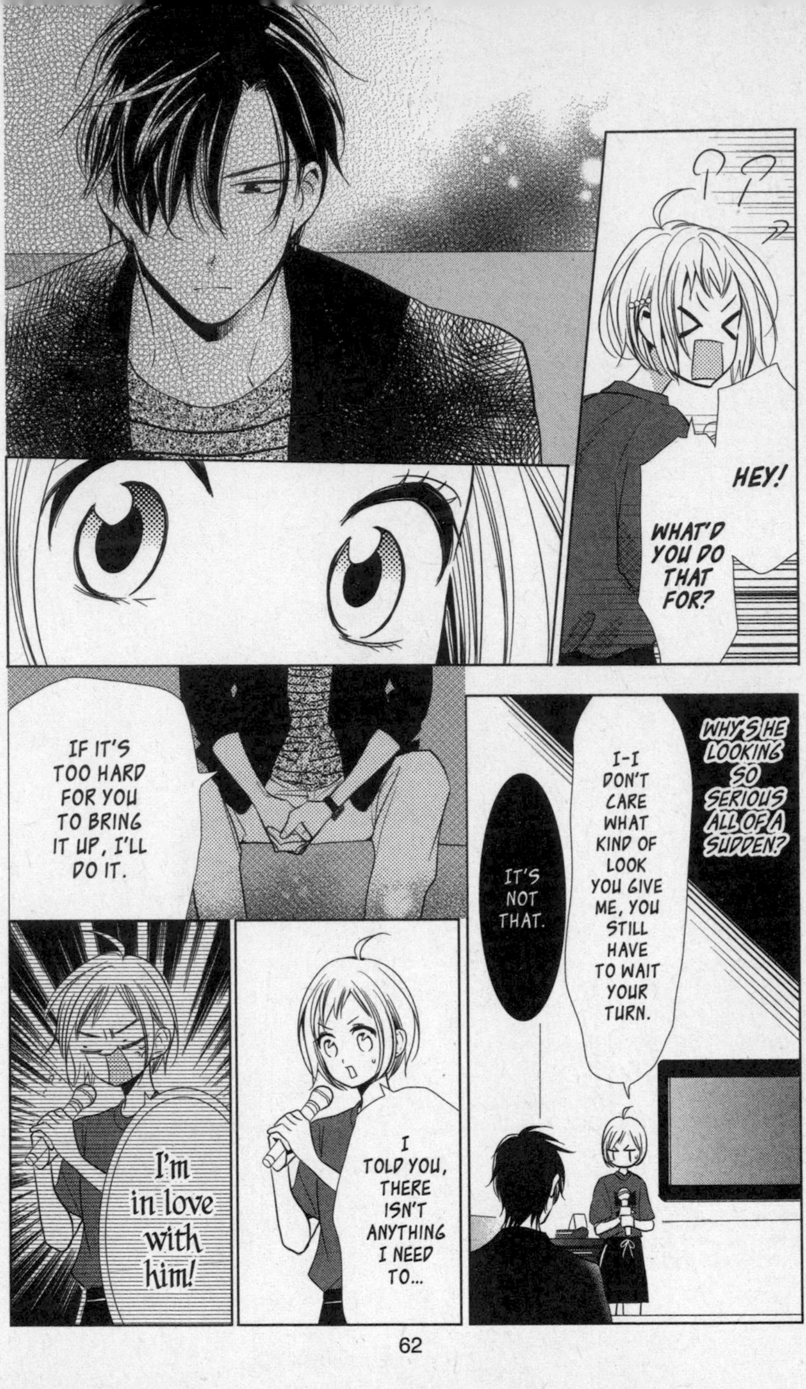
HEY!
WHAT'D YOU DO THAT FOR?
WHY'S HE LOOKING SO SERIOUS ALL OF A SUDDEN?
I-I DON'T CARE WHAT KIND OF LOOK YOU GIVE ME, YOU STILL HAVE TO WAIT YOUR TURN.
IT'S NOT THAT.
IF IT'S TOO HARD FOR YOU TO BRING IT UP, I'LL DO IT.
I TOLD YOU, THERE ISN'T ANYTHING I NEED TO...
I'm in love with him!

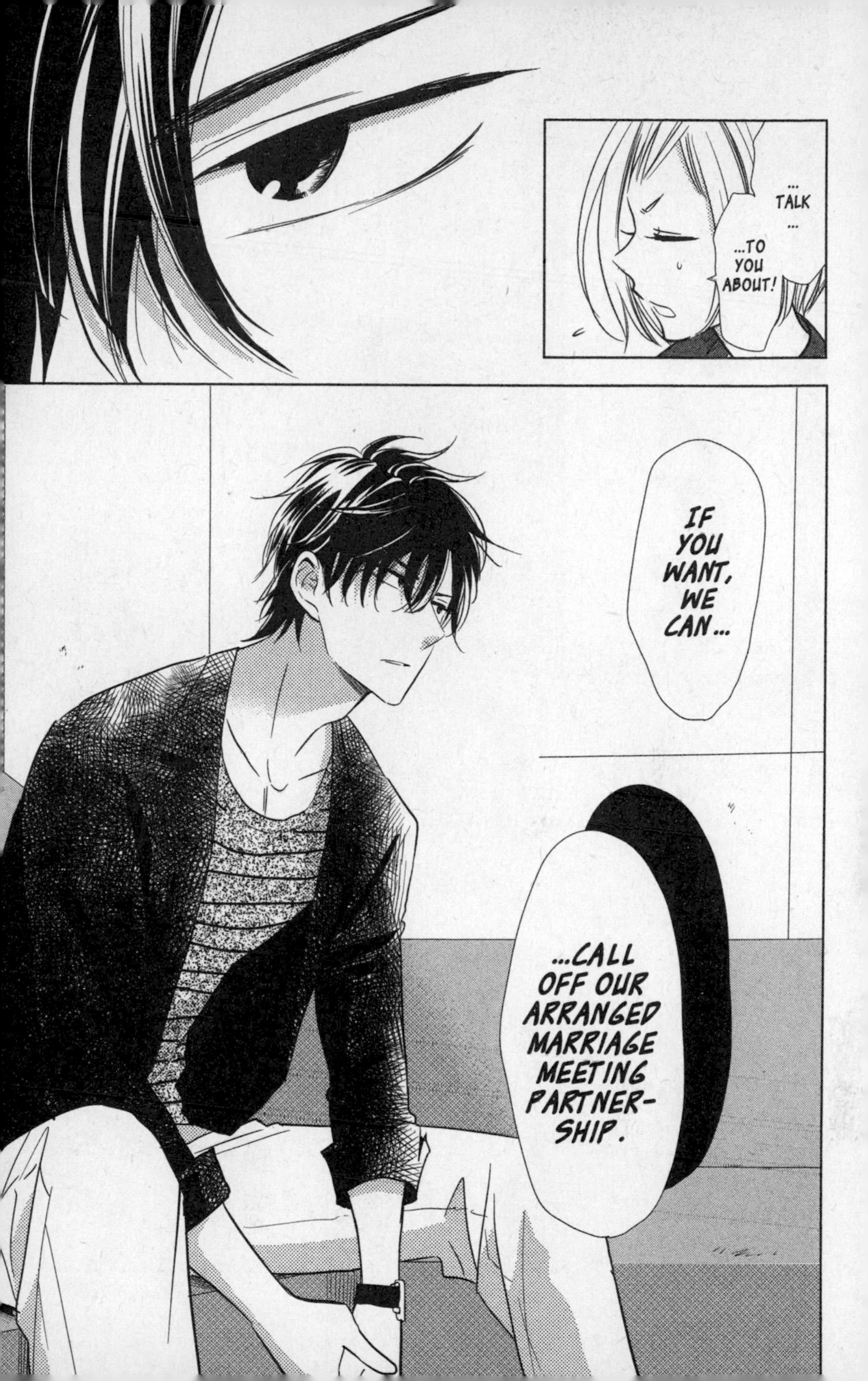
... TALK ...
...TO YOU ABOUT!
IF YOU WANT, WE CAN...
...CALL OFF OUR ARRANGED MARRIAGE MEETING PARTNER-SHIP.

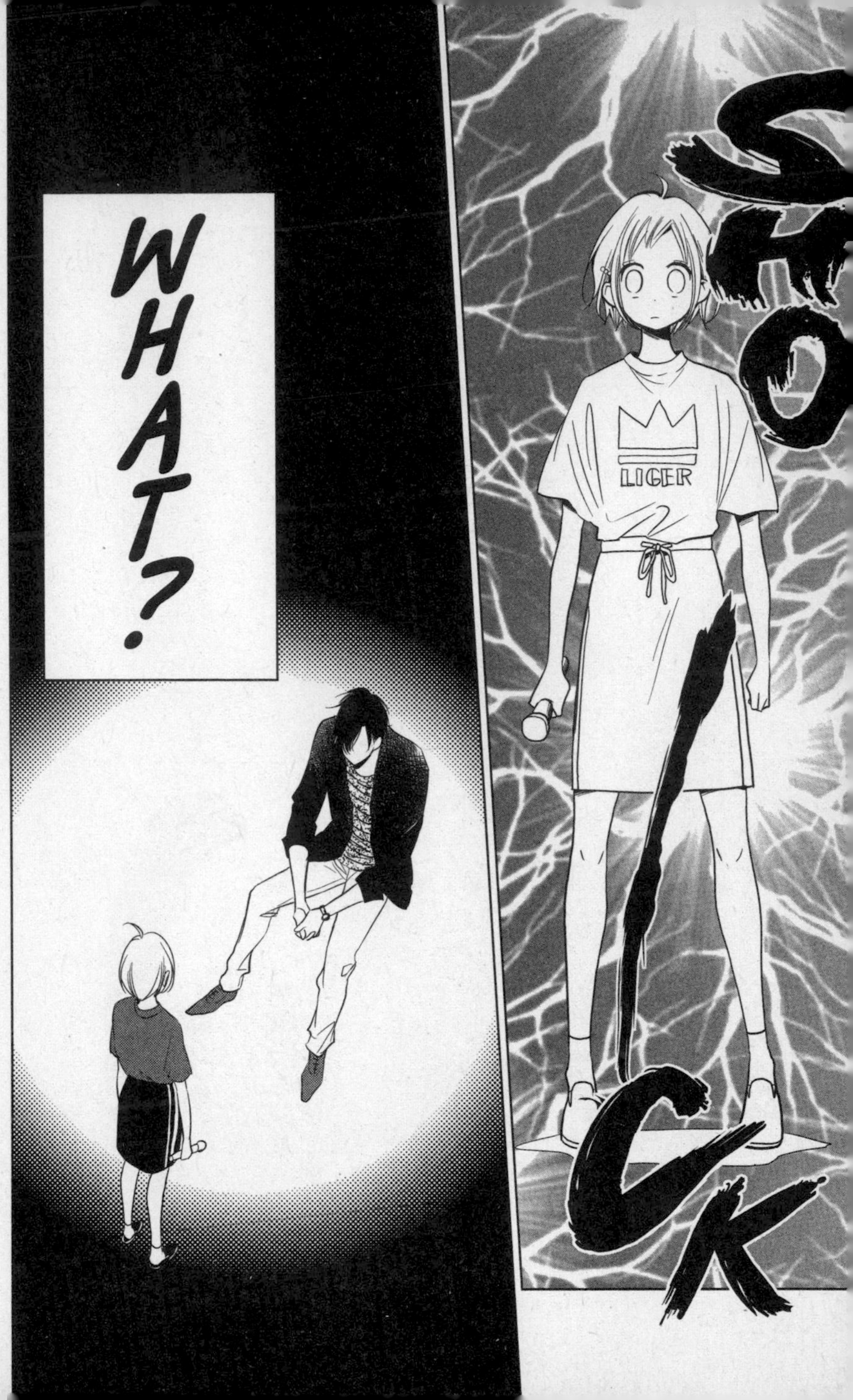
SHOCK
LIGER
WHAT?

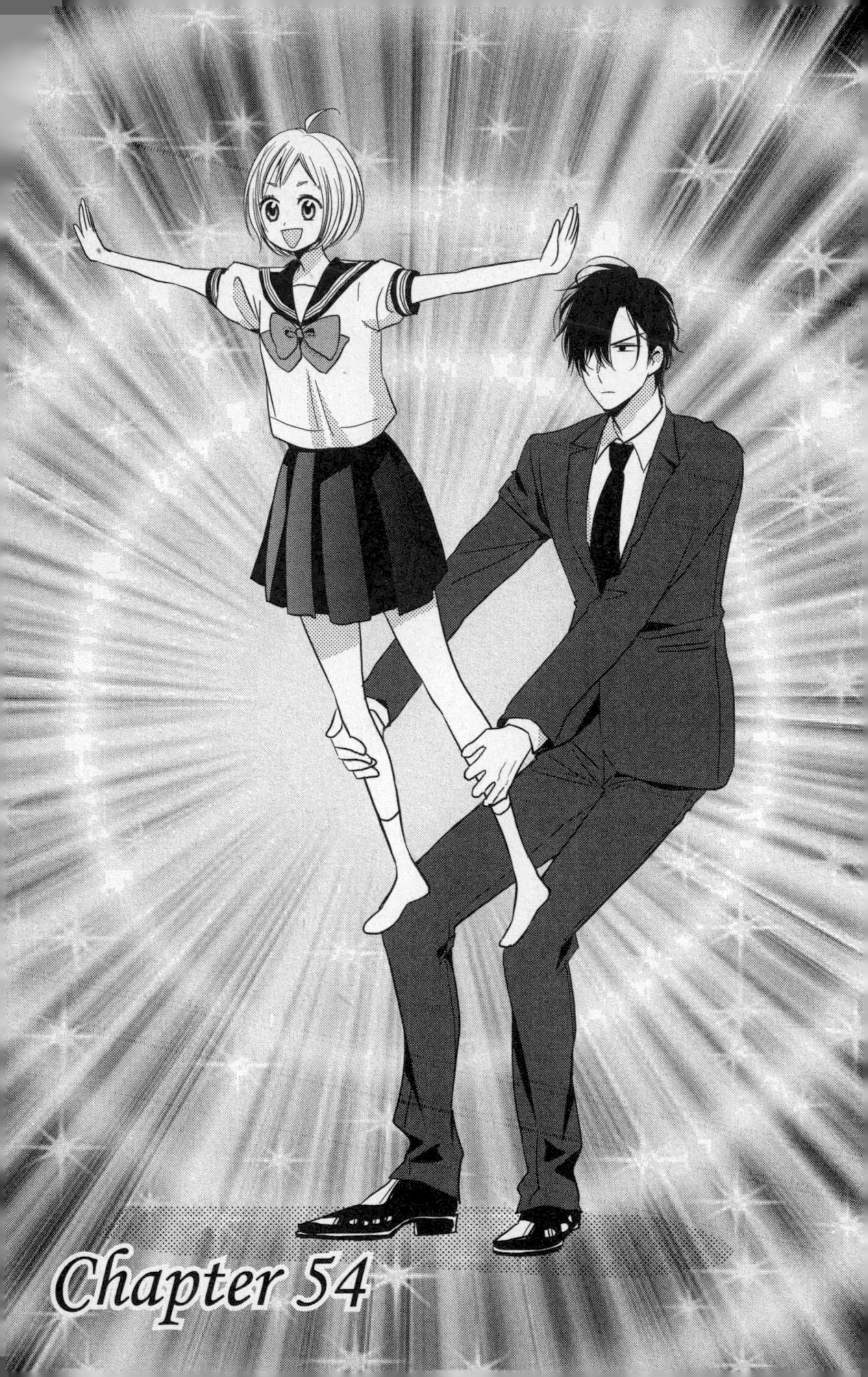
Chapter 54

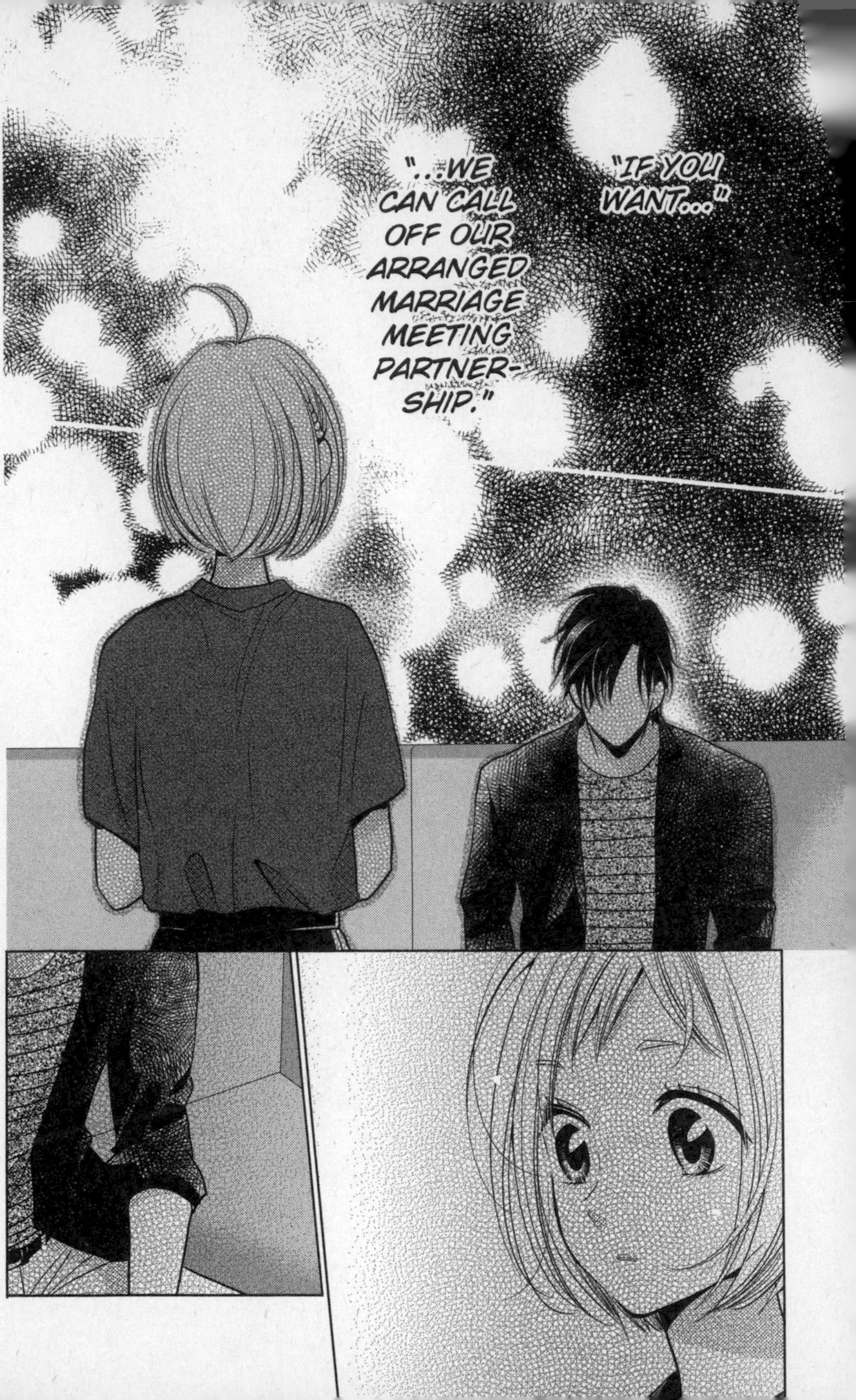
"IF YOU WANT..."
"...WE CAN CALL OFF OUR ARRANGED MARRIAGE MEETING PARTNER-SHIP."

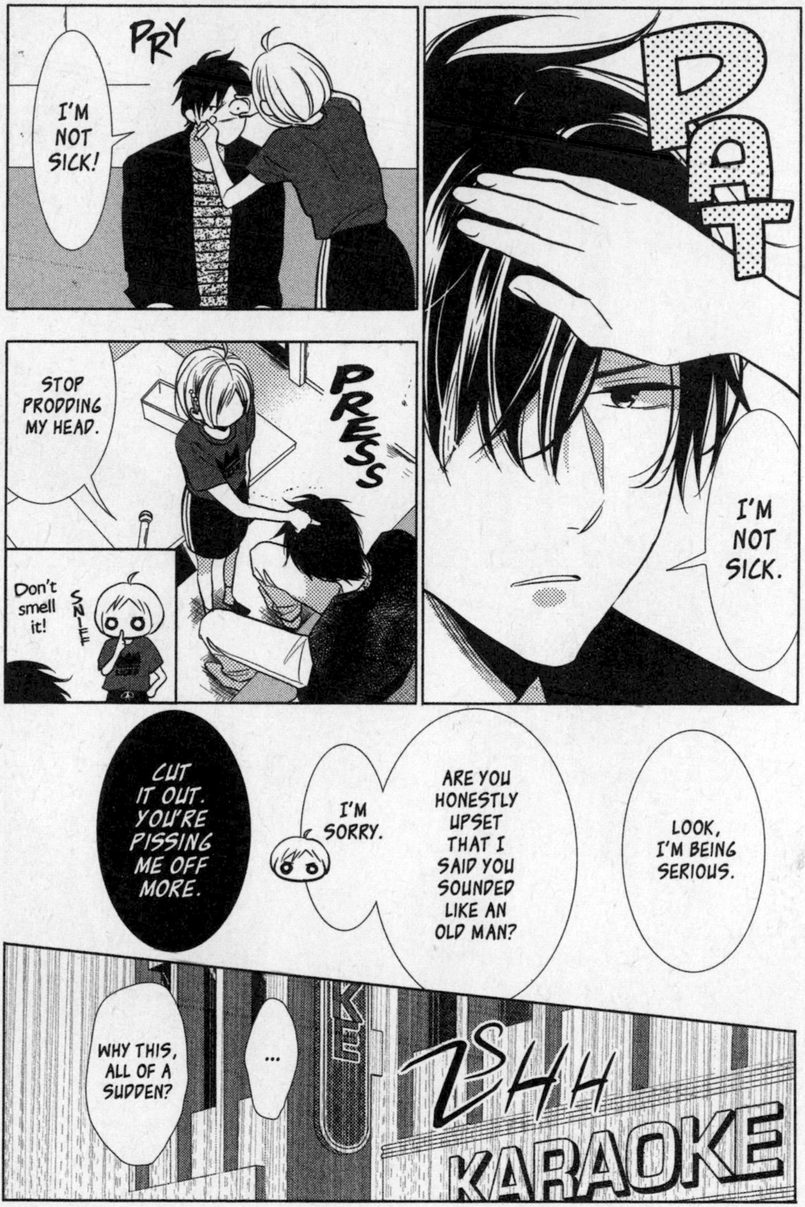
PAT
I'M NOT SICK.
PRY
I'M NOT SICK!
PRESS
STOP PRODDING MY HEAD.
SNIFF
Don't smell it!
LOOK, I'M BEING SERIOUS.
ARE YOU HONESTLY UPSET THAT I SAID YOU SOUNDED LIKE AN OLD MAN?
I'M SORRY.
CUT IT OUT. YOU'RE PISSING ME OFF MORE.
ZSHH
KARAOKE
...
WHY THIS, ALL OF A SUDDEN?

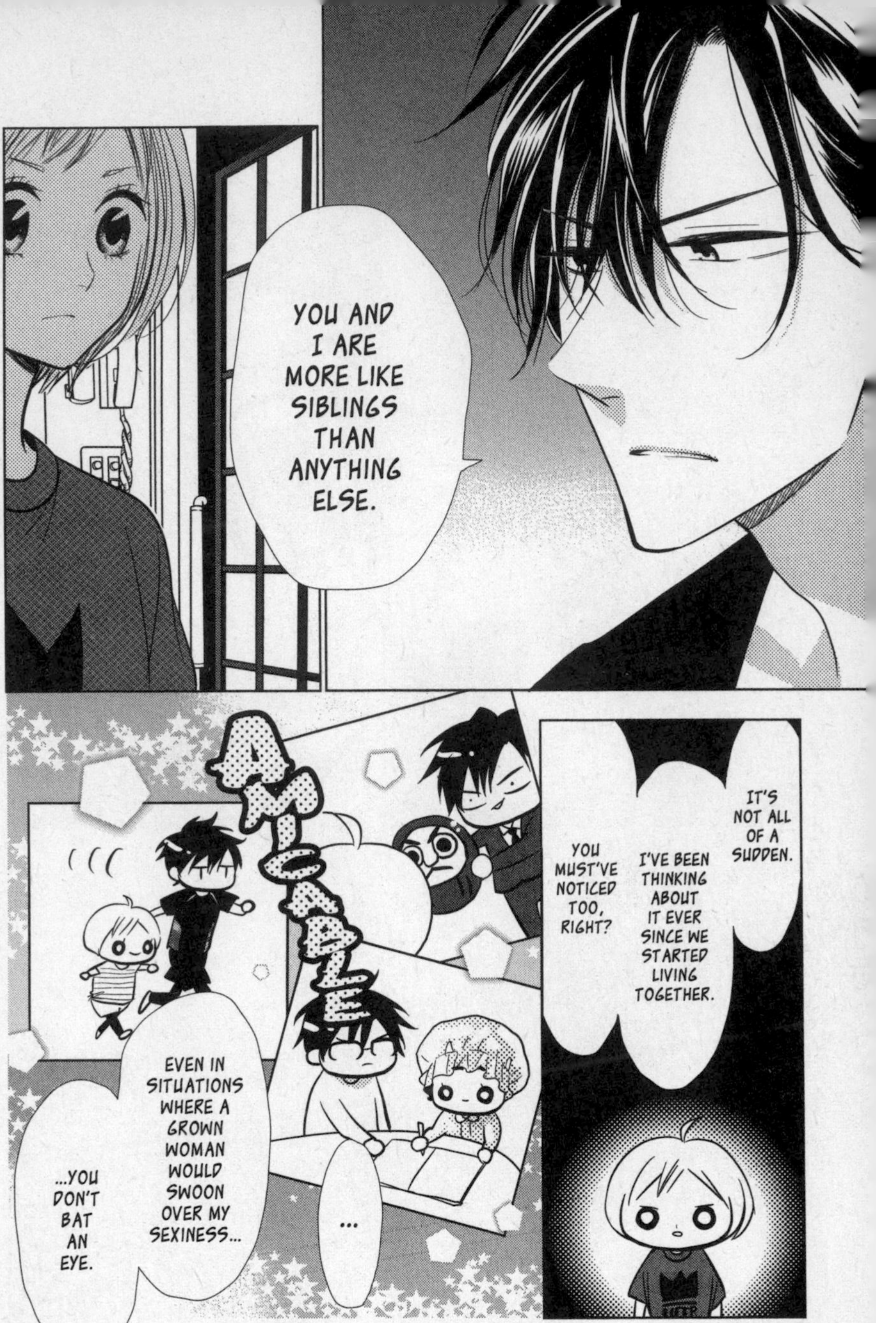
YOU AND I ARE MORE LIKE SIBLINGS THAN ANYTHING ELSE.
IT'S NOT ALL OF A SUDDEN.
I'VE BEEN THINKING ABOUT IT EVER SINCE WE STARTED LIVING TOGETHER.
YOU MUST'VE NOTICED TOO, RIGHT?
AMICABLE
EVEN IN SITUATIONS WHERE A GROWN WOMAN WOULD SWOON OVER MY SEXINESS...
...YOU DON'T BAT AN EYE.
...

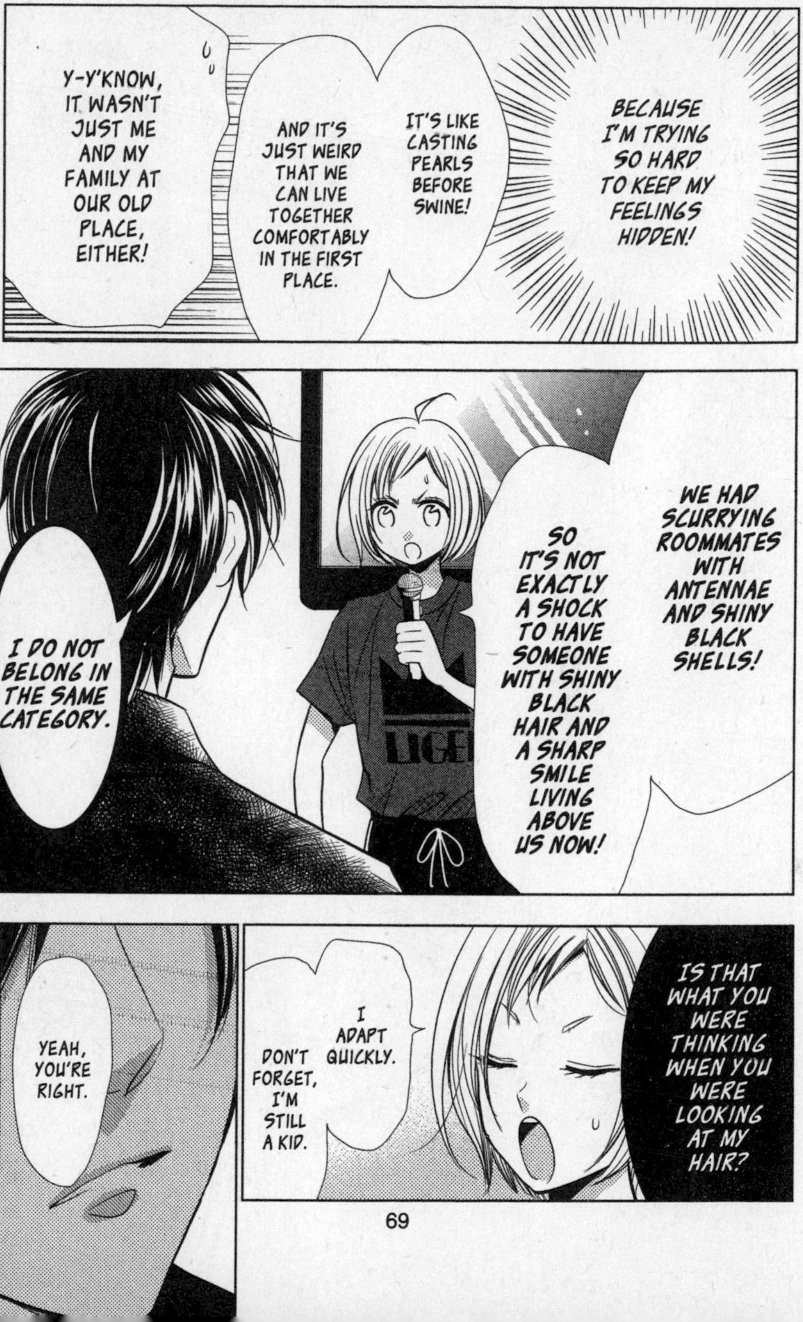
BECAUSE I'M TRYING SO HARD TO KEEP MY FEELINGS HIDDEN!
IT'S LIKE CASTING PEARLS BEFORE SWINE!
AND IT'S JUST WEIRD THAT WE CAN LIVE TOGETHER COMFORTABLY IN THE FIRST PLACE.
Y-Y'KNOW, IT WASN'T JUST ME AND MY FAMILY AT OUR OLD PLACE, EITHER!
WE HAD SCURRYING ROOMMATES WITH ANTENNAE AND SHINY BLACK SHELLS!
SO IT'S NOT EXACTLY A SHOCK TO HAVE SOMEONE WITH SHINY BLACK HAIR AND A SHARP SMILE LIVING ABOVE US NOW!
I DO NOT BELONG IN THE SAME CATEGORY.
IS THAT WHAT YOU WERE THINKING WHEN YOU WERE LOOKING AT MY HAIR?
I ADAPT QUICKLY.
DON'T FORGET, I'M STILL A KID.
YEAH, YOU'RE RIGHT.

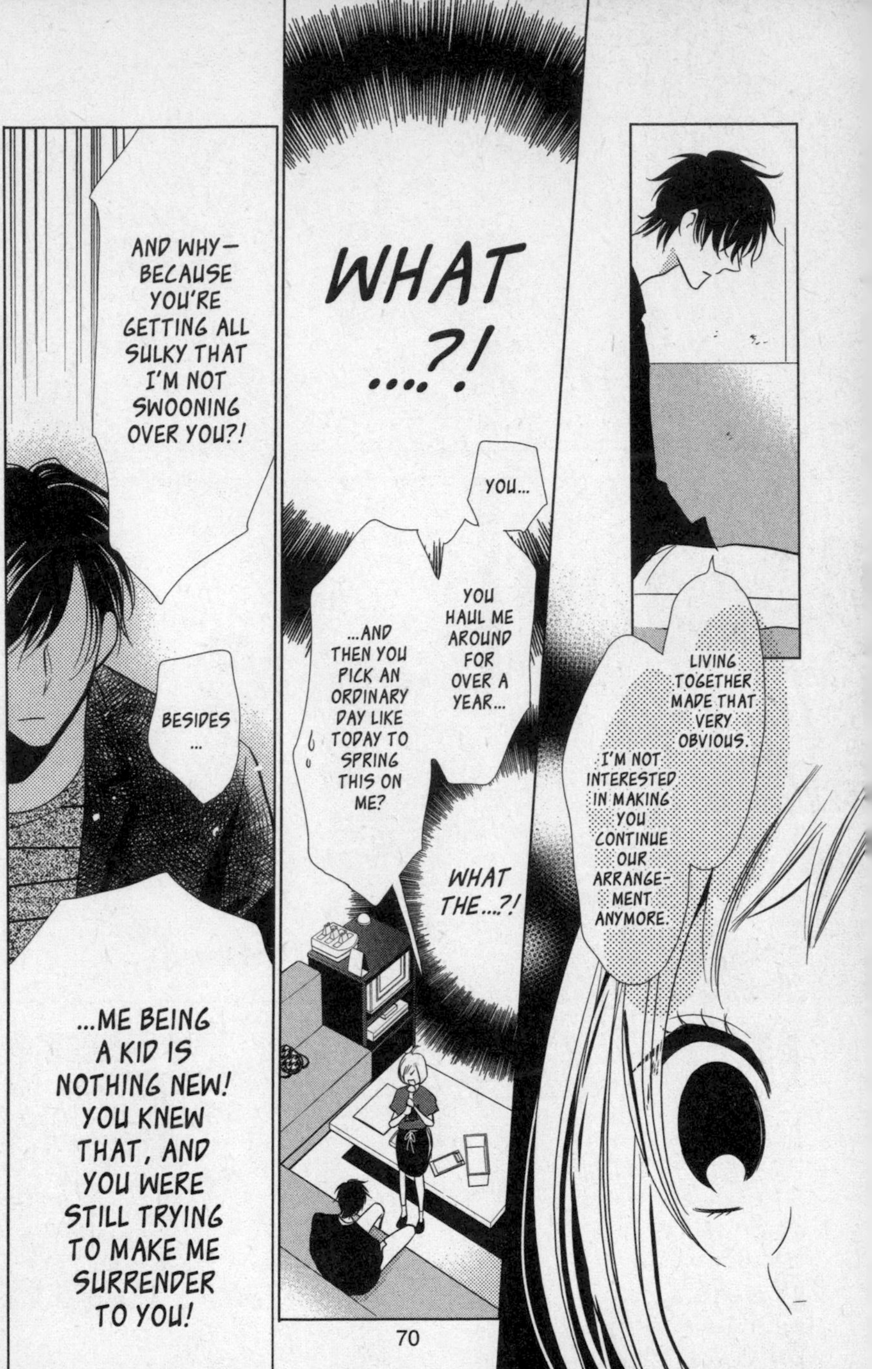
LIVING TOGETHER MADE THAT VERY OBVIOUS.
I'M NOT INTERESTED IN MAKING YOU CONTINUE OUR ARRANGEMENT ANYMORE.
WHAT ...?!
YOU...
YOU HAUL ME AROUND FOR OVER A YEAR...
...AND THEN YOU PICK AN ORDINARY DAY LIKE TODAY TO SPRING THIS ON ME?
WHAT THE...?!
AND WHY—BECAUSE YOU'RE GETTING ALL SULKY THAT I'M NOT SWOONING OVER YOU?!
BESIDES...
...ME BEING A KID IS NOTHING NEW! YOU KNEW THAT, AND YOU WERE STILL TRYING TO MAKE ME SURRENDER TO YOU!

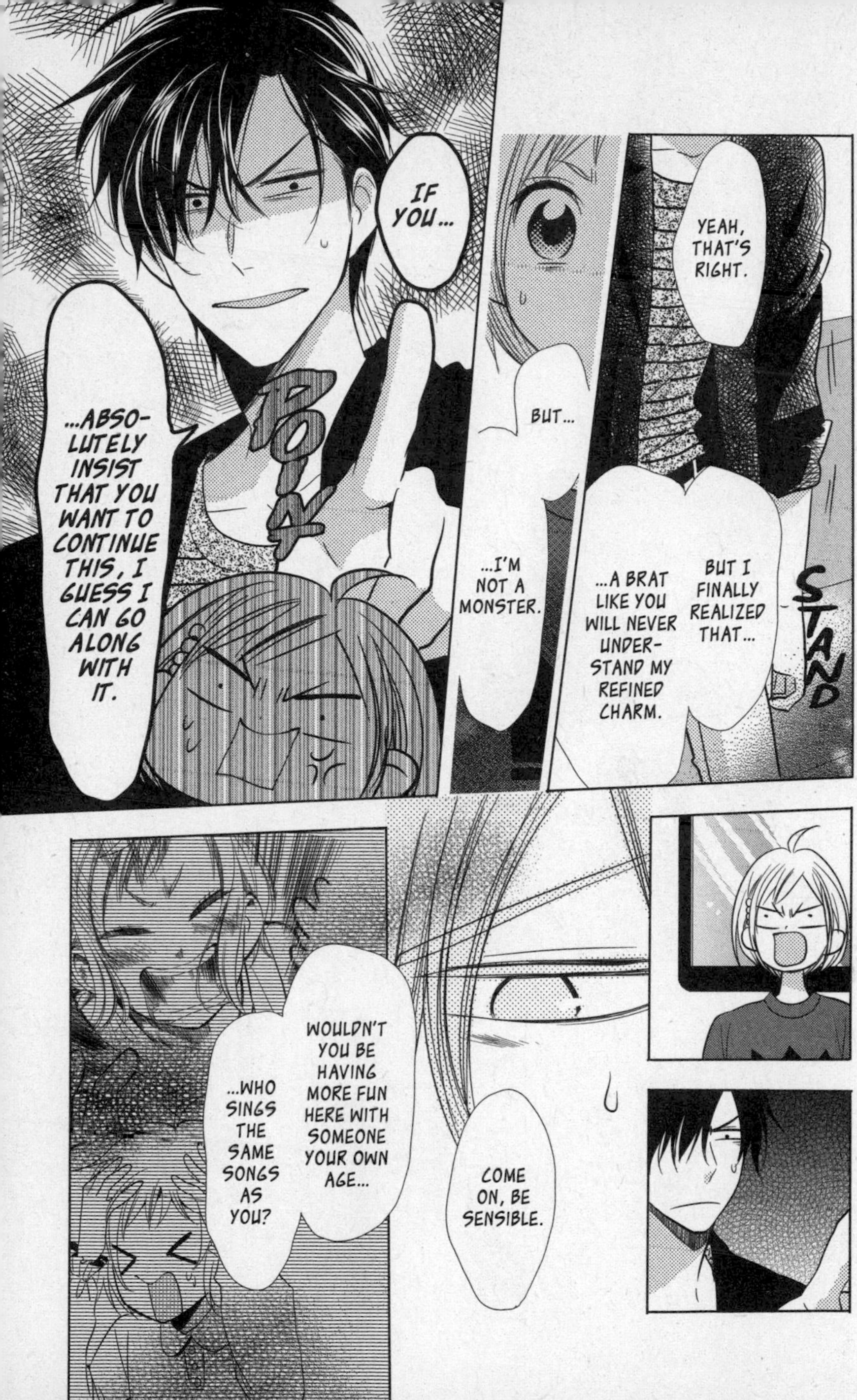
YEAH, THAT'S RIGHT.
BUT I FINALLY REALIZED THAT...
...A BRAT LIKE YOU WILL NEVER UNDER-STAND MY REFINED CHARM.
STAND
BUT...
...I'M NOT A MONSTER.
IF YOU...
...ABSO-LUTELY INSIST THAT YOU WANT TO CONTINUE THIS, I GUESS I CAN GO ALONG WITH IT.
POIK
COME ON, BE SENSIBLE.
WOULDN'T YOU BE HAVING MORE FUN HERE WITH SOMEONE YOUR OWN AGE...
...WHO SINGS THE SAME SONGS AS YOU?

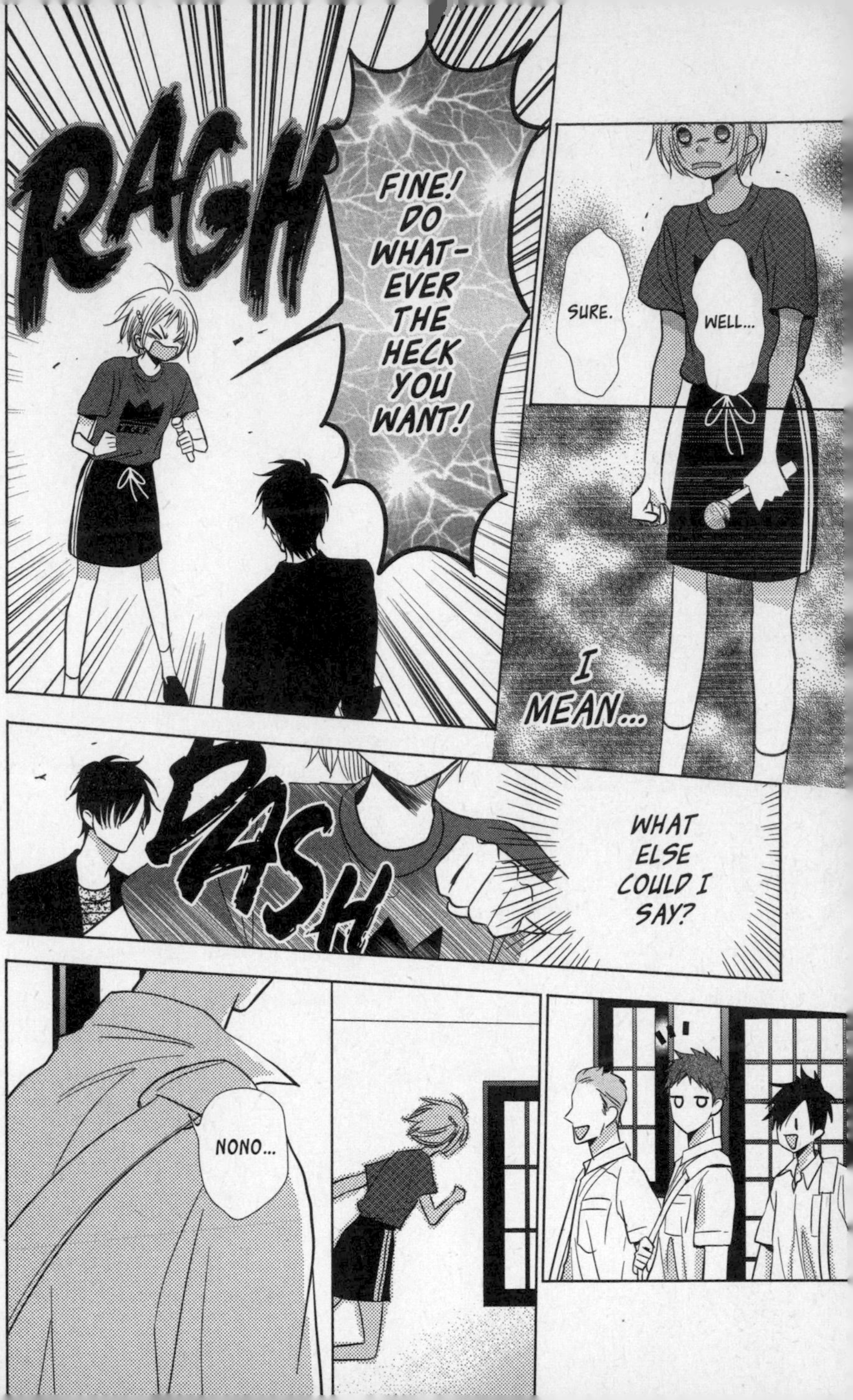
WELL...
SURE.
I MEAN...
RAGH
FINE! DO WHATEVER THE HECK YOU WANT!
WHAT ELSE COULD I SAY?
VASH
NONO...

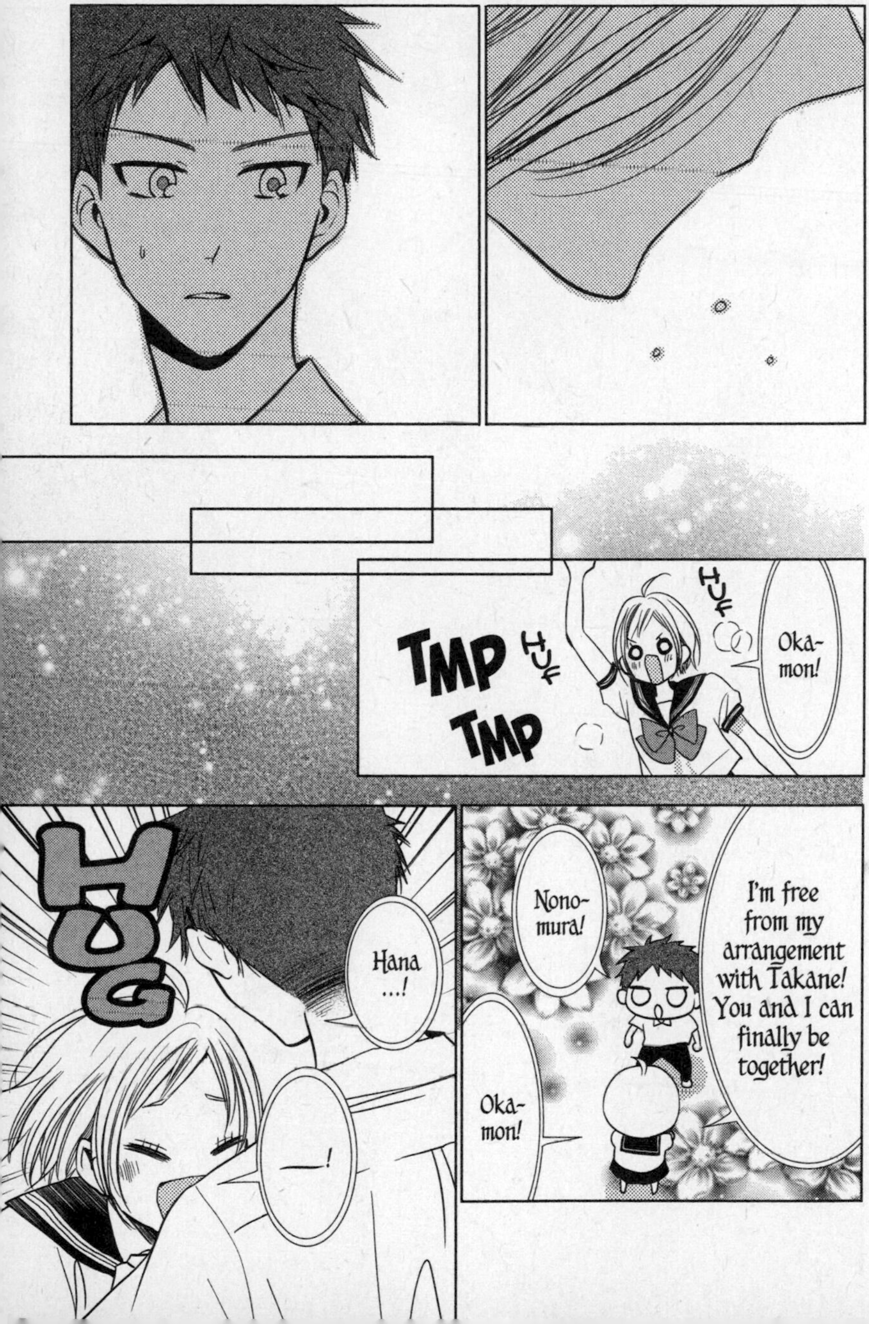
HUF
Oka-mon!
HUF
TMP
TMP
I'm free from my arrangement with Takane! You and I can finally be together!
Nono-mura!
Oka-mon!
Hana ...!
HUG
—!

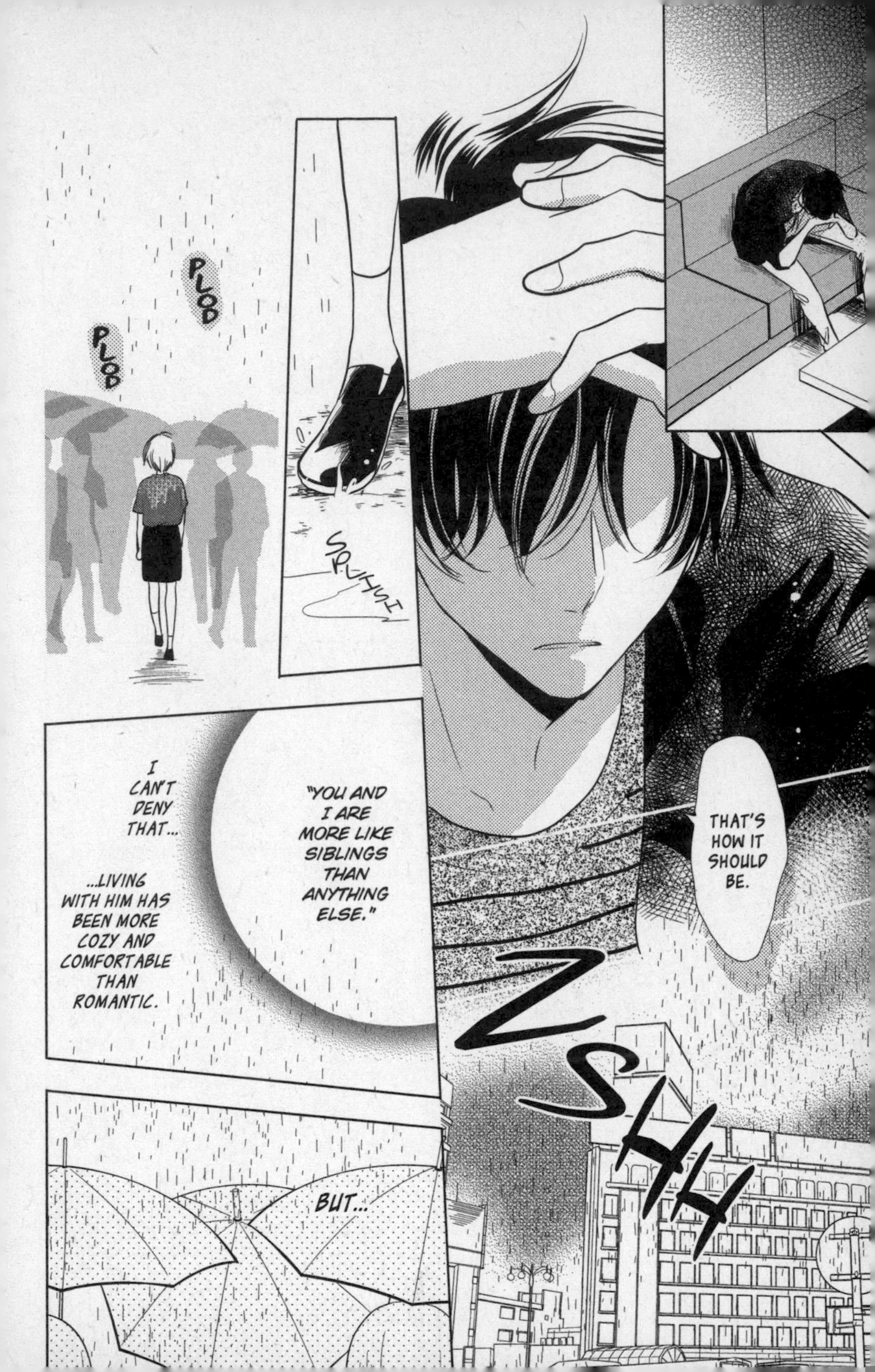

SPLISH
PLOD
PLOD
THAT'S HOW IT SHOULD BE.
"YOU AND I ARE MORE LIKE SIBLINGS THAN ANYTHING ELSE."
I CAN'T DENY THAT...
...LIVING WITH HIM HAS BEEN MORE COZY AND COMFORTABLE THAN ROMANTIC.
ZSHH
BUT...

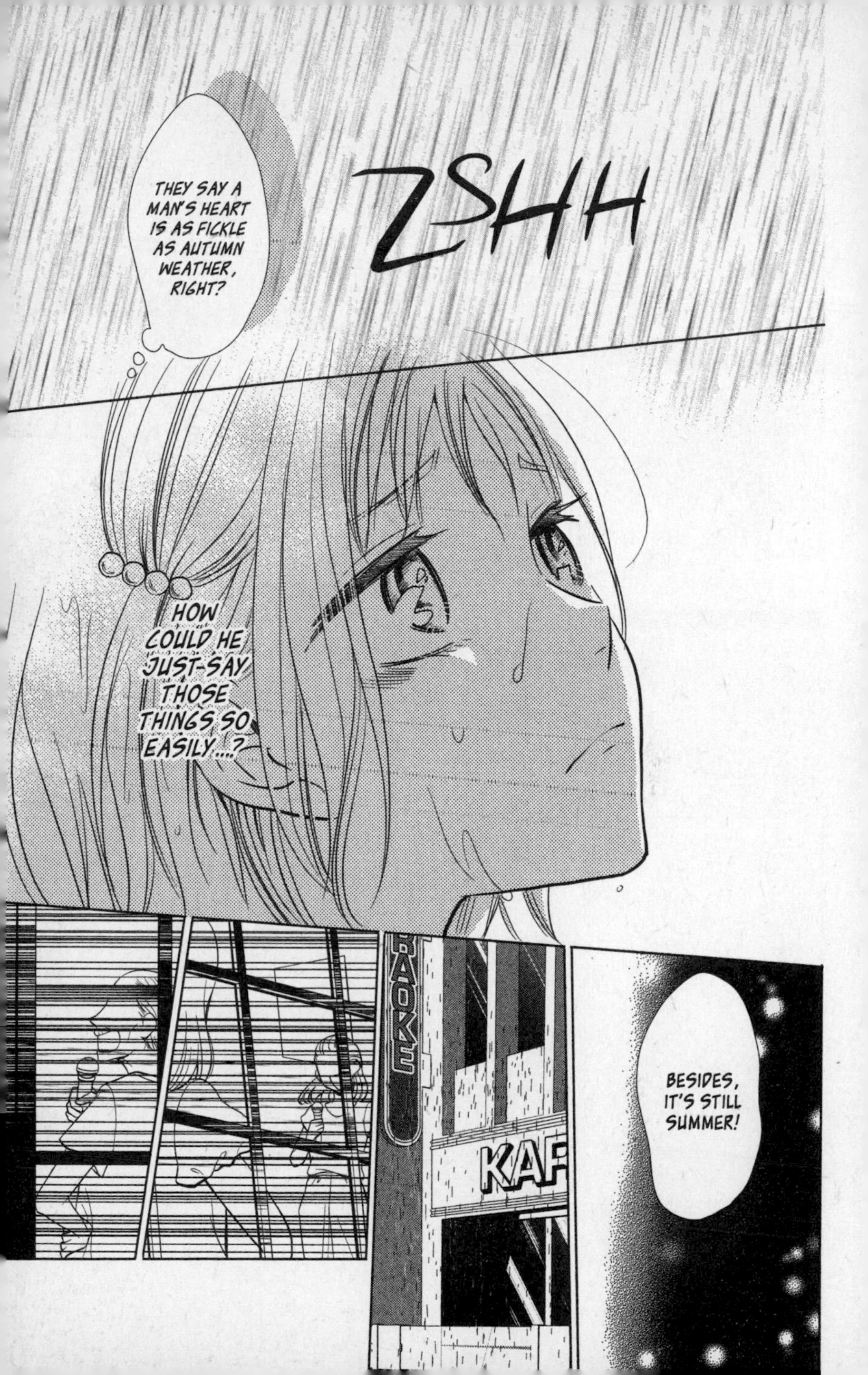
ZSHH
THEY SAY A MAN'S HEART IS AS FICKLE AS AUTUMN WEATHER, RIGHT?
HOW COULD HE JUST SAY THOSE THINGS SO EASILY...?
BESIDES, IT'S STILL SUMMER!
RAOKE
KAR

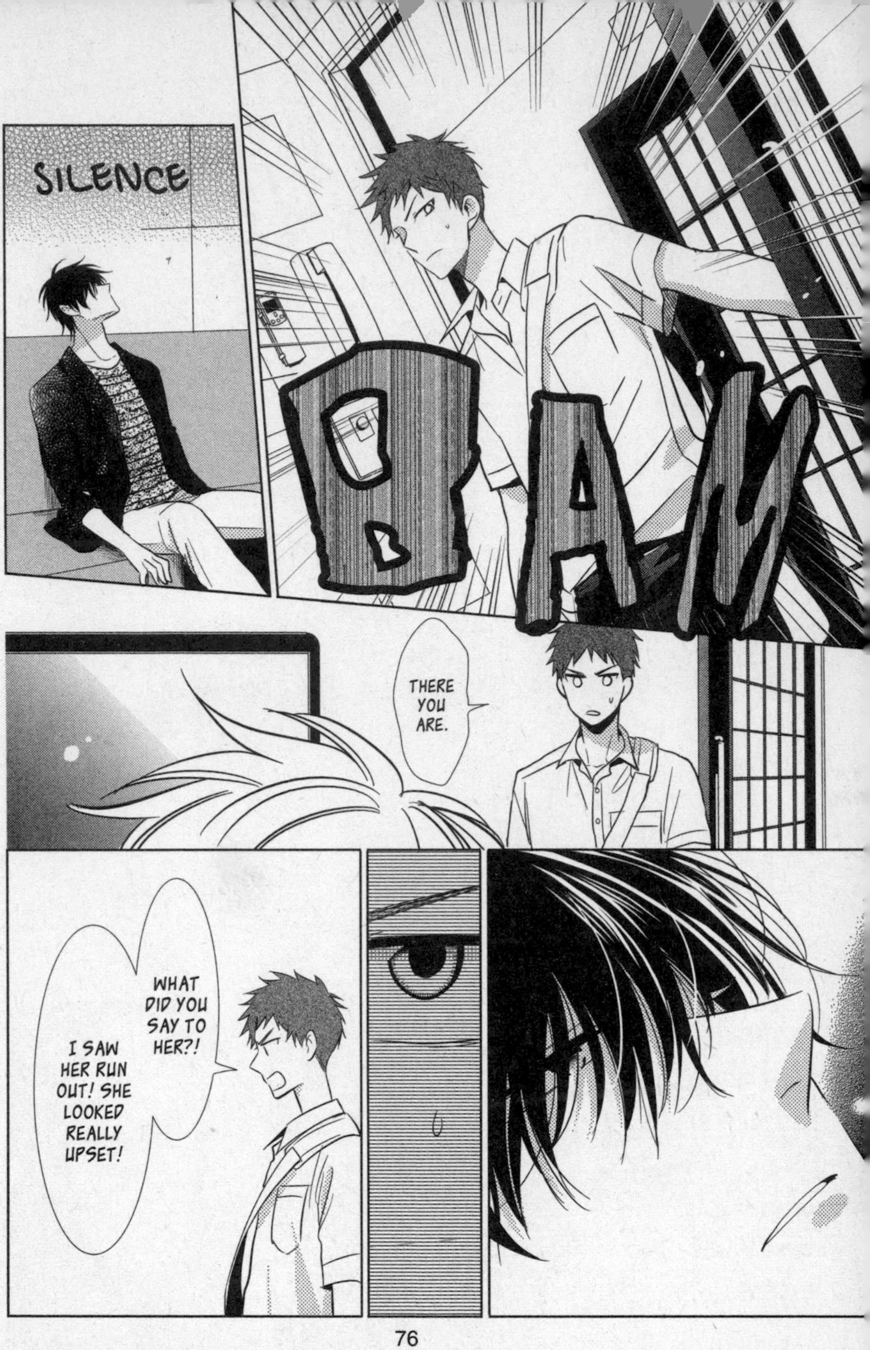
BAM
SILENCE
THERE YOU ARE.
WHAT DID YOU SAY TO HER?!
I SAW HER RUN OUT! SHE LOOKED REALLY UPSET!

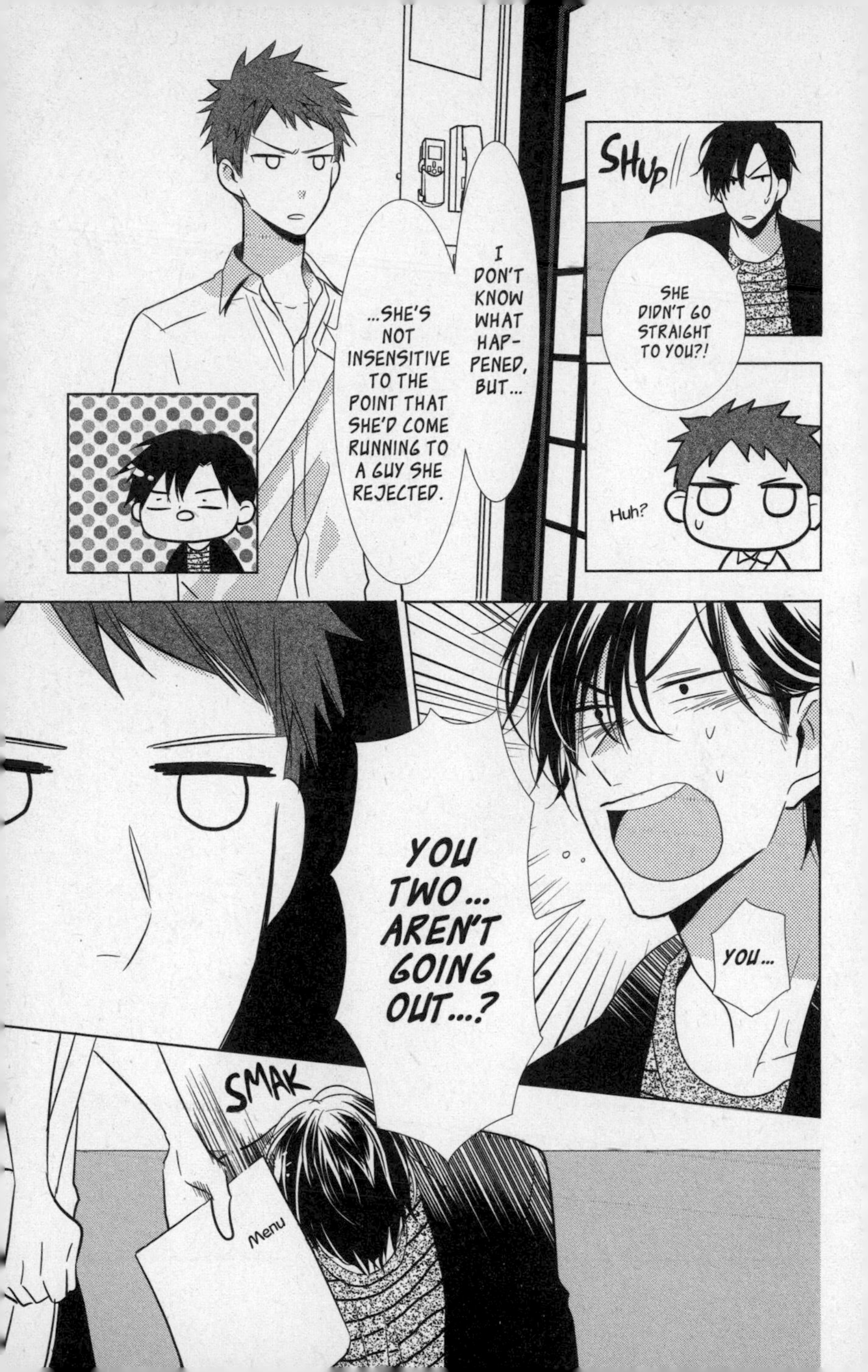
SHUP
SHE DIDN'T GO STRAIGHT TO YOU?!
Huh?
I DON'T KNOW WHAT HAP-PENED, BUT...
...SHE'S NOT INSENSITIVE TO THE POINT THAT SHE'D COME RUNNING TO A GUY SHE REJECTED.
YOU...
YOU TWO... AREN'T GOING OUT...?
SMAK
Menu

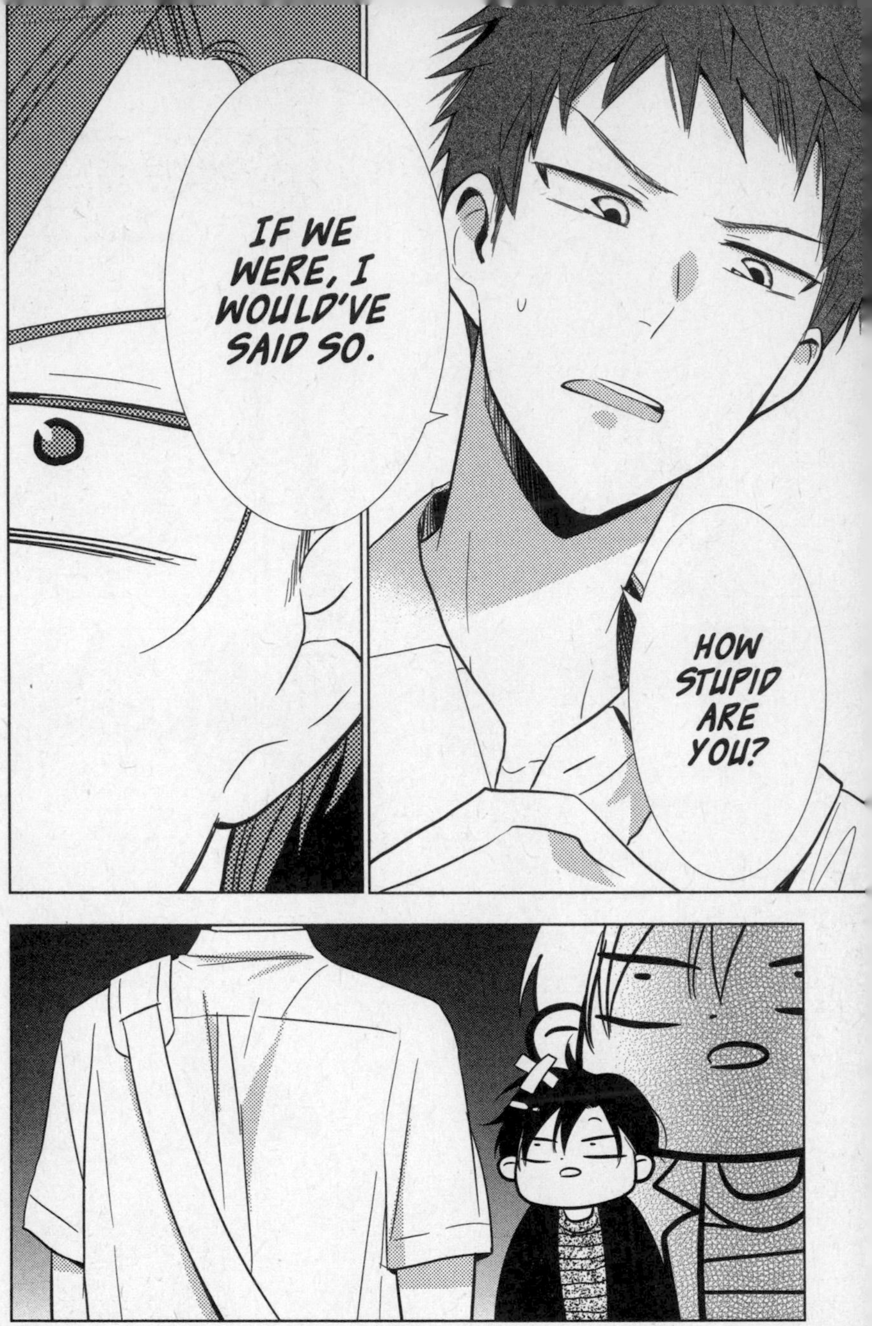
IF WE WERE, I WOULD'VE SAID SO.
HOW STUPID ARE YOU?

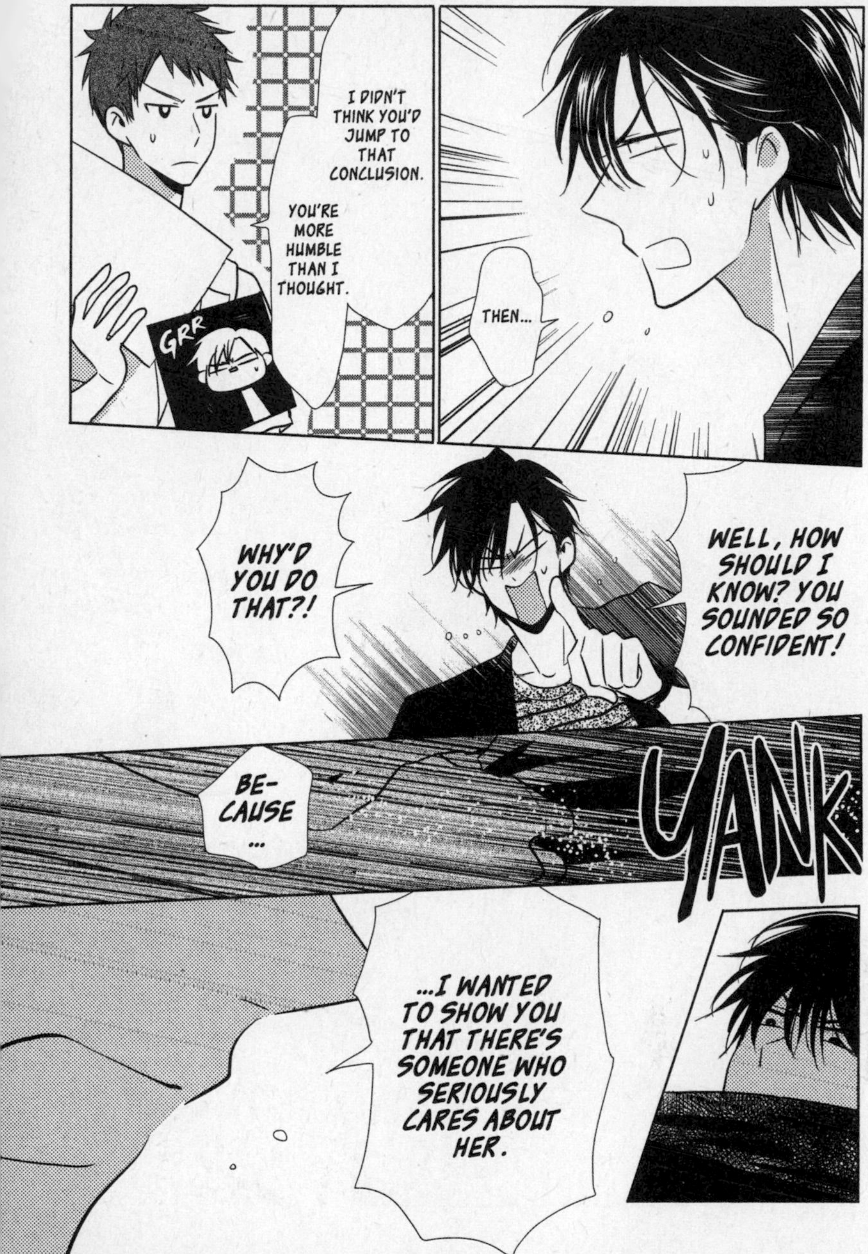
THEN...
I DIDN'T THINK YOU'D JUMP TO THAT CONCLUSION.
YOU'RE MORE HUMBLE THAN I THOUGHT.
GRR
WELL, HOW SHOULD I KNOW? YOU SOUNDED SO CONFIDENT!
WHY'D YOU DO THAT?!
YANK
BE-CAUSE ...
...I WANTED TO SHOW YOU THAT THERE'S SOMEONE WHO SERIOUSLY CARES ABOUT HER.

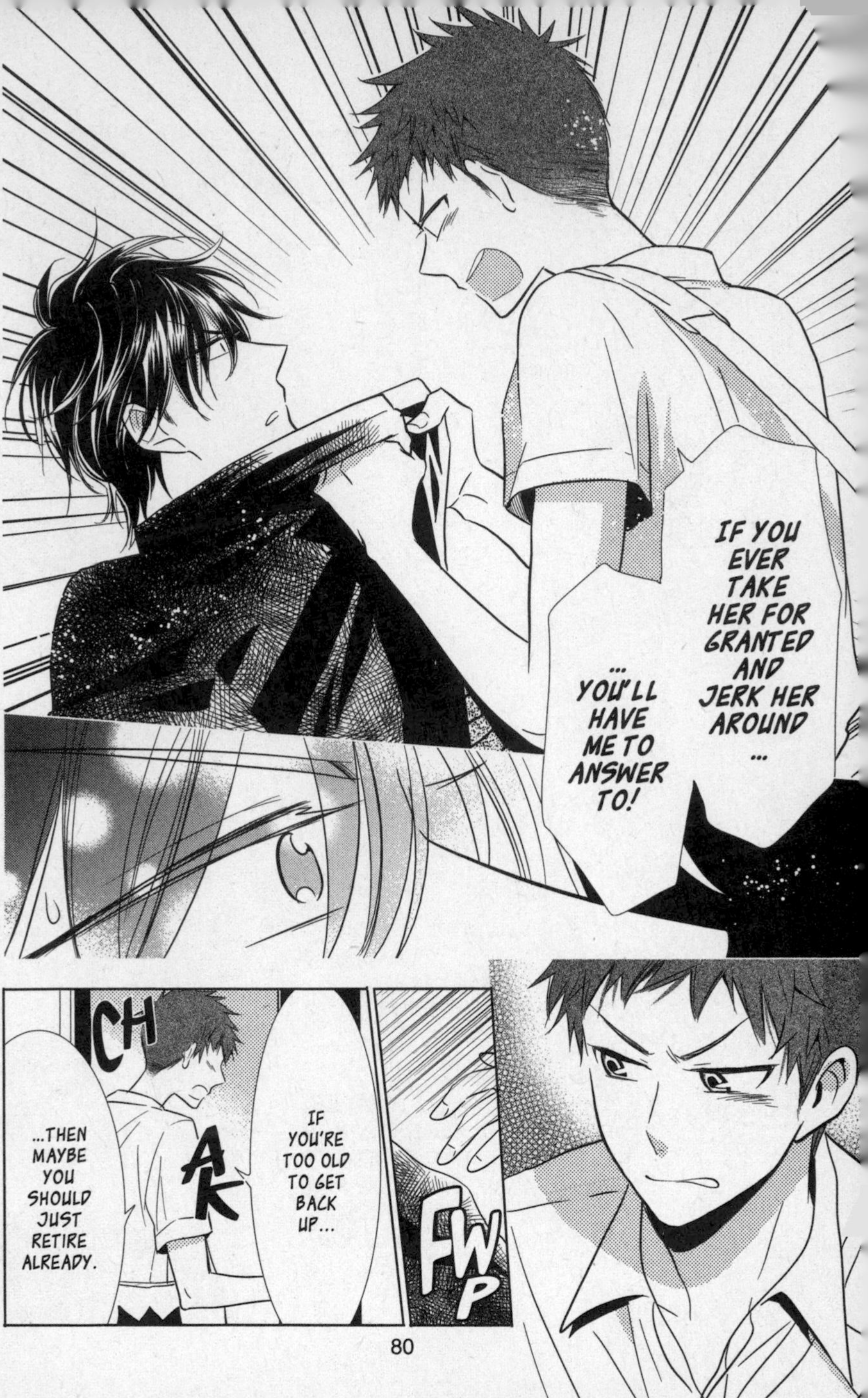
IF YOU EVER TAKE HER FOR GRANTED AND JERK HER AROUND...
...YOU'LL HAVE ME TO ANSWER TO!
FWP
IF YOU'RE TOO OLD TO GET BACK UP...
CHAK
...THEN MAYBE YOU SHOULD JUST RETIRE ALREADY.

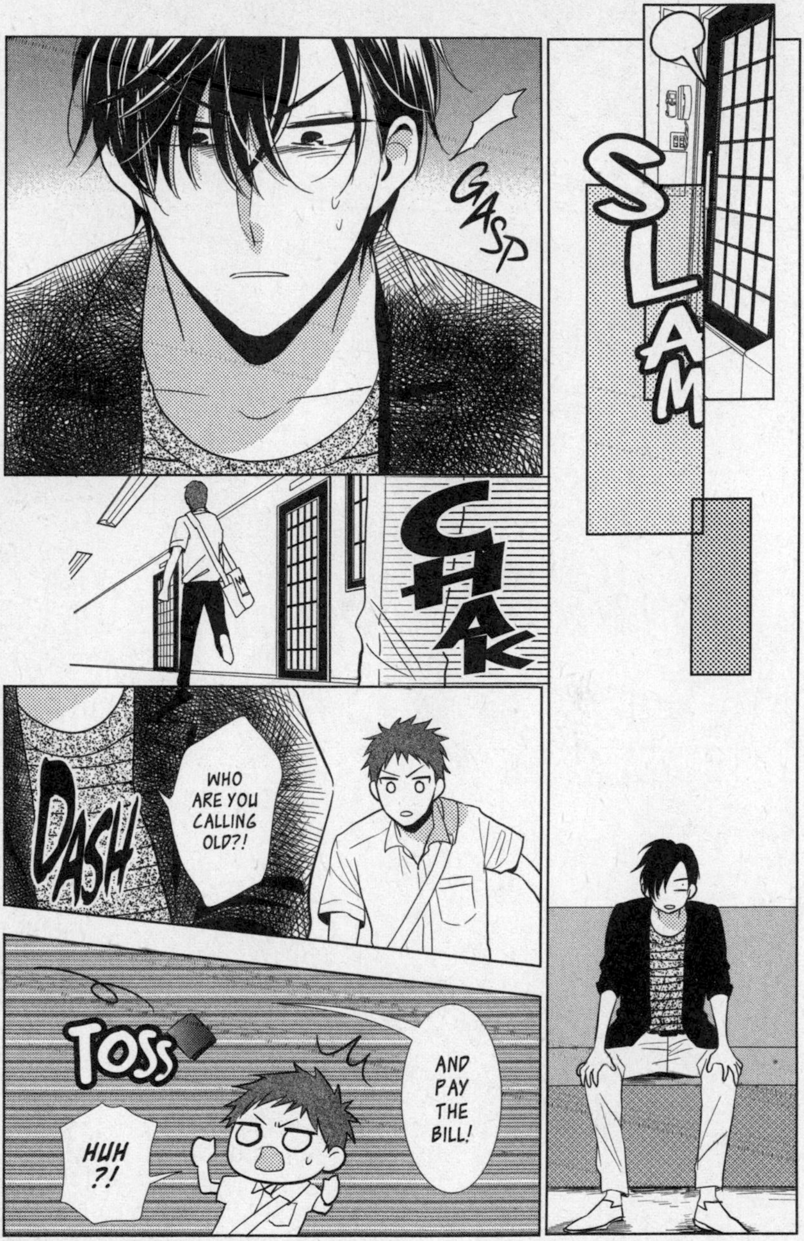
SLAM
GASP
CHAK
WHO ARE YOU CALLING OLD?!
DASH
AND PAY THE BILL!
TOSS
HUH?!

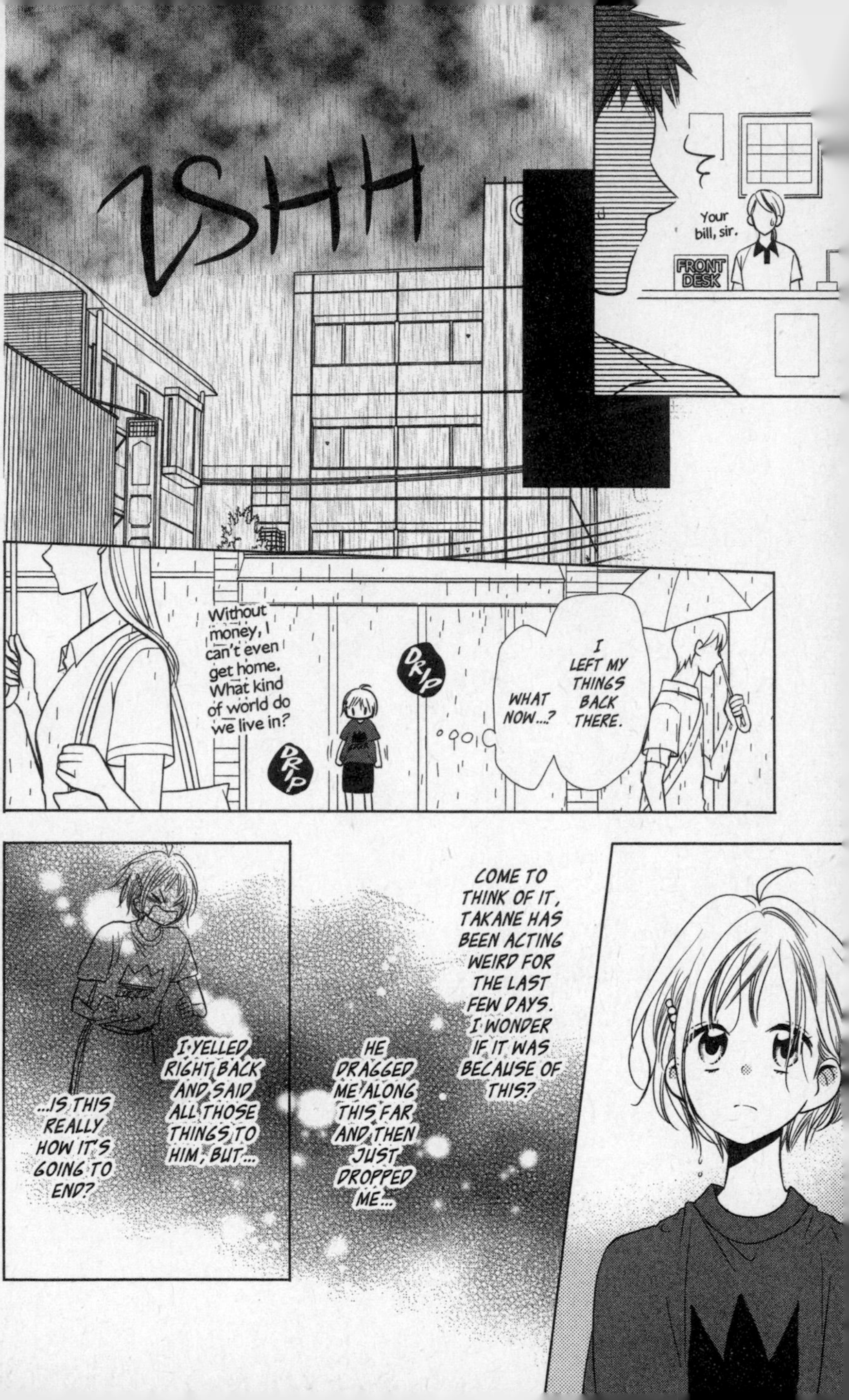

Your bill, sir.
FRONT DESK
ZSHH
I LEFT MY THINGS BACK THERE.
WHAT NOW...?
DRIP
Without money, I can't even get home. What kind of world do we live in?
DRIP
COME TO THINK OF IT, TAKANE HAS BEEN ACTING WEIRD FOR THE LAST FEW DAYS. I WONDER IF IT WAS BECAUSE OF THIS?
HE DRAGGED ME ALONG THIS FAR AND THEN JUST DROPPED ME...
I YELLED RIGHT BACK AND SAID ALL THOSE THINGS TO HIM, BUT...
...IS THIS REALLY HOW IT'S GOING TO END?

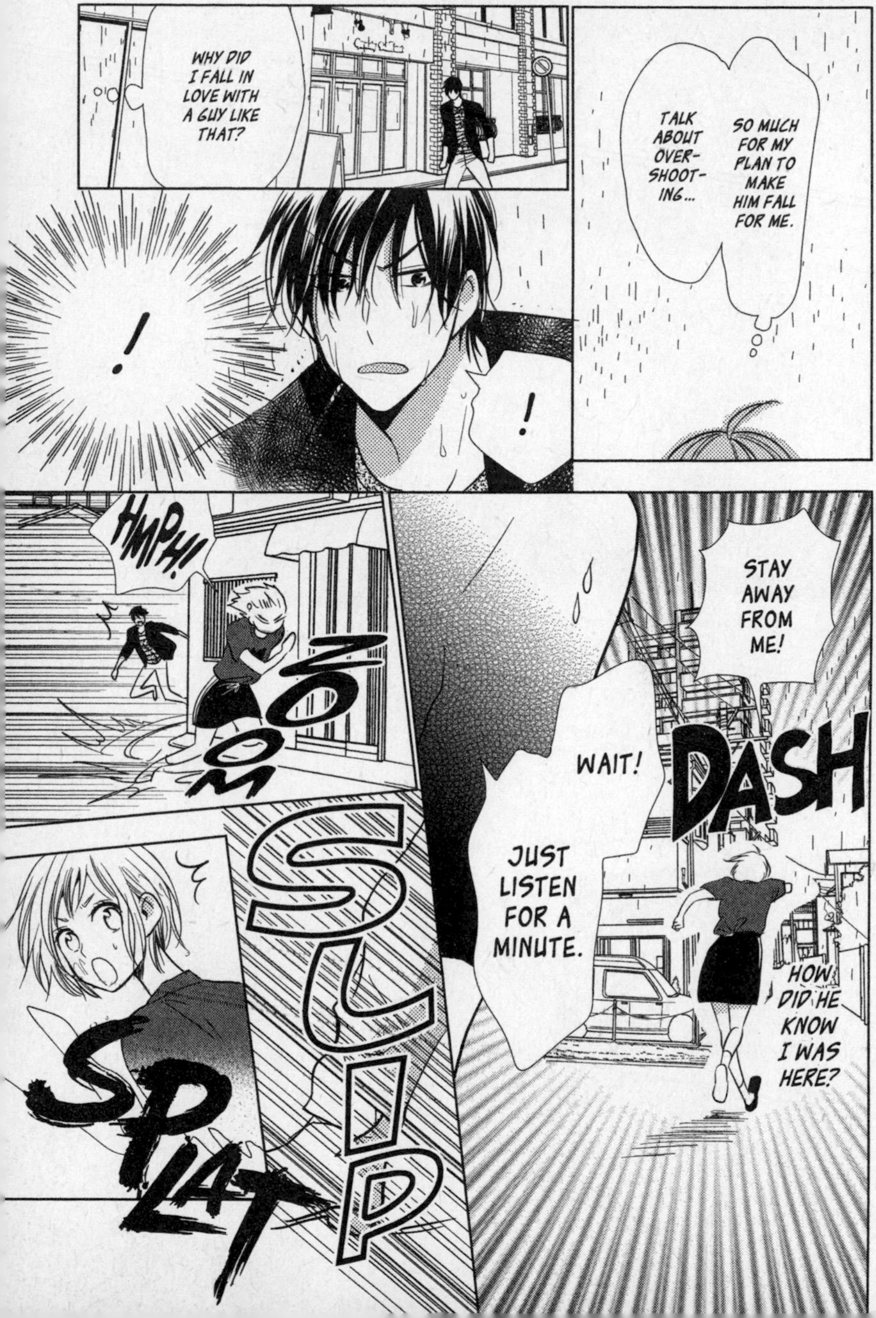
SO MUCH FOR MY PLAN TO MAKE HIM FALL FOR ME.
TALK ABOUT OVER-SHOOTING...
WHY DID I FALL IN LOVE WITH A GUY LIKE THAT?
!
!
STAY AWAY FROM ME!
DASH
HOW DID HE KNOW I WAS HERE?
WAIT!
JUST LISTEN FOR A MINUTE.
HMPH!
ZOOM
SLIP
SPLAT

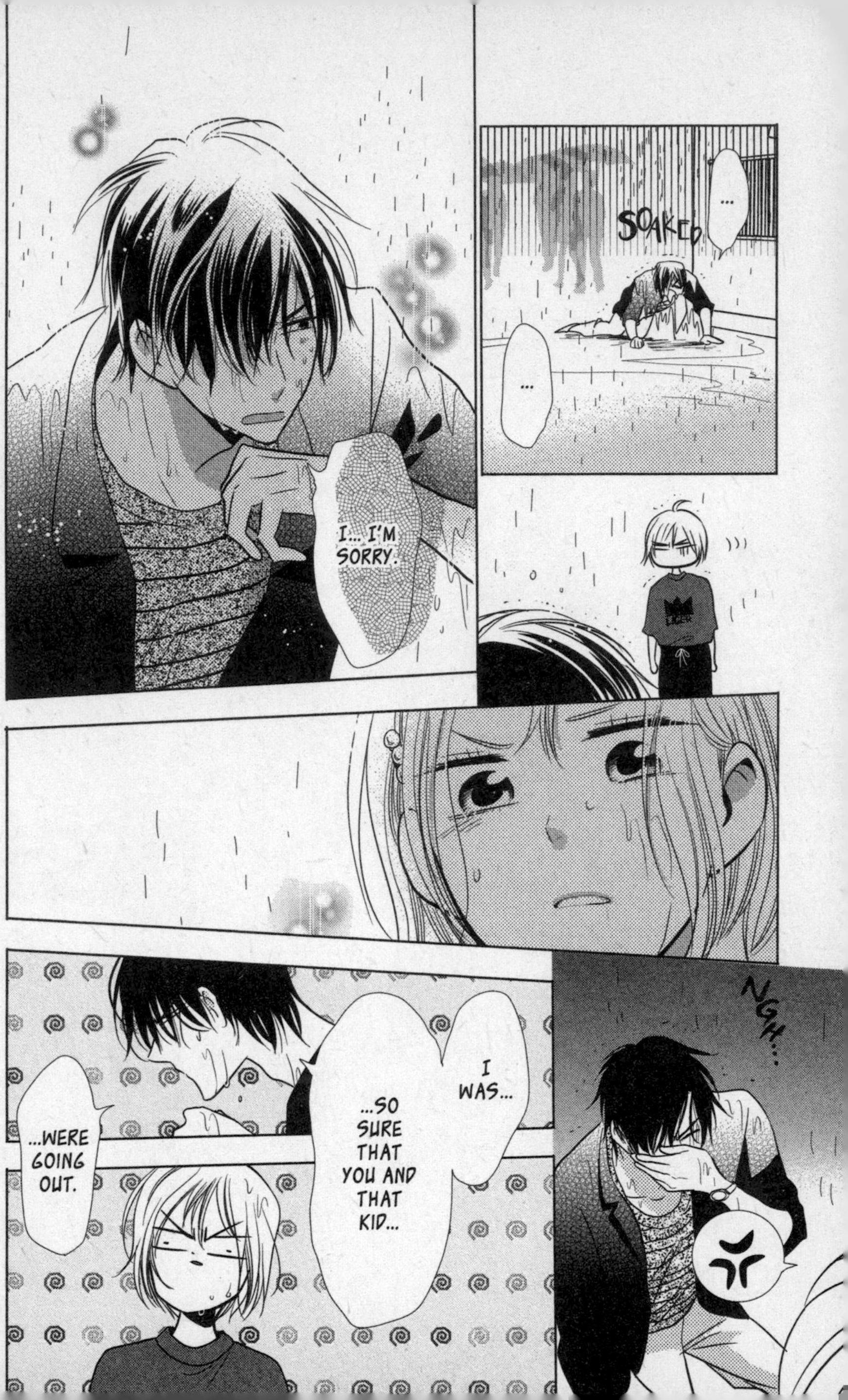
...
SOAKED
...
I... I'M SORRY.
NGH...
I WAS...
...SO SURE THAT YOU AND THAT KID...
...WERE GOING OUT.

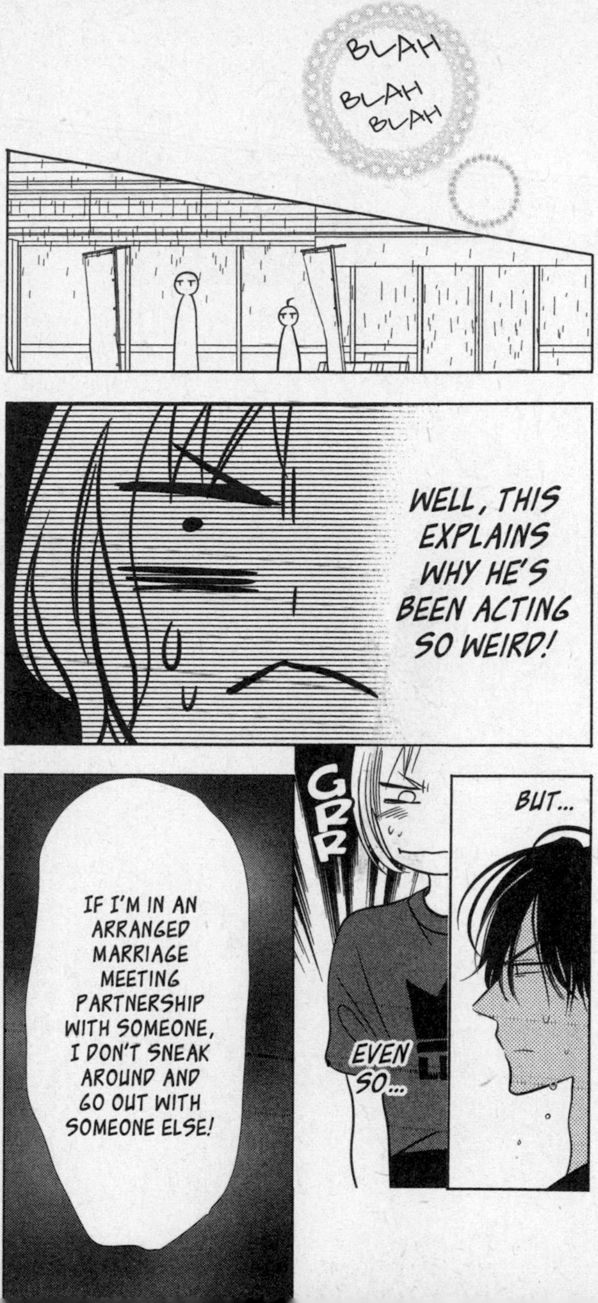
BLAH
BLAH
BLAH
WELL, THIS EXPLAINS WHY HE'S BEEN ACTING SO WEIRD!
BUT...
EVEN SO...
GRR
IF I'M IN AN ARRANGED MARRIAGE MEETING PARTNERSHIP WITH SOMEONE, I DON'T SNEAK AROUND AND GO OUT WITH SOMEONE ELSE!

● Karaoke 2 ●

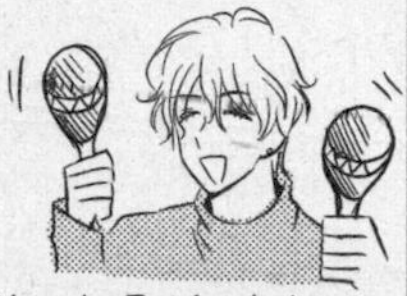

He sucks. But since he knows that, he devotes himself to being the life of the party. He's fantastic at clapping along and cheering. When you try to give him the mic, he'll keep smiling but flatly refuse.

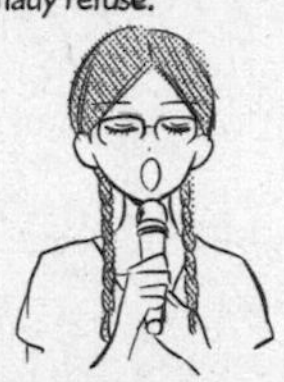

With her voice, she should be in a choir. She sounds weird singing pop songs, but that doesn't stop her from singing songs she likes.

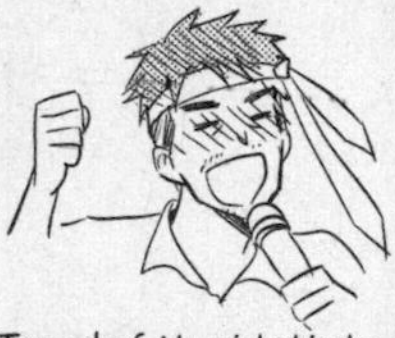

Tone-deaf. He might hit the wrong notes, but he always picks the right song. He's a mood maker.

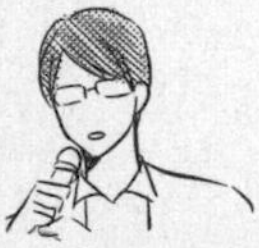

He doesn't realize he's tone-deaf, and the aura he gives off makes it hard for anyone to tell him. He doesn't do anything fancy.

And that concludes the section where I dis the characters' singing abilities.

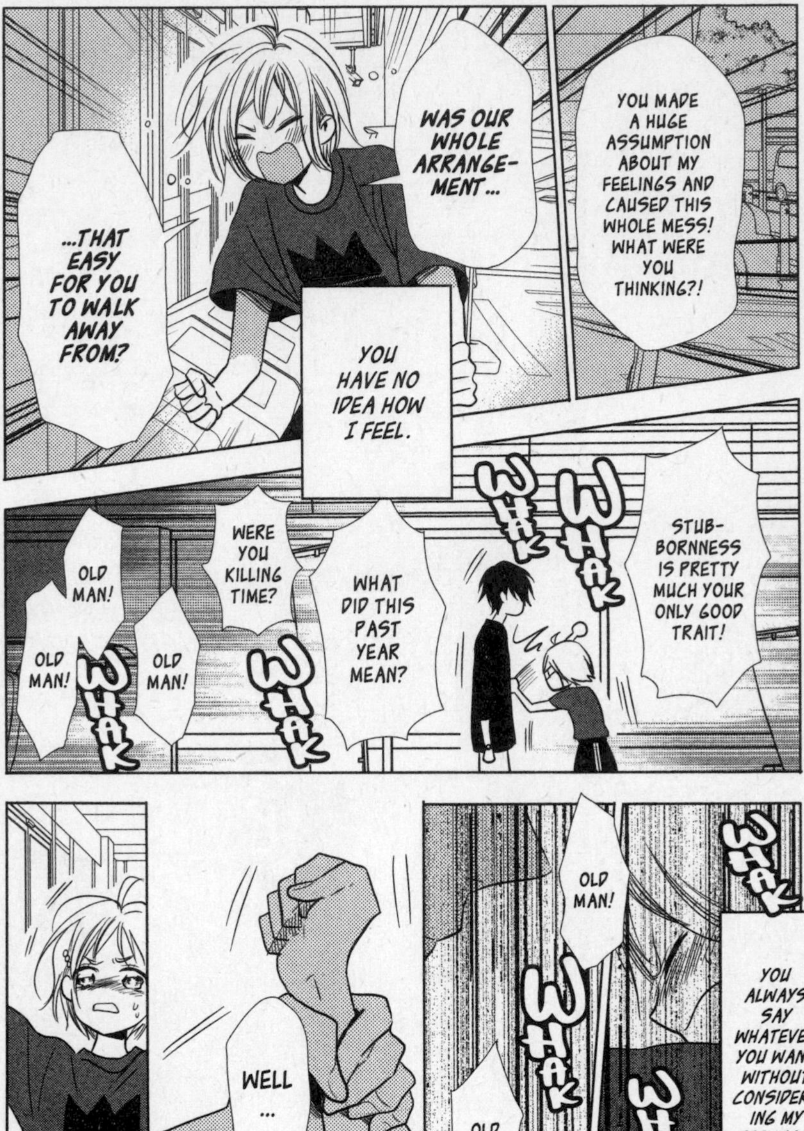
YOU MADE A HUGE ASSUMPTION ABOUT MY FEELINGS AND CAUSED THIS WHOLE MESS! WHAT WERE YOU THINKING?!
WAS OUR WHOLE ARRANGE-MENT...
...THAT EASY FOR YOU TO WALK AWAY FROM?
YOU HAVE NO IDEA HOW I FEEL.
STUB-BORNNESS IS PRETTY MUCH YOUR ONLY GOOD TRAIT!
WHAK
WHAK
WHAT DID THIS PAST YEAR MEAN?
WHAK
WERE YOU KILLING TIME?
OLD MAN!
OLD MAN!
WHAK
OLD MAN!
WHAK
YOU ALWAYS SAY WHATEVER YOU WANT WITHOUT CONSIDER-ING MY FEELINGS.
OLD MAN!
WHAK
WHAK
OLD MAN!
WELL ...
LIGER

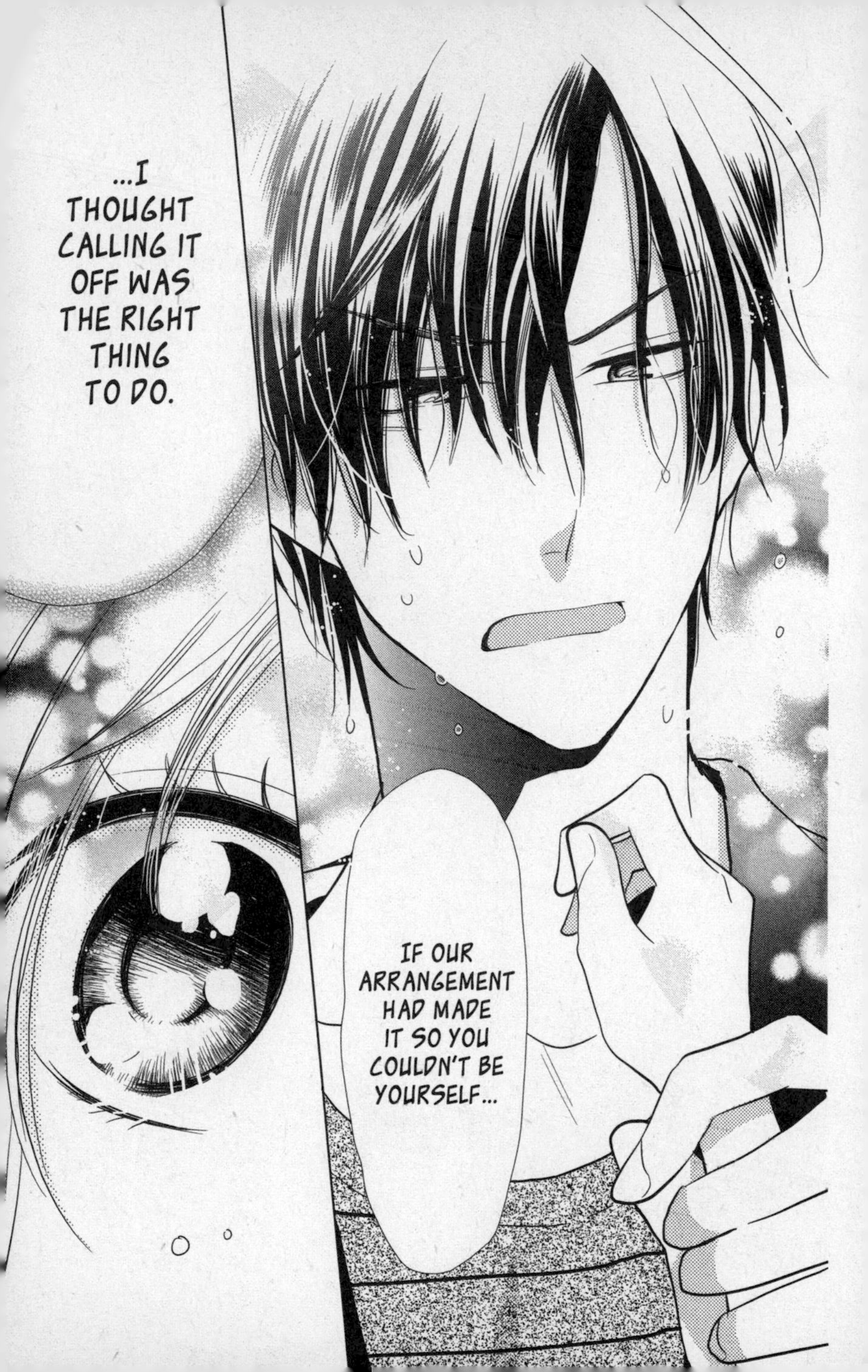
IF OUR ARRANGEMENT HAD MADE IT SO YOU COULDN'T BE YOURSELF...
...I THOUGHT CALLING IT OFF WAS THE RIGHT THING TO DO.

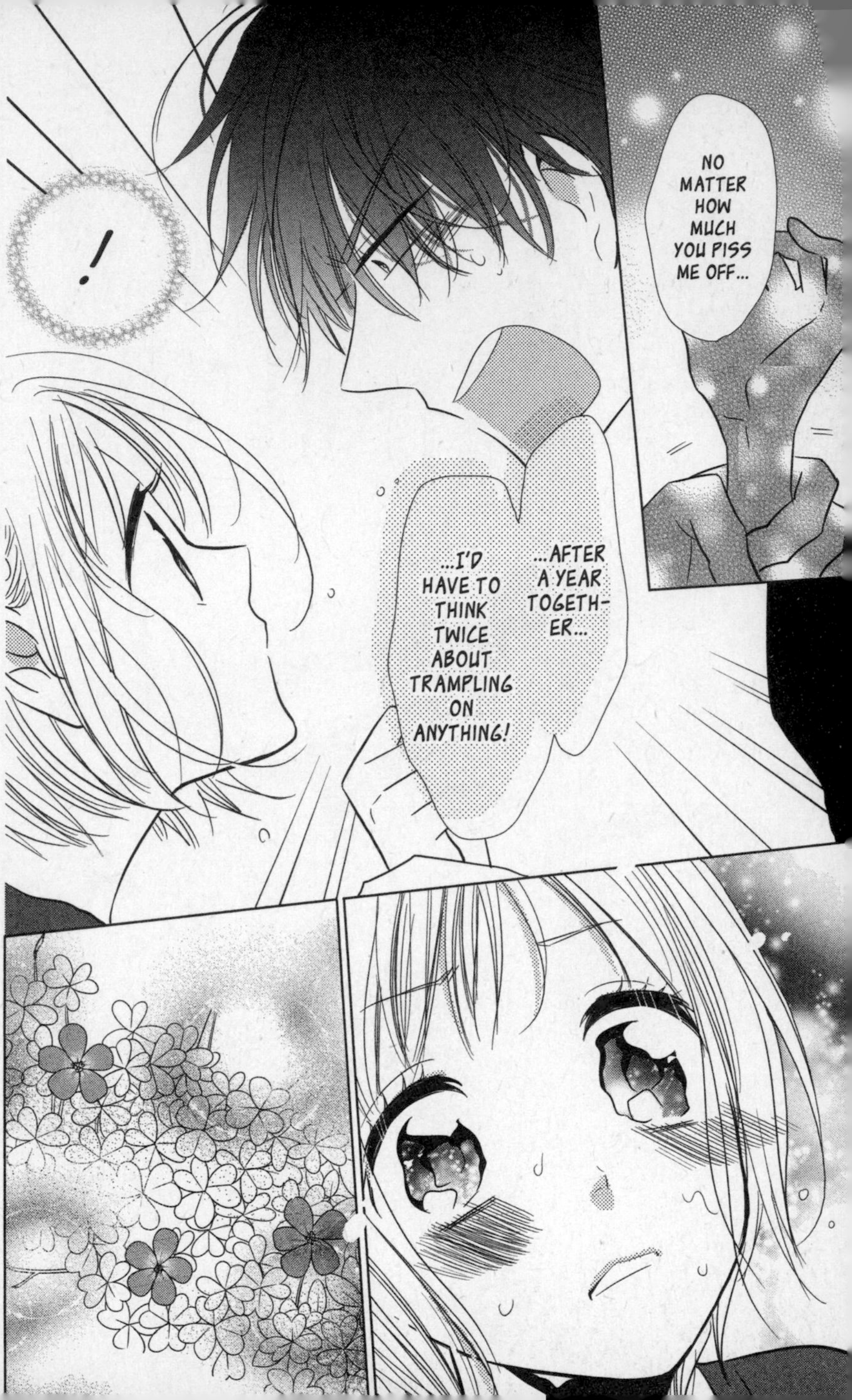
NO MATTER HOW MUCH YOU PISS ME OFF...
!
...AFTER A YEAR TOGETHER...
...I'D HAVE TO THINK TWICE ABOUT TRAMPLING ON ANYTHING!

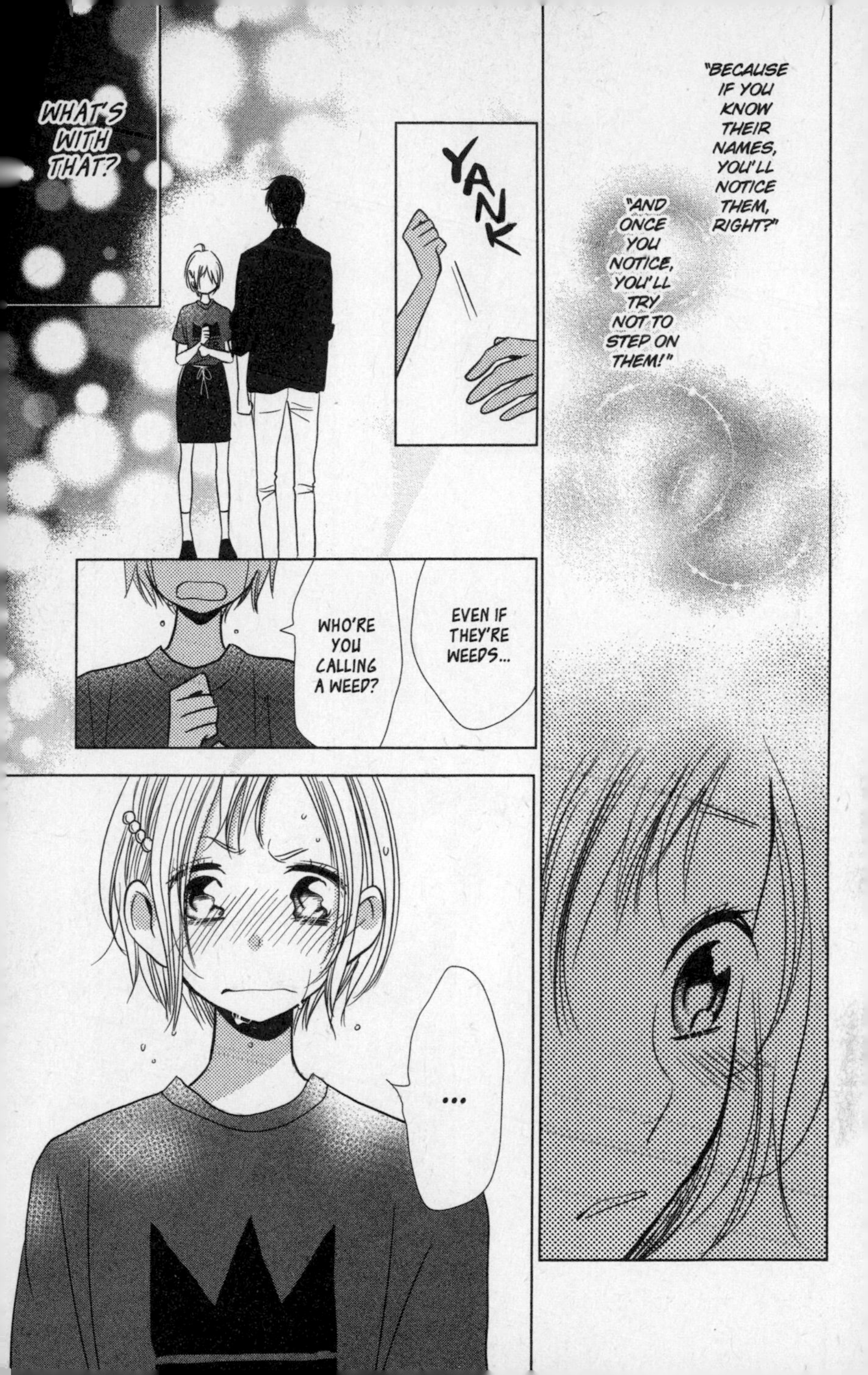
"BECAUSE IF YOU KNOW THEIR NAMES, YOU'LL NOTICE THEM, RIGHT?"
"AND ONCE YOU NOTICE, YOU'LL TRY NOT TO STEP ON THEM!"
YANK
WHAT'S WITH THAT?
EVEN IF THEY'RE WEEDS...
WHO'RE YOU CALLING A WEED?
...

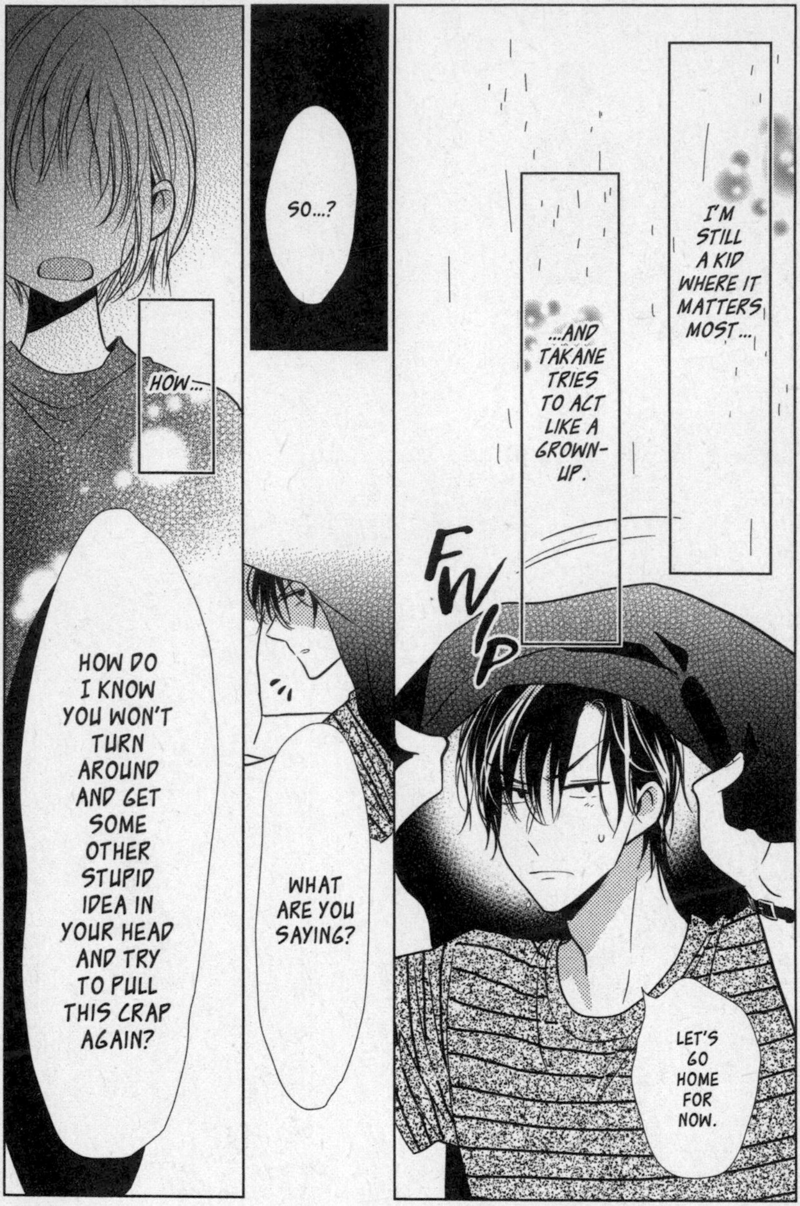
I'M STILL A KID WHERE IT MATTERS MOST...
...AND TAKANE TRIES TO ACT LIKE A GROWN-UP.
FWIP
LET'S GO HOME FOR NOW.
SO...?
WHAT ARE YOU SAYING?
HOW...
HOW DO I KNOW YOU WON'T TURN AROUND AND GET SOME OTHER STUPID IDEA IN YOUR HEAD AND TRY TO PULL THIS CRAP AGAIN?

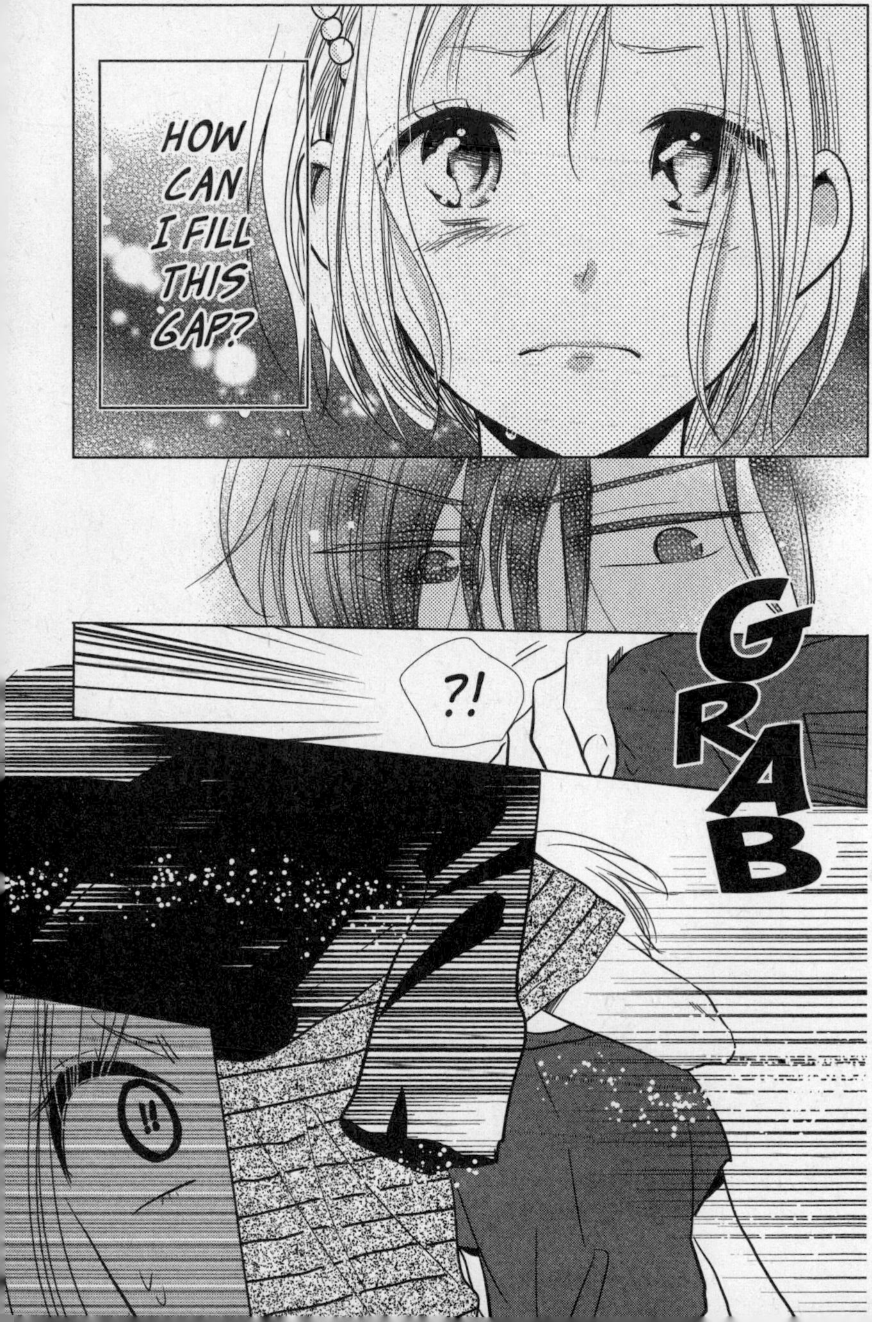
HOW CAN I FILL THIS GAP?
GRAB
?!
!!

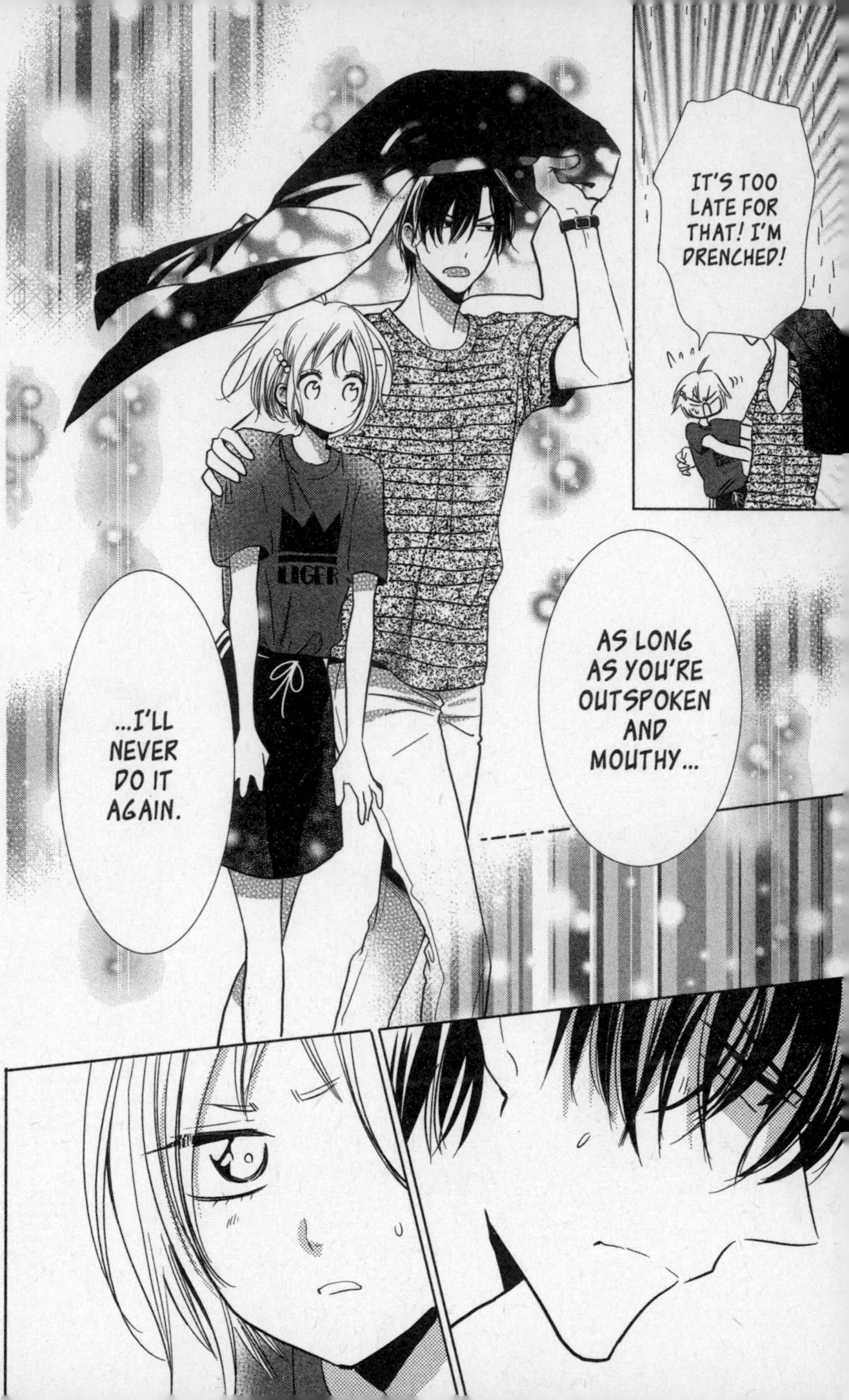
IT'S TOO LATE FOR THAT! I'M DRENCHED!
AS LONG AS YOU'RE OUTSPOKEN AND MOUTHY...
...I'LL NEVER DO IT AGAIN.

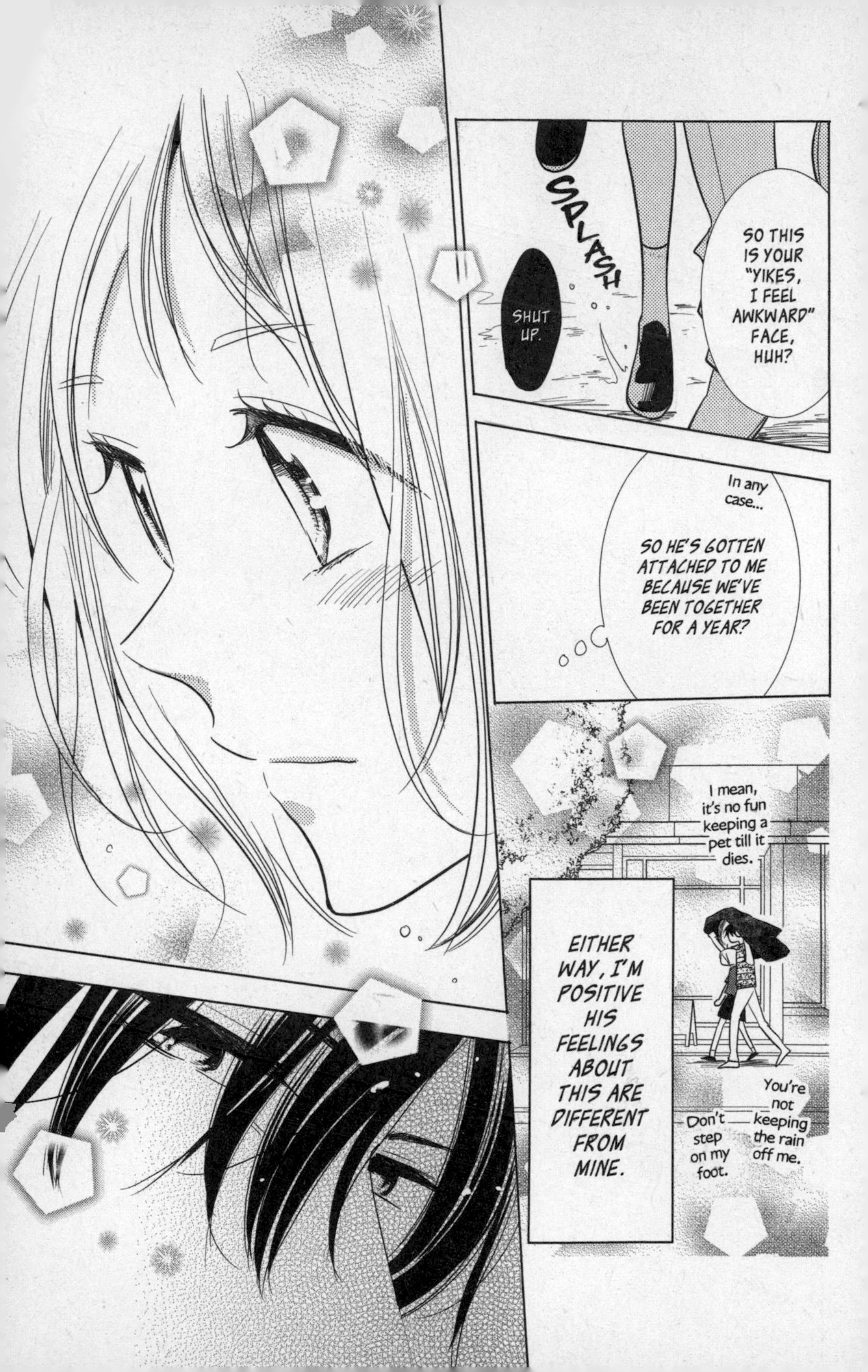
SO THIS IS YOUR "YIKES, I FEEL AWKWARD" FACE, HUH?
SPLASH
SHUT UP.
In any case...
SO HE'S GOTTEN ATTACHED TO ME BECAUSE WE'VE BEEN TOGETHER FOR A YEAR?
I mean, it's no fun keeping a pet till it dies.
EITHER WAY, I'M POSITIVE HIS FEELINGS ABOUT THIS ARE DIFFERENT FROM MINE.
You're not keeping the rain off me.
Don't step on my foot.

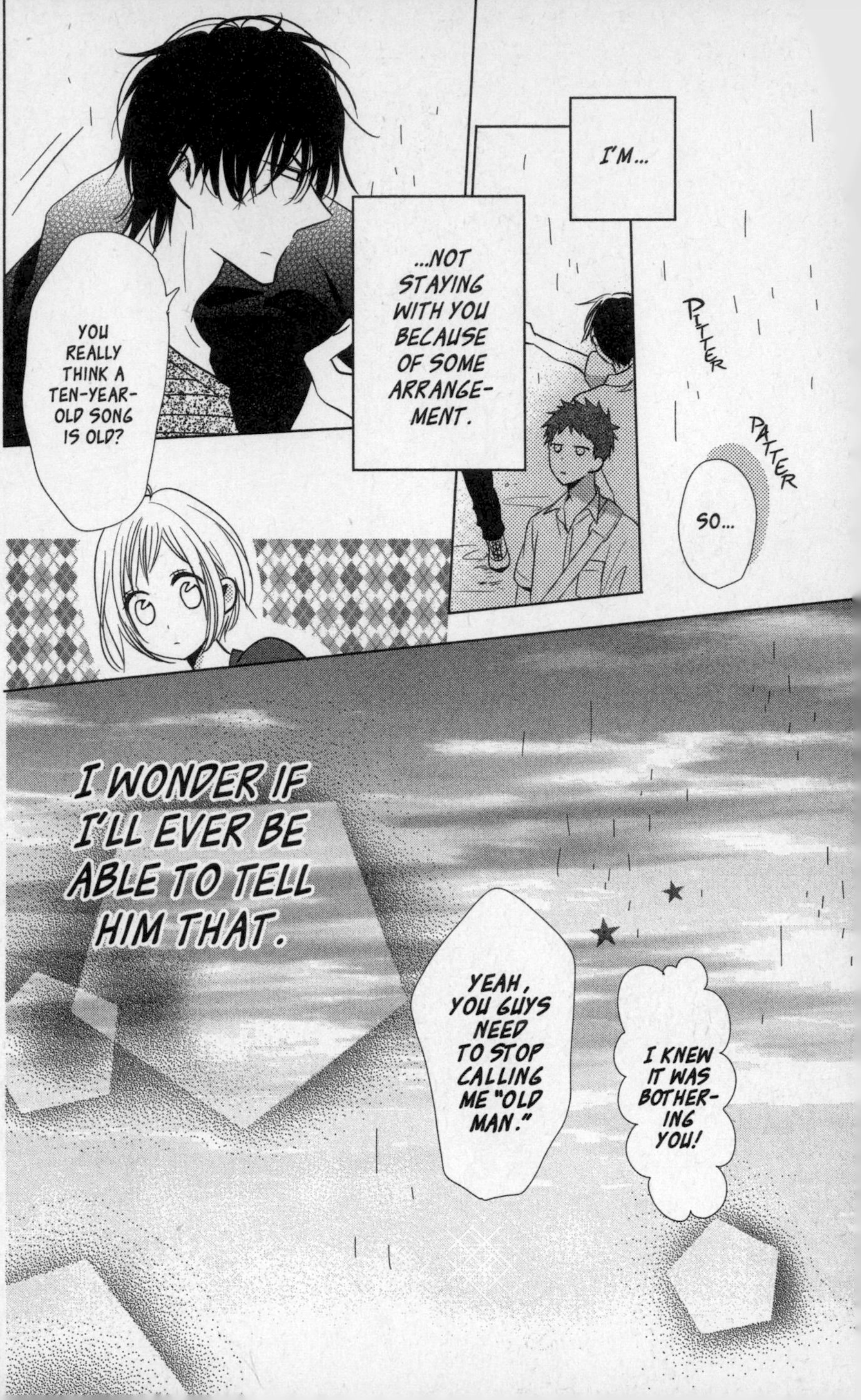
I'M...
...NOT STAYING WITH YOU BECAUSE OF SOME ARRANGEMENT.
PITTER
PATTER
SO...
YOU REALLY THINK A TEN-YEAR-OLD SONG IS OLD?
I KNEW IT WAS BOTHERING YOU!
YEAH, YOU GUYS NEED TO STOP CALLING ME "OLD MAN."
I WONDER IF I'LL EVER BE ABLE TO TELL HIM THAT.

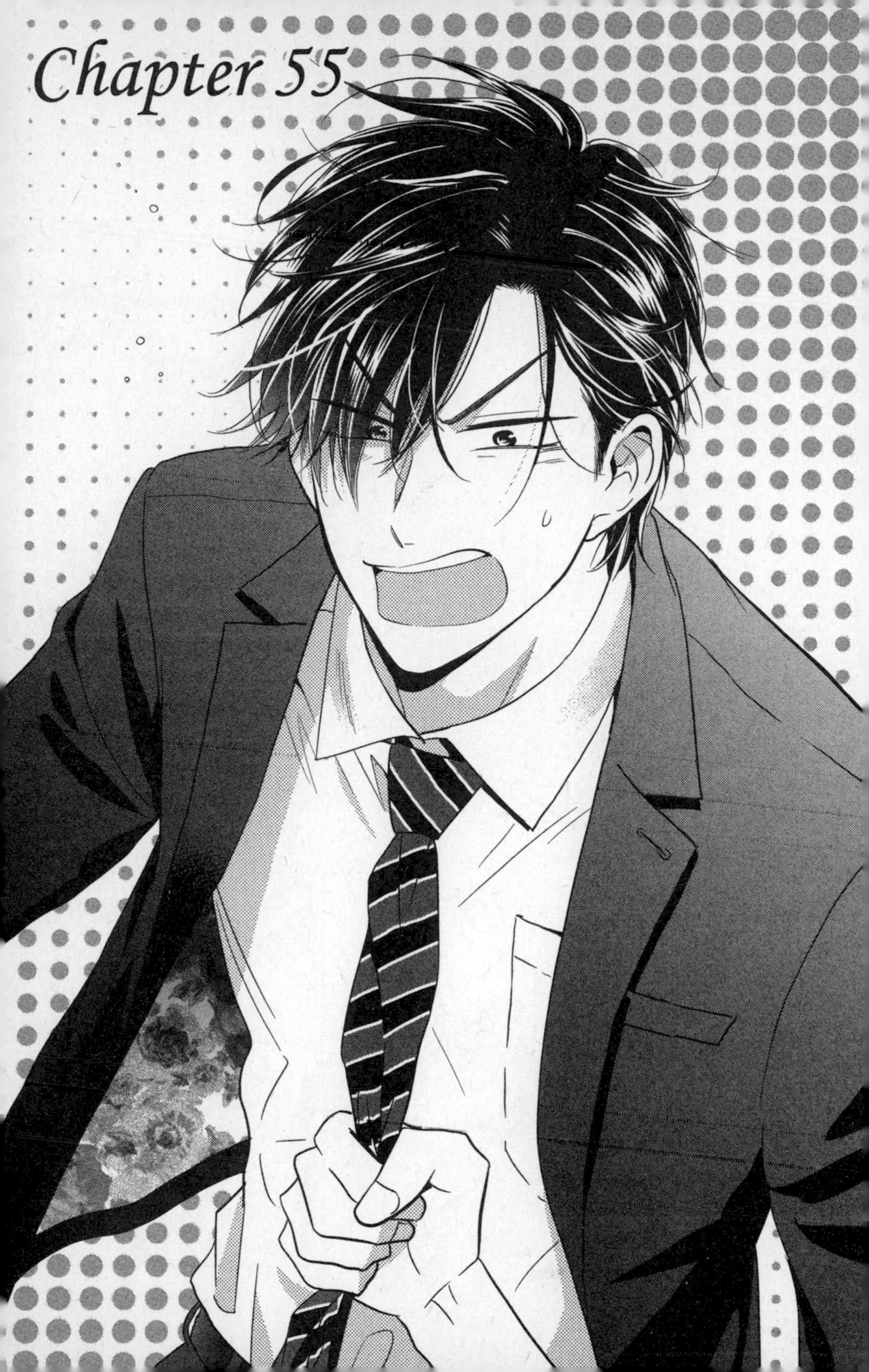
Chapter 55

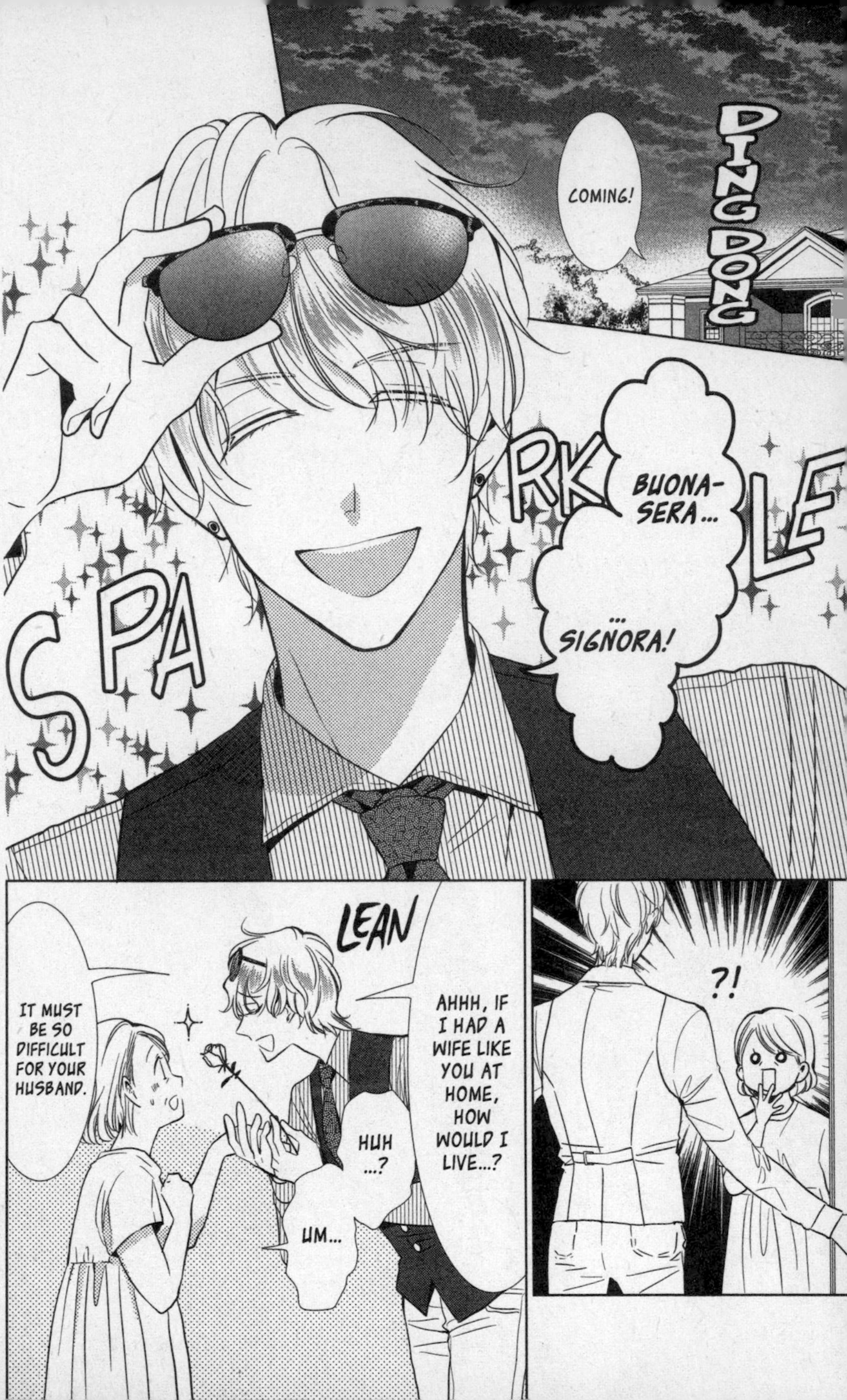
DING DONG
COMING!
SPARKLE
BUONA-SERA...
...SIGNORA!
?!
LEAN
AHHH, IF I HAD A WIFE LIKE YOU AT HOME, HOW WOULD I LIVE...?
HUH ...?
IT MUST BE SO DIFFICULT FOR YOUR HUSBAND.
UM...

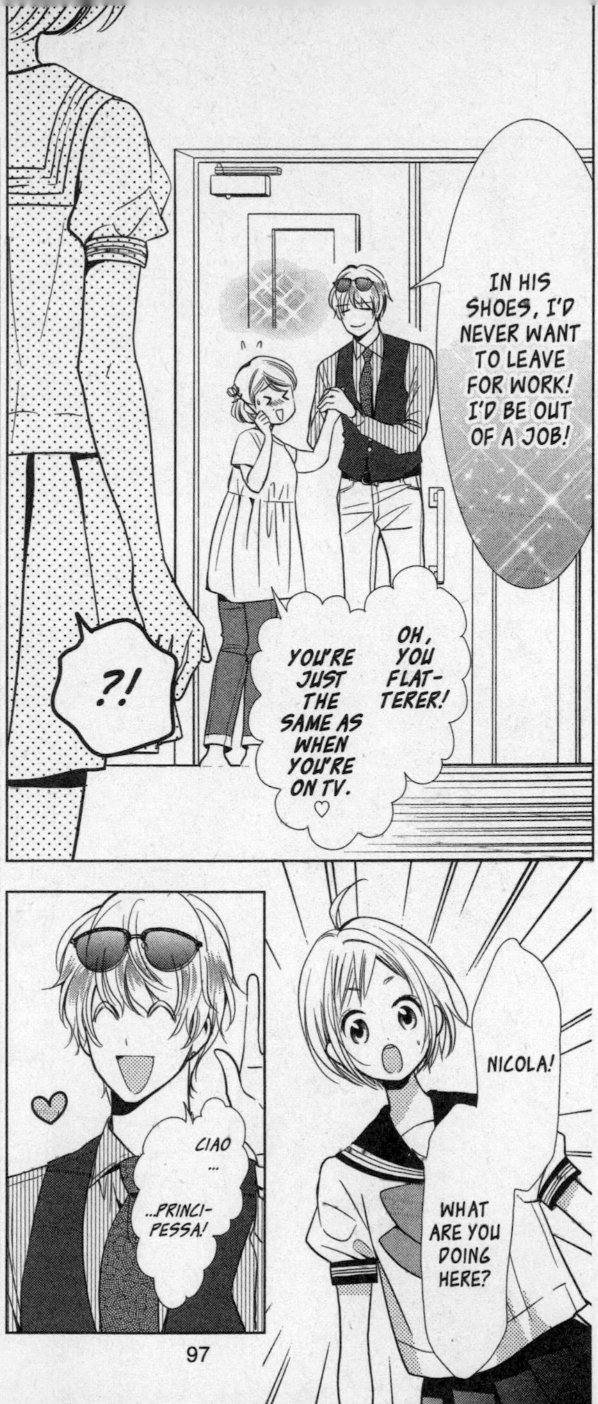
IN HIS SHOES, I'D NEVER WANT TO LEAVE FOR WORK! I'D BE OUT OF A JOB!
OH, YOU FLATTERER!
YOU'RE JUST THE SAME AS WHEN YOU'RE ON TV. ♡
?!
NICOLA!
WHAT ARE YOU DOING HERE?
CIAO...
...PRINCIPESSA!

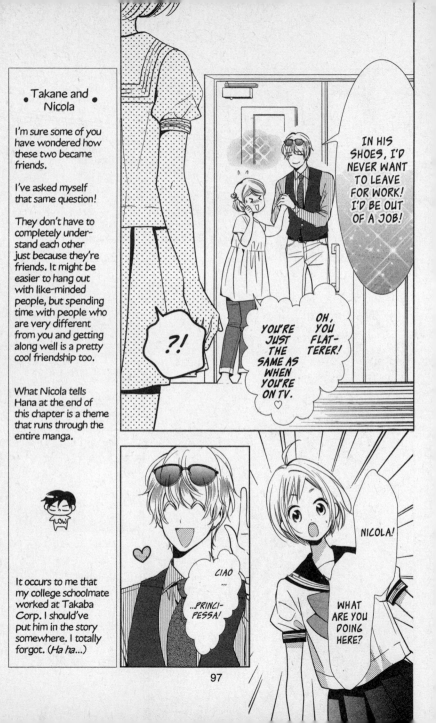

Takane and Nicola

I'm sure some of you have wondered how these two became friends.

I've asked myself that same question!

They don't have to completely understand each other just because they're friends. It might be easier to hang out with like-minded people, but spending time with people who are very different from you and getting along well is a pretty cool friendship too.

What Nicola tells Hana at the end of this chapter is a theme that runs through the entire manga.

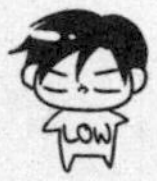
LOW

It occurs to me that my college schoolmate worked at Takaba Corp. I should've put him in the story somewhere. I totally forgot. (*Ha ha...*)

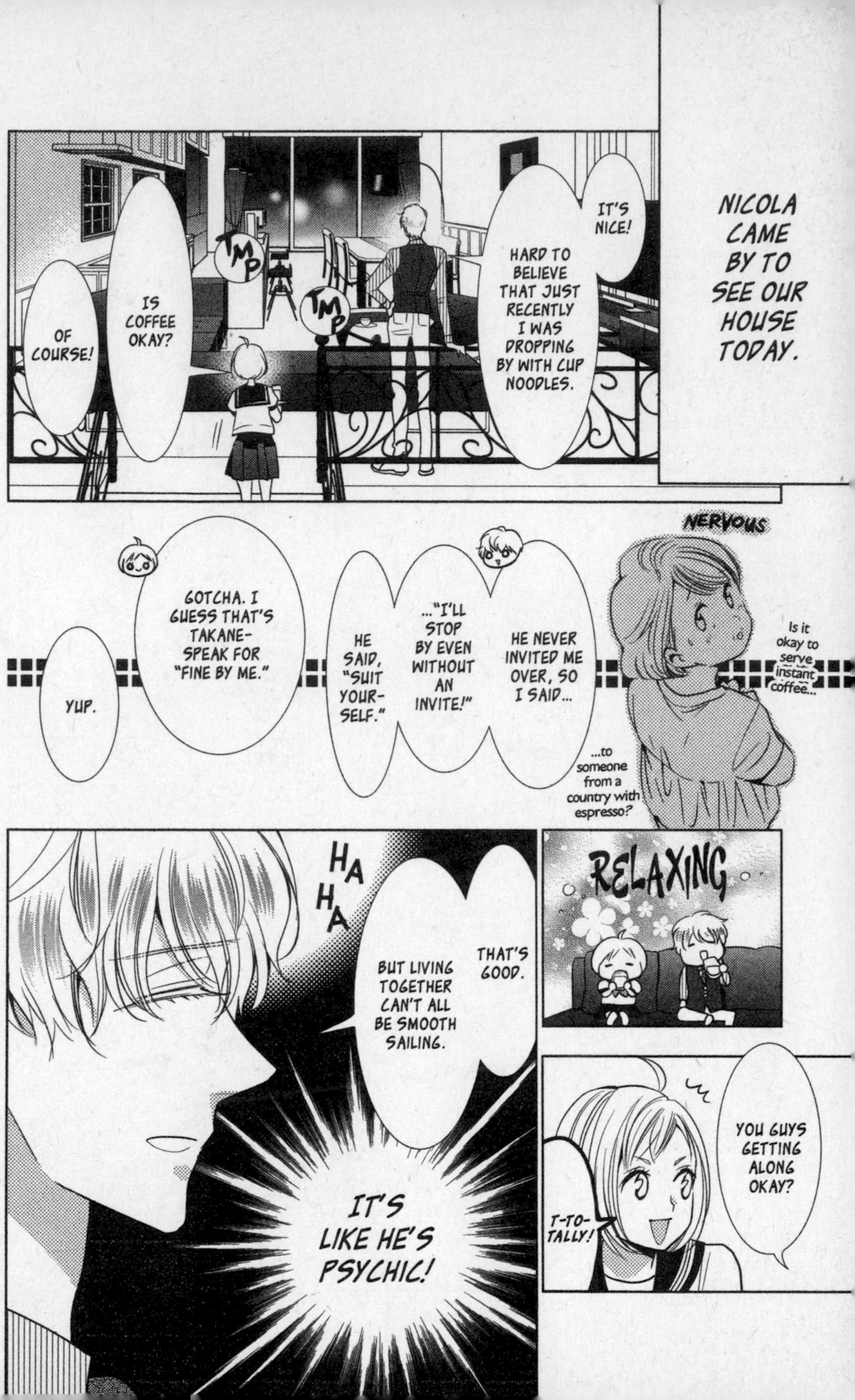
NICOLA CAME BY TO SEE OUR HOUSE TODAY.
IT'S NICE!
HARD TO BELIEVE THAT JUST RECENTLY I WAS DROPPING BY WITH CUP NOODLES.
TMP
TMP
IS COFFEE OKAY?
OF COURSE!
NERVOUS
Is it okay to serve instant coffee...
...to someone from a country with espresso?
HE NEVER INVITED ME OVER, SO I SAID...
..."I'LL STOP BY EVEN WITHOUT AN INVITE!"
HE SAID, "SUIT YOURSELF."
GOTCHA. I GUESS THAT'S TAKANE-SPEAK FOR "FINE BY ME."
YUP.
RELAXING
YOU GUYS GETTING ALONG OKAY?
T-TO-TALLY!
THAT'S GOOD.
BUT LIVING TOGETHER CAN'T ALL BE SMOOTH SAILING.
HA HA HA
IT'S LIKE HE'S PSYCHIC!

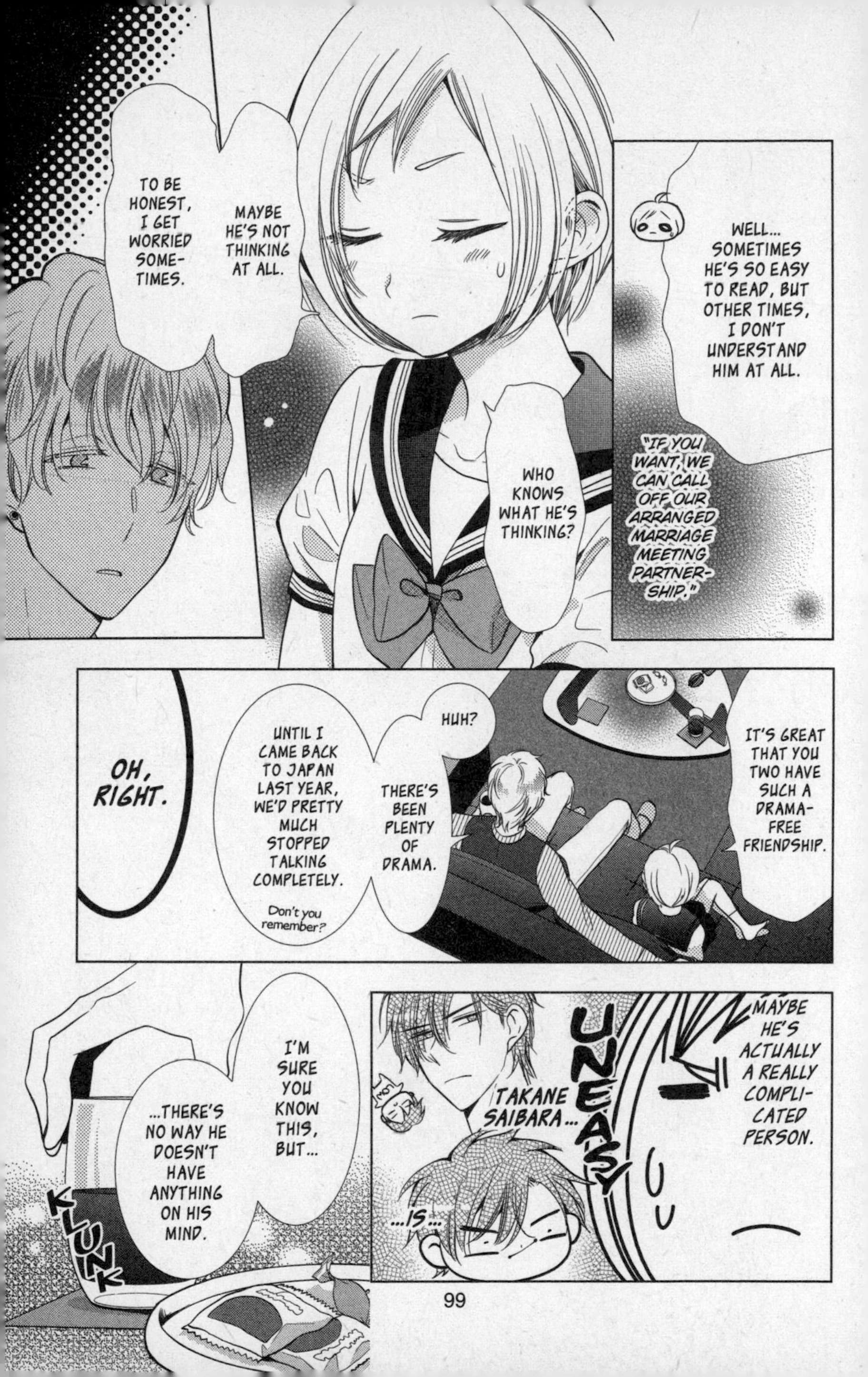
WELL... SOMETIMES HE'S SO EASY TO READ, BUT OTHER TIMES, I DON'T UNDERSTAND HIM AT ALL.
"IF YOU WANT, WE CAN CALL OFF OUR ARRANGED MARRIAGE MEETING PARTNERSHIP."
WHO KNOWS WHAT HE'S THINKING?
MAYBE HE'S NOT THINKING AT ALL.
TO BE HONEST, I GET WORRIED SOMETIMES.
IT'S GREAT THAT YOU TWO HAVE SUCH A DRAMA-FREE FRIENDSHIP.
HUH?
THERE'S BEEN PLENTY OF DRAMA.
UNTIL I CAME BACK TO JAPAN LAST YEAR, WE'D PRETTY MUCH STOPPED TALKING COMPLETELY.
Don't you remember?
OH, RIGHT.
MAYBE HE'S ACTUALLY A REALLY COMPLICATED PERSON.
UNEASY
TAKANE SAIBARA...
...IS...
I'M SURE YOU KNOW THIS, BUT...
...THERE'S NO WAY HE DOESN'T HAVE ANYTHING ON HIS MIND.
KLUNK

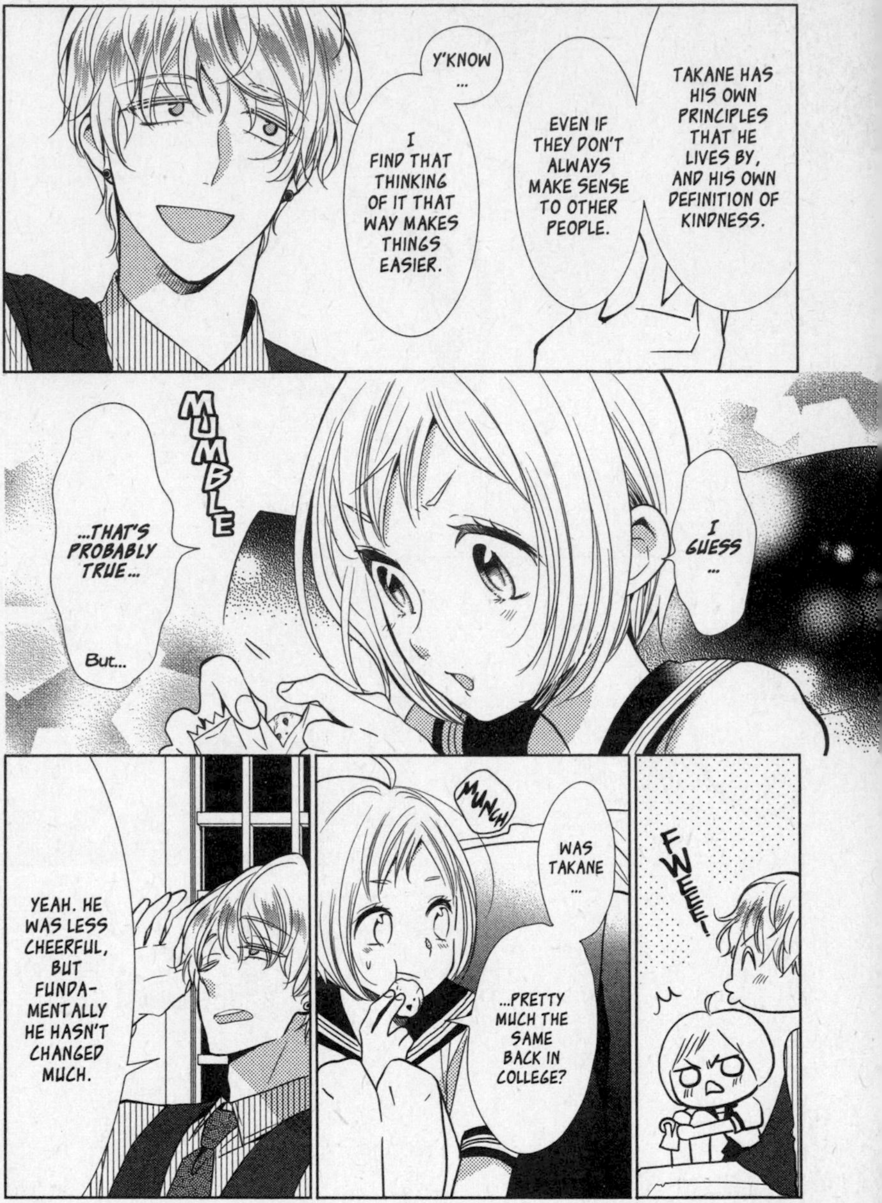
TAKANE HAS HIS OWN PRINCIPLES THAT HE LIVES BY, AND HIS OWN DEFINITION OF KINDNESS.
EVEN IF THEY DON'T ALWAYS MAKE SENSE TO OTHER PEOPLE.
Y'KNOW ...
I FIND THAT THINKING OF IT THAT WAY MAKES THINGS EASIER.
I GUESS ...
MUMBLE
...THAT'S PROBABLY TRUE...
But...
FWEEE!
MUNCH
WAS TAKANE ...
...PRETTY MUCH THE SAME BACK IN COLLEGE?
YEAH. HE WAS LESS CHEERFUL, BUT FUNDA-MENTALLY HE HASN'T CHANGED MUCH.

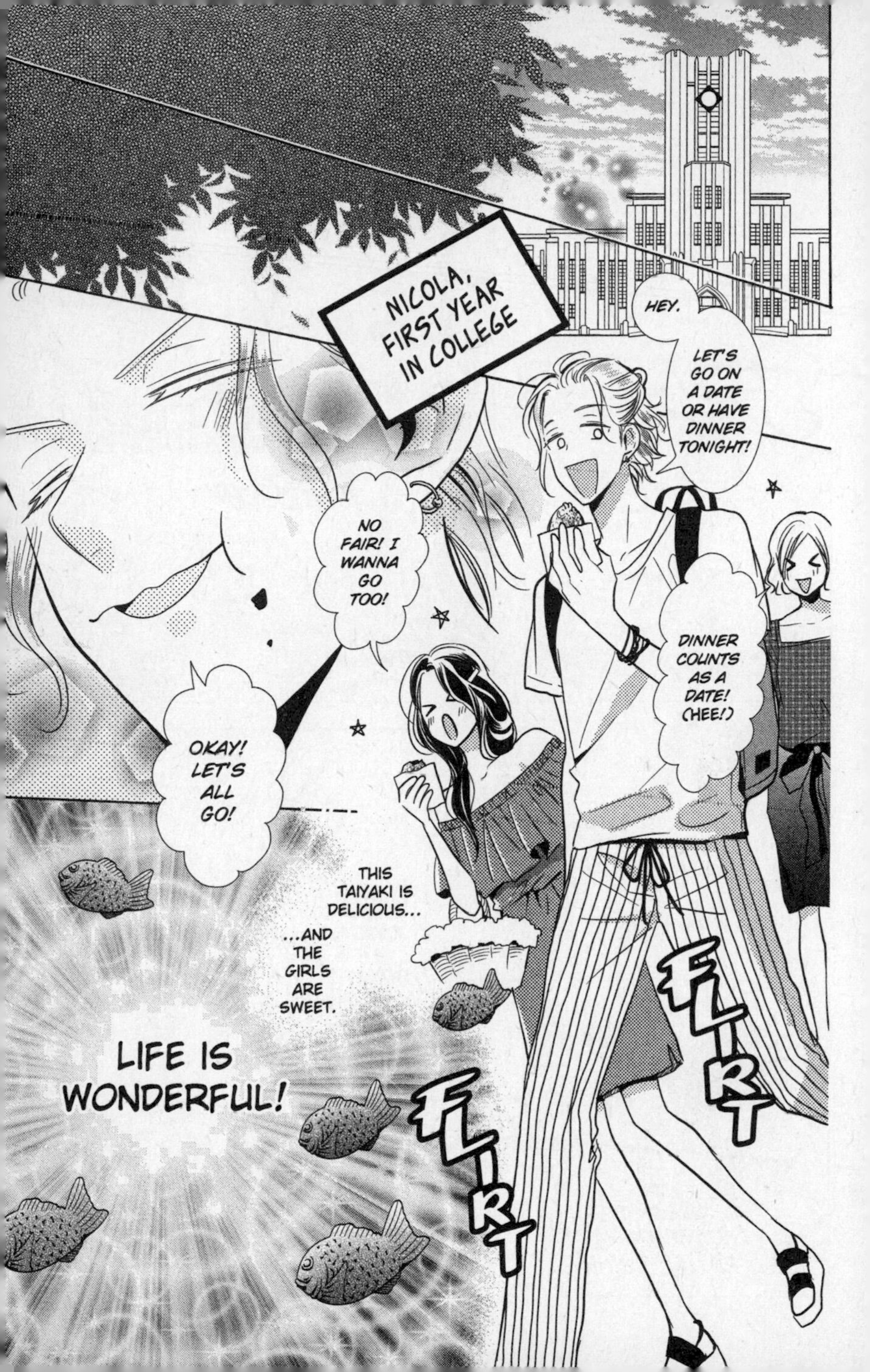
NICOLA, FIRST YEAR IN COLLEGE
HEY.
LET'S GO ON A DATE OR HAVE DINNER TONIGHT!
DINNER COUNTS AS A DATE! (HEE!)
NO FAIR! I WANNA GO TOO!
OKAY! LET'S ALL GO!
THIS TAIYAKI IS DELICIOUS...
...AND THE GIRLS ARE SWEET.
FLIRT
FLIRT
LIFE IS WONDERFUL!

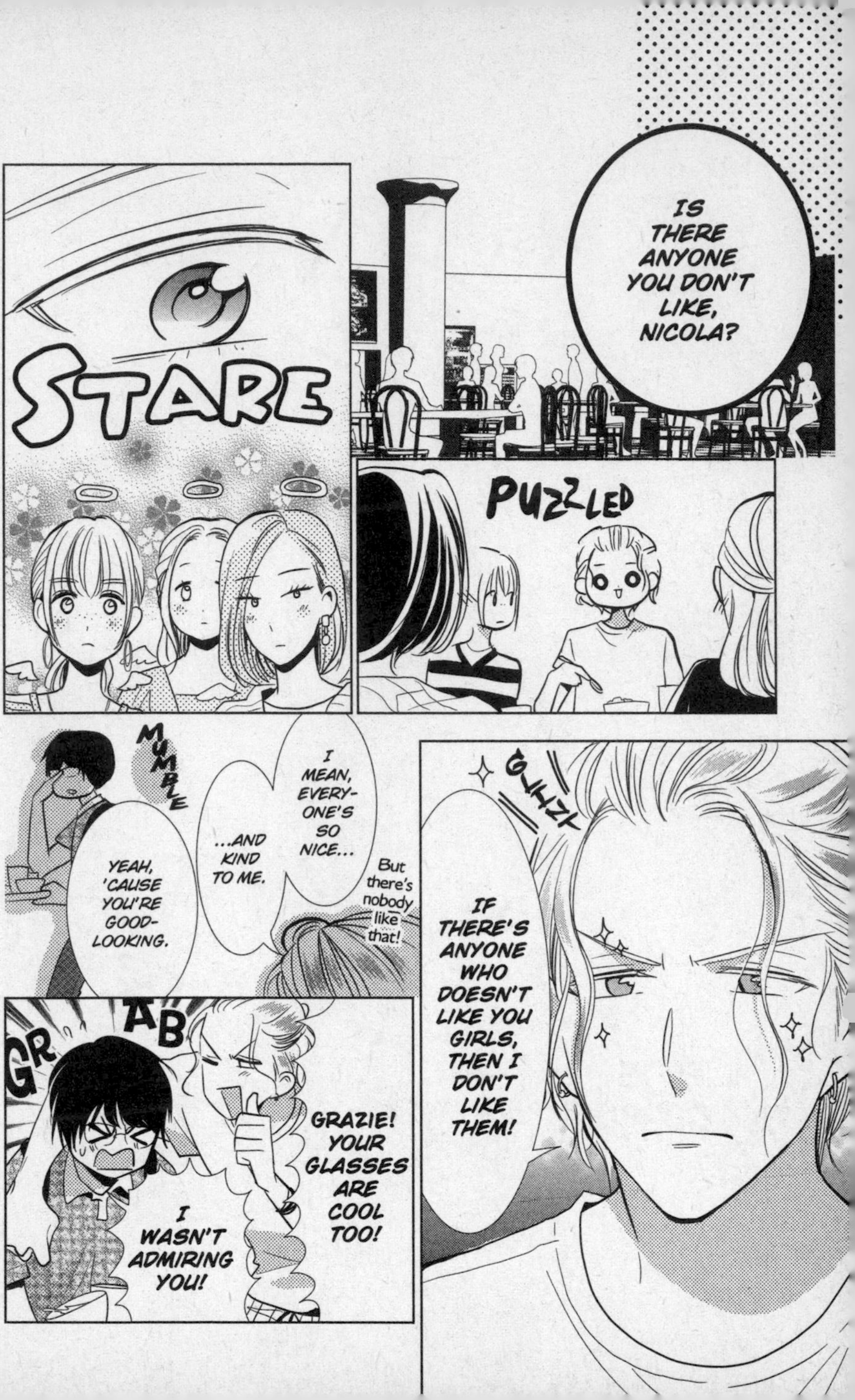
IS THERE ANYONE YOU DON'T LIKE, NICOLA?
PUZZLED
STARE
GLINT
IF THERE'S ANYONE WHO DOESN'T LIKE YOU GIRLS, THEN I DON'T LIKE THEM!
I MEAN, EVERYONE'S SO NICE...
...AND KIND TO ME.
But there's nobody like that!
MUMBLE
YEAH, 'CAUSE YOU'RE GOOD-LOOKING.
GRAB
GRAZIE! YOUR GLASSES ARE COOL TOO!
I WASN'T ADMIRING YOU!

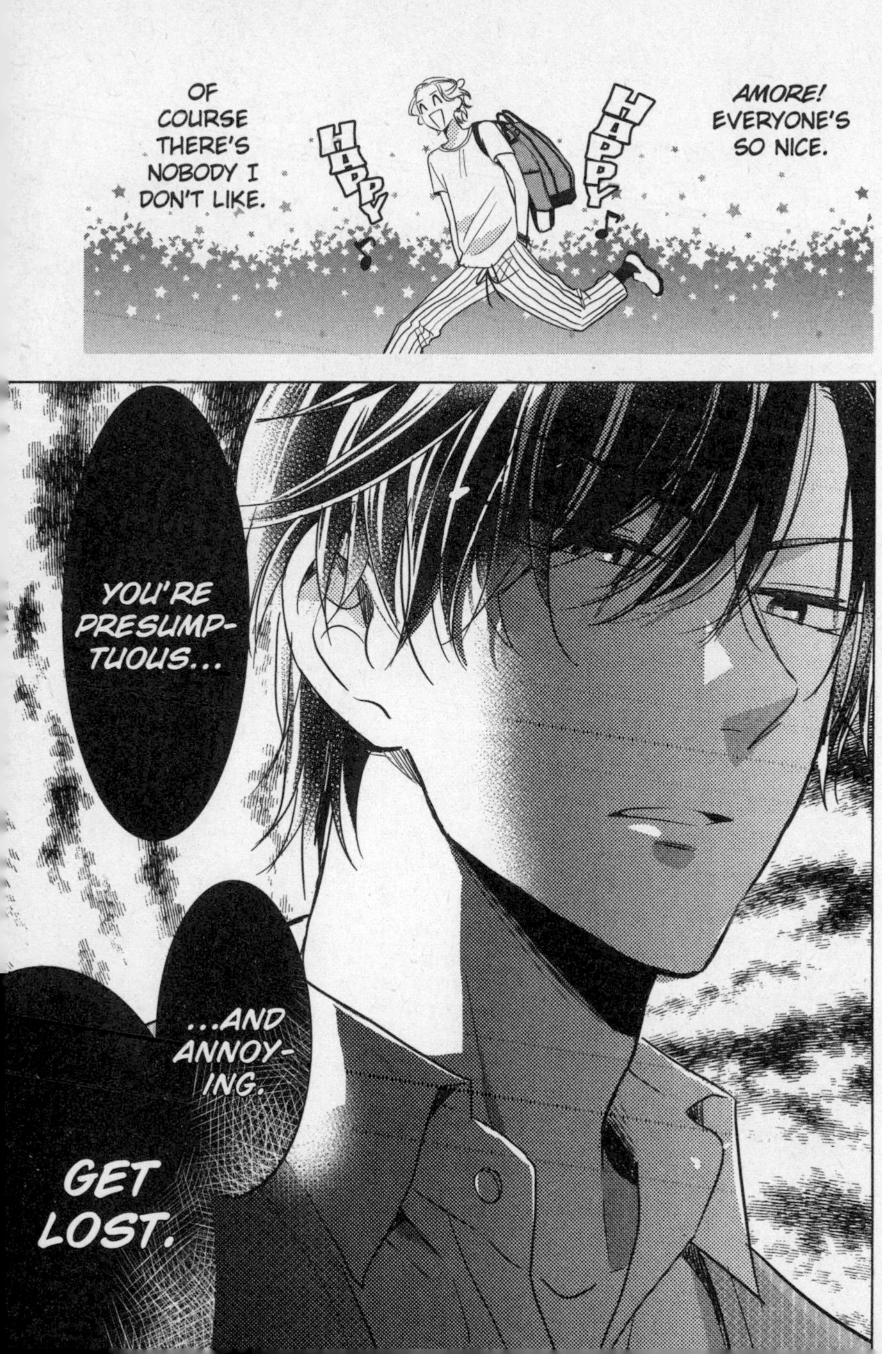
AMORE! EVERYONE'S SO NICE.
HAPPY
HAPPY
OF COURSE THERE'S NOBODY I DON'T LIKE.
YOU'RE PRESUMPTUOUS...
...AND ANNOYING.
GET LOST.

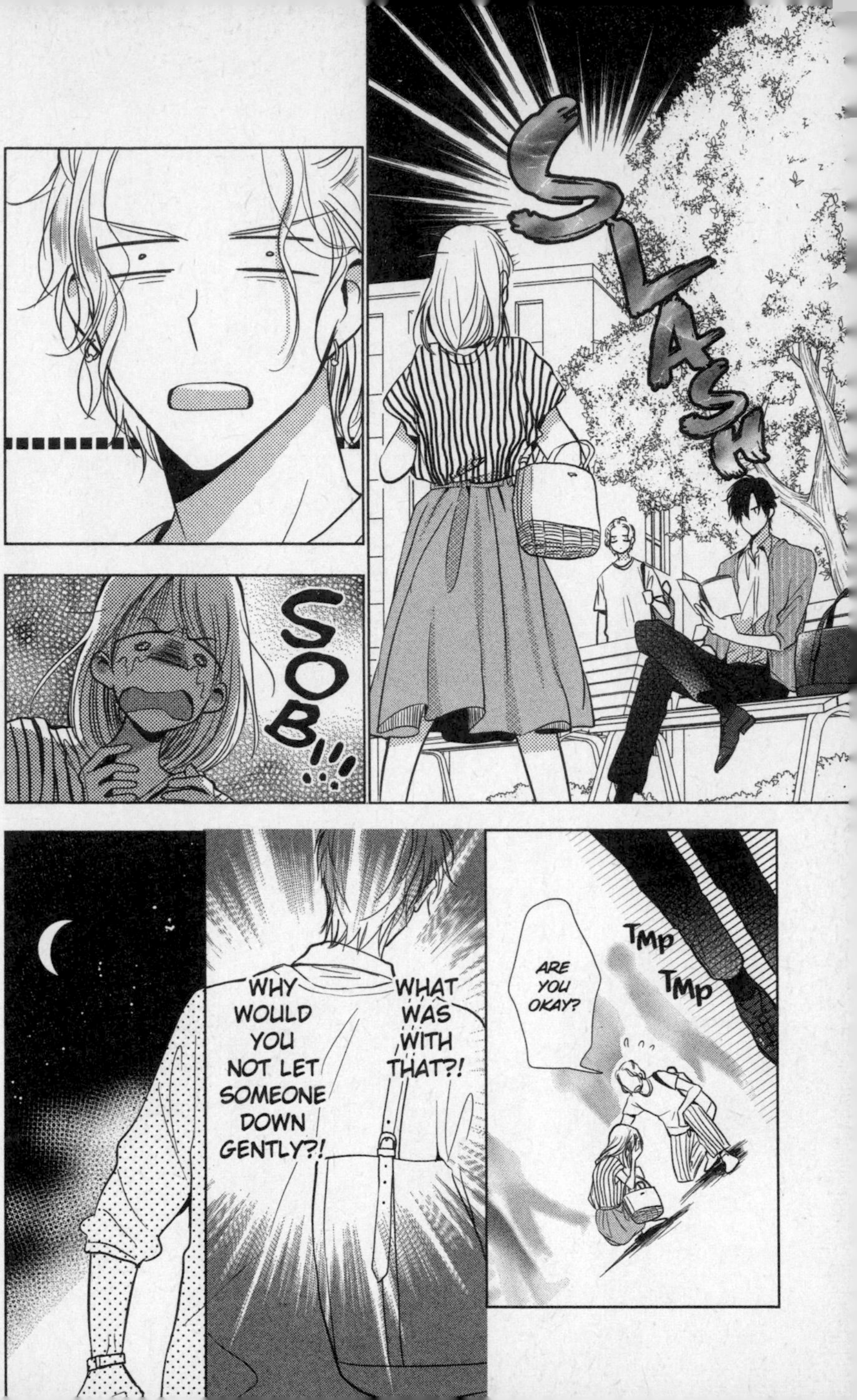
SLASH
SOB!!!
ARE YOU OKAY?
TMP
TMP
WHAT WAS WITH THAT?!
WHY WOULD YOU NOT LET SOMEONE DOWN GENTLY?!

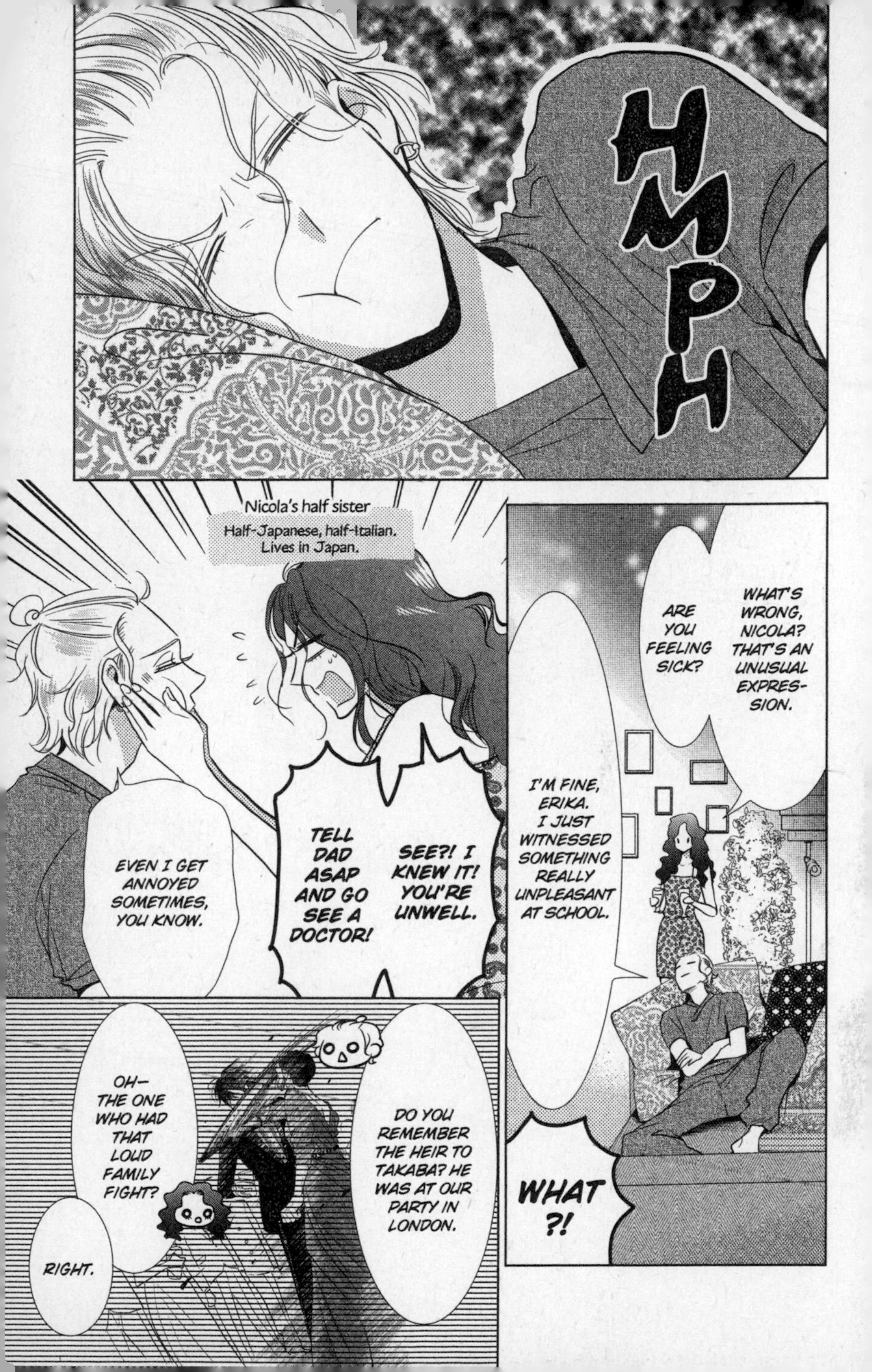
HMPH
WHAT'S WRONG, NICOLA? THAT'S AN UNUSUAL EXPRES-SION.
ARE YOU FEELING SICK?
I'M FINE, ERIKA. I JUST WITNESSED SOMETHING REALLY UNPLEASANT AT SCHOOL.
WHAT?!
Nicola's half sister
Half-Japanese, half-Italian. Lives in Japan.
SEE?! I KNEW IT! YOU'RE UNWELL.
TELL DAD ASAP AND GO SEE A DOCTOR!
EVEN I GET ANNOYED SOMETIMES, YOU KNOW.
DO YOU REMEMBER THE HEIR TO TAKABA? HE WAS AT OUR PARTY IN LONDON.
OH— THE ONE WHO HAD THAT LOUD FAMILY FIGHT?
RIGHT.

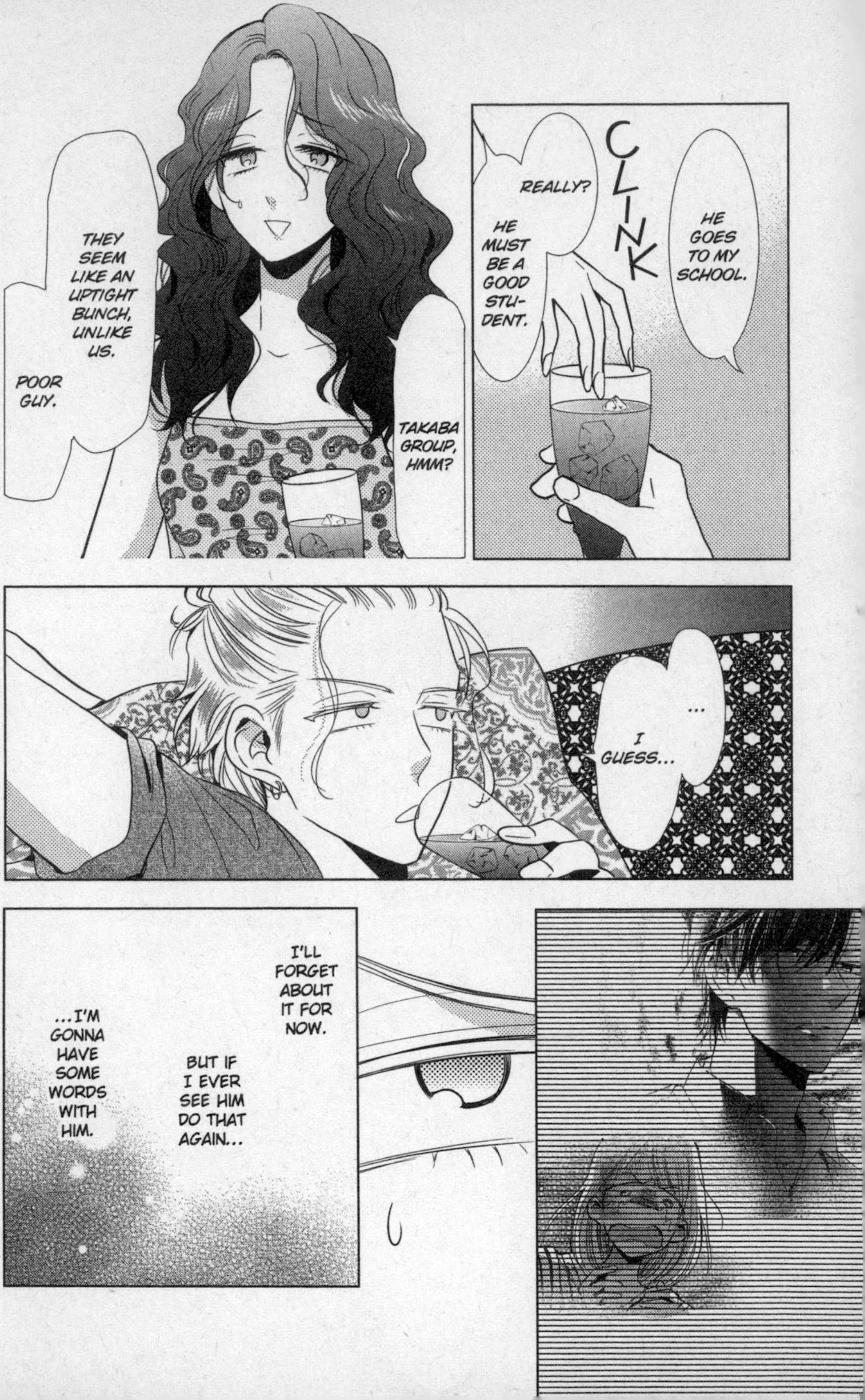
HE GOES TO MY SCHOOL.
CLINK
REALLY?
HE MUST BE A GOOD STUDENT.
TAKABA GROUP, HMM?
THEY SEEM LIKE AN UPTIGHT BUNCH, UNLIKE US.
POOR GUY.
... I GUESS...
I'LL FORGET ABOUT IT FOR NOW.
BUT IF I EVER SEE HIM DO THAT AGAIN...
...I'M GONNA HAVE SOME WORDS WITH HIM.

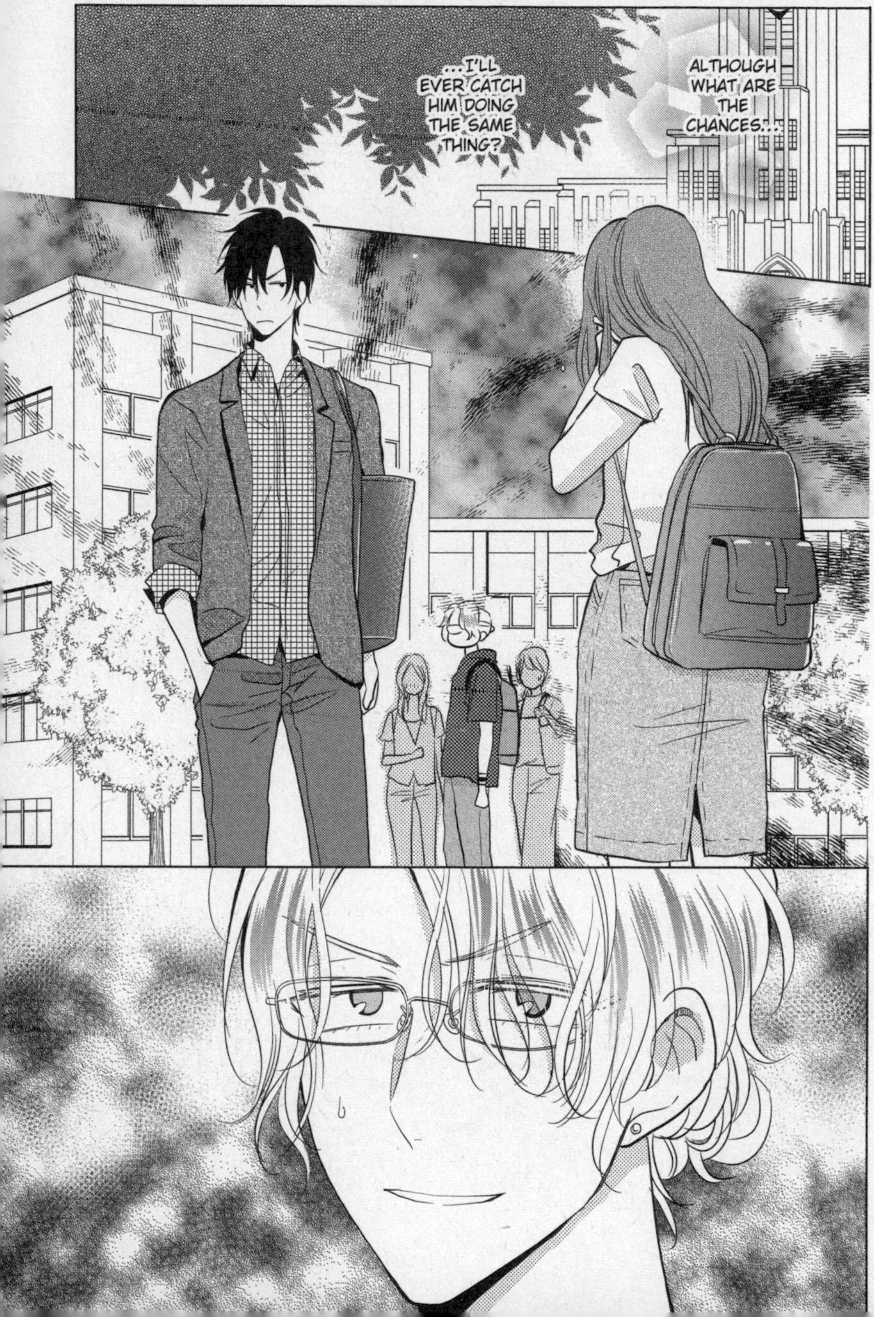
ALTHOUGH WHAT ARE THE CHANCES...
...I'LL EVER CATCH HIM DOING THE SAME THING?

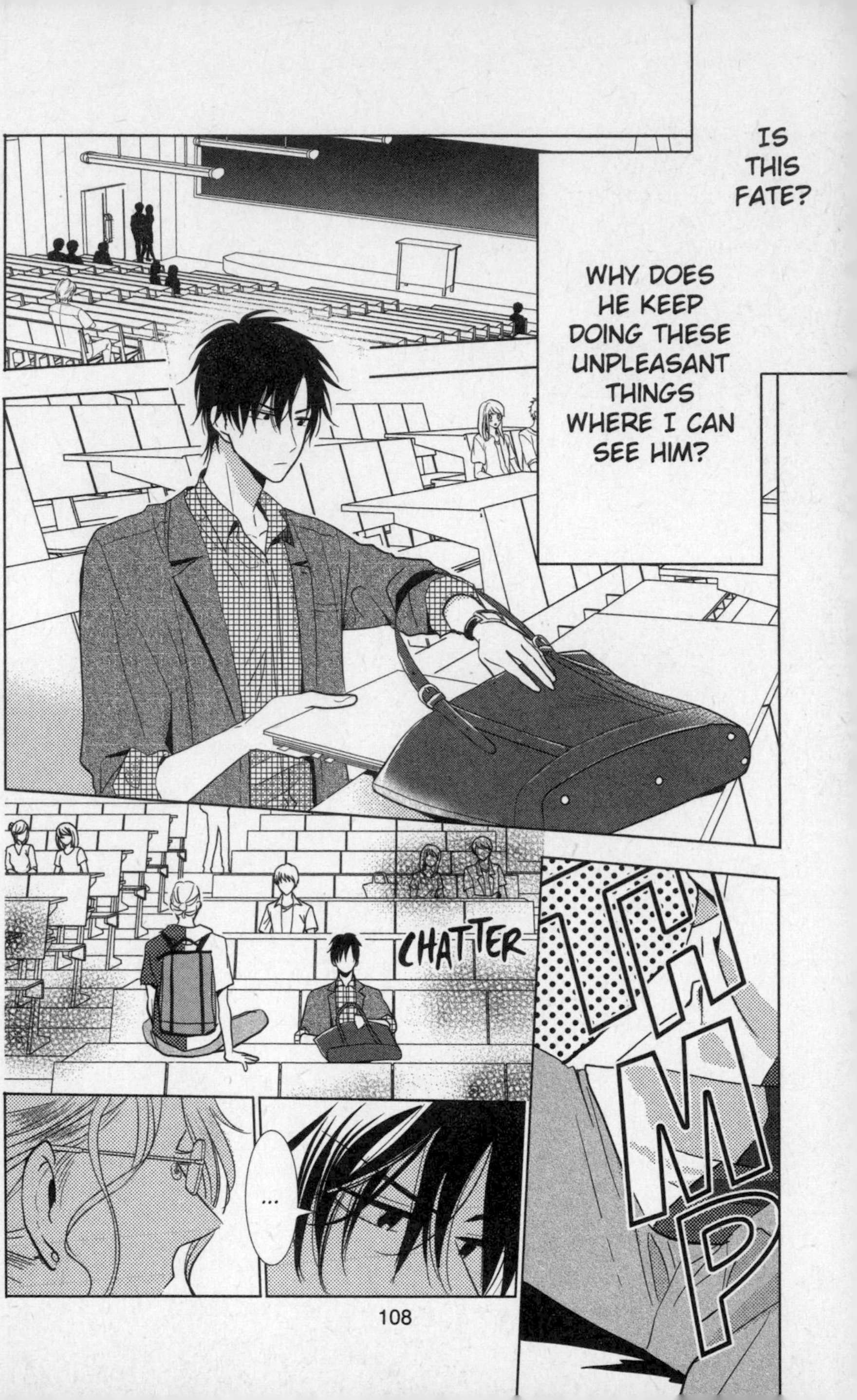
IS THIS FATE?
WHY DOES HE KEEP DOING THESE UNPLEASANT THINGS WHERE I CAN SEE HIM?
THMP
CHATTER
...

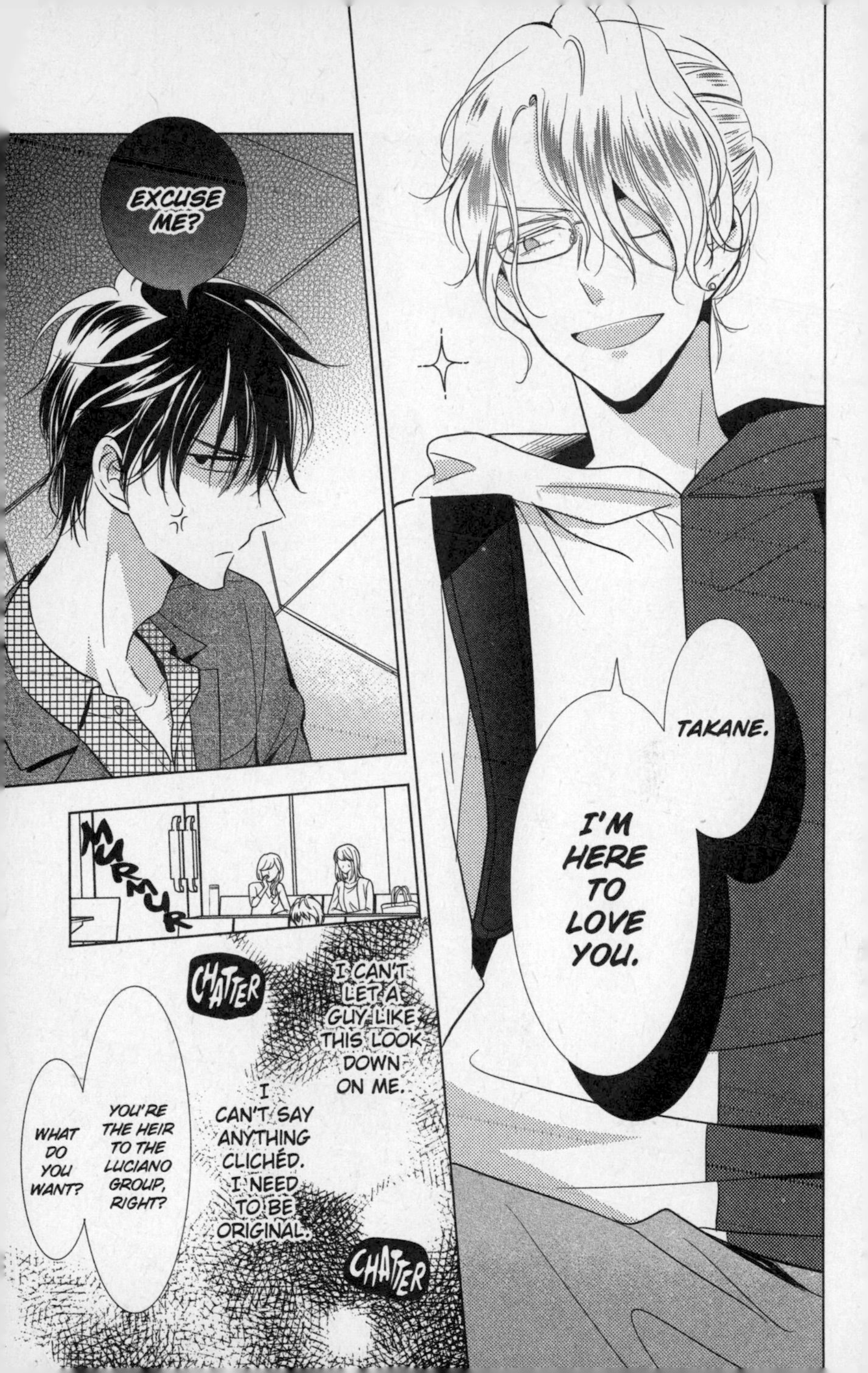
TAKANE.
I'M HERE TO LOVE YOU.
EXCUSE ME?
MURMUR
CHATTER
I CAN'T LET A GUY LIKE THIS LOOK DOWN ON ME.
I CAN'T SAY ANYTHING CLICHÉD. I NEED TO BE ORIGINAL.
CHATTER
YOU'RE THE HEIR TO THE LUCIANO GROUP, RIGHT?
WHAT DO YOU WANT?

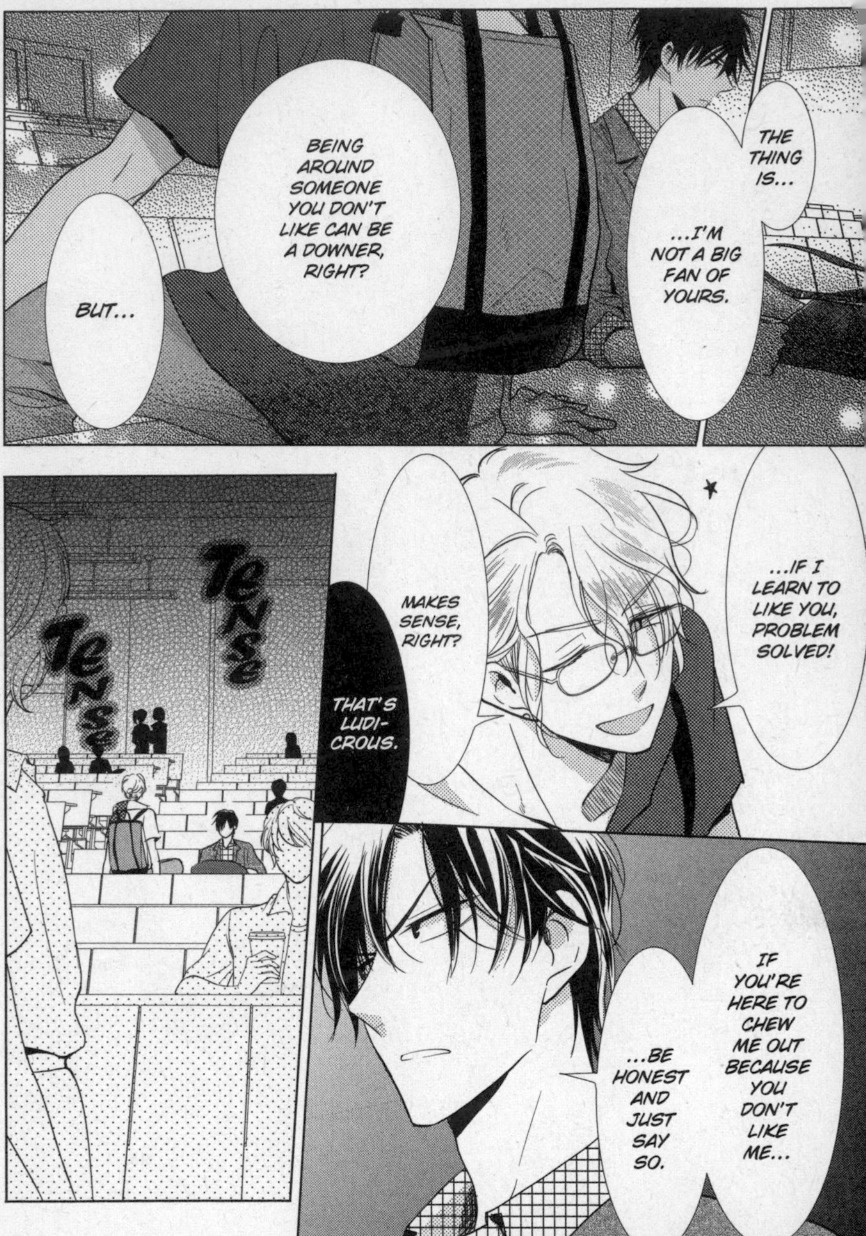
THE THING IS...
...I'M NOT A BIG FAN OF YOURS.
BEING AROUND SOMEONE YOU DON'T LIKE CAN BE A DOWNER, RIGHT?
BUT...
...IF I LEARN TO LIKE YOU, PROBLEM SOLVED!
MAKES SENSE, RIGHT?
THAT'S LUDI-CROUS.
IF YOU'RE HERE TO CHEW ME OUT BECAUSE YOU DON'T LIKE ME...
...BE HONEST AND JUST SAY SO.
TENSE
TENSE

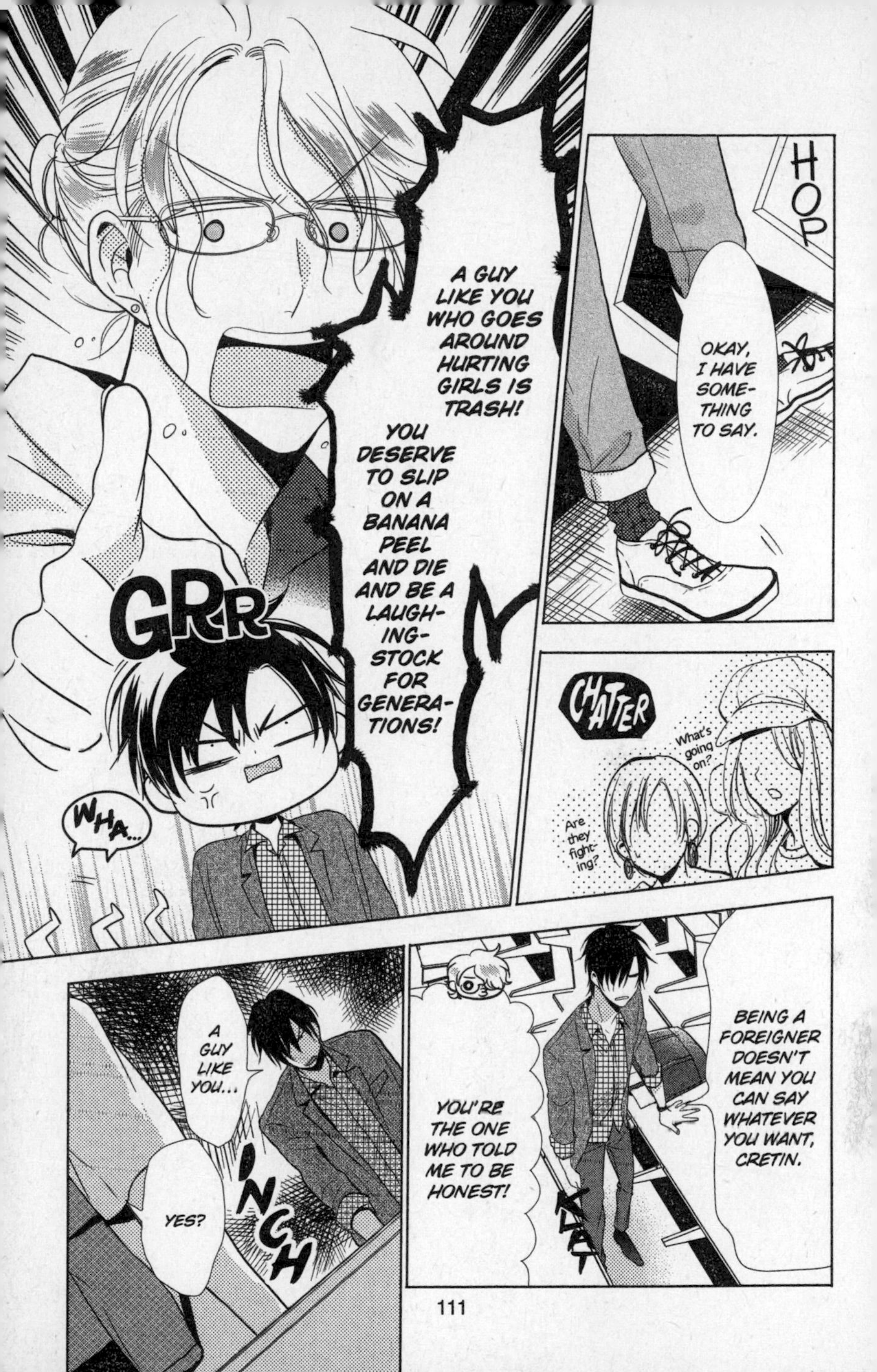
HOP
OKAY, I HAVE SOMETHING TO SAY.
CHATTER
What's going on?
Are they fighting?
A GUY LIKE YOU WHO GOES AROUND HURTING GIRLS IS TRASH!
YOU DESERVE TO SLIP ON A BANANA PEEL AND DIE AND BE A LAUGHINGSTOCK FOR GENERATIONS!
GRR
WHA...
BEING A FOREIGNER DOESN'T MEAN YOU CAN SAY WHATEVER YOU WANT, CRETIN.
YOU'RE THE ONE WHO TOLD ME TO BE HONEST!
A GUY LIKE YOU...
YES?

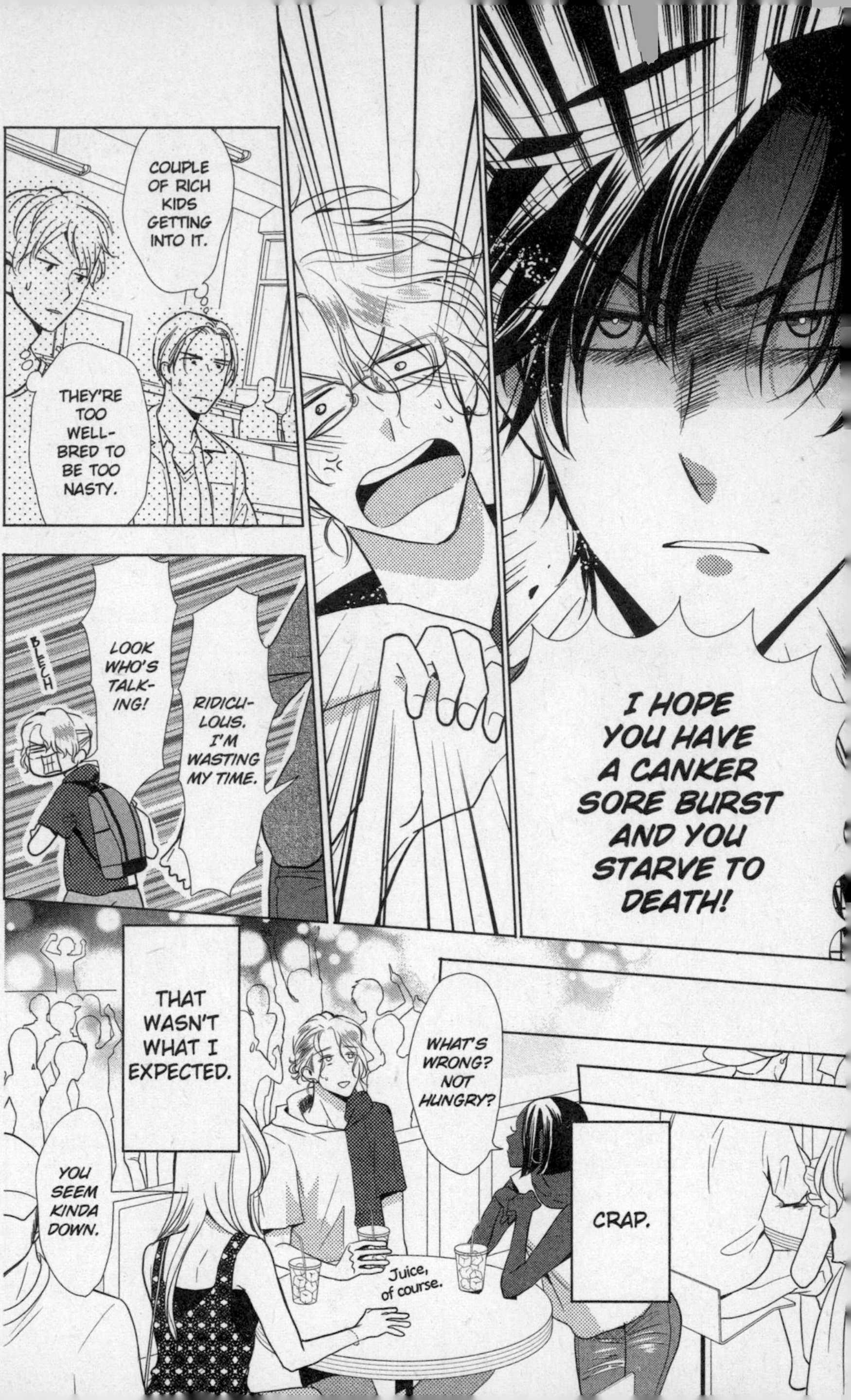
I HOPE YOU HAVE A CANKER SORE BURST AND YOU STARVE TO DEATH!
COUPLE OF RICH KIDS GETTING INTO IT.
THEY'RE TOO WELL-BRED TO BE TOO NASTY.
RIDICULOUS. I'M WASTING MY TIME.
LOOK WHO'S TALKING!
BLECH
WHAT'S WRONG? NOT HUNGRY?
THAT WASN'T WHAT I EXPECTED.
YOU SEEM KINDA DOWN.
Juice, of course.
CRAP.

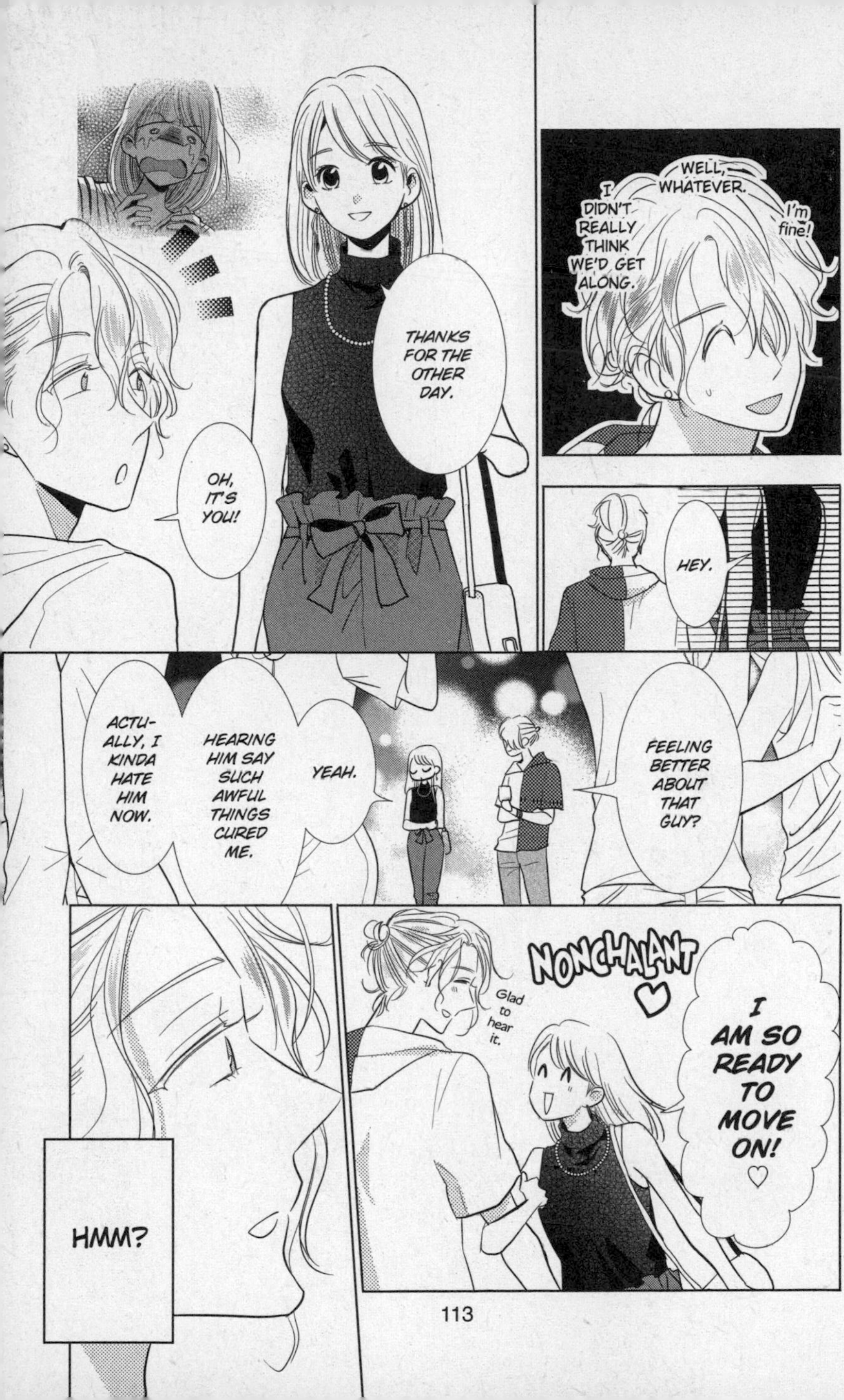
WELL, WHATEVER.
I DIDN'T REALLY THINK WE'D GET ALONG.
I'm fine!
HEY.
THANKS FOR THE OTHER DAY.
OH, IT'S YOU!
FEELING BETTER ABOUT THAT GUY?
YEAH.
HEARING HIM SAY SUCH AWFUL THINGS CURED ME.
ACTU-ALLY, I KINDA HATE HIM NOW.
I AM SO READY TO MOVE ON! ♡
NONCHALANT ♥
Glad to hear it.
HMM?

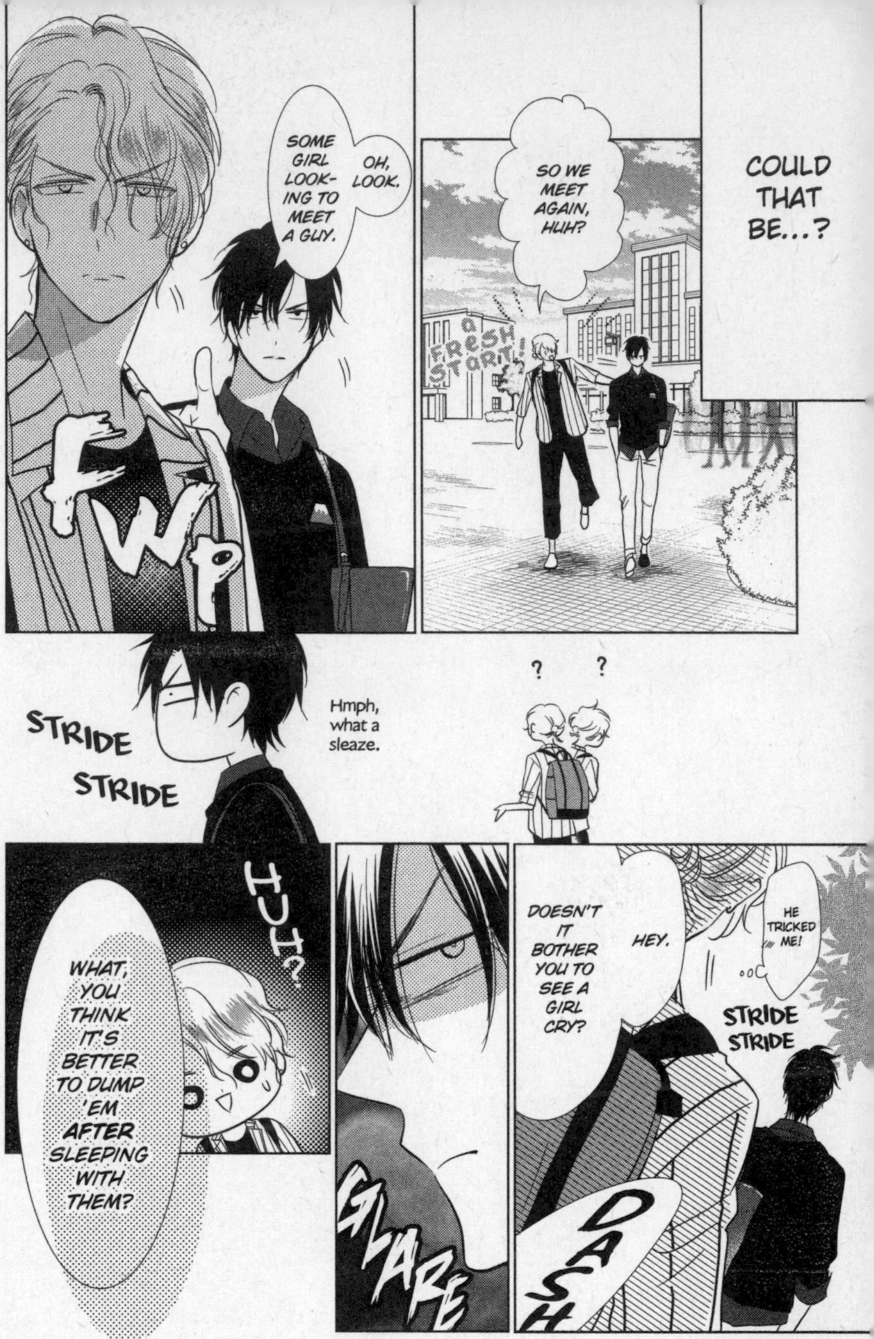
COULD THAT BE...?
SO WE MEET AGAIN, HUH?
A FRESH START!
OH, LOOK.
SOME GIRL LOOKING TO MEET A GUY.
FWP
? ?
Hmph, what a sleaze.
STRIDE STRIDE
HE TRICKED ME!
STRIDE STRIDE
HEY.
DOESN'T IT BOTHER YOU TO SEE A GIRL CRY?
DASH
GLARE
HUH?
WHAT, YOU THINK IT'S BETTER TO DUMP 'EM AFTER SLEEPING WITH THEM?

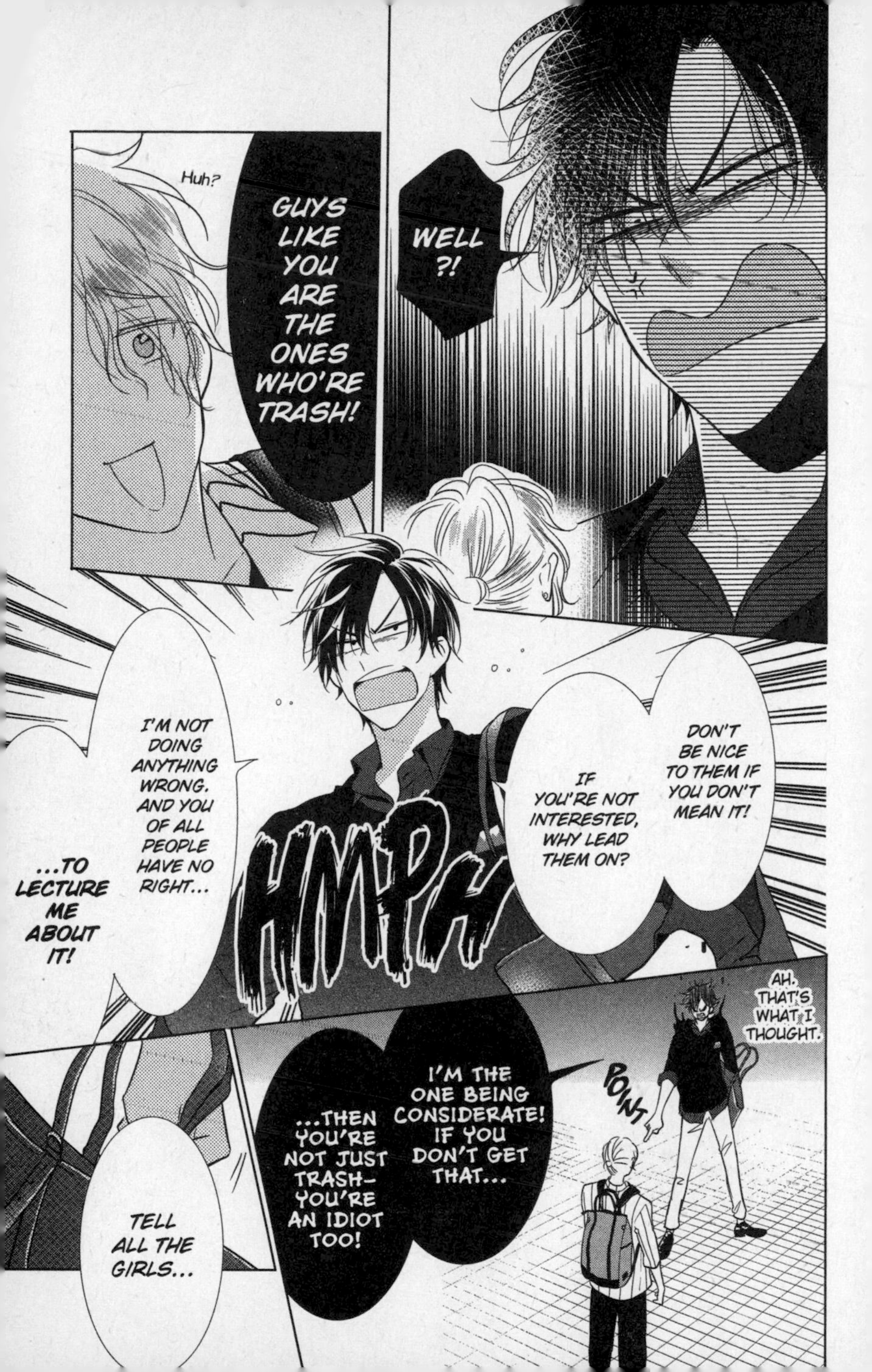
WELL ?!
Huh?
GUYS LIKE YOU ARE THE ONES WHO'RE TRASH!
DON'T BE NICE TO THEM IF YOU DON'T MEAN IT!
IF YOU'RE NOT INTERESTED, WHY LEAD THEM ON?
HMPH
I'M NOT DOING ANYTHING WRONG. AND YOU OF ALL PEOPLE HAVE NO RIGHT...
...TO LECTURE ME ABOUT IT!
AH. THAT'S WHAT I THOUGHT.
POINT
I'M THE ONE BEING CONSIDERATE! IF YOU DON'T GET THAT...
...THEN YOU'RE NOT JUST TRASH-YOU'RE AN IDIOT TOO!
TELL ALL THE GIRLS...

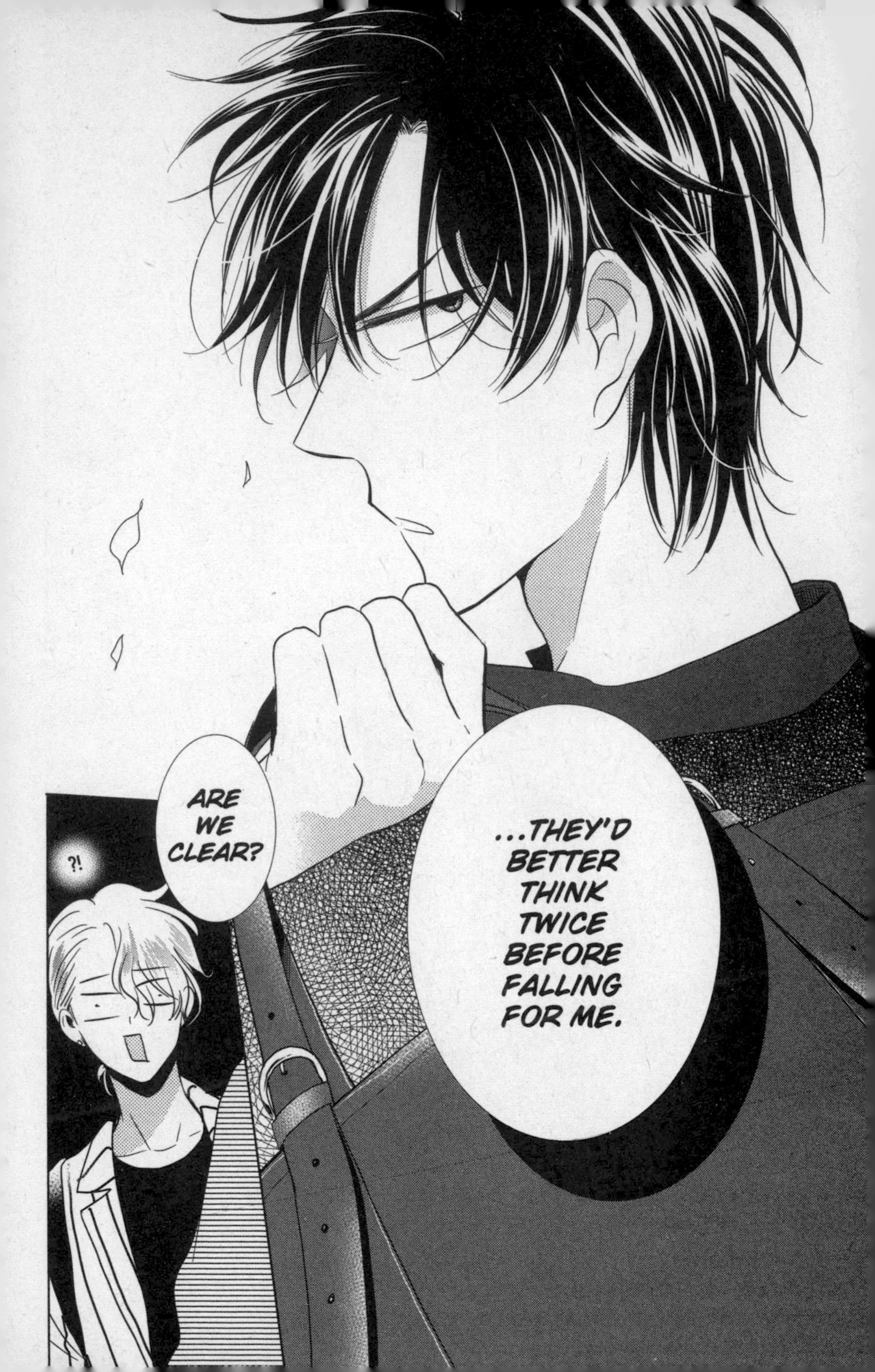
...THEY'D BETTER THINK TWICE BEFORE FALLING FOR ME.
ARE WE CLEAR?
?!

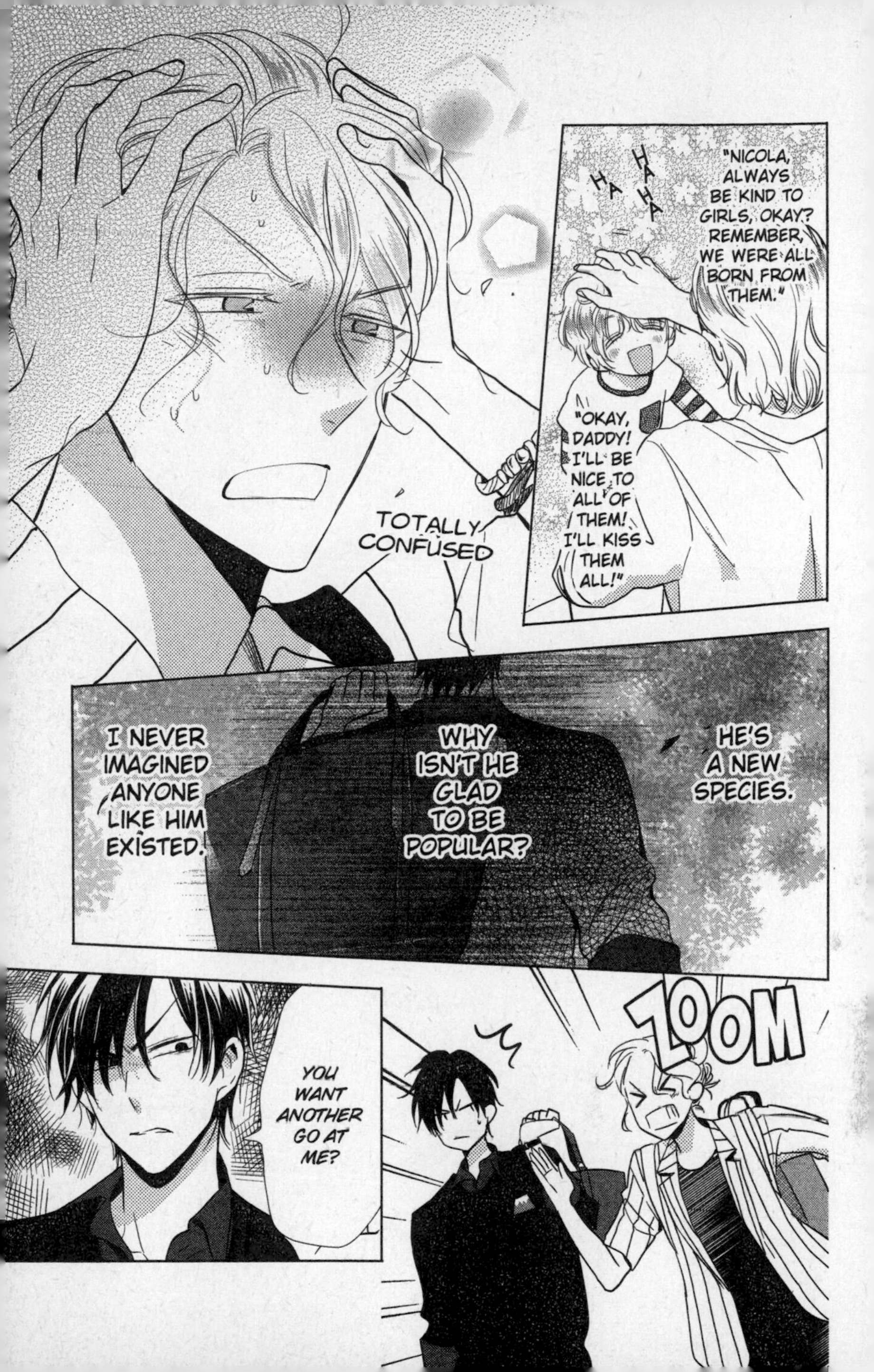
HA HA HA HA
"NICOLA, ALWAYS BE KIND TO GIRLS, OKAY? REMEMBER, WE WERE ALL BORN FROM THEM."
"OKAY, DADDY! I'LL BE NICE TO ALL OF THEM! I'LL KISS THEM ALL!"
TOTALLY CONFUSED
HE'S A NEW SPECIES.
WHY ISN'T HE GLAD TO BE POPULAR?
I NEVER IMAGINED ANYONE LIKE HIM EXISTED.
ZOOM
YOU WANT ANOTHER GO AT ME?

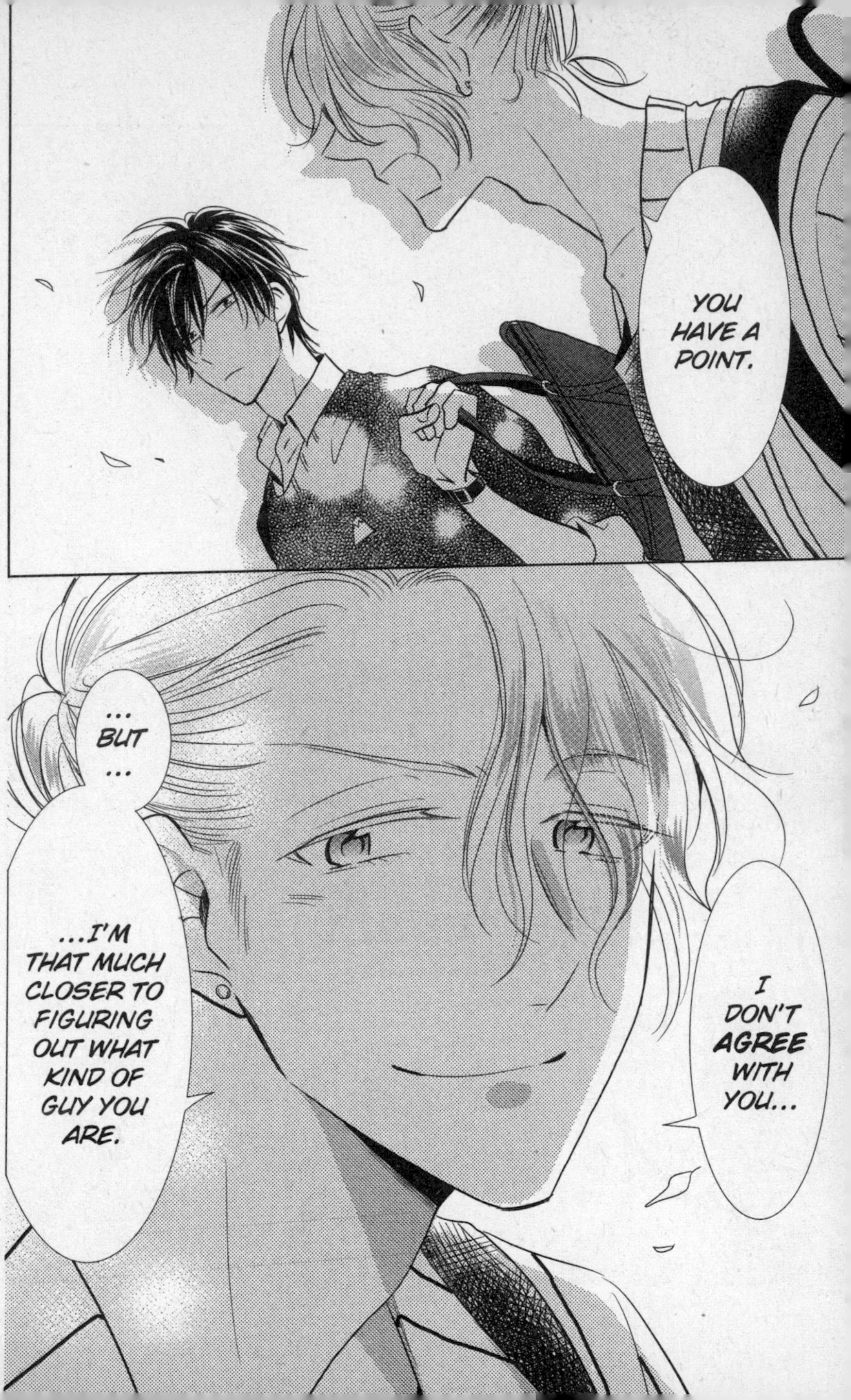
YOU HAVE A POINT.
I DON'T AGREE WITH YOU...
...BUT...
...I'M THAT MUCH CLOSER TO FIGURING OUT WHAT KIND OF GUY YOU ARE.

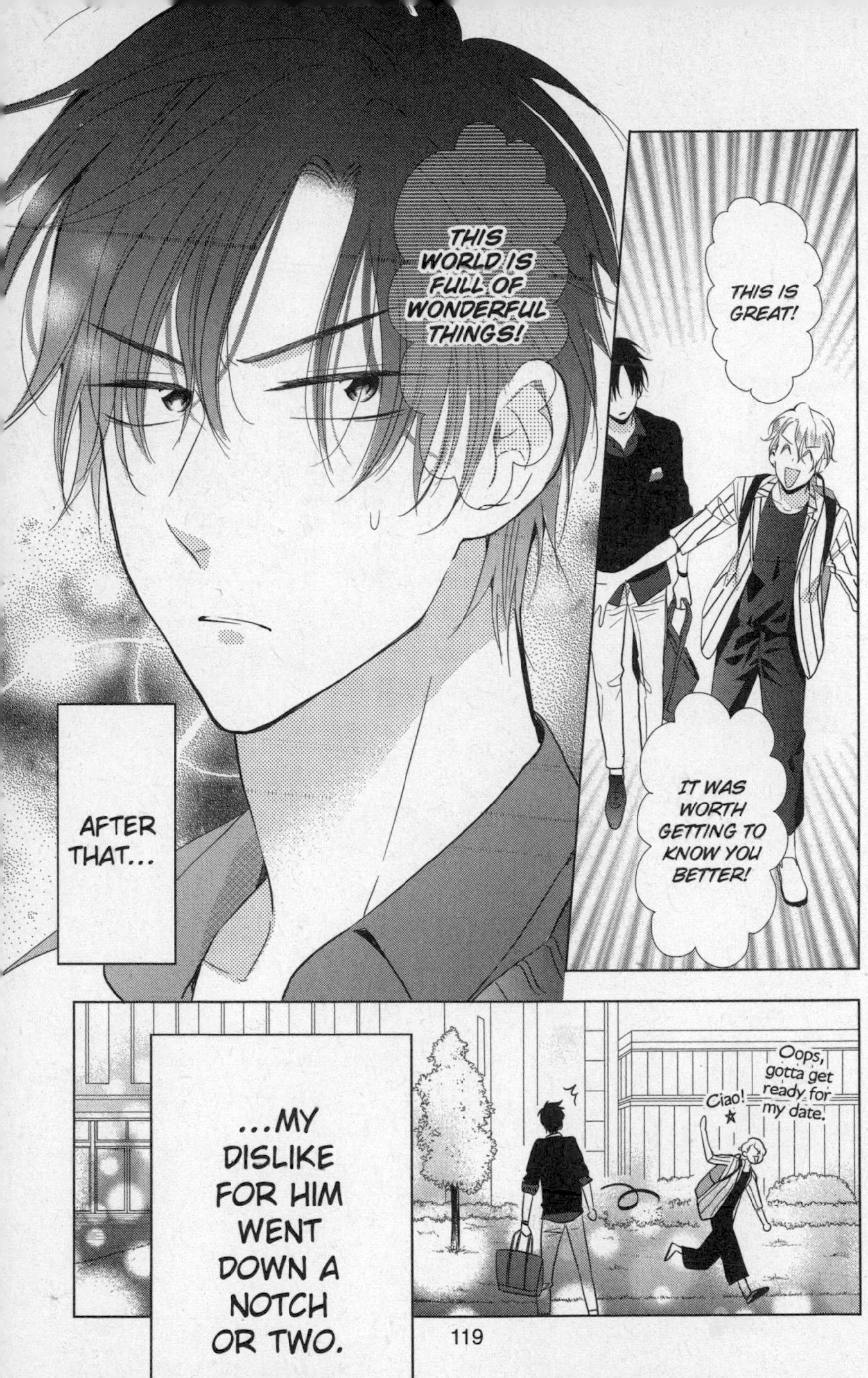
THIS IS GREAT!
IT WAS WORTH GETTING TO KNOW YOU BETTER!
THIS WORLD IS FULL OF WONDERFUL THINGS!
AFTER THAT...
Oops, gotta get ready for my date.
Ciao! ☆
...MY DISLIKE FOR HIM WENT DOWN A NOTCH OR TWO.

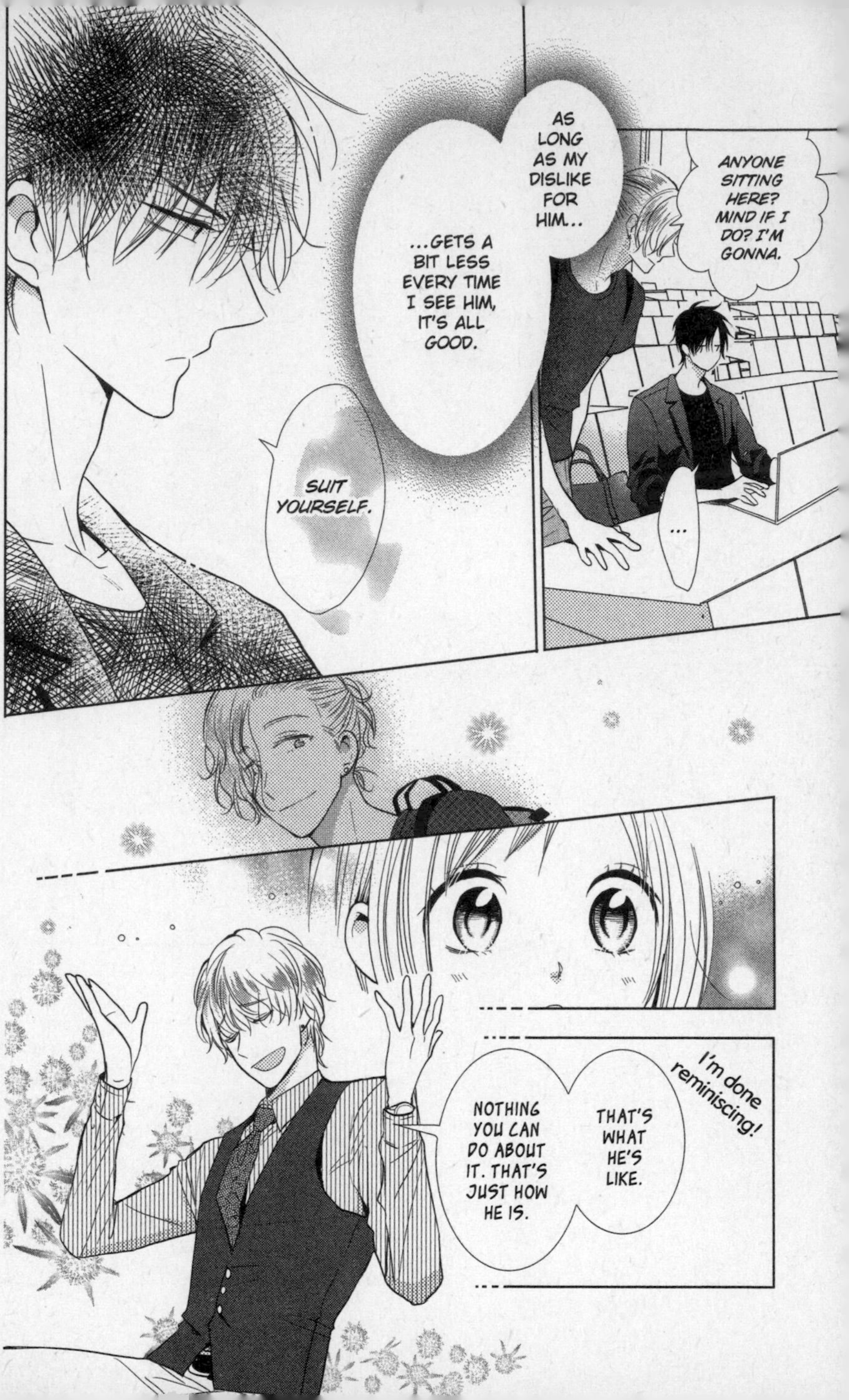
ANYONE SITTING HERE? MIND IF I DO? I'M GONNA.
...
AS LONG AS MY DISLIKE FOR HIM...
...GETS A BIT LESS EVERY TIME I SEE HIM, IT'S ALL GOOD.
SUIT YOURSELF.
I'm done reminiscing!
THAT'S WHAT HE'S LIKE.
NOTHING YOU CAN DO ABOUT IT. THAT'S JUST HOW HE IS.

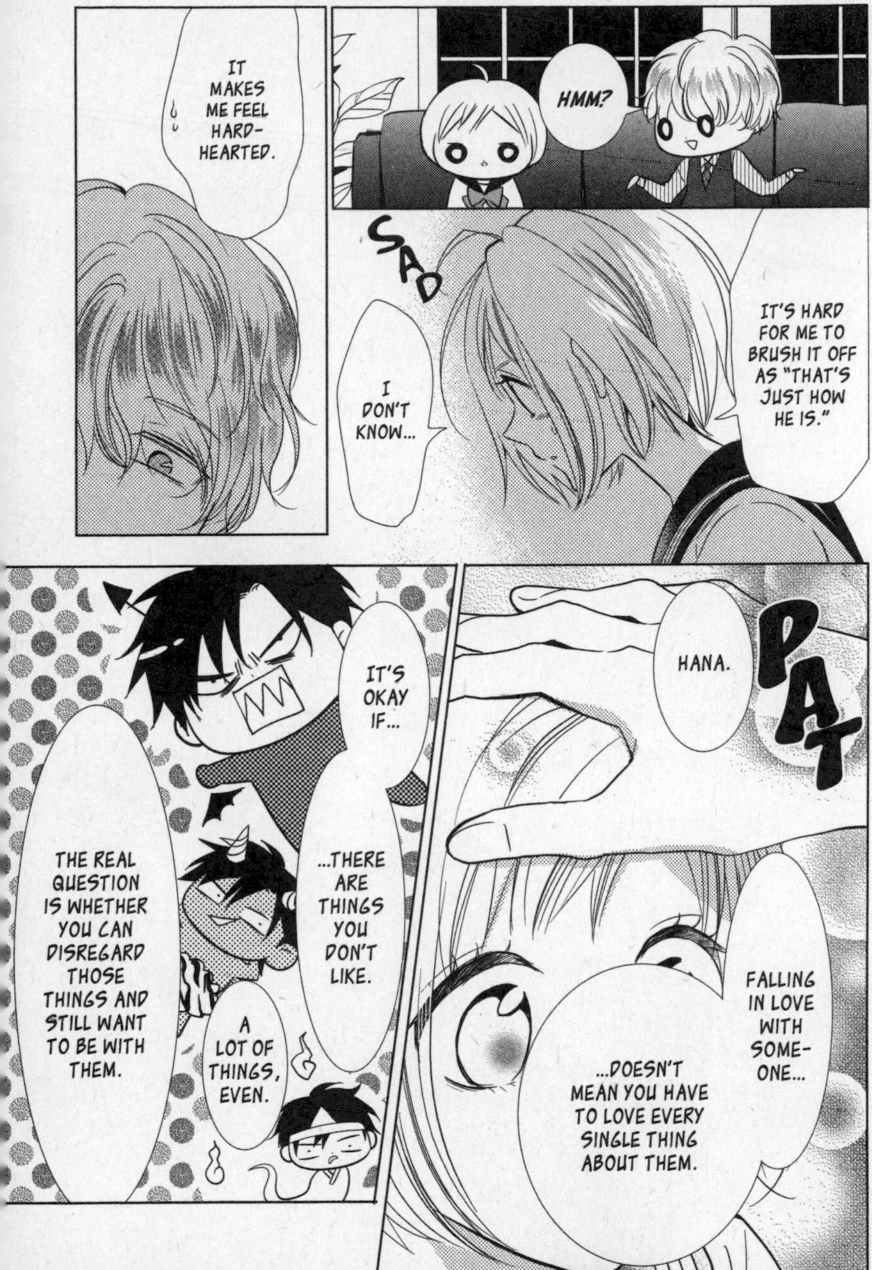
HMM?
SAD
IT'S HARD FOR ME TO BRUSH IT OFF AS "THAT'S JUST HOW HE IS."
I DON'T KNOW...
IT MAKES ME FEEL HARD-HEARTED.
PAT
HANA.
FALLING IN LOVE WITH SOME-ONE...
...DOESN'T MEAN YOU HAVE TO LOVE EVERY SINGLE THING ABOUT THEM.
IT'S OKAY IF...
...THERE ARE THINGS YOU DON'T LIKE.
A LOT OF THINGS, EVEN.
THE REAL QUESTION IS WHETHER YOU CAN DISREGARD THOSE THINGS AND STILL WANT TO BE WITH THEM.

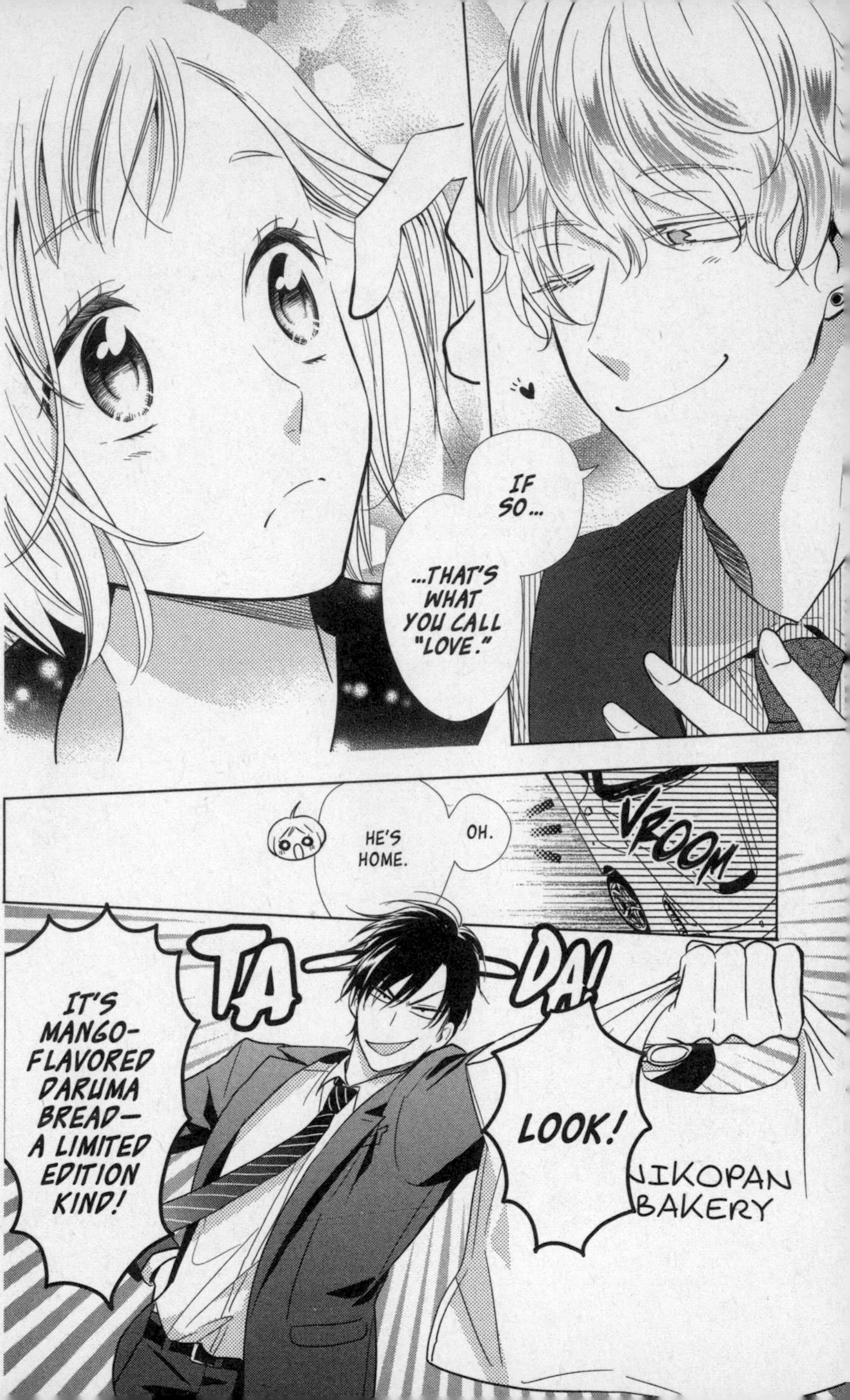
IF SO...
...THAT'S WHAT YOU CALL "LOVE."
VROOM
OH.
HE'S HOME.
TA-DA!
LOOK!
JIKOPAN BAKERY
IT'S MANGO-FLAVORED DARUMA BREAD—A LIMITED EDITION KIND!

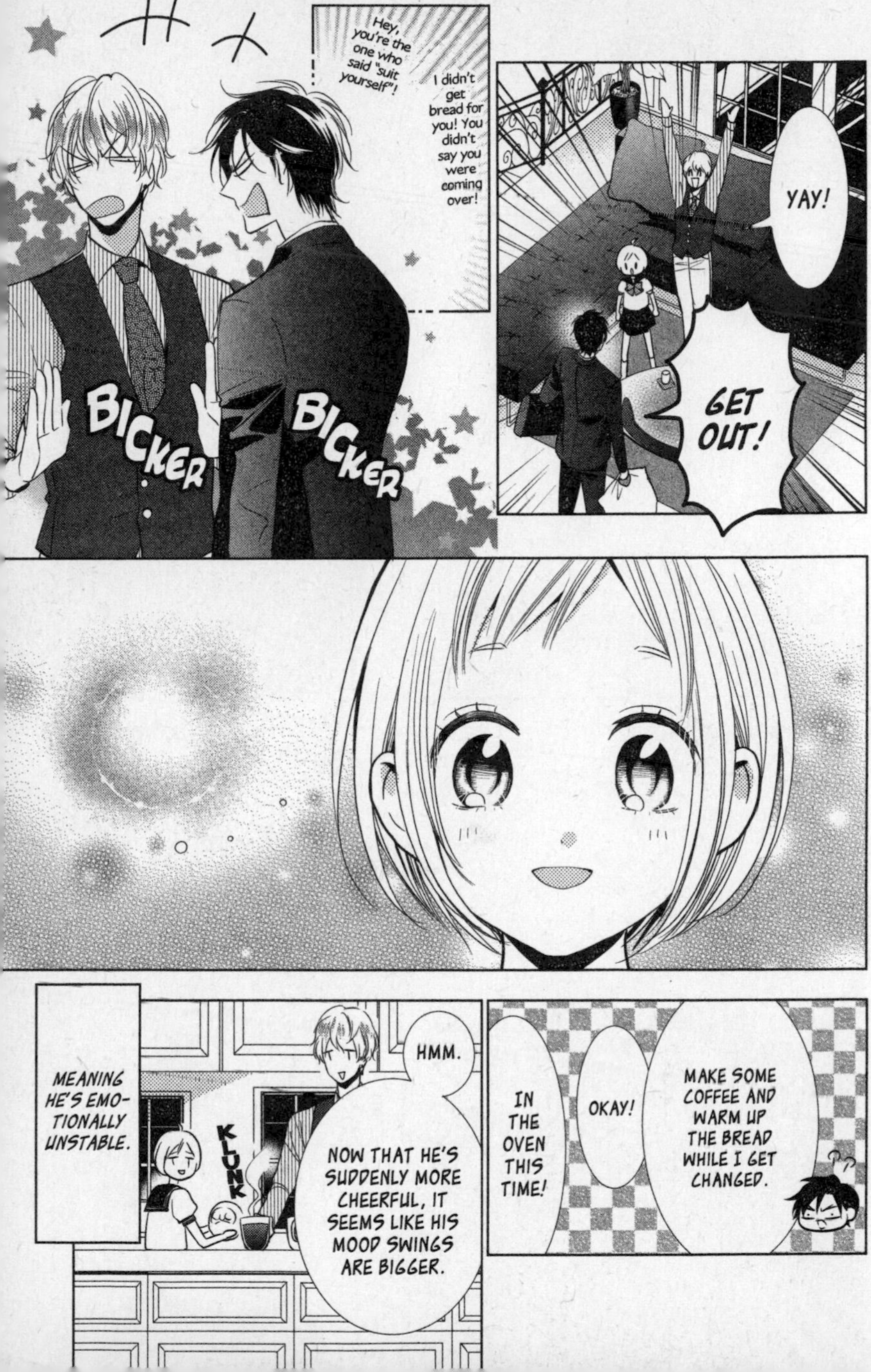
YAY!
GET OUT!
I didn't get bread for you! You didn't say you were coming over!
Hey, you're the one who said "suit yourself"!
BICKER
BICKER
MAKE SOME COFFEE AND WARM UP THE BREAD WHILE I GET CHANGED.
OKAY!
IN THE OVEN THIS TIME!
HMM.
NOW THAT HE'S SUDDENLY MORE CHEERFUL, IT SEEMS LIKE HIS MOOD SWINGS ARE BIGGER.
KLUNK
MEANING HE'S EMOTIONALLY UNSTABLE.

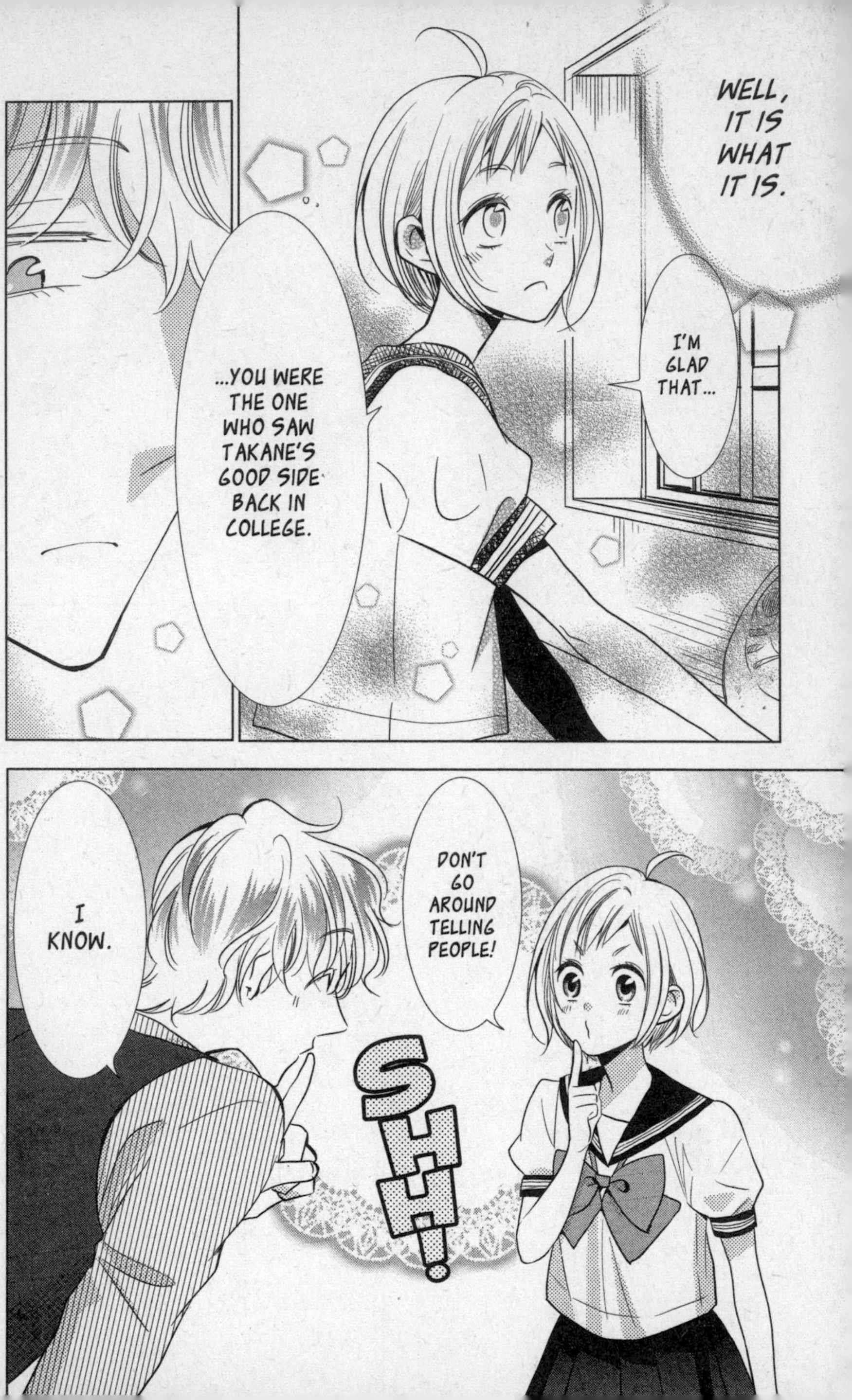
WELL, IT IS WHAT IT IS.
I'M GLAD THAT...
...YOU WERE THE ONE WHO SAW TAKANE'S GOOD SIDE BACK IN COLLEGE.
DON'T GO AROUND TELLING PEOPLE!
SHHH!
I KNOW.

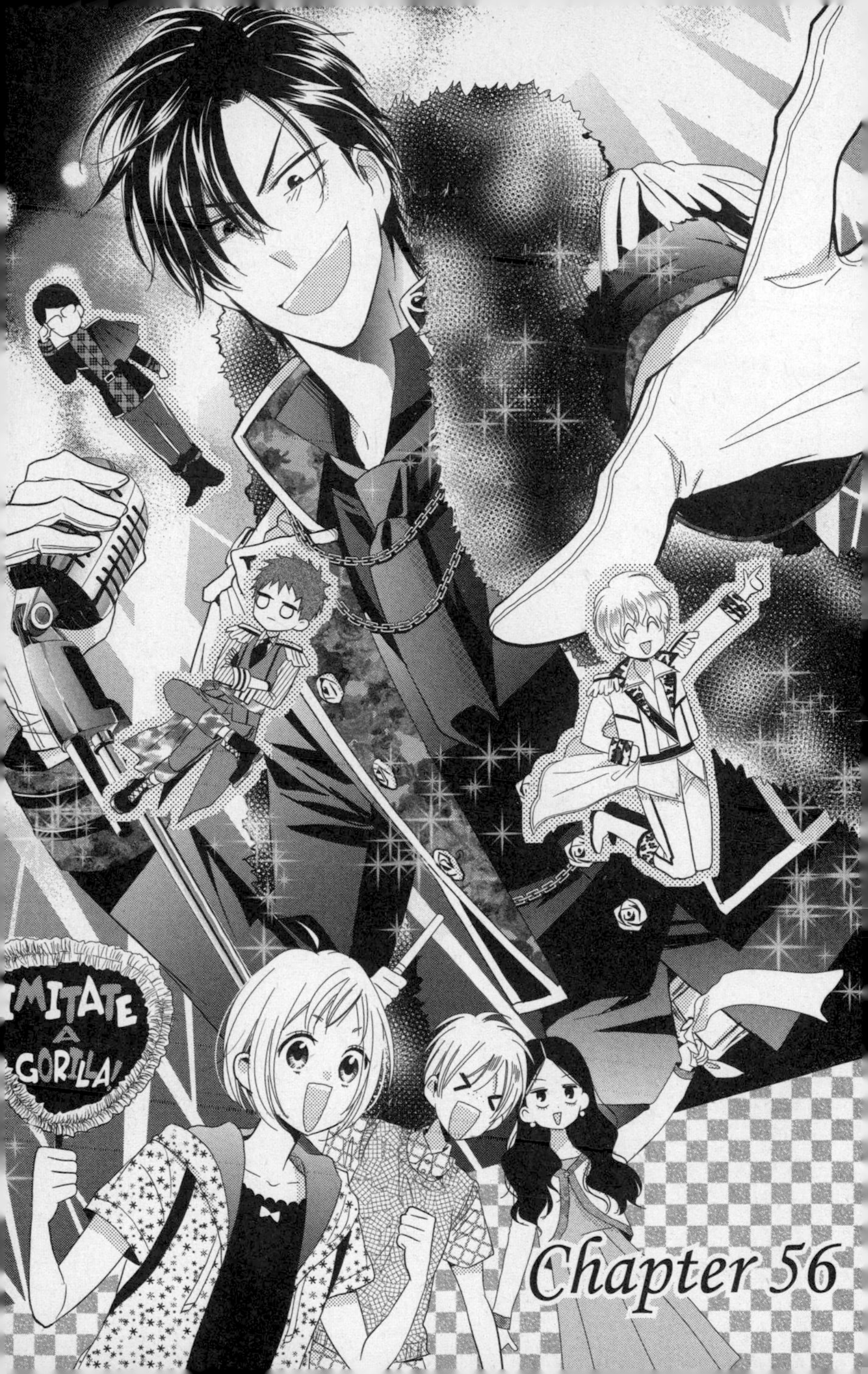
IMITATE A GORILLA!
Chapter 56

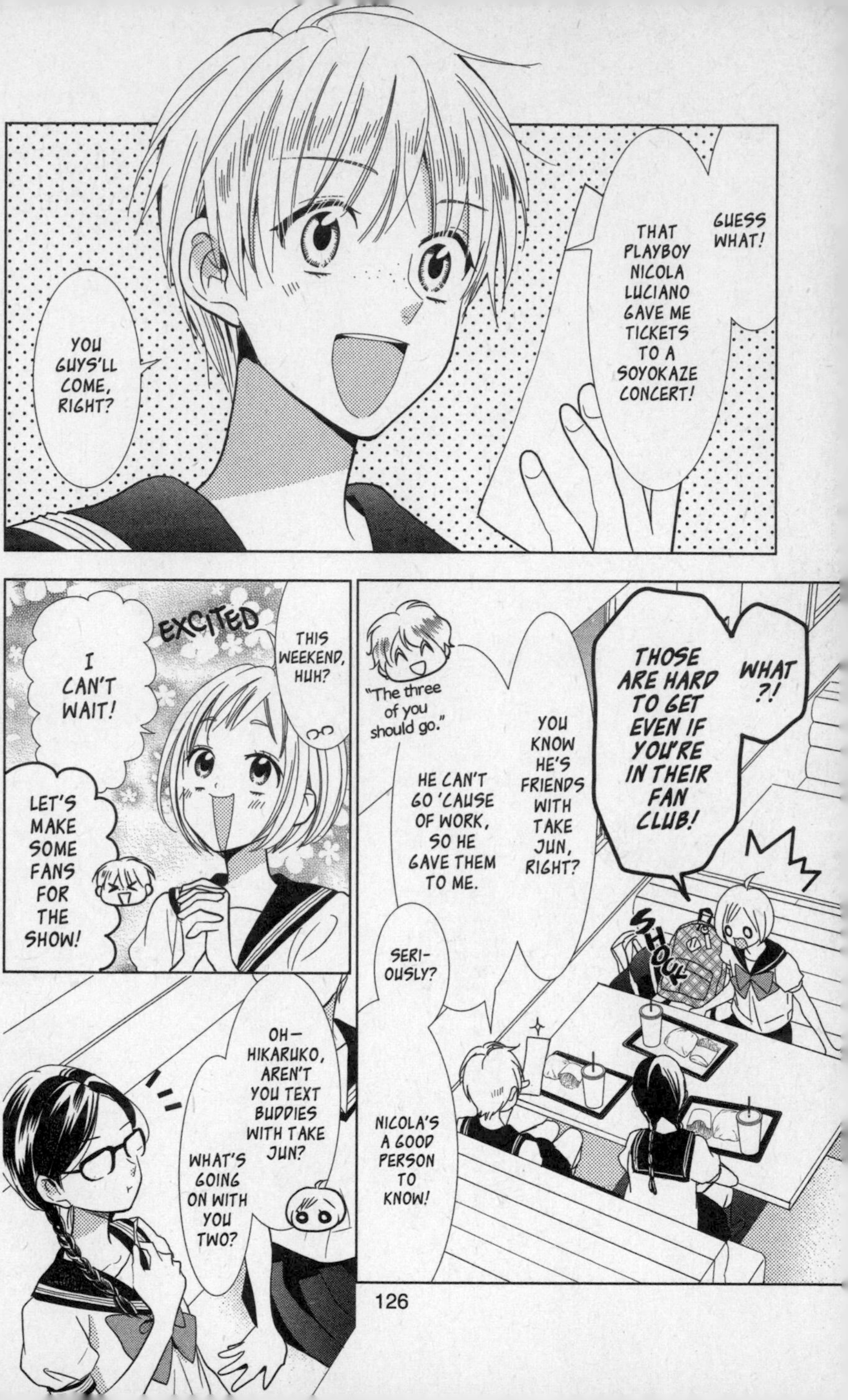
GUESS WHAT!
THAT PLAYBOY NICOLA LUCIANO GAVE ME TICKETS TO A SOYOKAZE CONCERT!
YOU GUYS'LL COME, RIGHT?
WHAT?!
THOSE ARE HARD TO GET EVEN IF YOU'RE IN THEIR FAN CLUB!
SHOCK
YOU KNOW HE'S FRIENDS WITH TAKE JUN, RIGHT?
HE CAN'T GO 'CAUSE OF WORK, SO HE GAVE THEM TO ME.
"The three of you should go."
SERIOUSLY?
NICOLA'S A GOOD PERSON TO KNOW!
THIS WEEKEND, HUH?
EXCITED
I CAN'T WAIT!
LET'S MAKE SOME FANS FOR THE SHOW!
OH— HIKARUKO, AREN'T YOU TEXT BUDDIES WITH TAKE JUN?
WHAT'S GOING ON WITH YOU TWO?

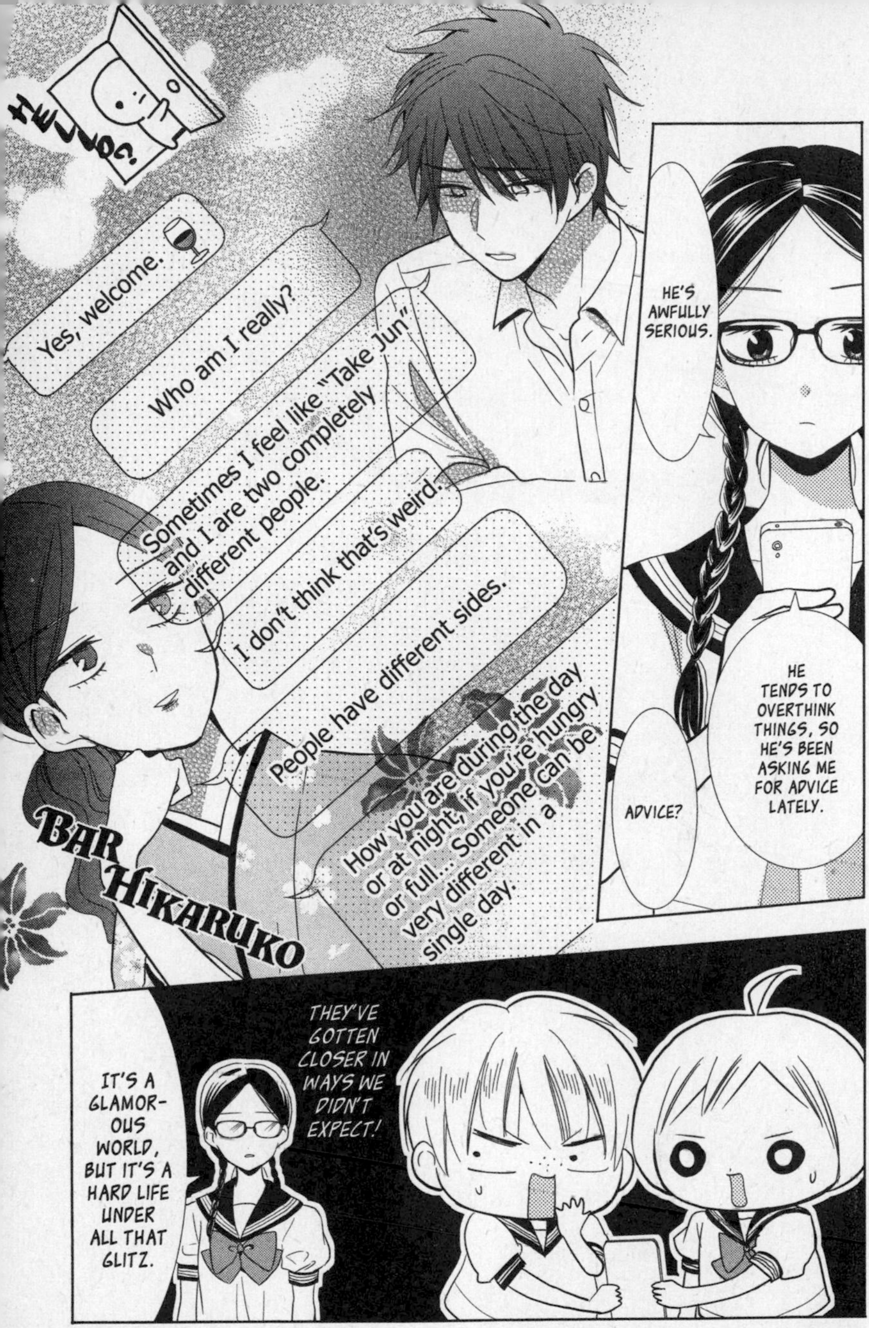
HE'S AWFULLY SERIOUS.
HE TENDS TO OVERTHINK THINGS, SO HE'S BEEN ASKING ME FOR ADVICE LATELY.
ADVICE?
HELLO?
Yes, welcome.
Who am I really?
Sometimes I feel like "Take Jun" and I are two completely different people.
I don't think that's weird.
People have different sides.
How you are during the day or at night, if you're hungry or full... Someone can be very different in a single day.
BAR HIKARUKO
THEY'VE GOTTEN CLOSER IN WAYS WE DIDN'T EXPECT!
IT'S A GLAMOROUS WORLD, BUT IT'S A HARD LIFE UNDER ALL THAT GLITZ.

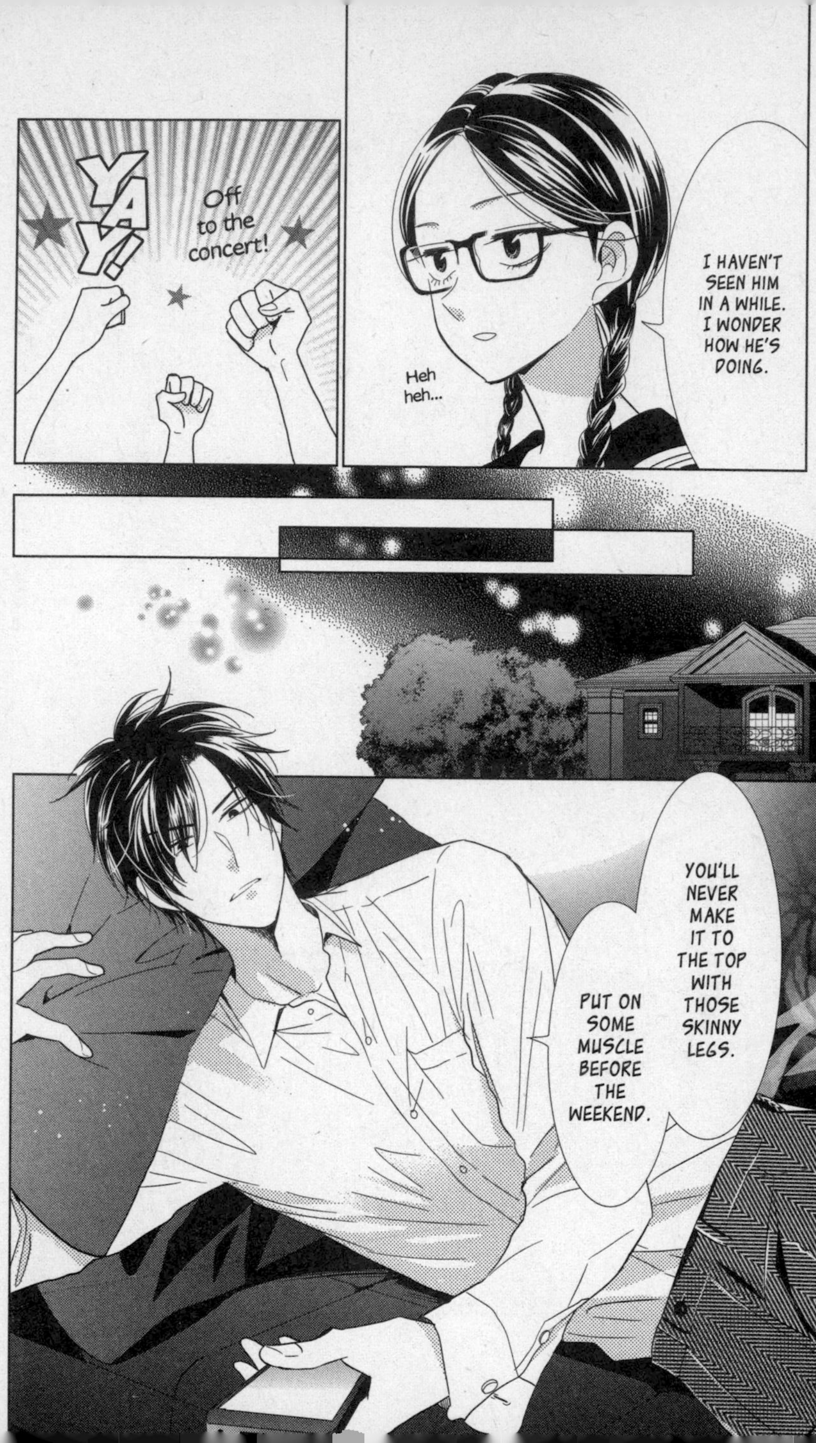
I HAVEN'T SEEN HIM IN A WHILE. I WONDER HOW HE'S DOING.
Heh heh...
YAY!
Off to the concert!
YOU'LL NEVER MAKE IT TO THE TOP WITH THOSE SKINNY LEGS.
PUT ON SOME MUSCLE BEFORE THE WEEKEND.

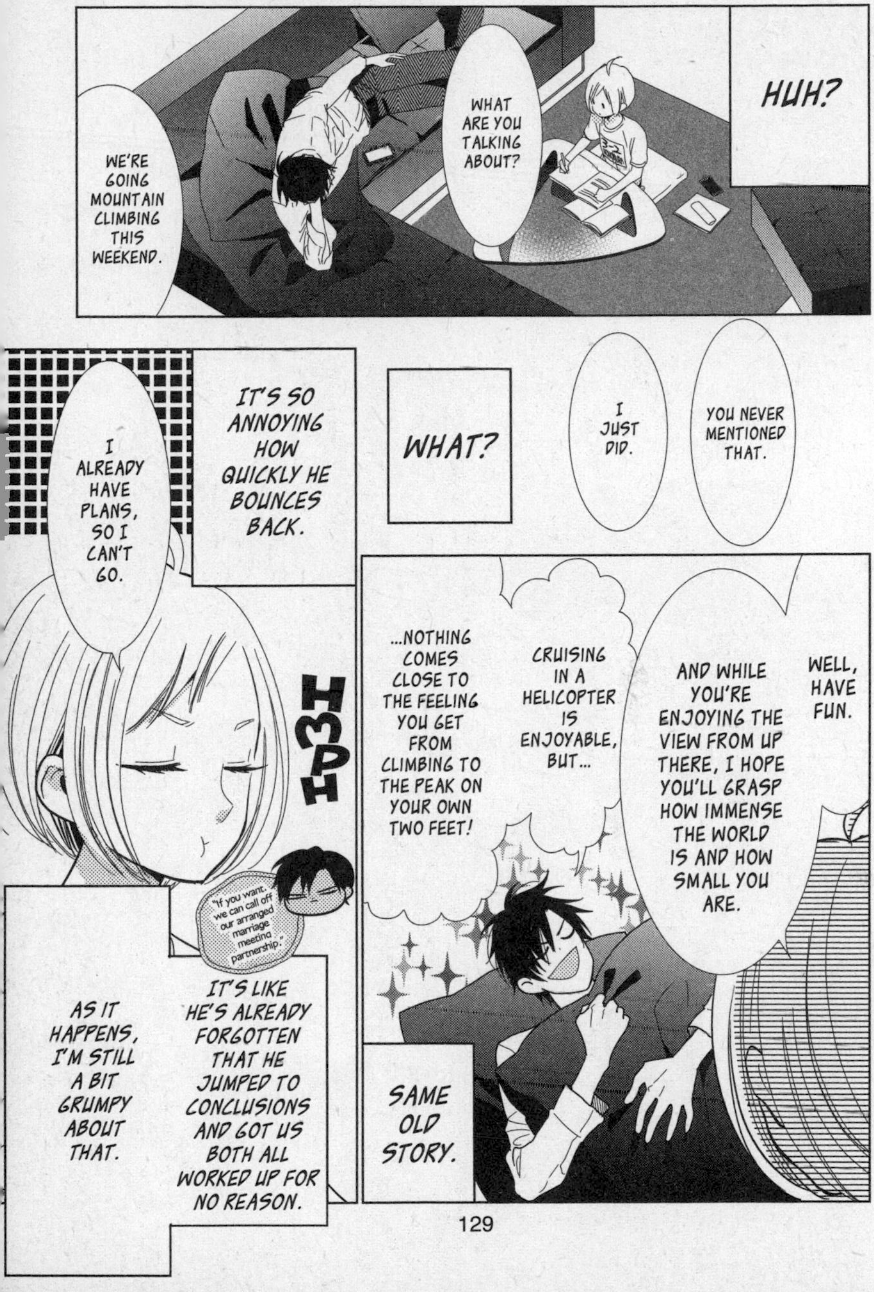
HUH?
WHAT ARE YOU TALKING ABOUT?
WE'RE GOING MOUNTAIN CLIMBING THIS WEEKEND.
YOU NEVER MENTIONED THAT.
I JUST DID.
WHAT?
WELL, HAVE FUN.
AND WHILE YOU'RE ENJOYING THE VIEW FROM UP THERE, I HOPE YOU'LL GRASP HOW IMMENSE THE WORLD IS AND HOW SMALL YOU ARE.
CRUISING IN A HELICOPTER IS ENJOYABLE, BUT...
...NOTHING COMES CLOSE TO THE FEELING YOU GET FROM CLIMBING TO THE PEAK ON YOUR OWN TWO FEET!
SAME OLD STORY.
IT'S SO ANNOYING HOW QUICKLY HE BOUNCES BACK.
I ALREADY HAVE PLANS, SO I CAN'T GO.
HMPH
"If you want, we can call off our arranged marriage meeting partnership."
IT'S LIKE HE'S ALREADY FORGOTTEN THAT HE JUMPED TO CONCLUSIONS AND GOT US BOTH ALL WORKED UP FOR NO REASON.
AS IT HAPPENS, I'M STILL A BIT GRUMPY ABOUT THAT.

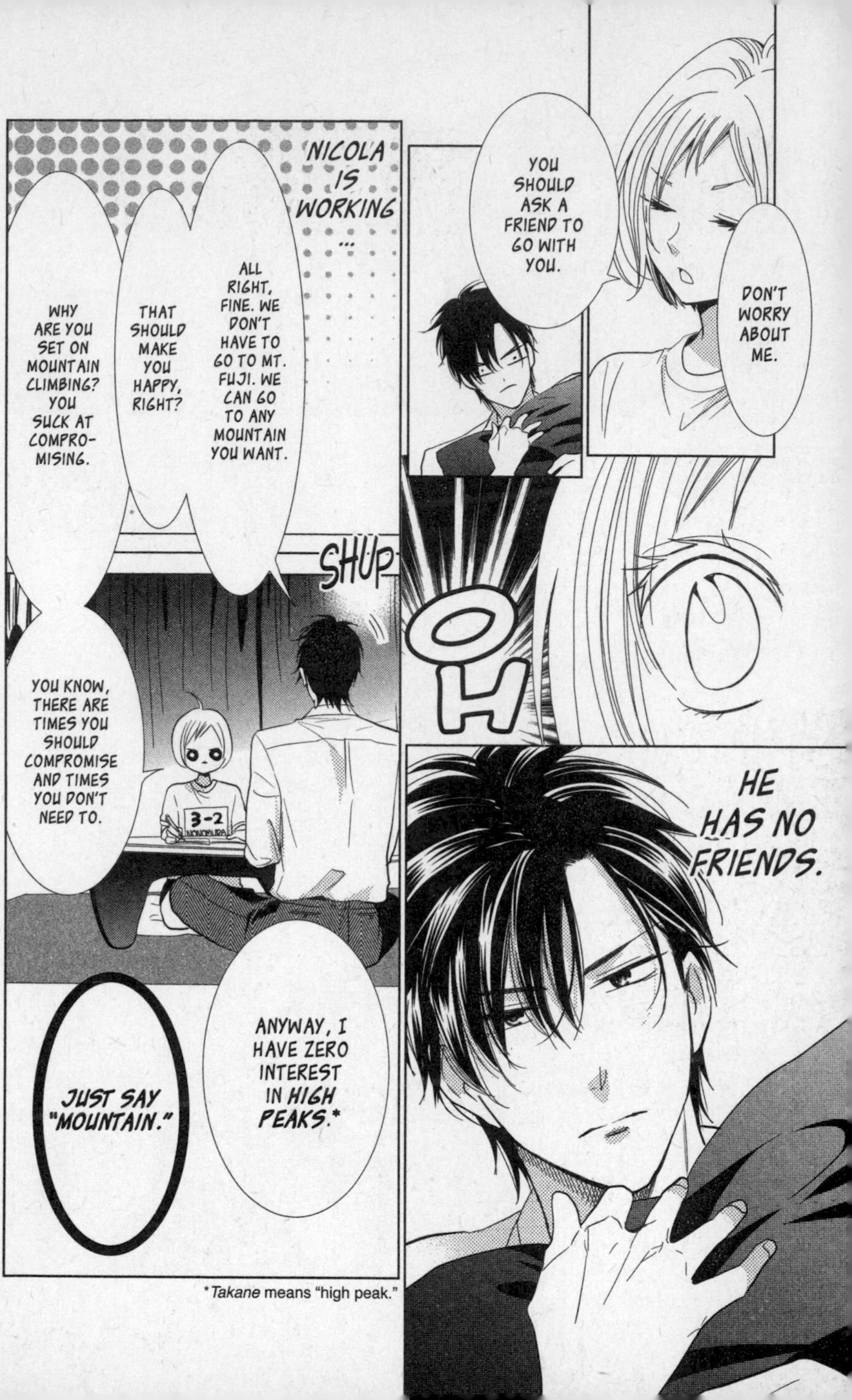
YOU SHOULD ASK A FRIEND TO GO WITH YOU.
DON'T WORRY ABOUT ME.
OH
HE HAS NO FRIENDS.
NICOLA IS WORKING...
ALL RIGHT, FINE. WE DON'T HAVE TO GO TO MT. FUJI. WE CAN GO TO ANY MOUNTAIN YOU WANT.
THAT SHOULD MAKE YOU HAPPY, RIGHT?
WHY ARE YOU SET ON MOUNTAIN CLIMBING? YOU SUCK AT COMPROMISING.
SHUP
YOU KNOW, THERE ARE TIMES YOU SHOULD COMPROMISE AND TIMES YOU DON'T NEED TO.
3-2
ANYWAY, I HAVE ZERO INTEREST IN HIGH PEAKS.*
JUST SAY "MOUNTAIN."

*Takane means "high peak."

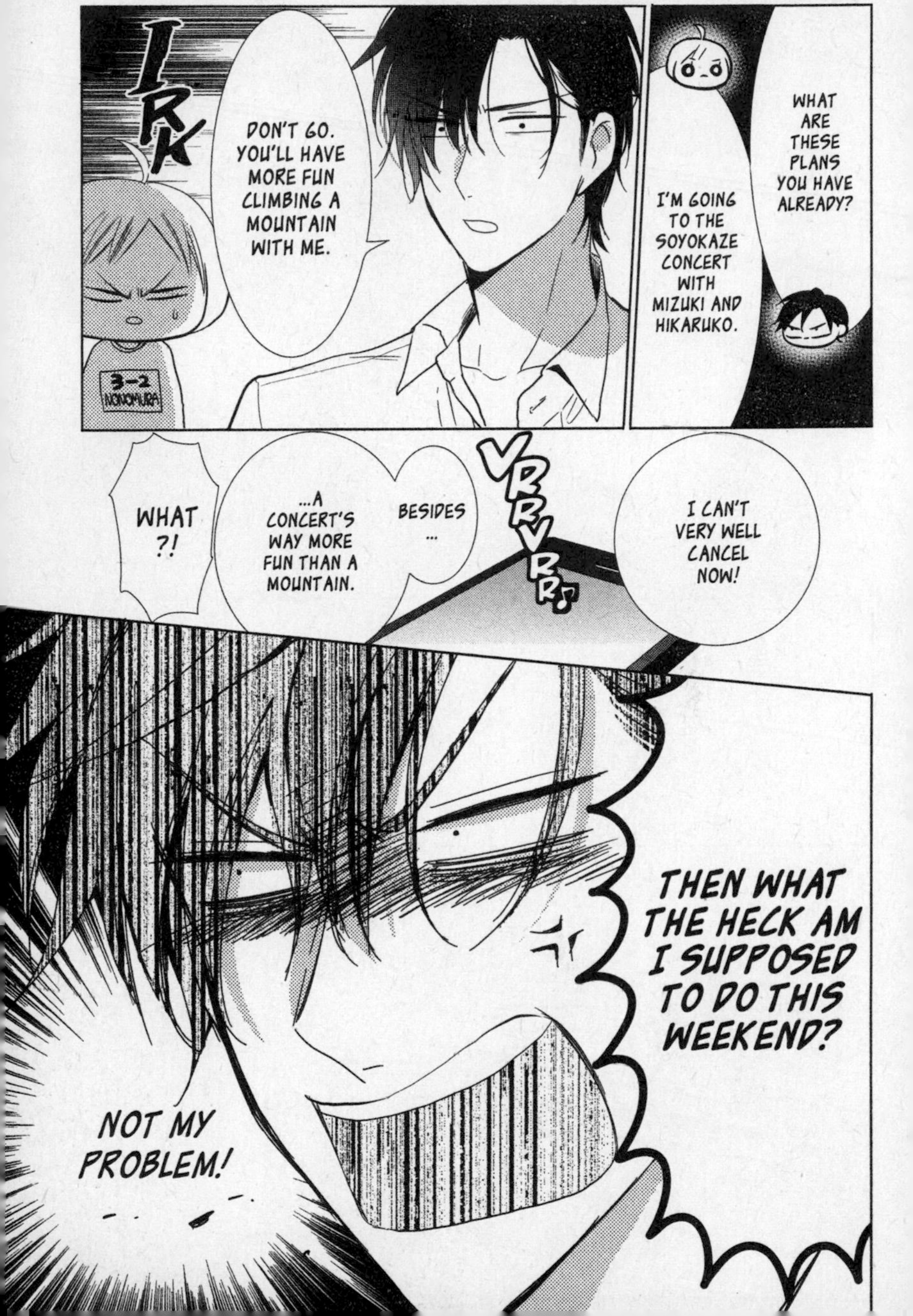
WHAT ARE THESE PLANS YOU HAVE ALREADY?
I'M GOING TO THE SOYOKAZE CONCERT WITH MIZUKI AND HIKARUKO.
DON'T GO. YOU'LL HAVE MORE FUN CLIMBING A MOUNTAIN WITH ME.
IRK
3-2 NONOMURA
I CAN'T VERY WELL CANCEL NOW!
VRRVRR
BESIDES...
...A CONCERT'S WAY MORE FUN THAN A MOUNTAIN.
WHAT?!
THEN WHAT THE HECK AM I SUPPOSED TO DO THIS WEEKEND?
NOT MY PROBLEM!

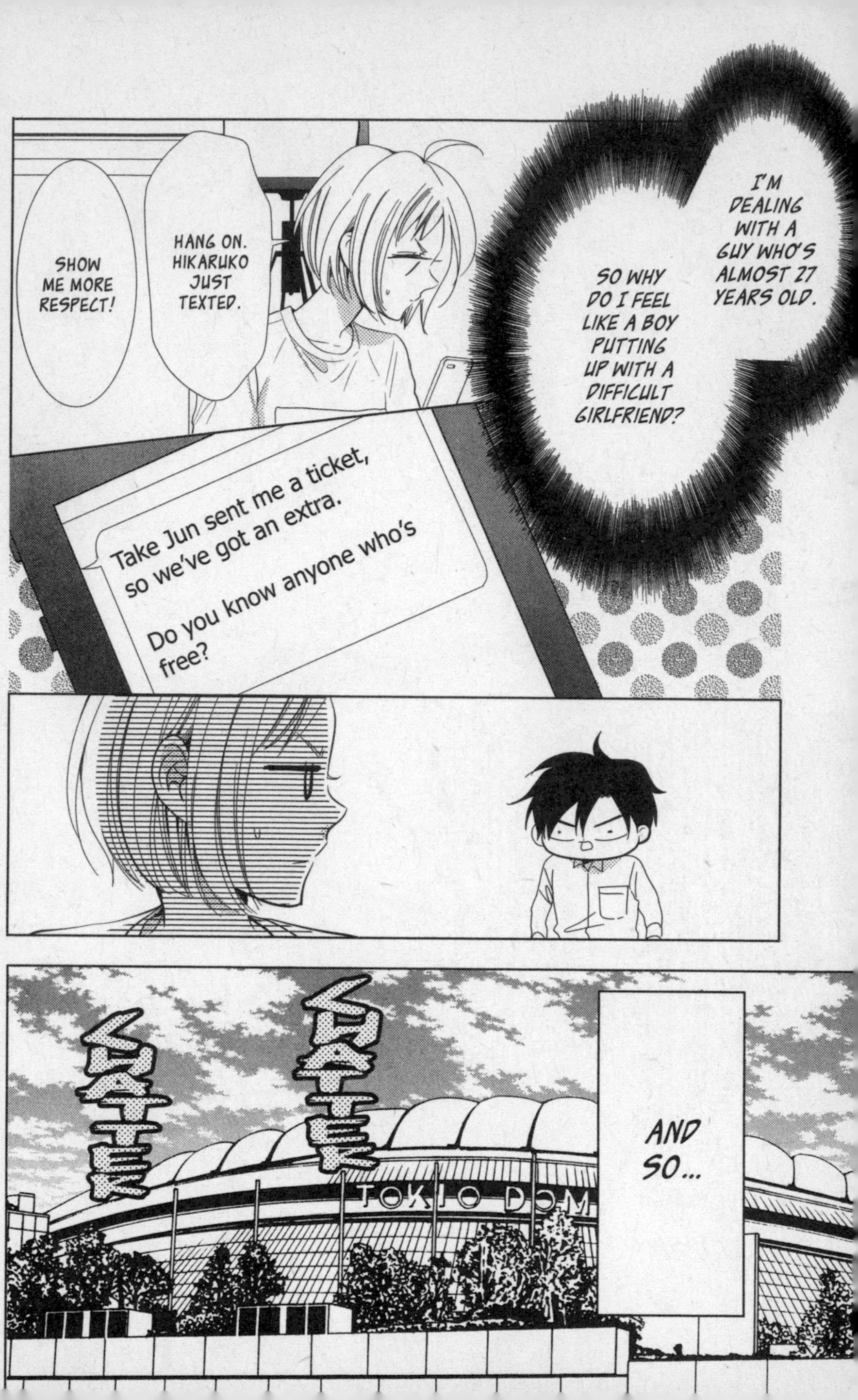
I'M DEALING WITH A GUY WHO'S ALMOST 27 YEARS OLD.
SO WHY DO I FEEL LIKE A BOY PUTTING UP WITH A DIFFICULT GIRLFRIEND?
HANG ON. HIKARUKO JUST TEXTED.
SHOW ME MORE RESPECT!
Take Jun sent me a ticket, so we've got an extra.
Do you know anyone who's free?
AND SO...
TOKIO DOM

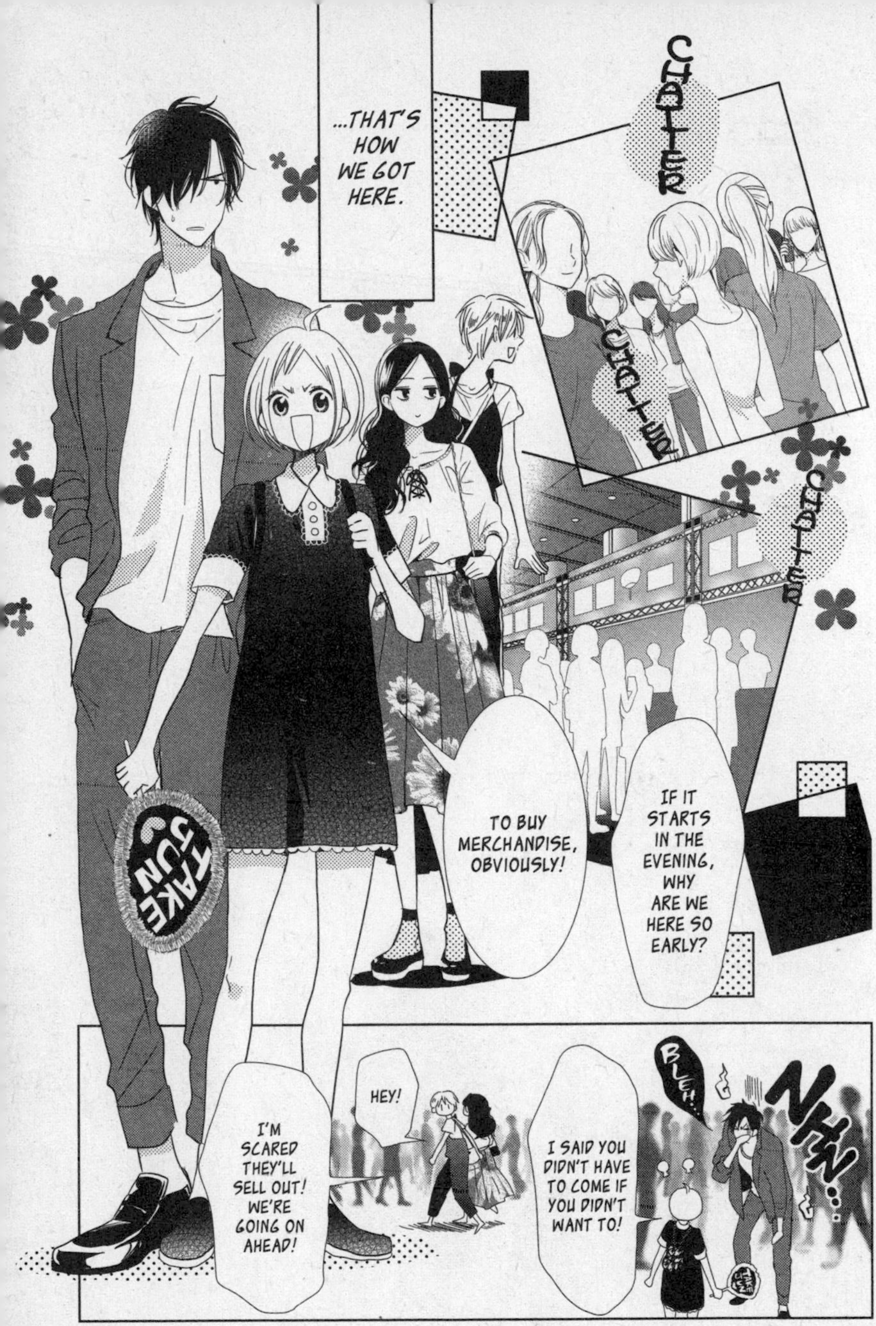
CHATTER
...THAT'S HOW WE GOT HERE.
CHATTER
CHATTER
IF IT STARTS IN THE EVENING, WHY ARE WE HERE SO EARLY?
TO BUY MERCHANDISE, OBVIOUSLY!
TAKE JUN
NHN...
BLEH!
I SAID YOU DIDN'T HAVE TO COME IF YOU DIDN'T WANT TO!
HEY!
I'M SCARED THEY'LL SELL OUT! WE'RE GOING ON AHEAD!

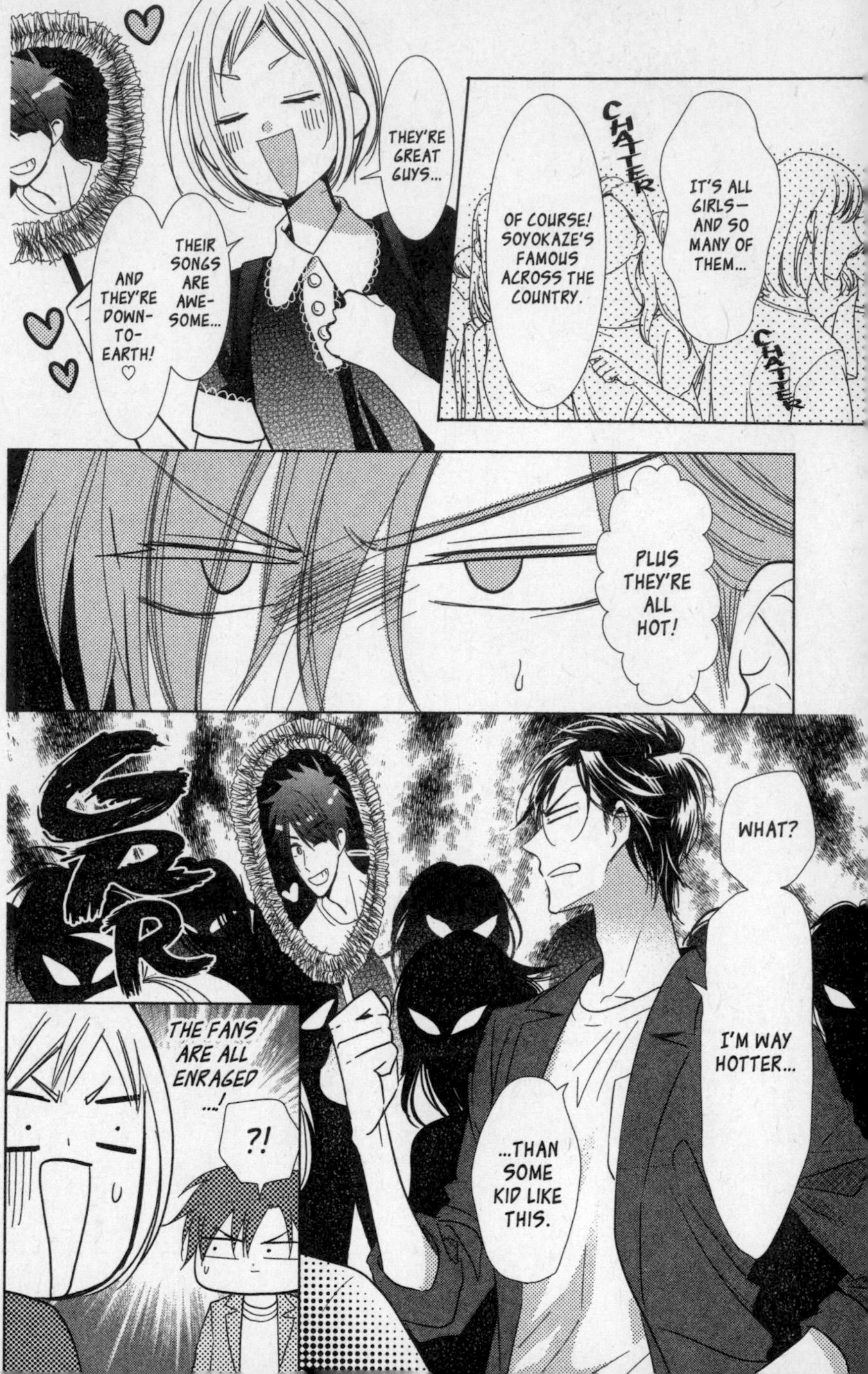

IT'S ALL GIRLS— AND SO MANY OF THEM...
CHATTER
CHATTER
OF COURSE! SOYOKAZE'S FAMOUS ACROSS THE COUNTRY.
THEY'RE GREAT GUYS...
THEIR SONGS ARE AWE-SOME...
AND THEY'RE DOWN-TO-EARTH! ♡
PLUS THEY'RE ALL HOT!
WHAT?
I'M WAY HOTTER...
...THAN SOME KID LIKE THIS.
GRR
THE FANS ARE ALL ENRAGED ...!
?!

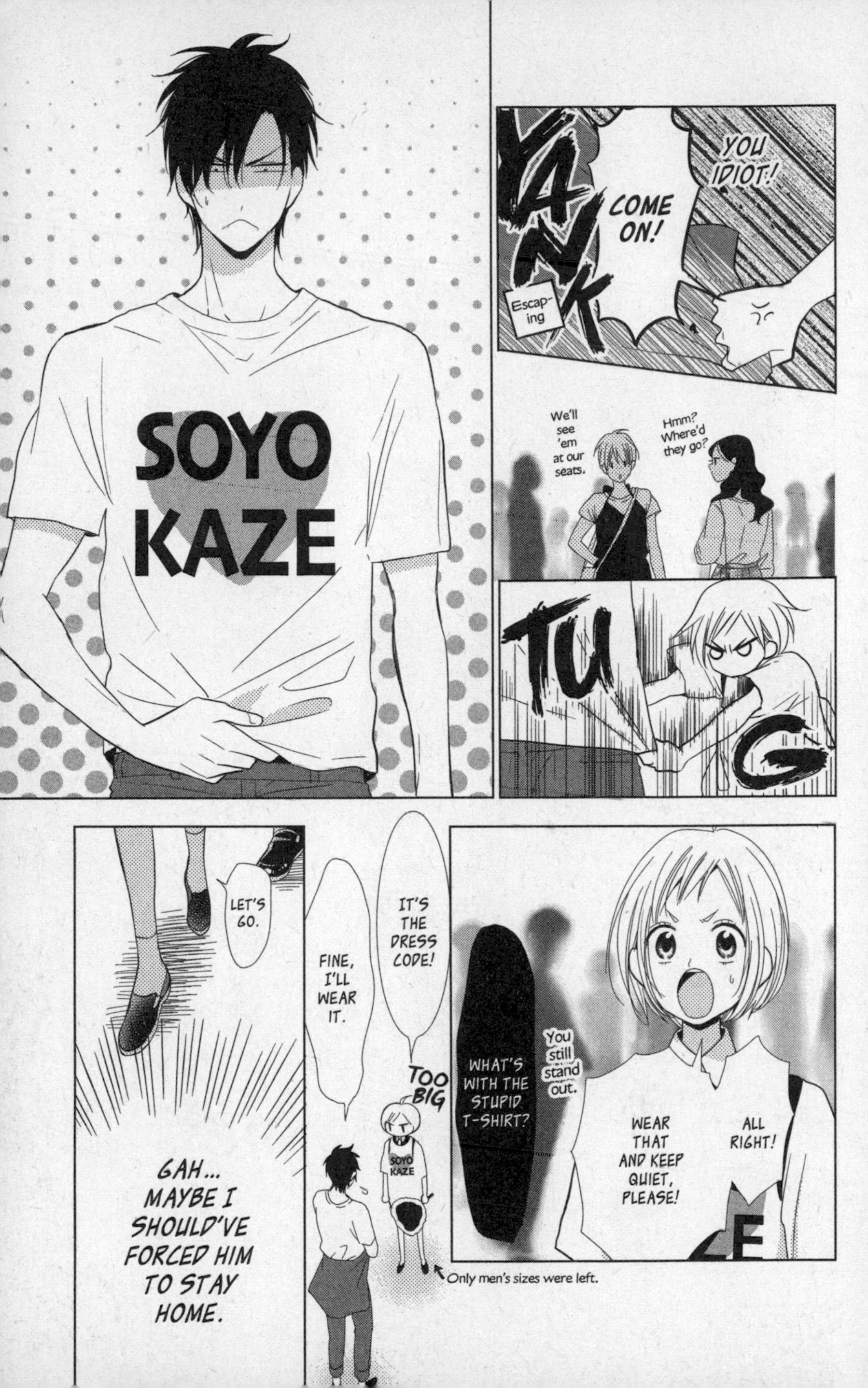
YANK
COME ON!
YOU IDIOT!
Escap-ing
Hmm? Where'd they go?
We'll see 'em at our seats.
TUG
SOYO KAZE
WHAT'S WITH THE STUPID T-SHIRT?
You still stand out.
WEAR THAT AND KEEP QUIET, PLEASE!
ALL RIGHT!
IT'S THE DRESS CODE!
FINE, I'LL WEAR IT.
LET'S GO.
TOO BIG
SOYO KAZE
GAH... MAYBE I SHOULD'VE FORCED HIM TO STAY HOME.
Only men's sizes were left.

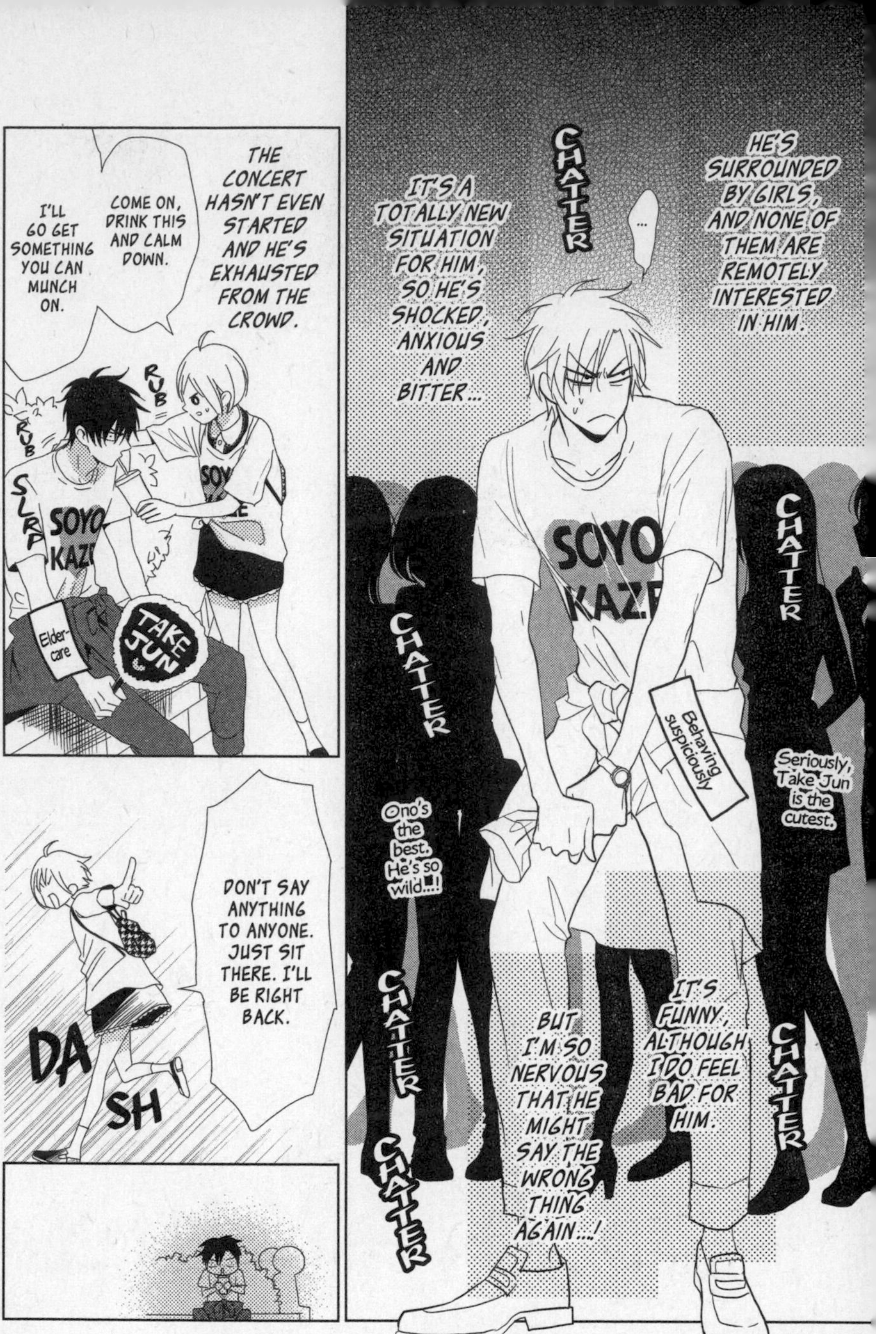
HE'S SURROUNDED BY GIRLS, AND NONE OF THEM ARE REMOTELY INTERESTED IN HIM.
CHATTER
...
IT'S A TOTALLY NEW SITUATION FOR HIM, SO HE'S SHOCKED, ANXIOUS AND BITTER...
CHATTER
SOYO KAZE
Seriously, Take Jun is the cutest.
Behaving suspiciously
CHATTER
Ono's the best. He's so wild...!
IT'S FUNNY, ALTHOUGH I DO FEEL BAD FOR HIM.
CHATTER
BUT I'M SO NERVOUS THAT HE MIGHT SAY THE WRONG THING AGAIN...!
CHATTER
CHATTER
THE CONCERT HASN'T EVEN STARTED AND HE'S EXHAUSTED FROM THE CROWD.
COME ON, DRINK THIS AND CALM DOWN.
I'LL GO GET SOMETHING YOU CAN MUNCH ON.
RUB
RUB
SLRP
SOYO KAZE
TAKE JUN
Elder-care
DON'T SAY ANYTHING TO ANYONE. JUST SIT THERE. I'LL BE RIGHT BACK.
DASH

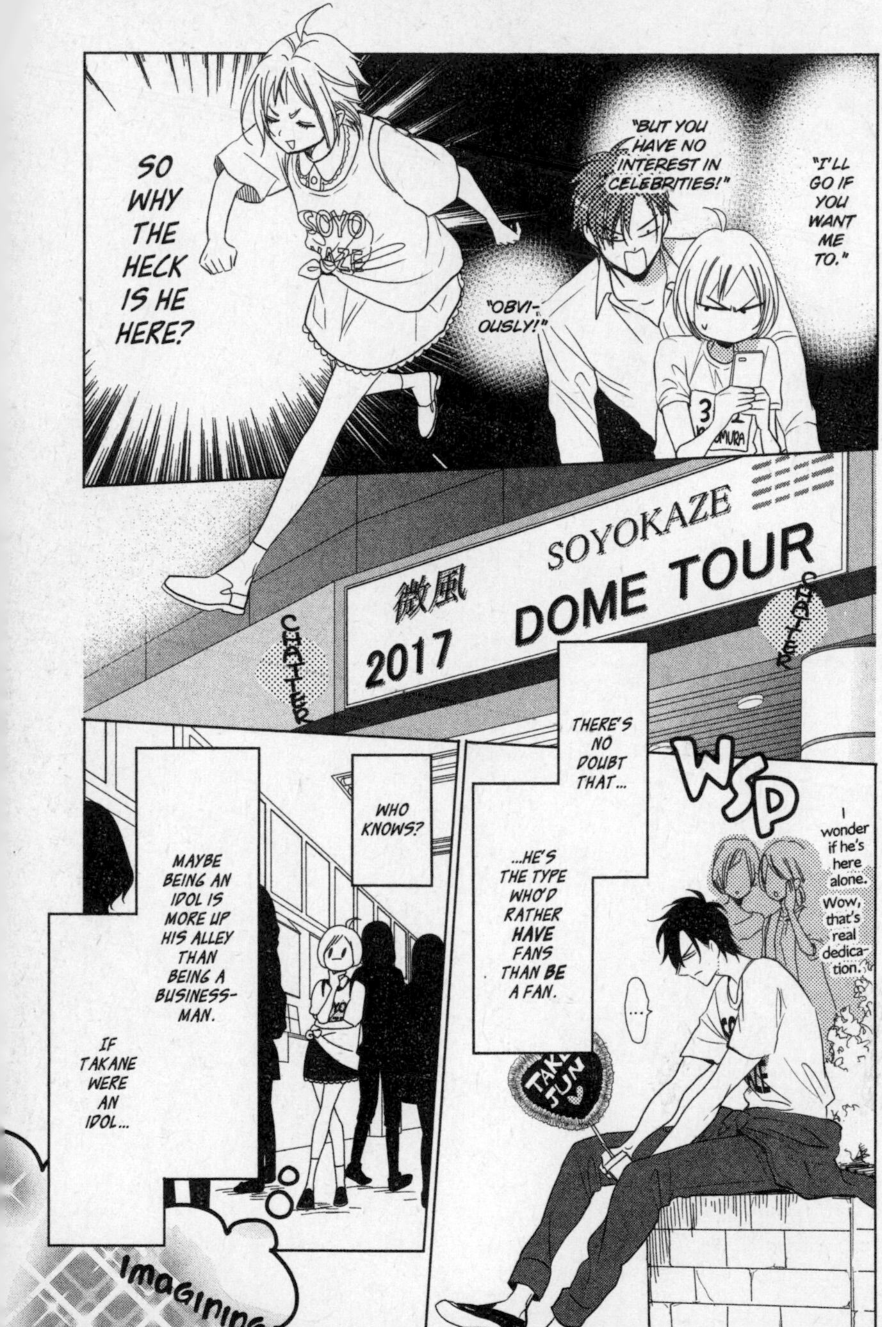
"I'LL GO IF YOU WANT ME TO."
"BUT YOU HAVE NO INTEREST IN CELEBRITIES!"
"OBVI-OUSLY!"
SO WHY THE HECK IS HE HERE?
SOYOKAZE
微風
2017 DOME TOUR
CHATTER
CHATTER
THERE'S NO DOUBT THAT...
WSP
I wonder if he's here alone. Wow, that's real dedication.
...HE'S THE TYPE WHO'D RATHER HAVE FANS THAN BE A FAN.
...
TAKE JUN
WHO KNOWS?
MAYBE BEING AN IDOL IS MORE UP HIS ALLEY THAN BEING A BUSINESS-MAN.
IF TAKANE WERE AN IDOL...
Imagining

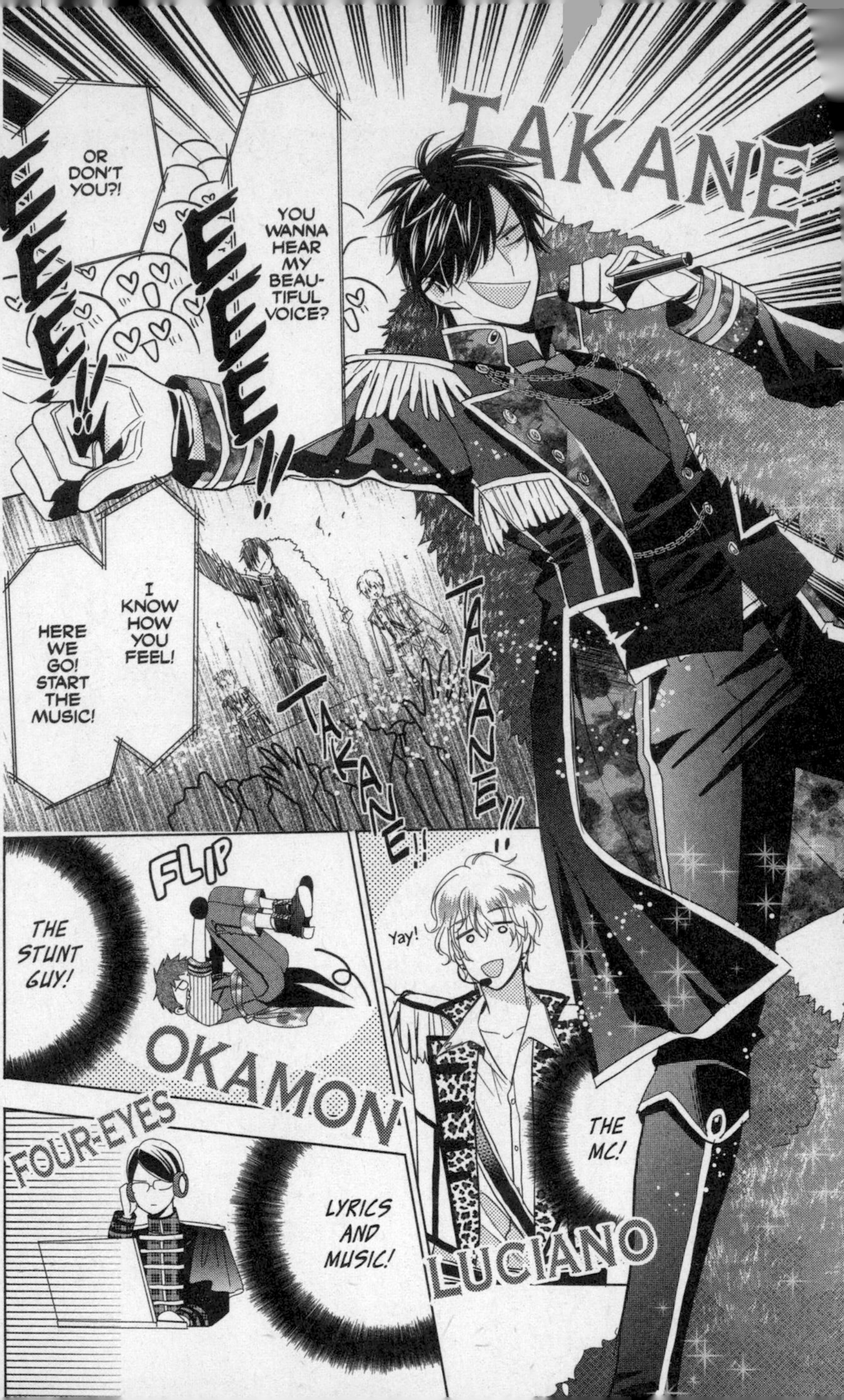
TAKANE
YOU WANNA HEAR MY BEAUTIFUL VOICE?
EEEE!!
OR DON'T YOU?!
EEEE!!
TAKANE!!
TAKANE!!
I KNOW HOW YOU FEEL!
HERE WE GO! START THE MUSIC!
Yay!
THE MC!
LUCIANO
FLIP
THE STUNT GUY!
OKAMON
LYRICS AND MUSIC!
FOUR-EYES

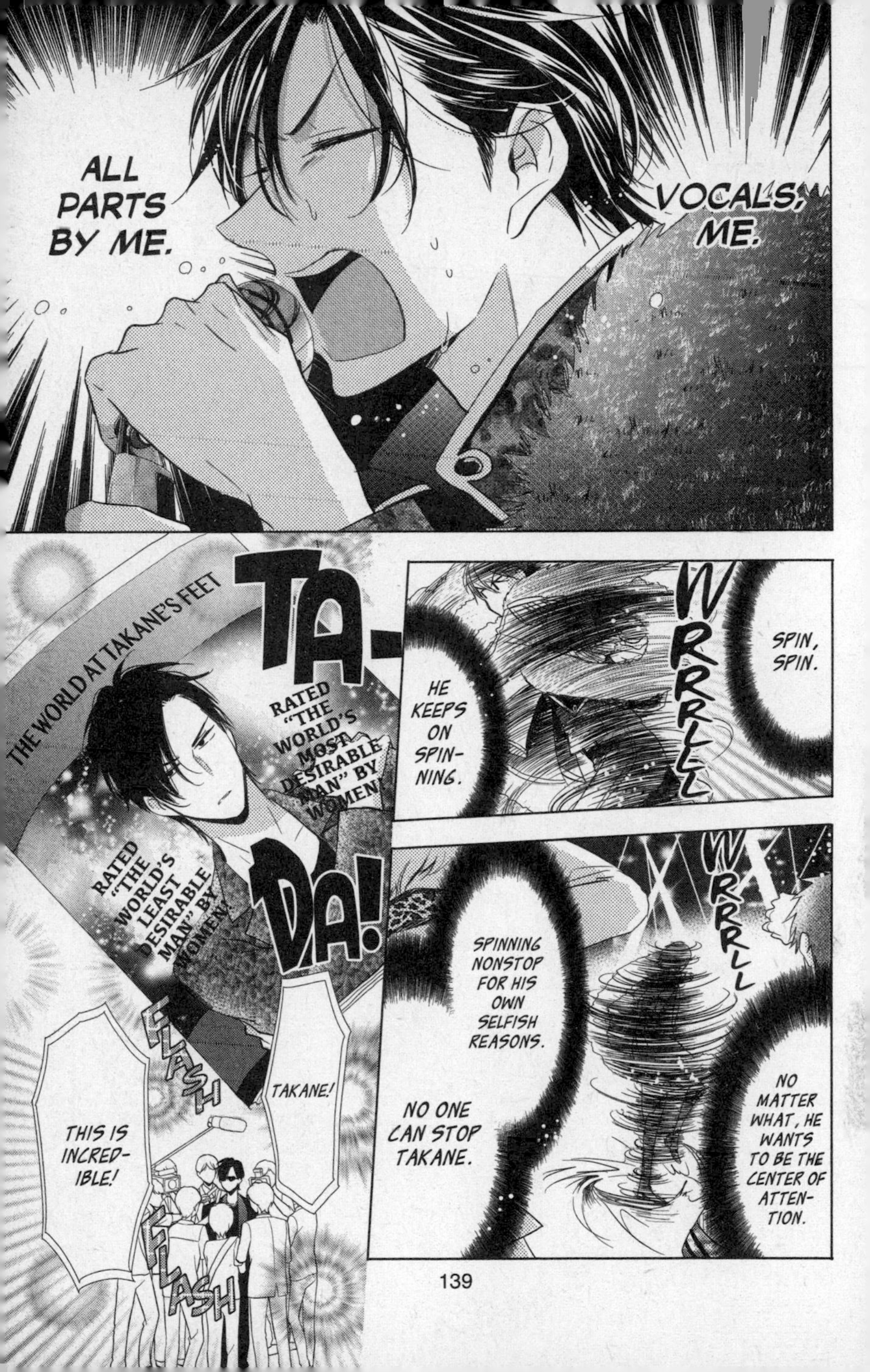
VOCALS, ME.
ALL PARTS BY ME.
WRRRLLL
SPIN, SPIN.
HE KEEPS ON SPIN-NING.
WRRRLL
NO MATTER WHAT, HE WANTS TO BE THE CENTER OF ATTEN-TION.
SPINNING NONSTOP FOR HIS OWN SELFISH REASONS.
NO ONE CAN STOP TAKANE.
TA-
DA!
THE WORLD AT TAKANE'S FEET
RATED "THE WORLD'S MOST DESIRABLE MAN" BY WOMEN!
RATED "THE WORLD'S LEAST DESIRABLE MAN" BY WOMEN!
FLASH
TAKANE!
THIS IS INCRED-IBLE!
FLASH
FLASH

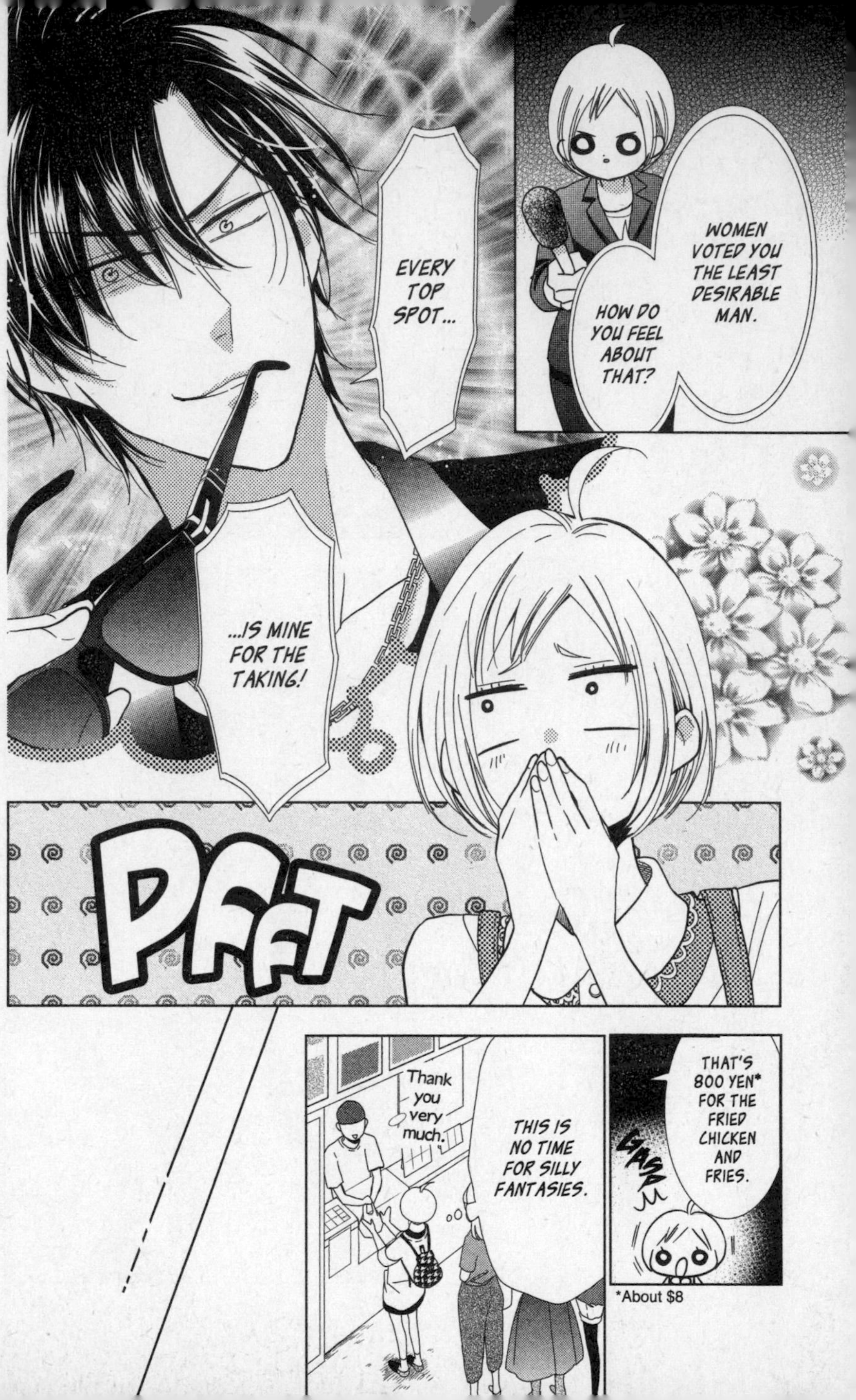
WOMEN VOTED YOU THE LEAST DESIRABLE MAN.
HOW DO YOU FEEL ABOUT THAT?
EVERY TOP SPOT...
...IS MINE FOR THE TAKING!
PFFT
THAT'S 800 YEN* FOR THE FRIED CHICKEN AND FRIES.
GASP
THIS IS NO TIME FOR SILLY FANTASIES.
Thank you very much.

*About $8

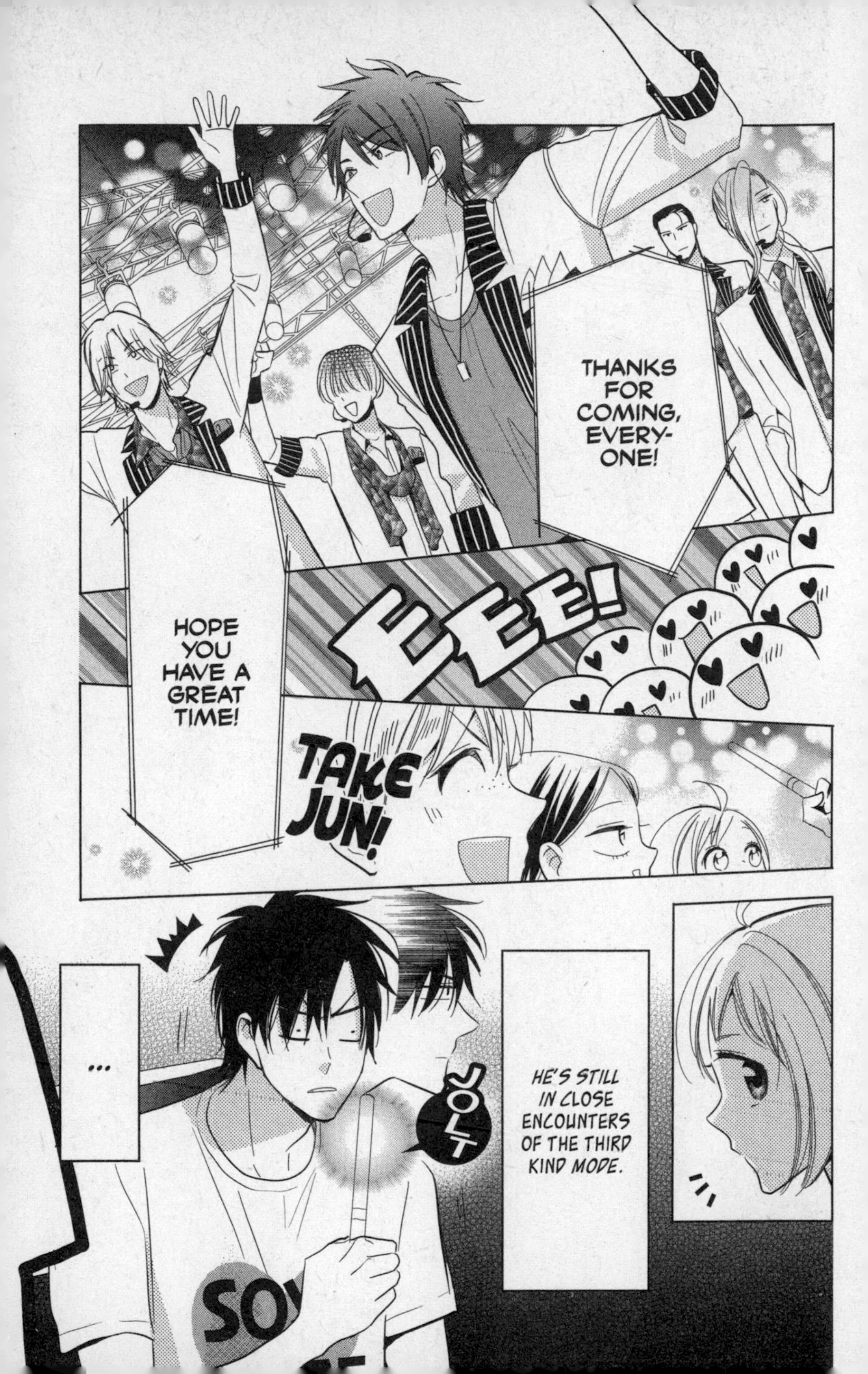
THANKS FOR COMING, EVERY-ONE!
HOPE YOU HAVE A GREAT TIME!
EEE!
TAKE JUN!
HE'S STILL IN CLOSE ENCOUNTERS OF THE THIRD KIND MODE.
JOLT
...

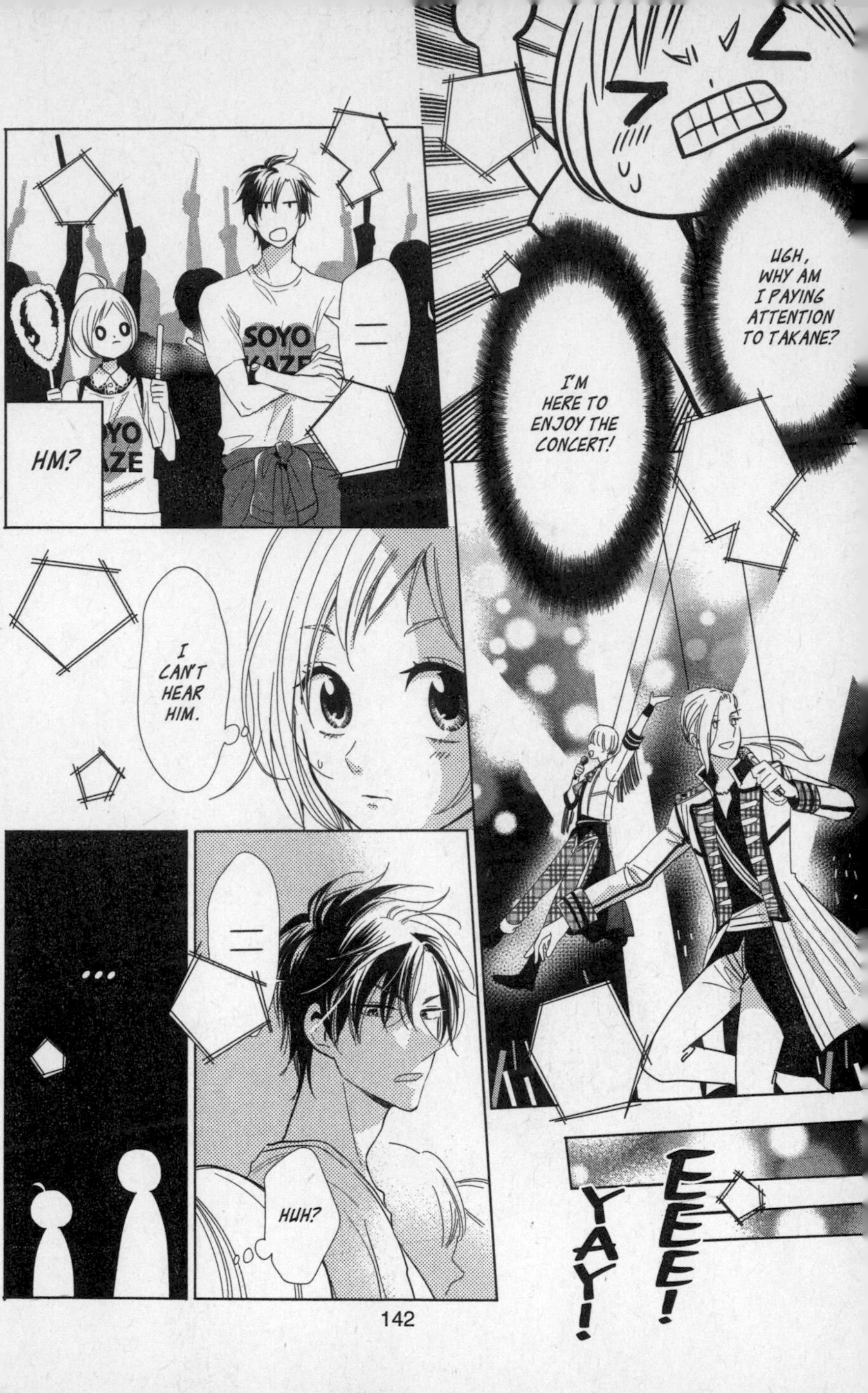
UGH, WHY AM I PAYING ATTENTION TO TAKANE?
I'M HERE TO ENJOY THE CONCERT!
EEEE!
YAY!
HM?
I CAN'T HEAR HIM.
HUH?
...

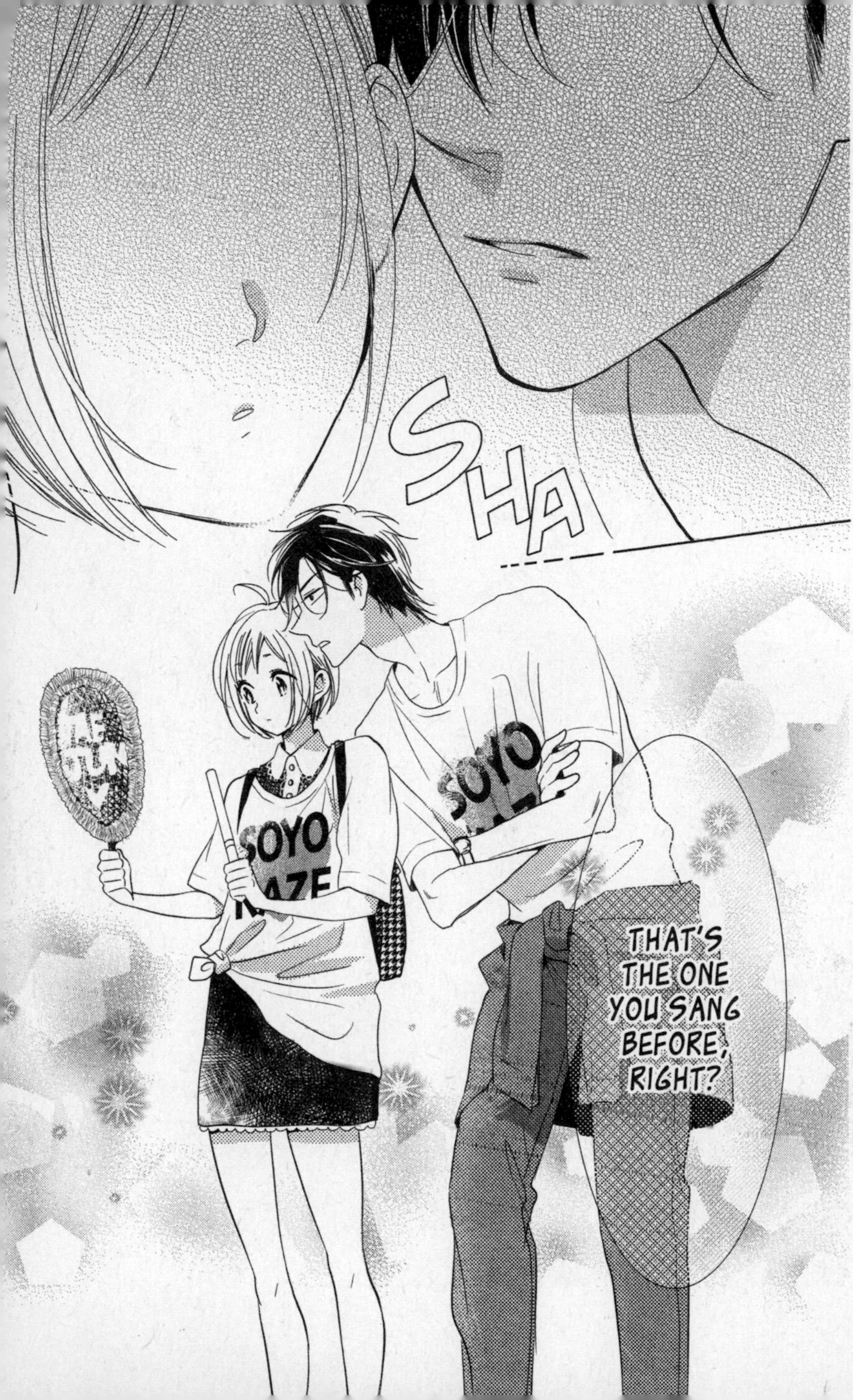
SHA
THAT'S THE ONE YOU SANG BEFORE, RIGHT?

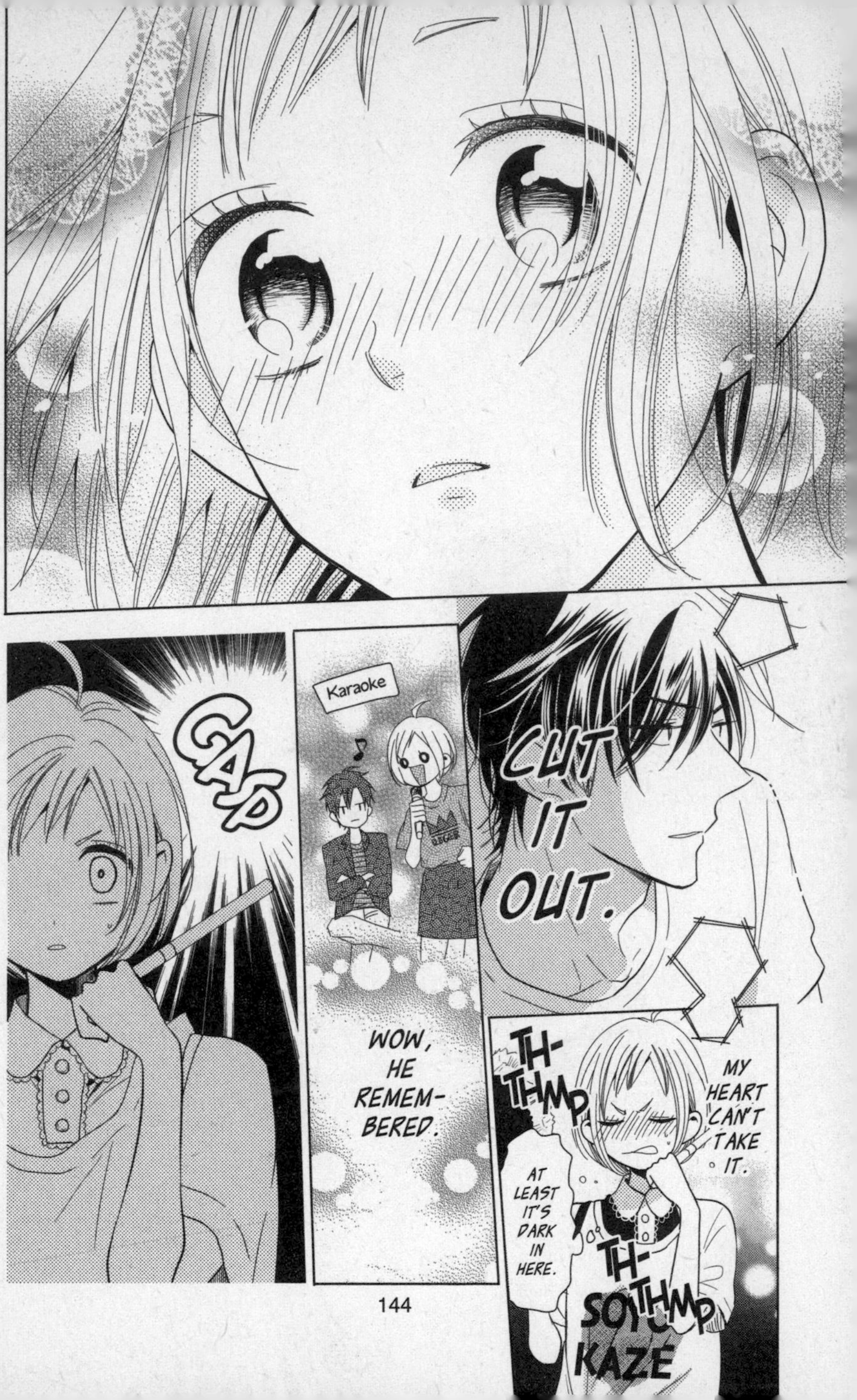
CUT IT OUT.
MY HEART CAN'T TAKE IT.
TH-THMP
AT LEAST IT'S DARK IN HERE.
TH-THMP
SOYOU KAZE
Karaoke
WOW, HE REMEMBERED.
GAP

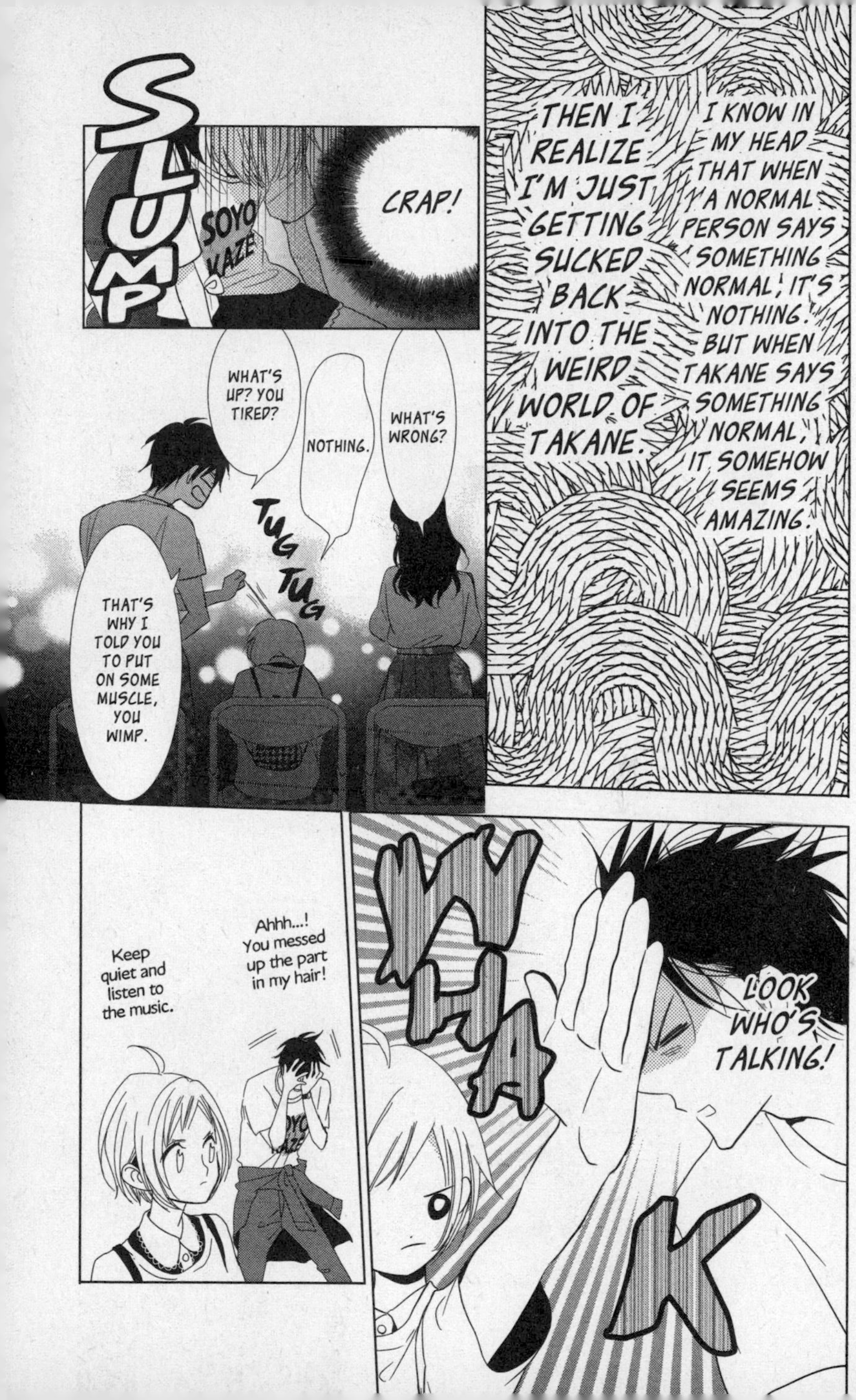
I KNOW IN MY HEAD THAT WHEN A NORMAL PERSON SAYS SOMETHING NORMAL, IT'S NOTHING. BUT WHEN TAKANE SAYS SOMETHING NORMAL, IT SOMEHOW SEEMS AMAZING.
THEN I REALIZE I'M JUST GETTING SUCKED BACK INTO THE WEIRD WORLD OF TAKANE.
CRAP!
SOYO KAZE
SLUMP
WHAT'S WRONG?
NOTHING.
WHAT'S UP? YOU TIRED?
TUG TUG
THAT'S WHY I TOLD YOU TO PUT ON SOME MUSCLE, YOU WIMP.
LOOK WHO'S TALKING!
WHAK
Ahhh...! You messed up the part in my hair!
Keep quiet and listen to the music.

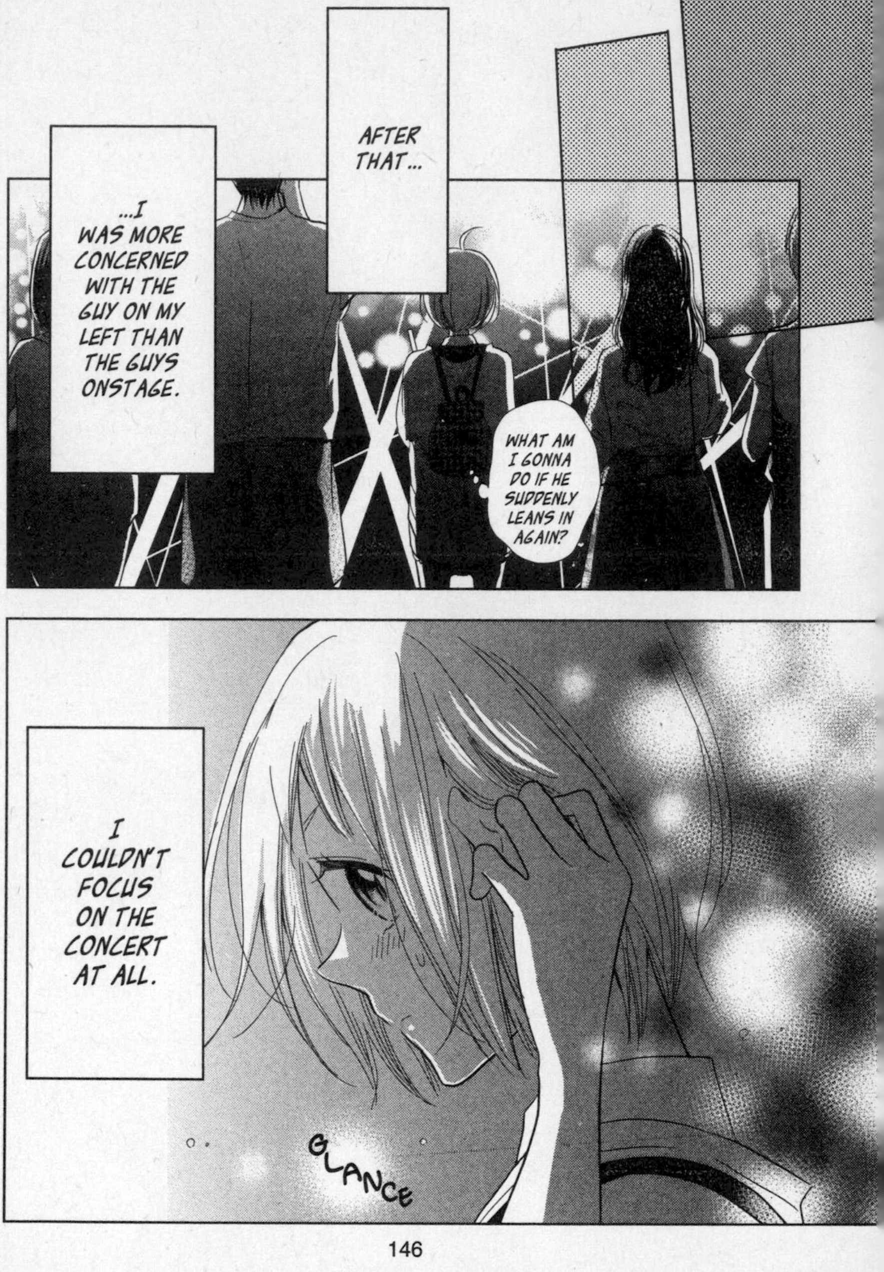
AFTER THAT...
...I WAS MORE CONCERNED WITH THE GUY ON MY LEFT THAN THE GUYS ONSTAGE.
WHAT AM I GONNA DO IF HE SUDDENLY LEANS IN AGAIN?
I COULDN'T FOCUS ON THE CONCERT AT ALL.
GLANCE

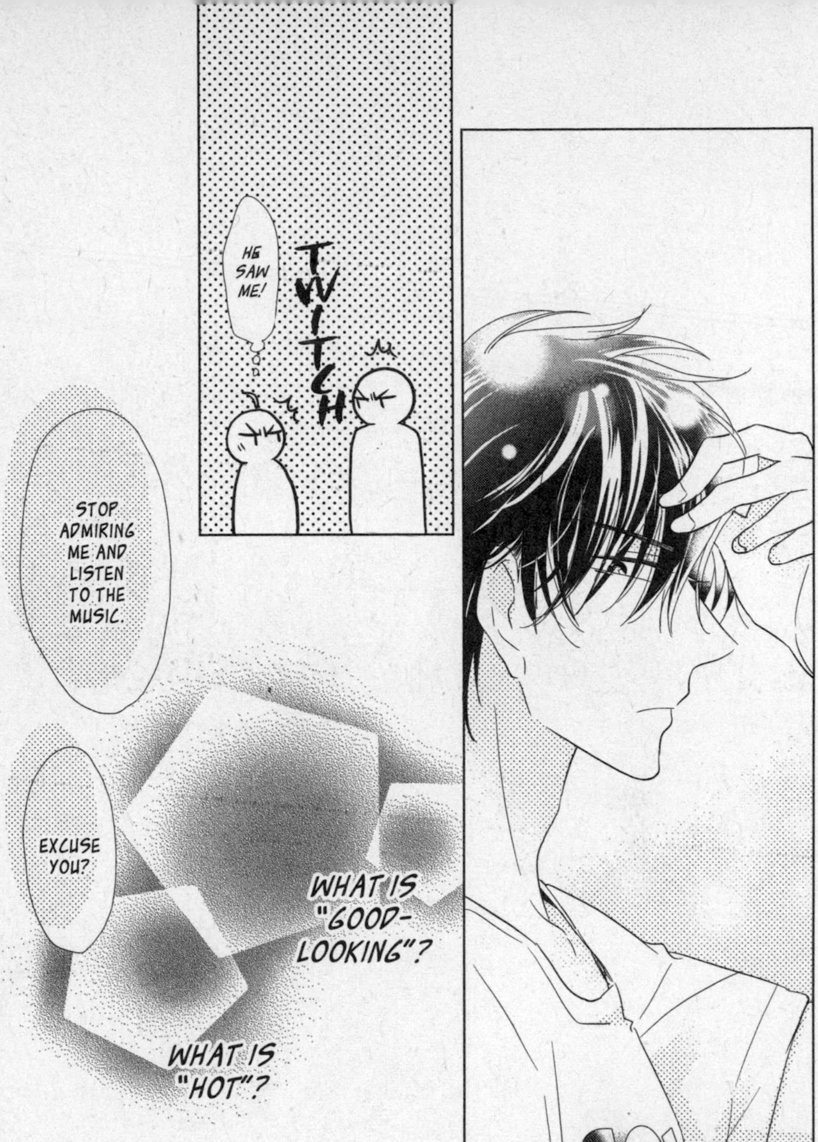
HE SAW ME!
TWITCH
STOP ADMIRING ME AND LISTEN TO THE MUSIC.
EXCUSE YOU?
WHAT IS "GOOD-LOOKING"?
WHAT IS "HOT"?

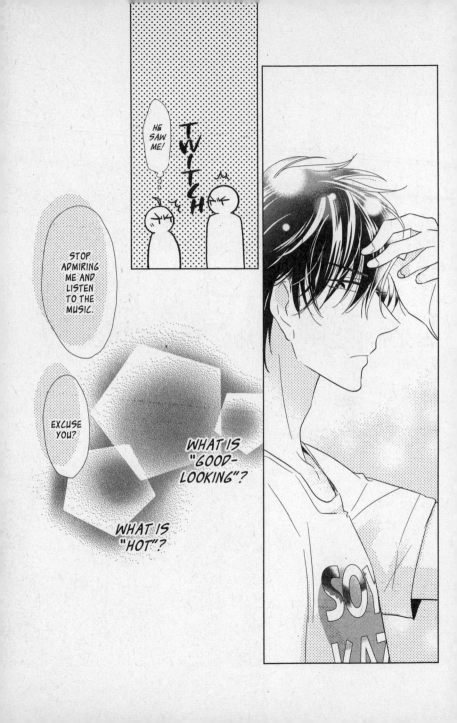

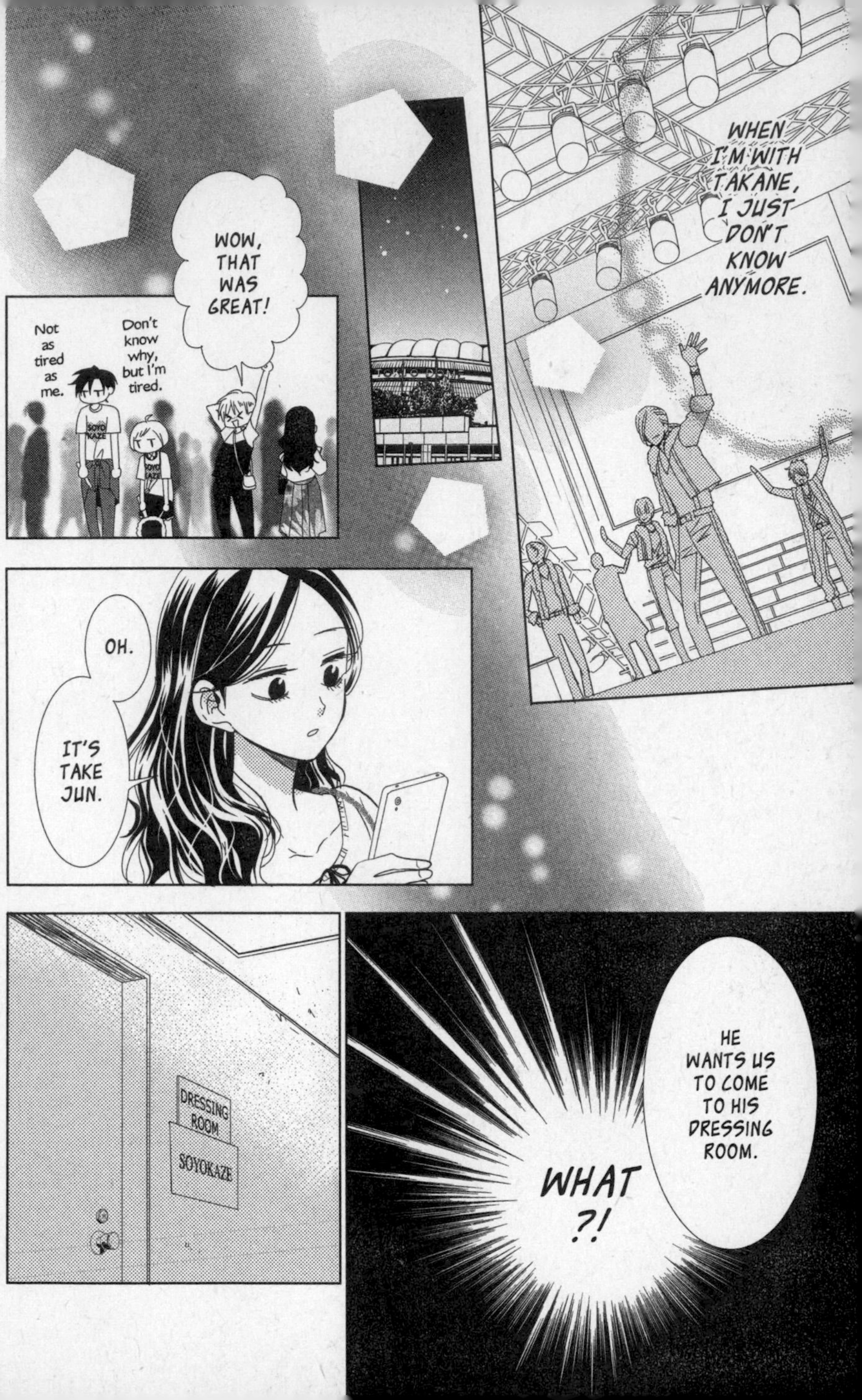
WHEN I'M WITH TAKANE, I JUST DON'T KNOW ANYMORE.
WOW, THAT WAS GREAT!
Don't know why, but I'm tired.
Not as tired as me.
OH.
IT'S TAKE JUN.
HE WANTS US TO COME TO HIS DRESSING ROOM.
WHAT?!
DRESSING ROOM
SOYOKAZE

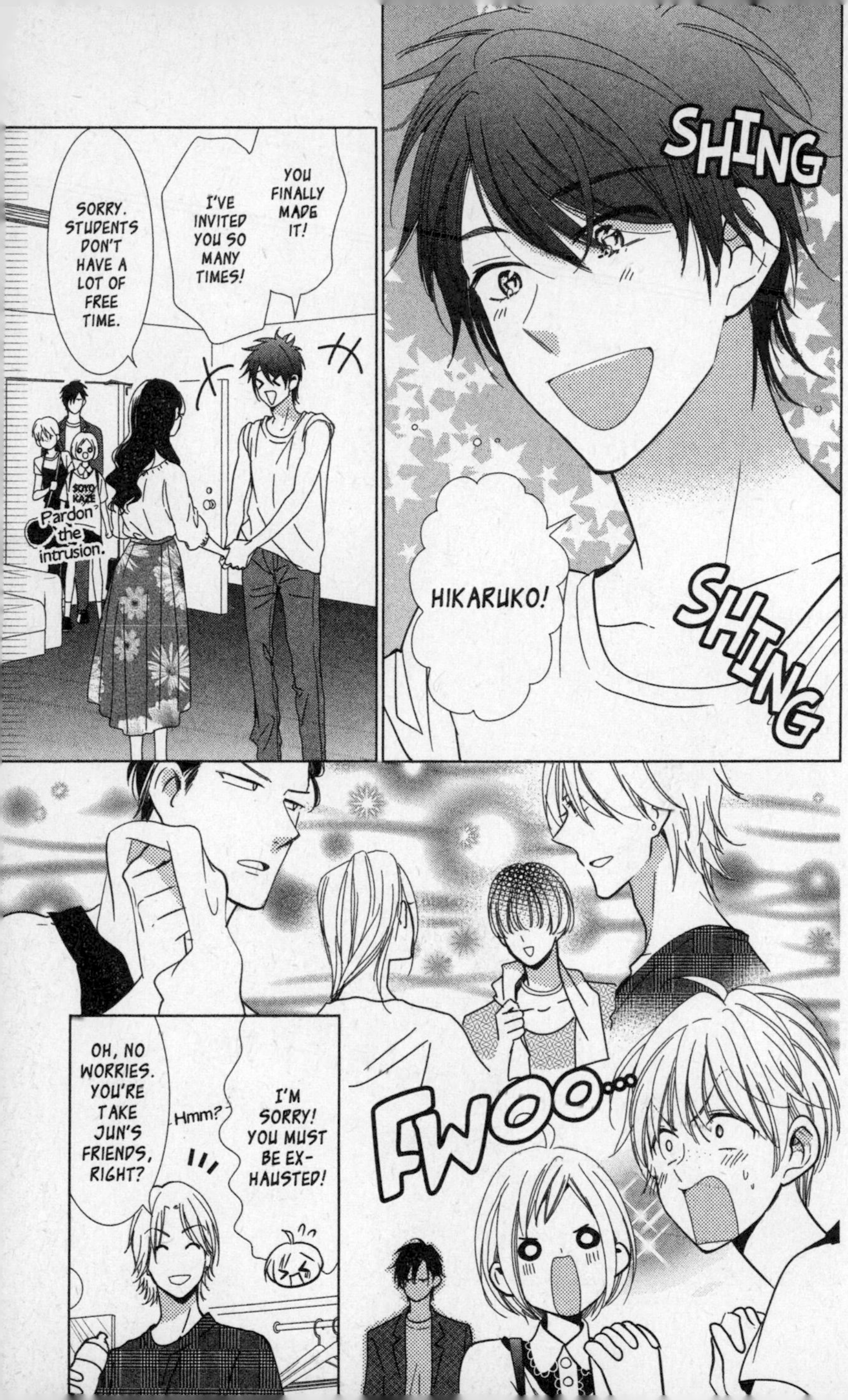
SHING
SHING
HIKARUKO!
YOU FINALLY MADE IT!
I'VE INVITED YOU SO MANY TIMES!
SORRY. STUDENTS DON'T HAVE A LOT OF FREE TIME.
SOYO KAZE
Pardon the intrusion.
FWOO...
I'M SORRY! YOU MUST BE EX- HAUSTED!
Hmm?
OH, NO WORRIES. YOU'RE TAKE JUN'S FRIENDS, RIGHT?

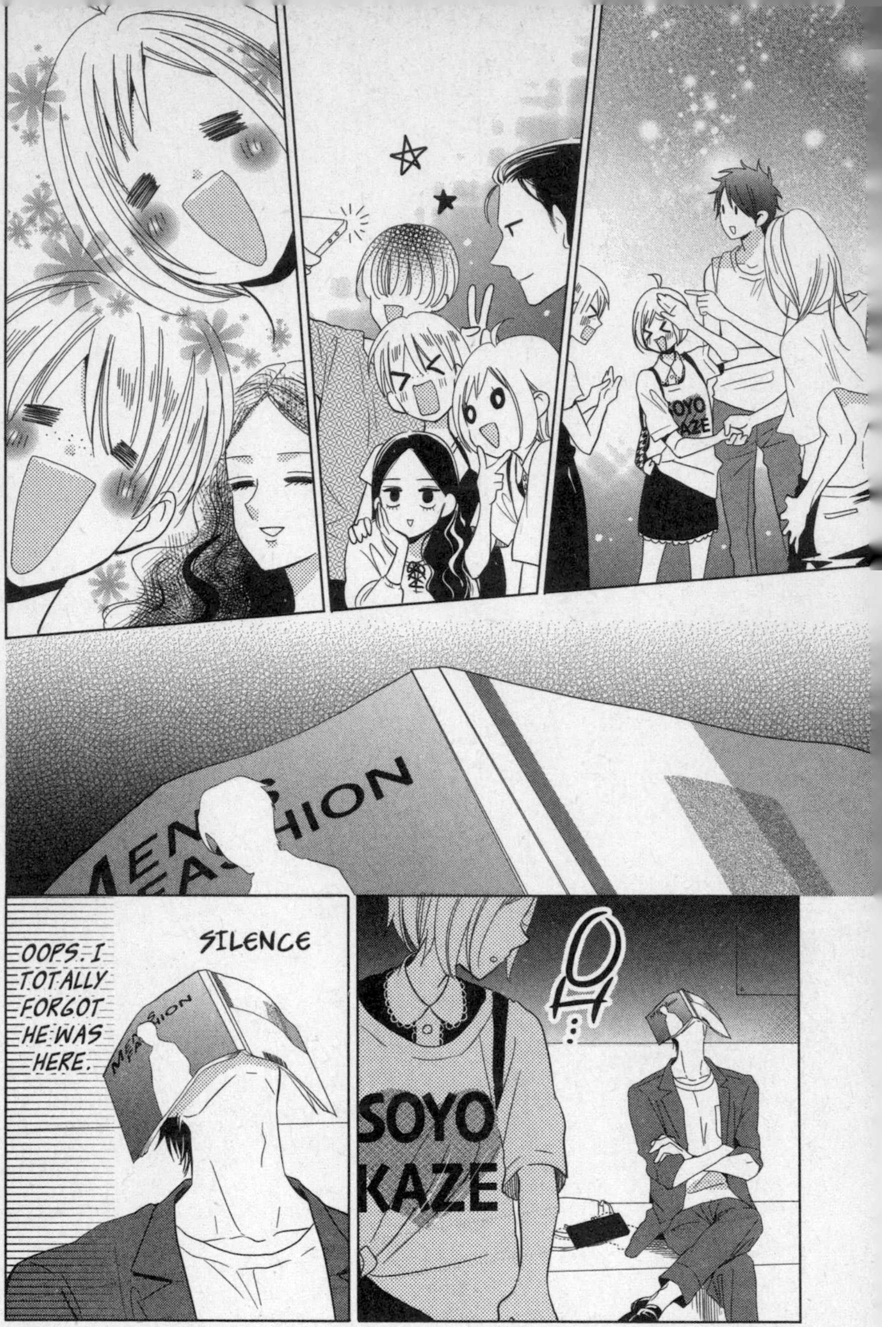
SOYO KAZE
SOYO KAZE
SILENCE
OOPS. I TOTALLY FORGOT HE WAS HERE.
Sleep sulking

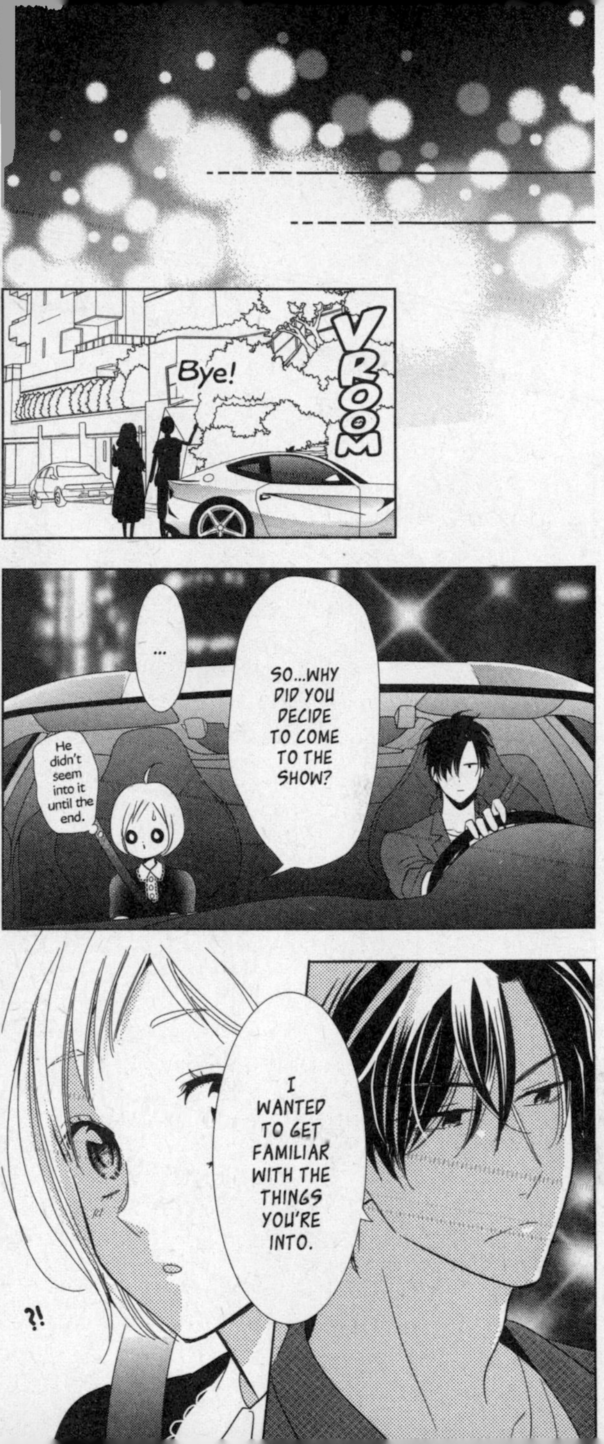
VROOM
Bye!
SO...WHY DID YOU DECIDE TO COME TO THE SHOW?
...
He didn't seem into it until the end.
I WANTED TO GET FAMILIAR WITH THE THINGS YOU'RE INTO.
?!

Find the one who's in good spirits!

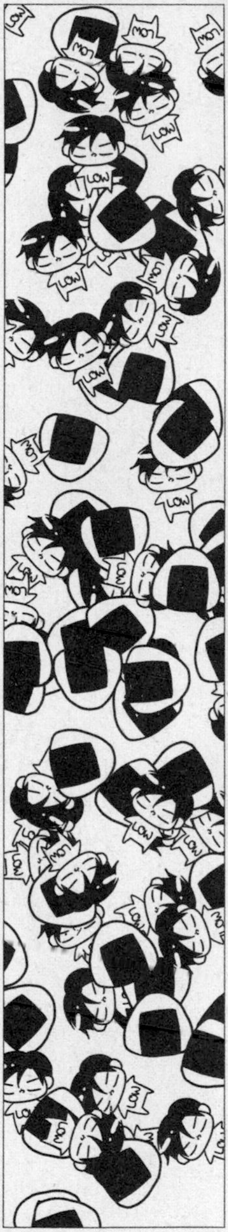
LOW

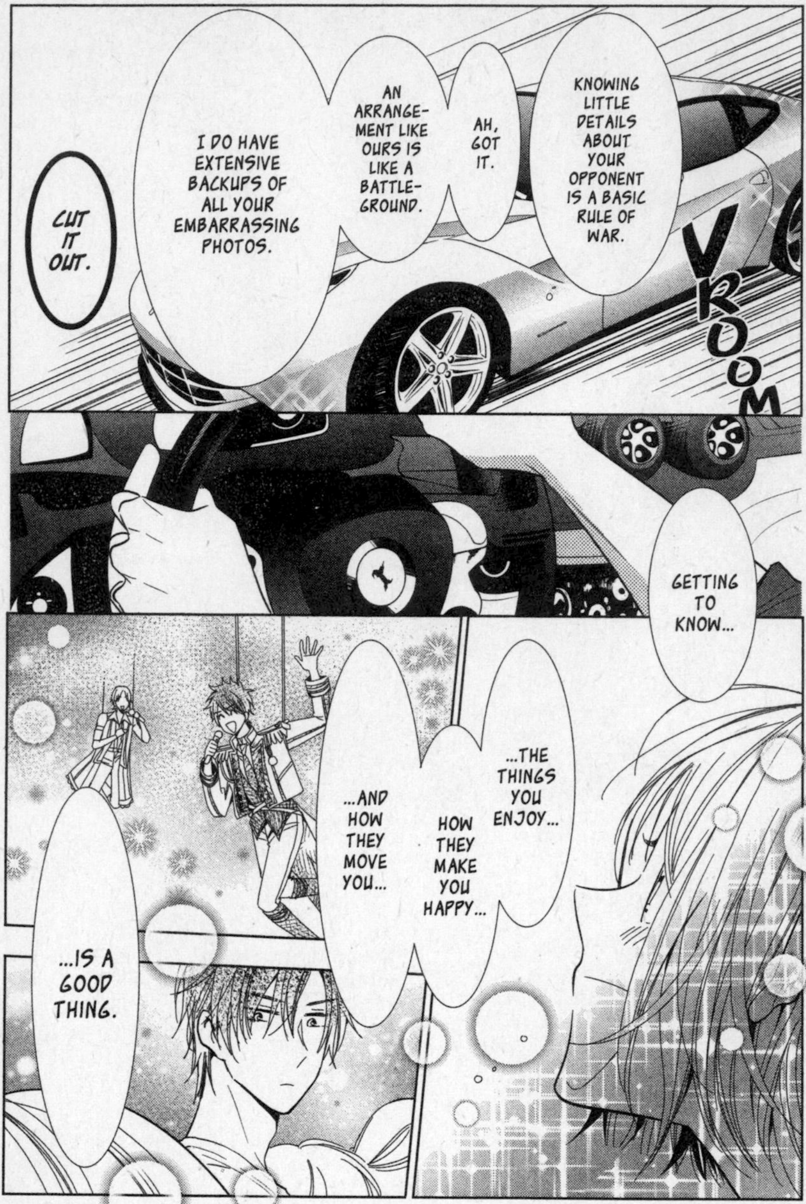
KNOWING LITTLE DETAILS ABOUT YOUR OPPONENT IS A BASIC RULE OF WAR.
VROOM
AH, GOT IT.
AN ARRANGEMENT LIKE OURS IS LIKE A BATTLEGROUND.
I DO HAVE EXTENSIVE BACKUPS OF ALL YOUR EMBARRASSING PHOTOS.
CUT IT OUT.
GETTING TO KNOW...
...THE THINGS YOU ENJOY...
HOW THEY MAKE YOU HAPPY...
...AND HOW THEY MOVE YOU...
...IS A GOOD THING.

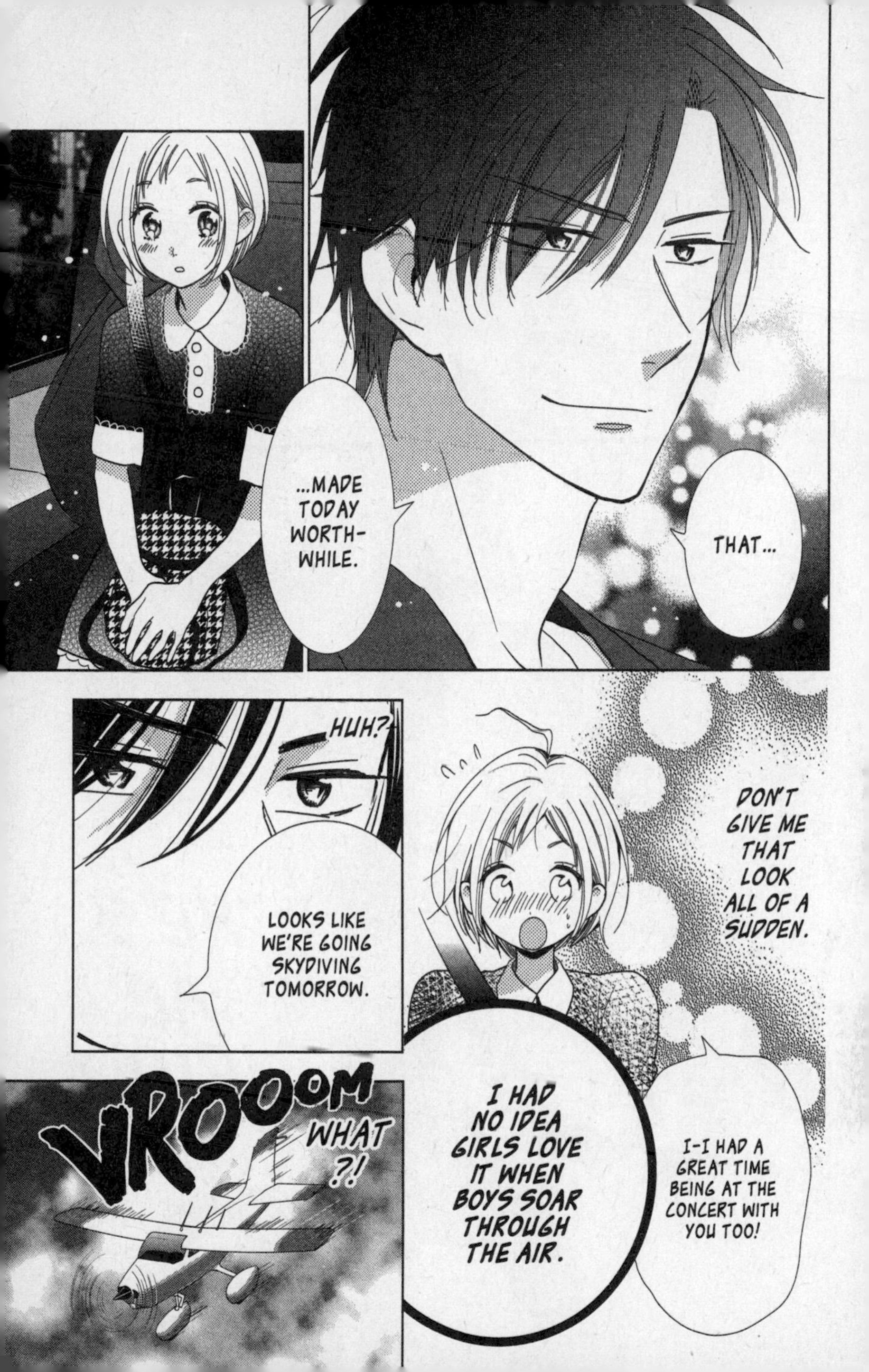
THAT...
...MADE TODAY WORTH-WHILE.
DON'T GIVE ME THAT LOOK ALL OF A SUDDEN.
I-I HAD A GREAT TIME BEING AT THE CONCERT WITH YOU TOO!
I HAD NO IDEA GIRLS LOVE IT WHEN BOYS SOAR THROUGH THE AIR.
HUH?
LOOKS LIKE WE'RE GOING SKYDIVING TOMORROW.
VROOOM
WHAT?!

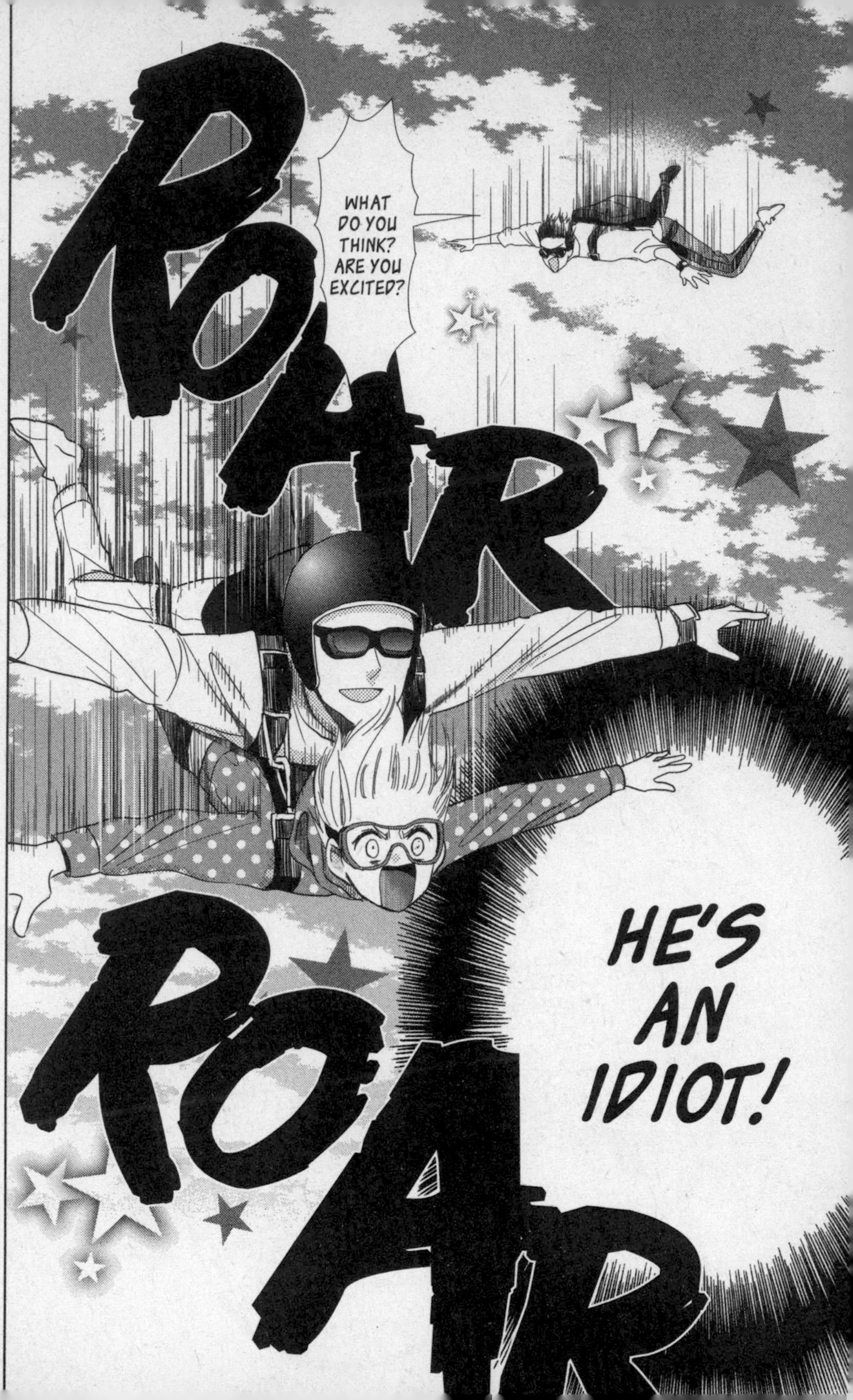
WHAT DO YOU THINK? ARE YOU EXCITED?
ROAR
HE'S AN IDIOT!
ROAR

Chapter 57

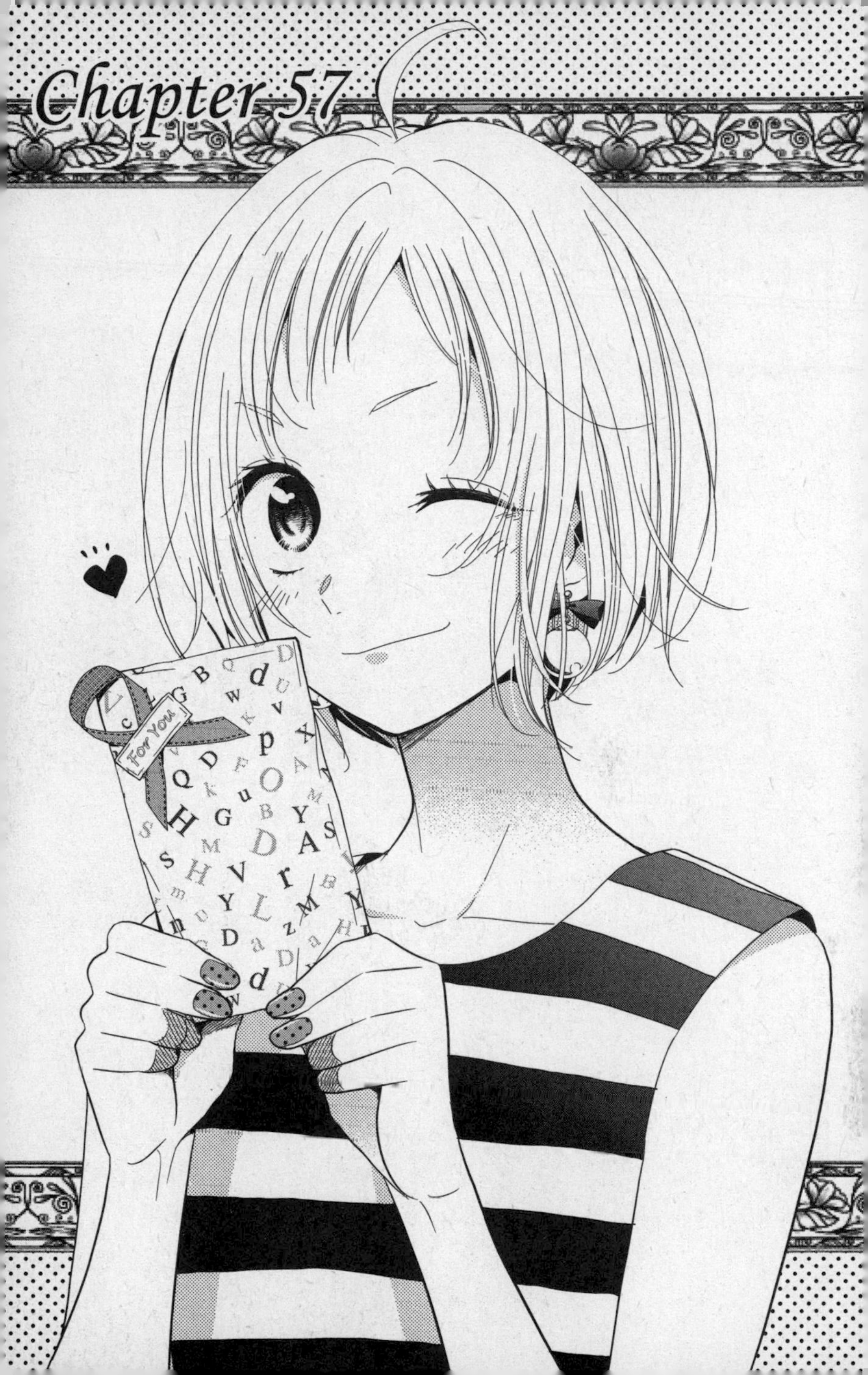
For You

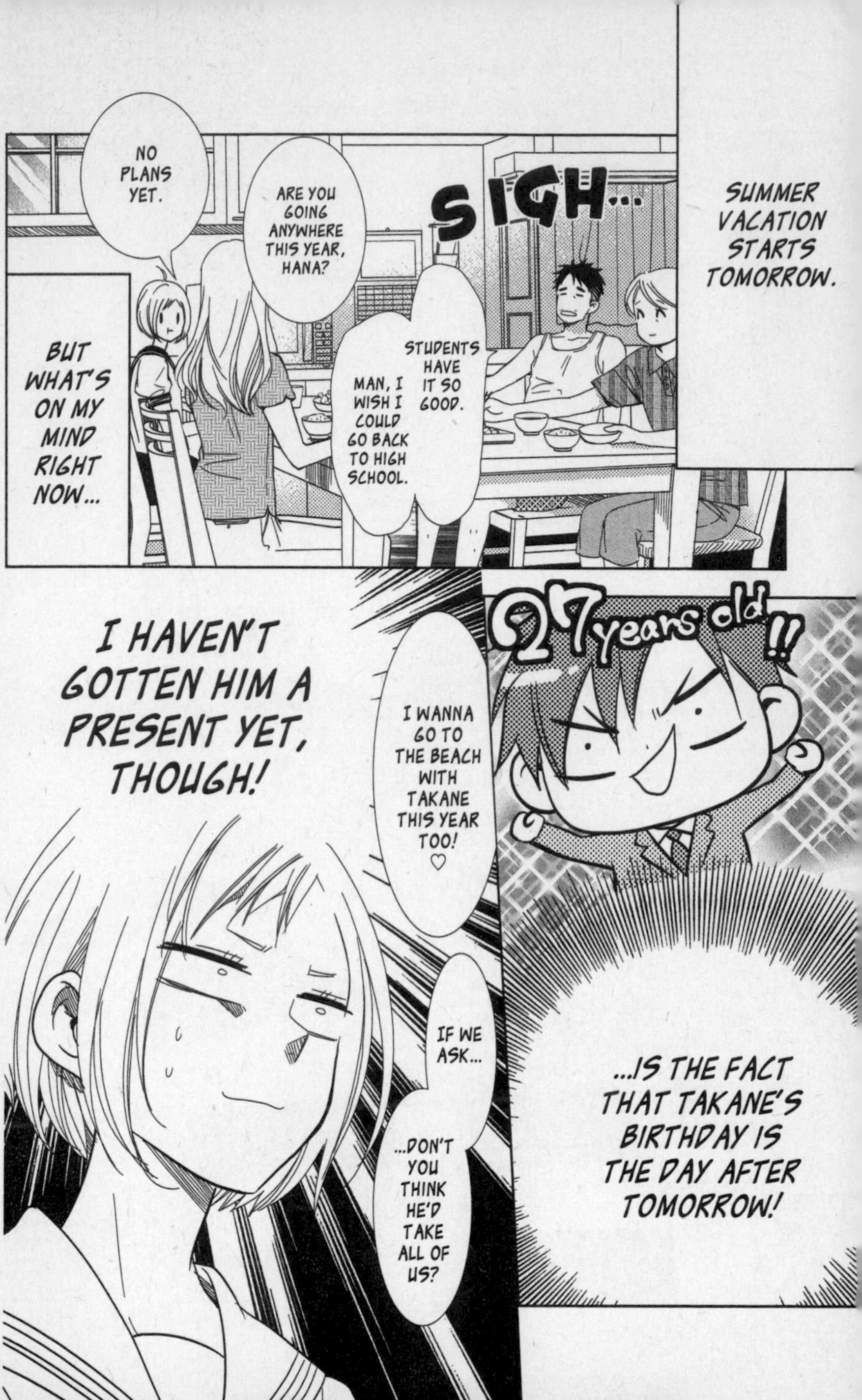
SUMMER VACATION STARTS TOMORROW.
SIGH...
ARE YOU GOING ANYWHERE THIS YEAR, HANA?
NO PLANS YET.
STUDENTS HAVE IT SO GOOD.
MAN, I WISH I COULD GO BACK TO HIGH SCHOOL.
BUT WHAT'S ON MY MIND RIGHT NOW...
27 years old!!
...IS THE FACT THAT TAKANE'S BIRTHDAY IS THE DAY AFTER TOMORROW!
I WANNA GO TO THE BEACH WITH TAKANE THIS YEAR TOO! ♡
IF WE ASK...
...DON'T YOU THINK HE'D TAKE ALL OF US?
I HAVEN'T GOTTEN HIM A PRESENT YET, THOUGH!

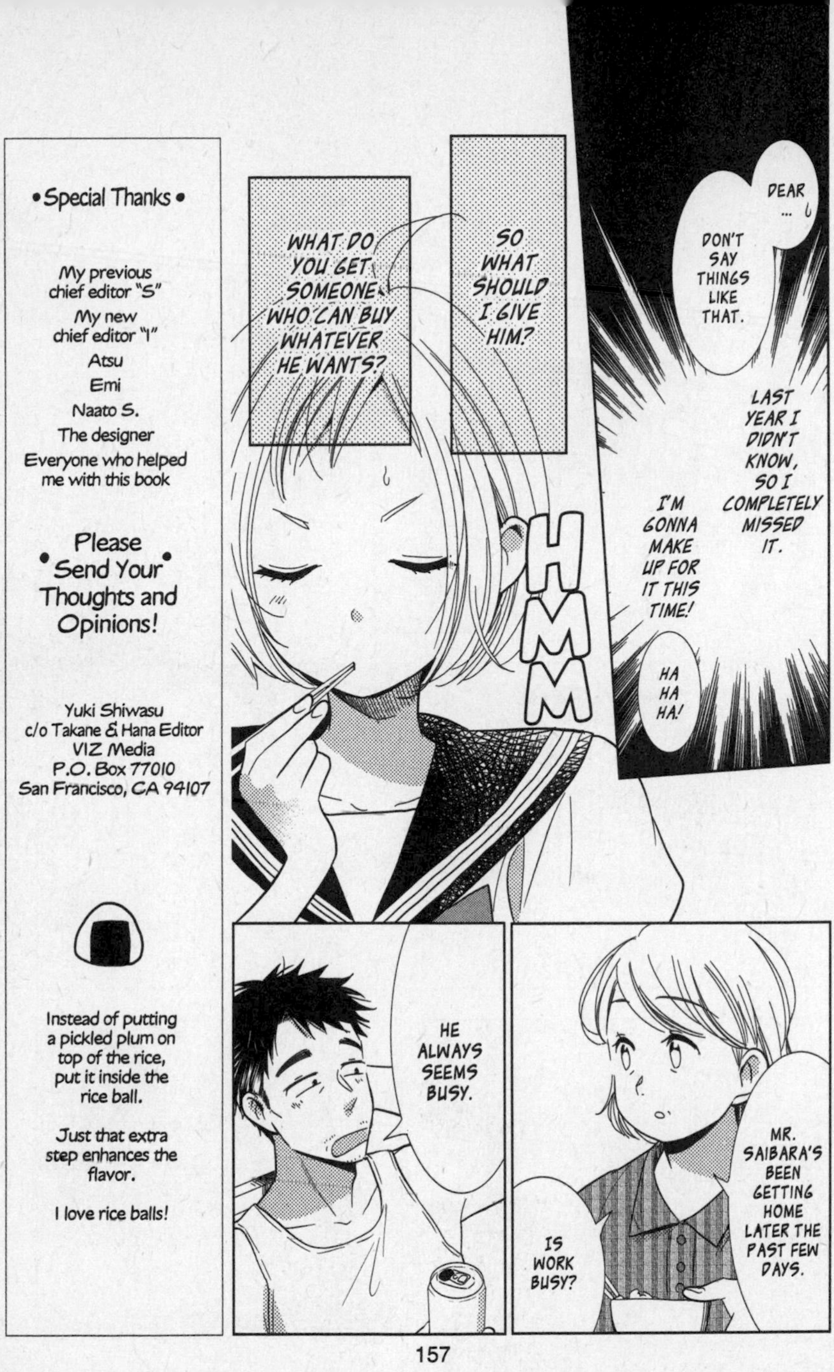
DEAR ... DON'T SAY THINGS LIKE THAT.
LAST YEAR I DIDN'T KNOW, SO I COMPLETELY MISSED IT.
I'M GONNA MAKE UP FOR IT THIS TIME!
HA HA HA!
SO WHAT SHOULD I GIVE HIM?
WHAT DO YOU GET SOMEONE WHO CAN BUY WHATEVER HE WANTS?
HMMM
MR. SAIBARA'S BEEN GETTING HOME LATER THE PAST FEW DAYS.
IS WORK BUSY?
HE ALWAYS SEEMS BUSY.

• Special Thanks •

My previous chief editor "S"
My new chief editor "I"
Atsu
Emi
Naato S.
The designer
Everyone who helped me with this book

• Please Send Your Thoughts and Opinions! •

Yuki Shiwasu
c/o Takane & Hana Editor
VIZ Media
P.O. Box 77010
San Francisco, CA 94107

Instead of putting a pickled plum on top of the rice, put it inside the rice ball.

Just that extra step enhances the flavor.

I love rice balls!

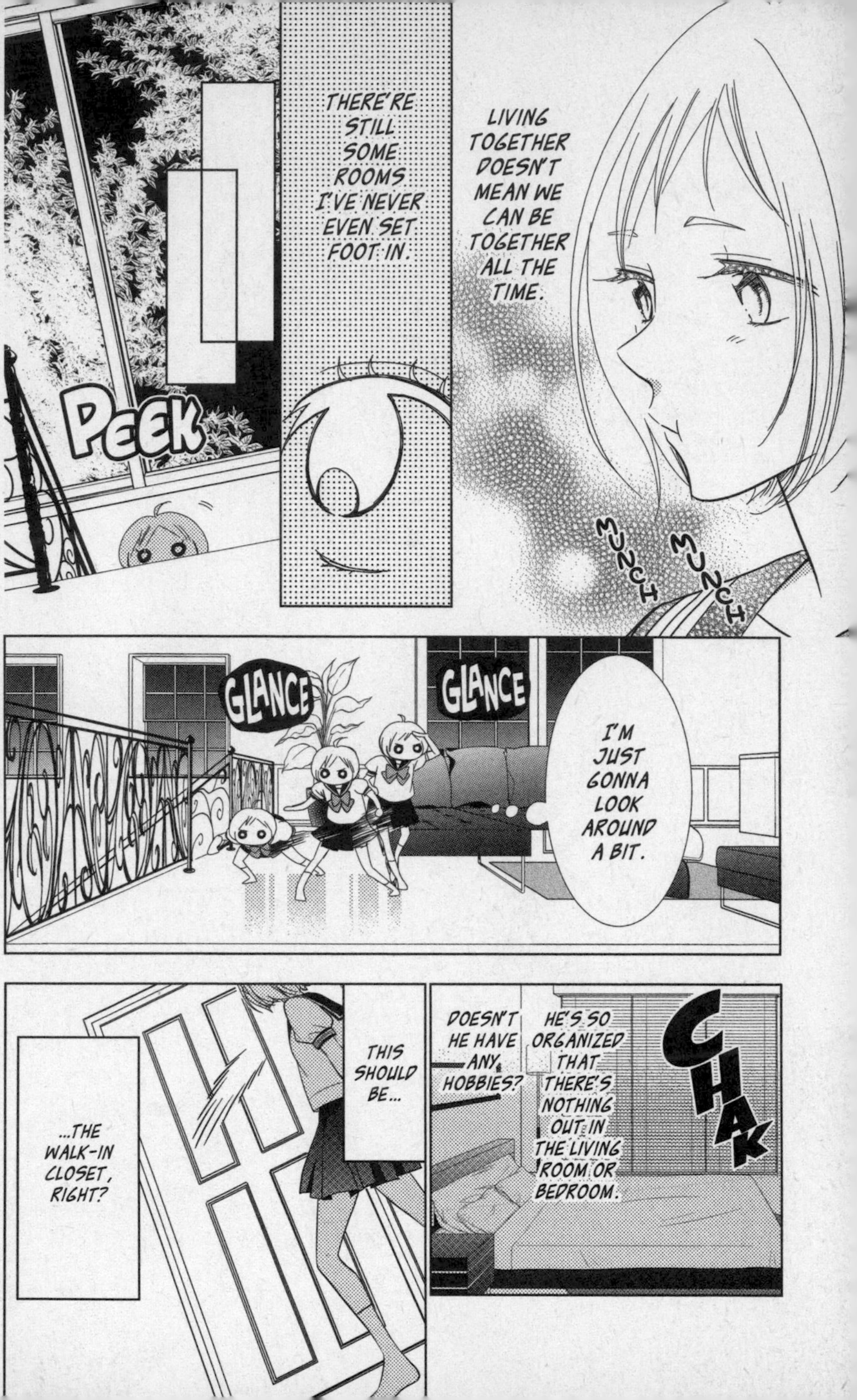
LIVING TOGETHER DOESN'T MEAN WE CAN BE TOGETHER ALL THE TIME.
MUNCH
MUNCH
THERE'RE STILL SOME ROOMS I'VE NEVER EVEN SET FOOT IN.
PEEK
GLANCE
GLANCE
I'M JUST GONNA LOOK AROUND A BIT.
CHAK
HE'S SO ORGANIZED THAT THERE'S NOTHING OUT IN THE LIVING ROOM OR BEDROOM.
DOESN'T HE HAVE ANY HOBBIES?
THIS SHOULD BE...
...THE WALK-IN CLOSET, RIGHT?

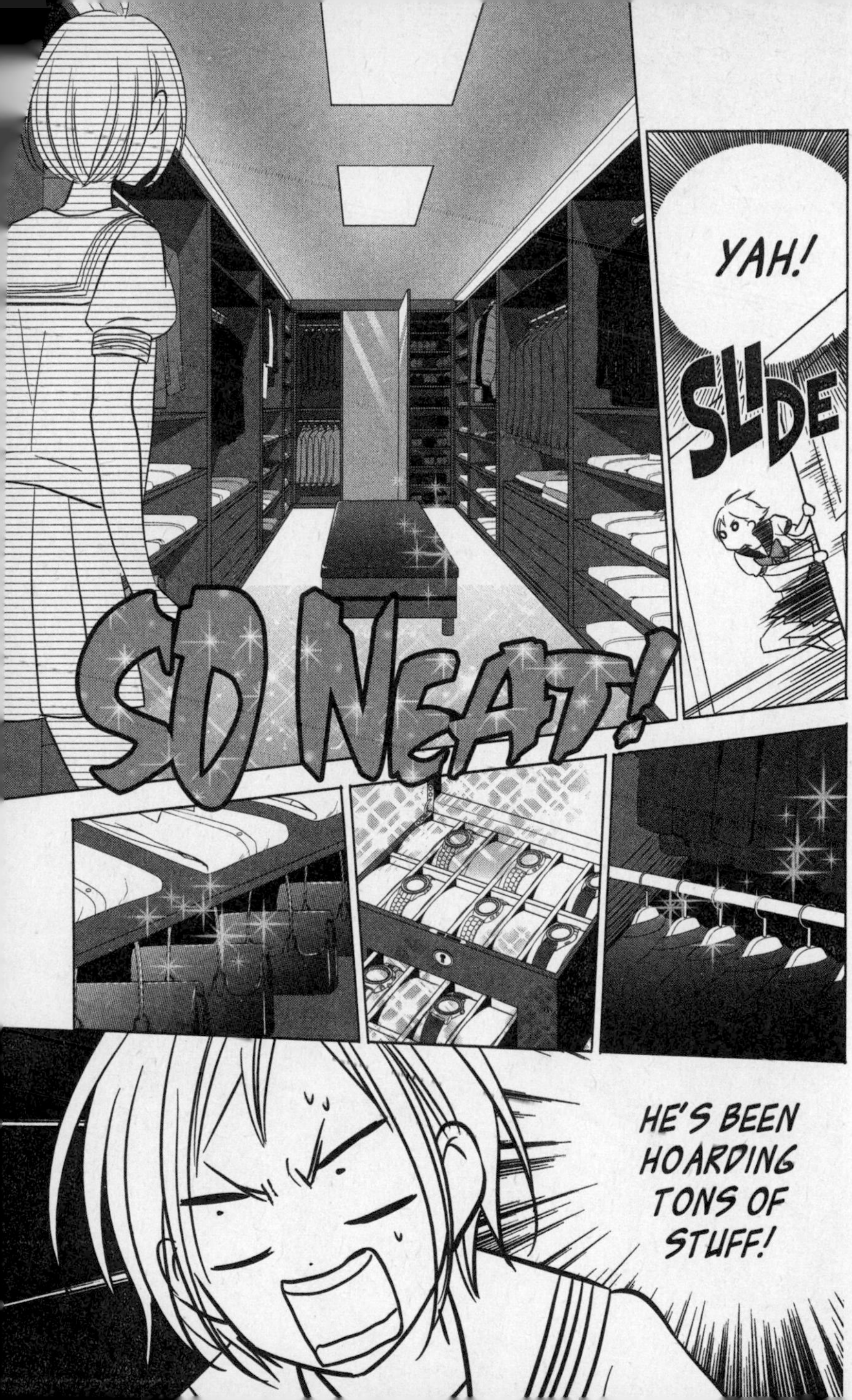
YAH!
SLIDE
SO NEAT!
HE'S BEEN HOARDING TONS OF STUFF!

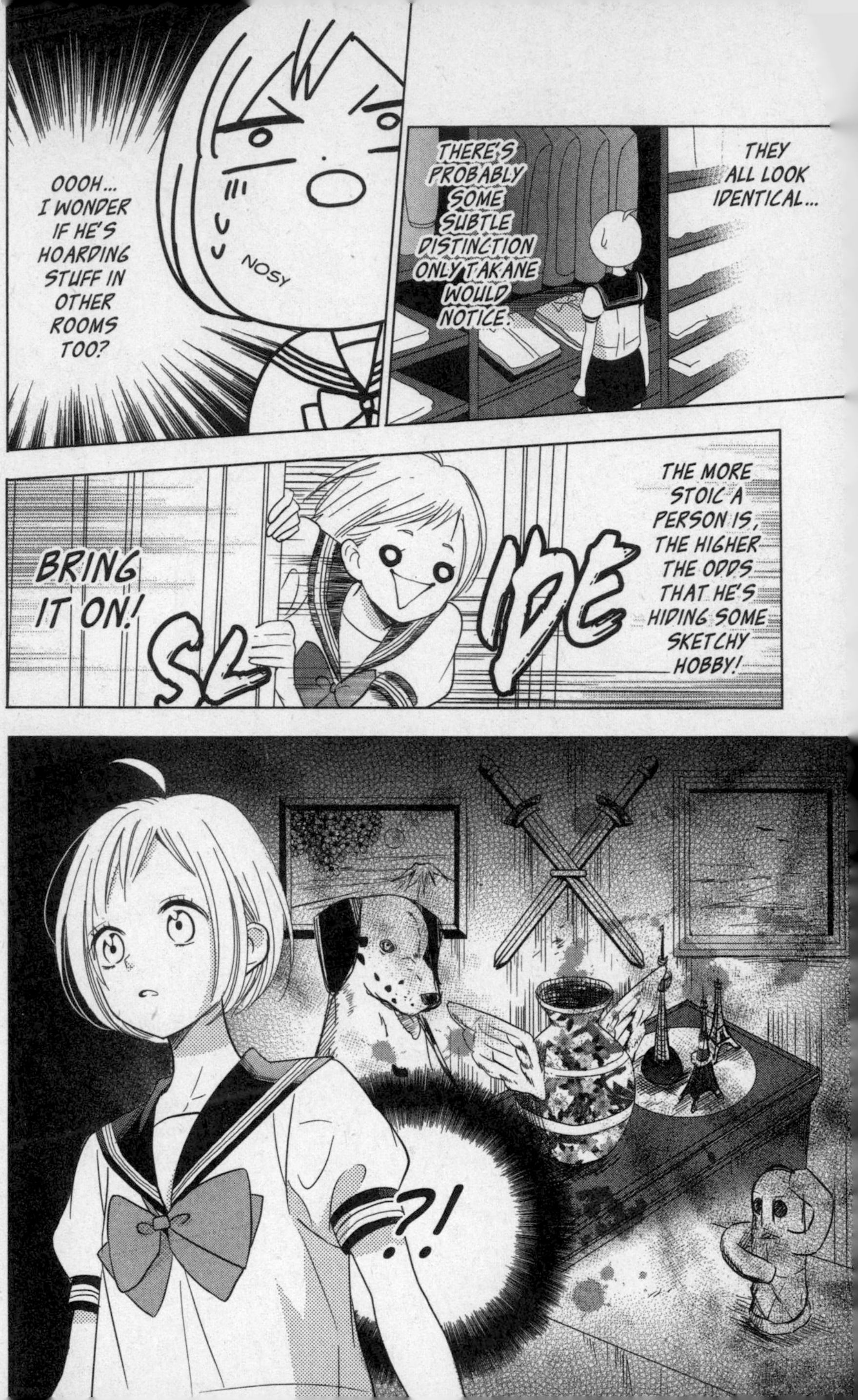
THEY ALL LOOK IDENTICAL...
THERE'S PROBABLY SOME SUBTLE DISTINCTION ONLY TAKANE WOULD NOTICE.
OOOH... I WONDER IF HE'S HOARDING STUFF IN OTHER ROOMS TOO?
NOSY
THE MORE STOIC A PERSON IS, THE HIGHER THE ODDS THAT HE'S HIDING SOME SKETCHY HOBBY!
SLIDE
BRING IT ON!
?!

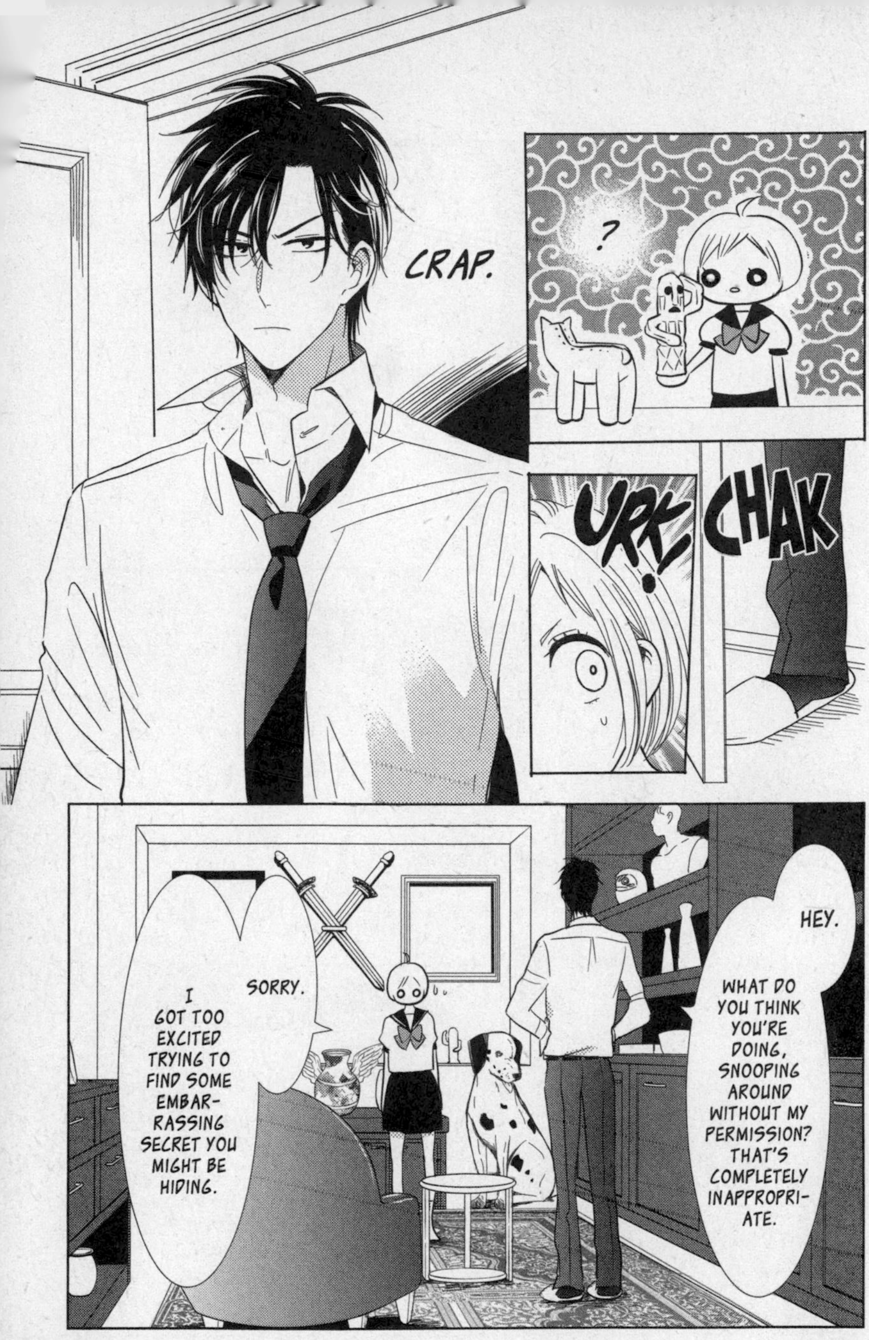
?
CHAK
URK!
CRAP.
HEY.
WHAT DO YOU THINK YOU'RE DOING, SNOOPING AROUND WITHOUT MY PERMISSION? THAT'S COMPLETELY INAPPROPRIATE.
SORRY.
I GOT TOO EXCITED TRYING TO FIND SOME EMBARRASSING SECRET YOU MIGHT BE HIDING.

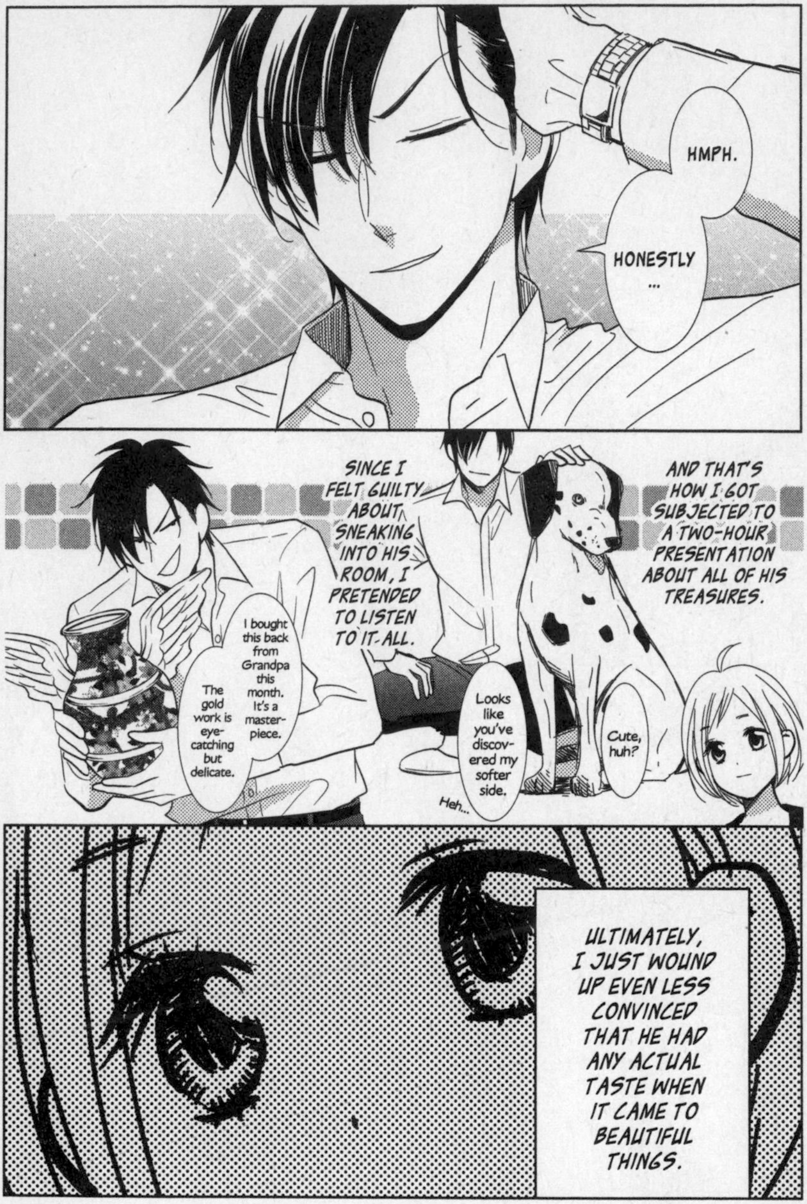
HMPH.
HONESTLY ...
AND THAT'S HOW I GOT SUBJECTED TO A TWO-HOUR PRESENTATION ABOUT ALL OF HIS TREASURES.
SINCE I FELT GUILTY ABOUT SNEAKING INTO HIS ROOM, I PRETENDED TO LISTEN TO IT ALL.
Cute, huh?
Looks like you've discovered my softer side.
Heh...
I bought this back from Grandpa this month. It's a masterpiece.
The gold work is eye-catching but delicate.
ULTIMATELY, I JUST WOUND UP EVEN LESS CONVINCED THAT HE HAD ANY ACTUAL TASTE WHEN IT CAME TO BEAUTIFUL THINGS.

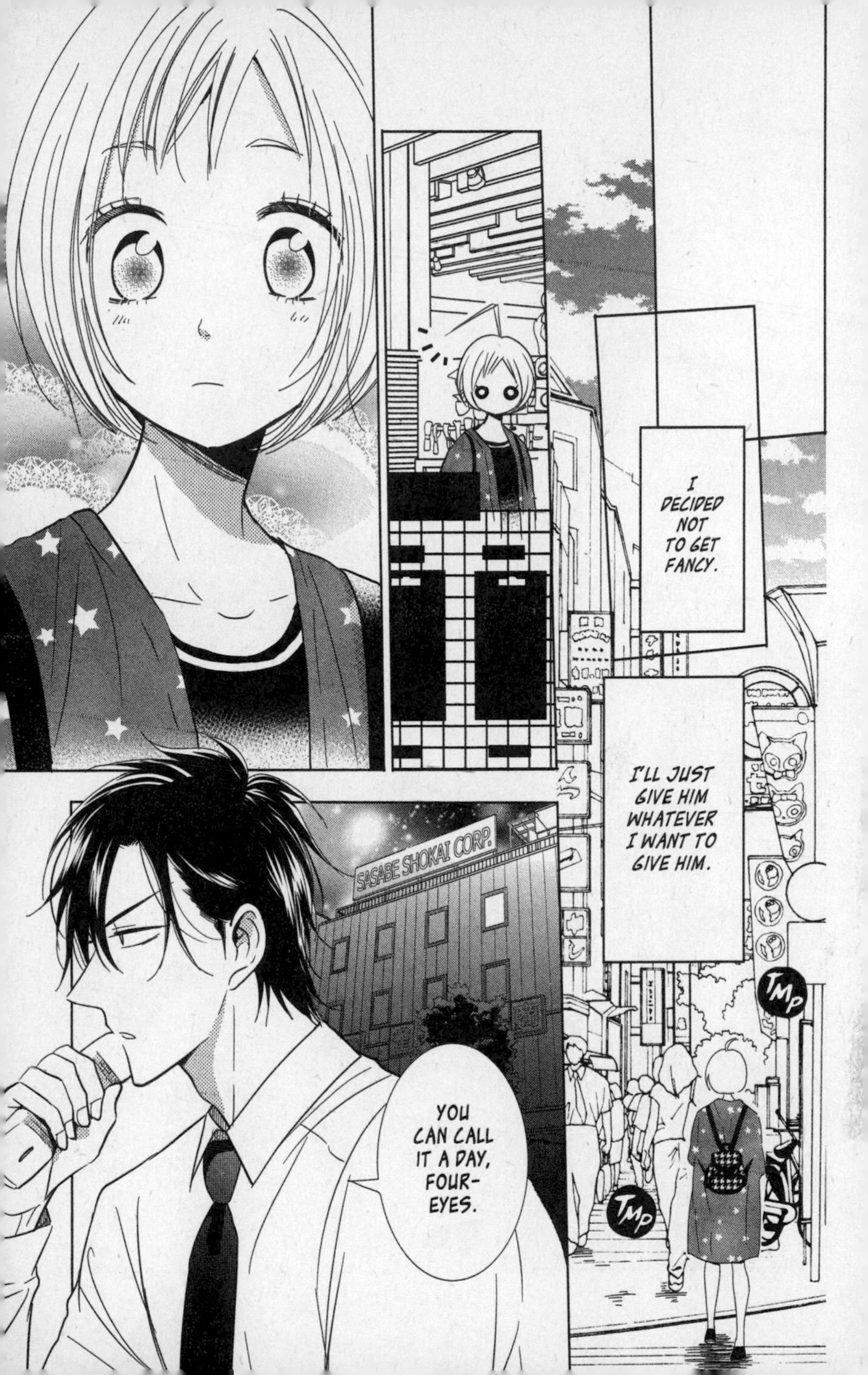
I DECIDED NOT TO GET FANCY.
I'LL JUST GIVE HIM WHATEVER I WANT TO GIVE HIM.
TMP
TMP
SASABE SHOKAI CORP.
YOU CAN CALL IT A DAY, FOUR-EYES.

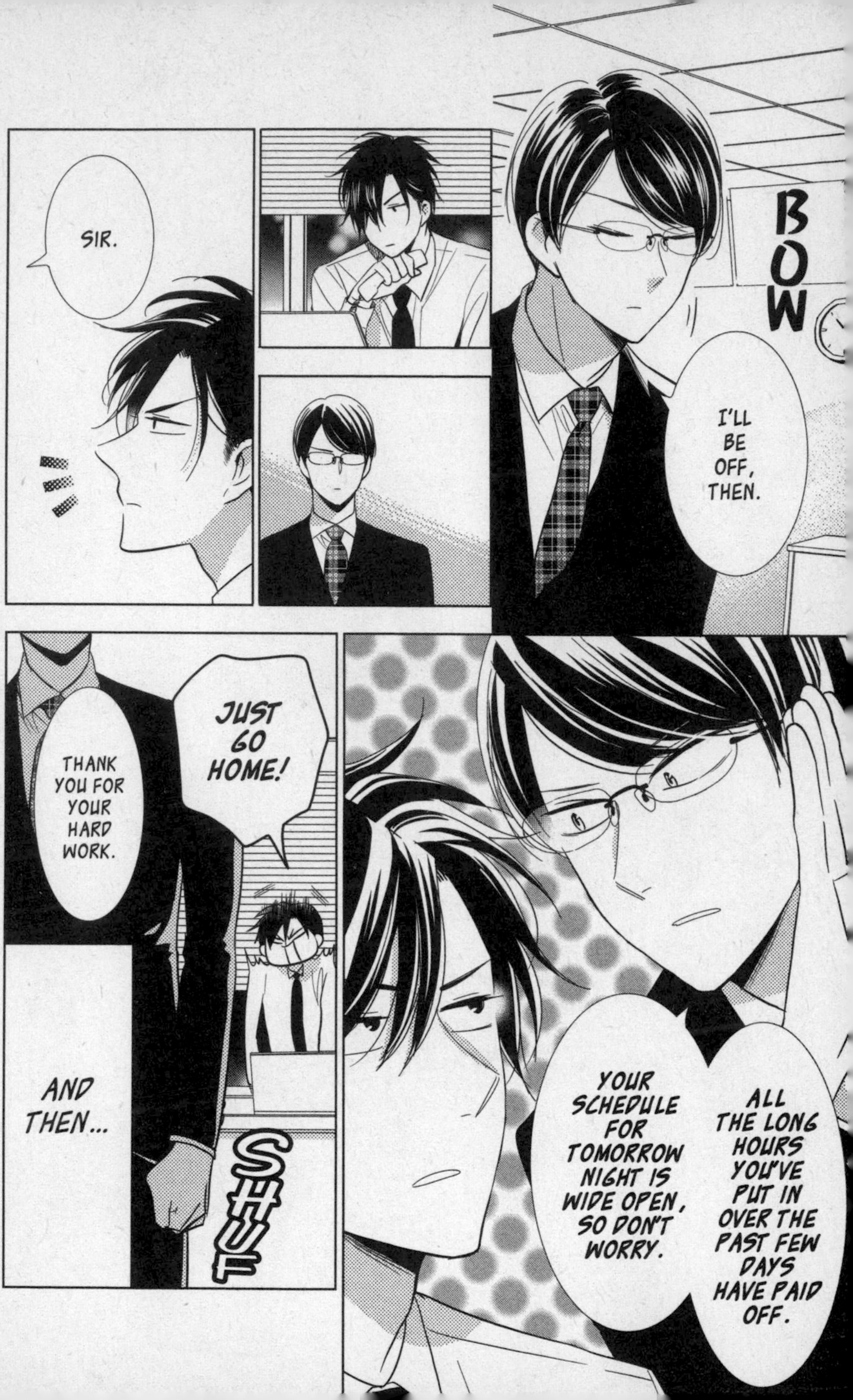
BOW
I'LL BE OFF, THEN.
SIR.
ALL THE LONG HOURS YOU'VE PUT IN OVER THE PAST FEW DAYS HAVE PAID OFF.
YOUR SCHEDULE FOR TOMORROW NIGHT IS WIDE OPEN, SO DON'T WORRY.
JUST GO HOME!
THANK YOU FOR YOUR HARD WORK.
SHUF
AND THEN...

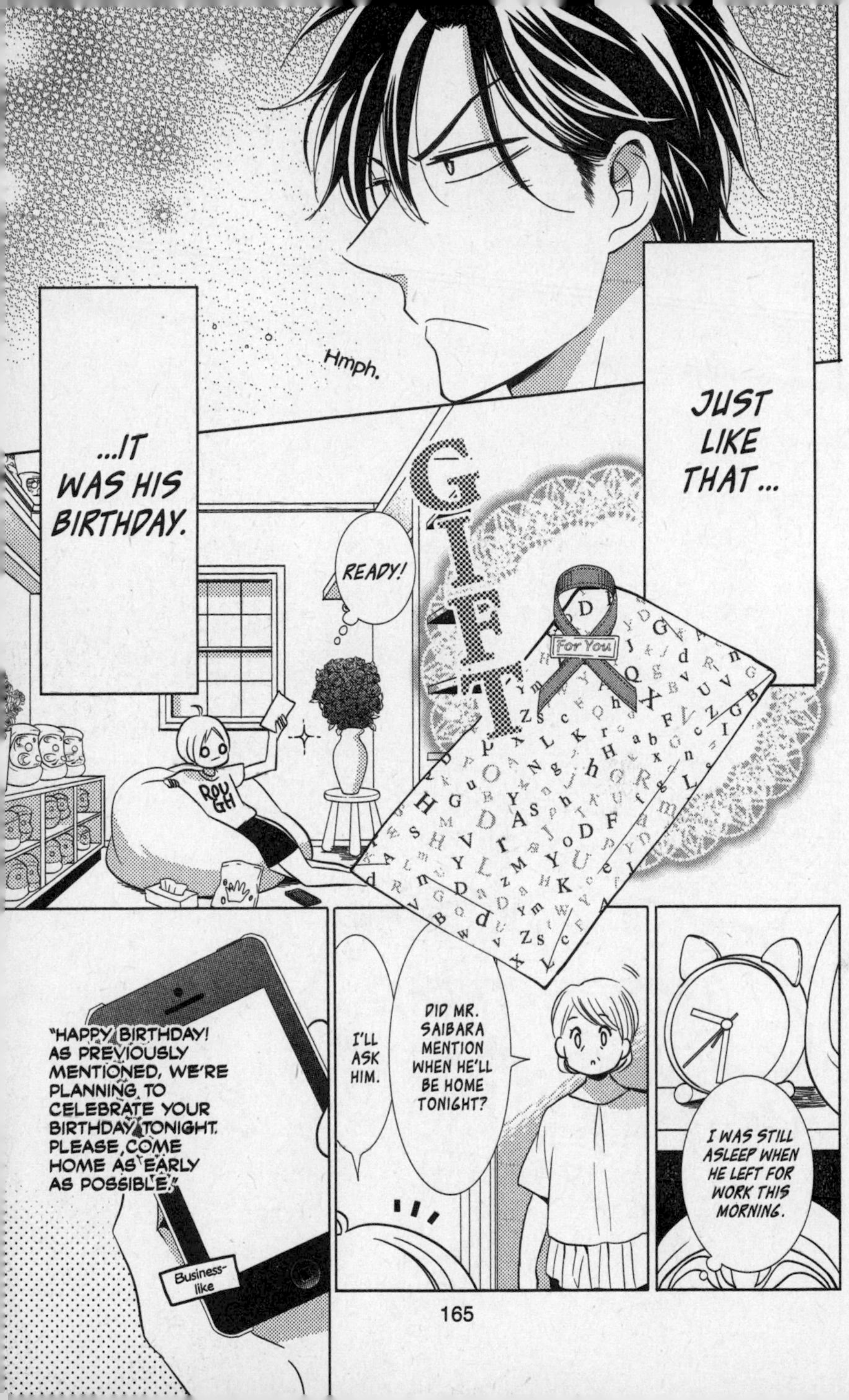
JUST LIKE THAT...
Hmph.
...IT WAS HIS BIRTHDAY.
GIFT
For You
READY!
I WAS STILL ASLEEP WHEN HE LEFT FOR WORK THIS MORNING.
DID MR. SAIBARA MENTION WHEN HE'LL BE HOME TONIGHT?
I'LL ASK HIM.
"HAPPY BIRTHDAY! AS PREVIOUSLY MENTIONED, WE'RE PLANNING TO CELEBRATE YOUR BIRTHDAY TONIGHT. PLEASE COME HOME AS EARLY AS POSSIBLE."
Business-like

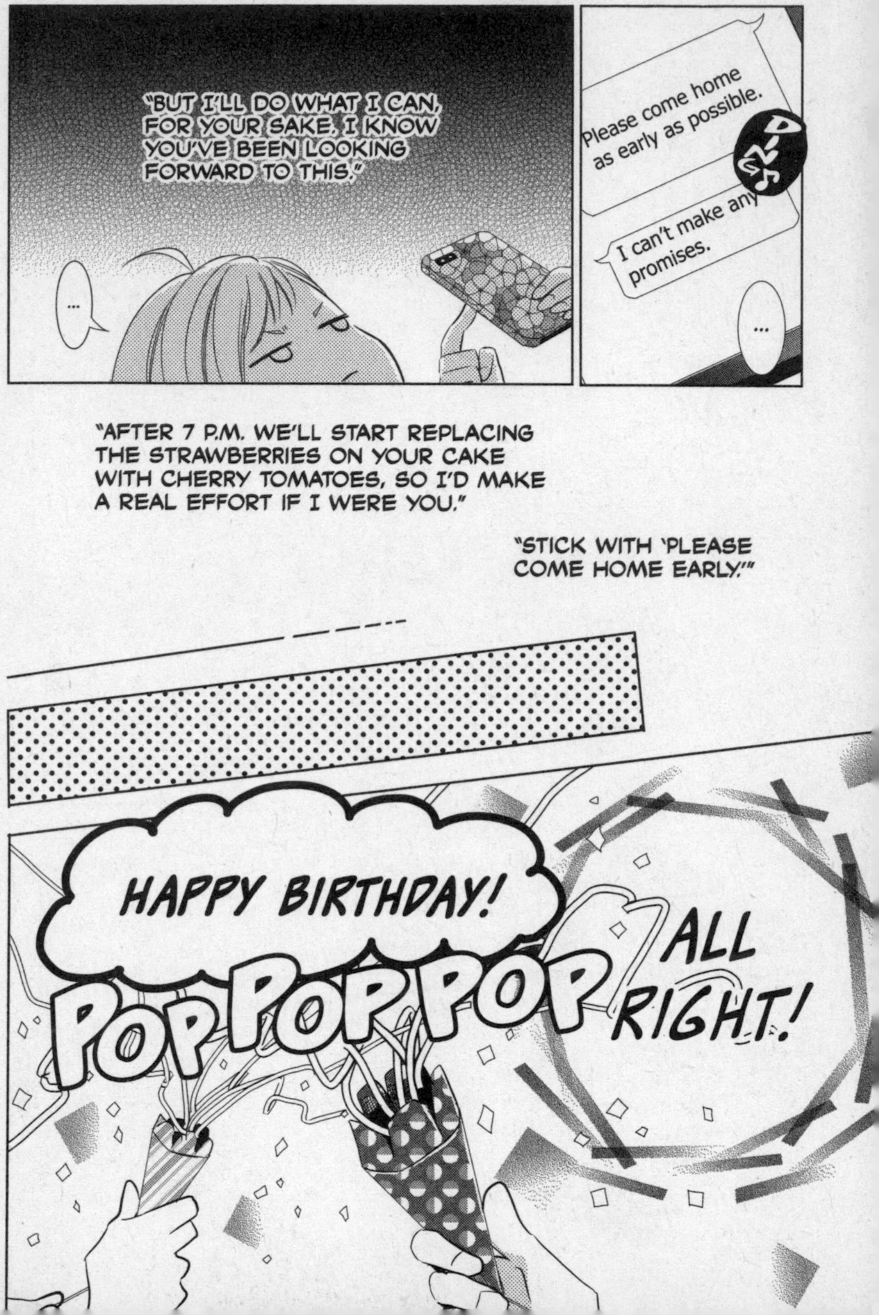
Please come home as early as possible.
DING♪
I can't make any promises.
...
"BUT I'LL DO WHAT I CAN, FOR YOUR SAKE. I KNOW YOU'VE BEEN LOOKING FORWARD TO THIS."
...
"AFTER 7 P.M. WE'LL START REPLACING THE STRAWBERRIES ON YOUR CAKE WITH CHERRY TOMATOES, SO I'D MAKE A REAL EFFORT IF I WERE YOU."
"STICK WITH 'PLEASE COME HOME EARLY.'"
ALL RIGHT!
HAPPY BIRTHDAY!
POP POP POP

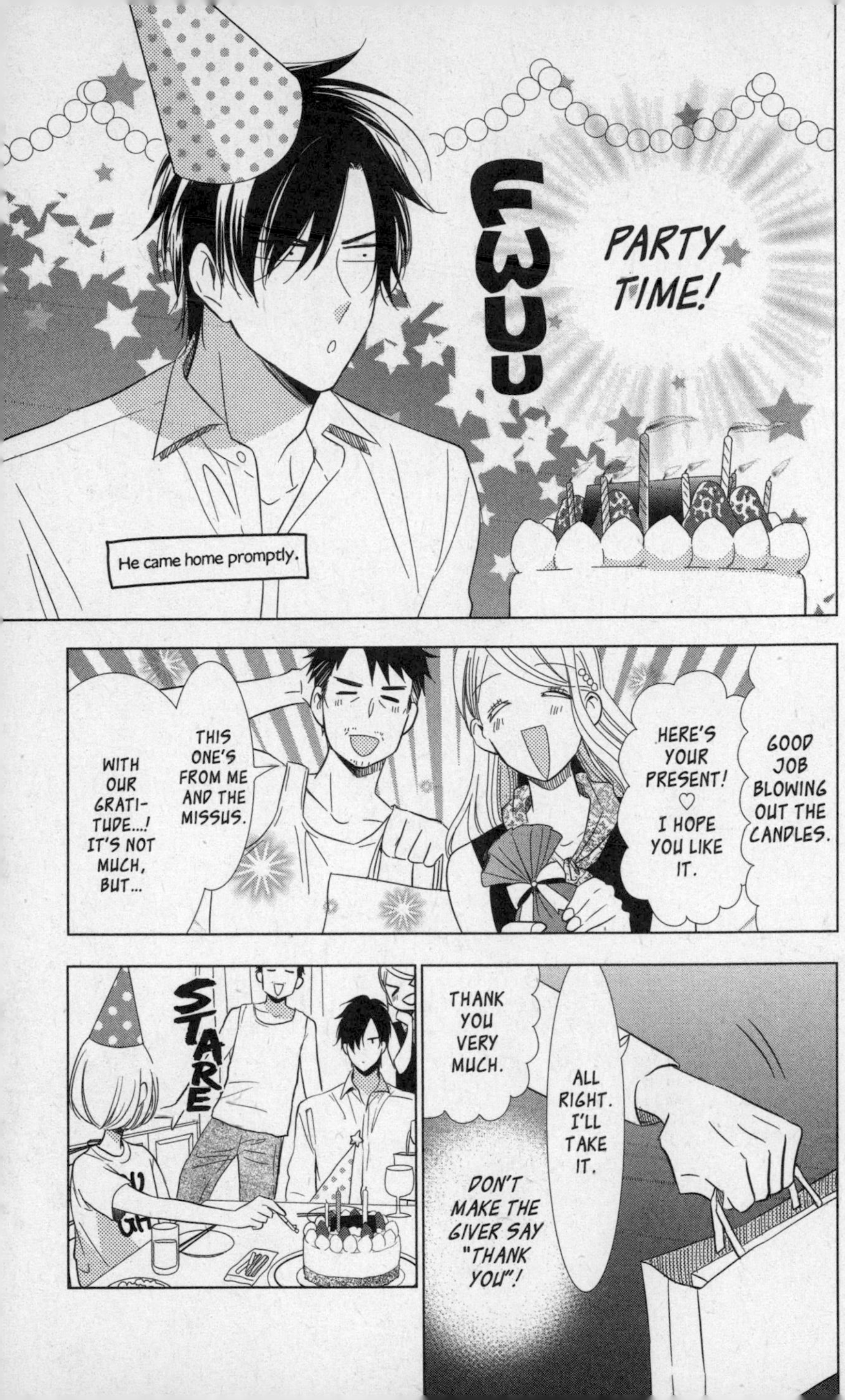
PARTY TIME!
FWUU
He came home promptly.
GOOD JOB BLOWING OUT THE CANDLES.
HERE'S YOUR PRESENT! ♡ I HOPE YOU LIKE IT.
THIS ONE'S FROM ME AND THE MISSUS.
WITH OUR GRATITUDE...! IT'S NOT MUCH, BUT...
ALL RIGHT. I'LL TAKE IT.
THANK YOU VERY MUCH.
DON'T MAKE THE GIVER SAY "THANK YOU"!
STARE

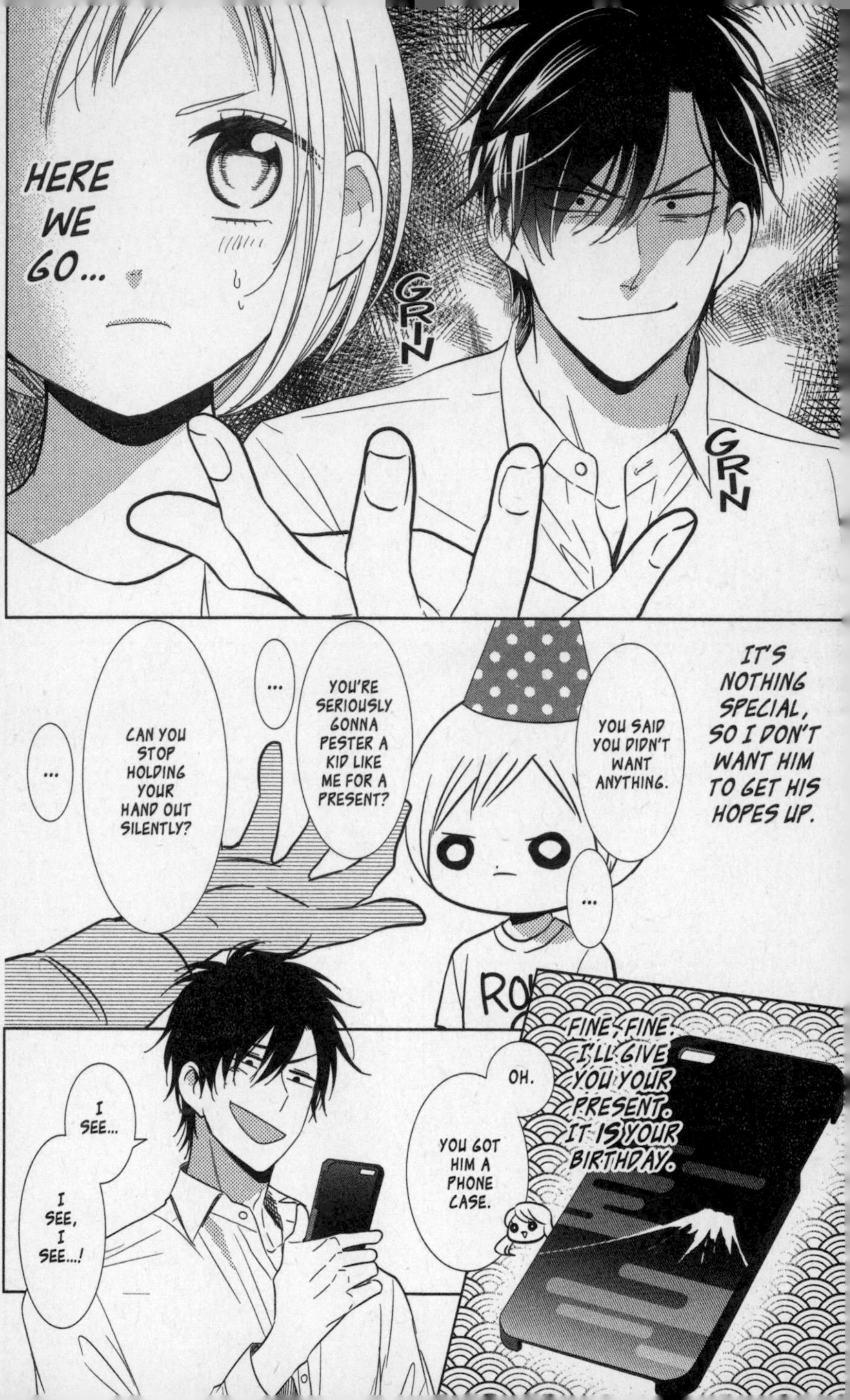
GRIN
GRIN
HERE WE GO...
IT'S NOTHING SPECIAL, SO I DON'T WANT HIM TO GET HIS HOPES UP.
YOU SAID YOU DIDN'T WANT ANYTHING.
...
YOU'RE SERIOUSLY GONNA PESTER A KID LIKE ME FOR A PRESENT?
...
CAN YOU STOP HOLDING YOUR HAND OUT SILENTLY?
...
FINE, FINE. I'LL GIVE YOU YOUR PRESENT. IT IS YOUR BIRTHDAY.
OH.
YOU GOT HIM A PHONE CASE.
I SEE...
I SEE, I SEE...!

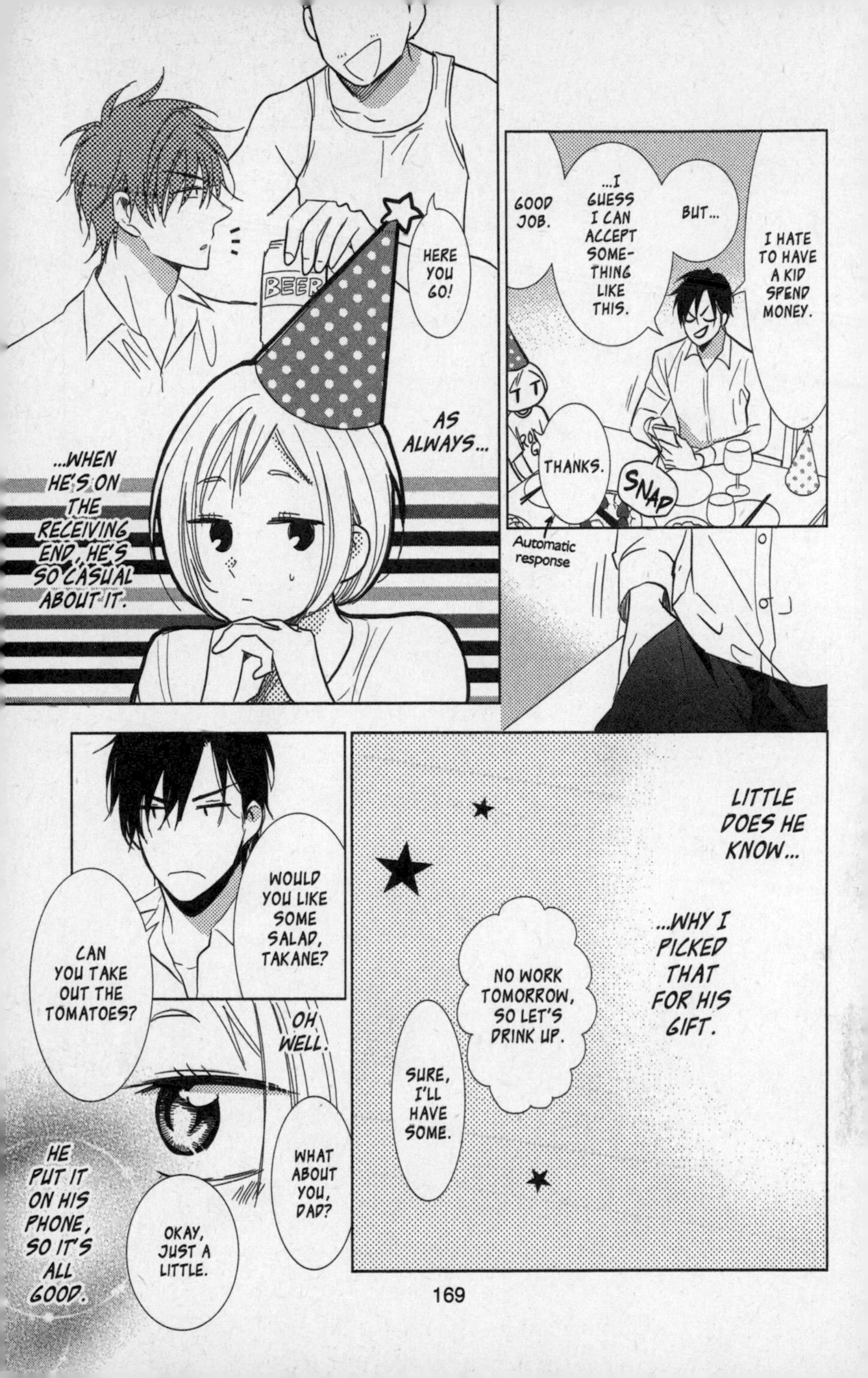
I HATE TO HAVE A KID SPEND MONEY.
BUT...
...I GUESS I CAN ACCEPT SOME-THING LIKE THIS.
GOOD JOB.
THANKS.
SNAP
Automatic response
HERE YOU GO!
BEER
AS ALWAYS...
...WHEN HE'S ON THE RECEIVING END, HE'S SO CASUAL ABOUT IT.
LITTLE DOES HE KNOW...
...WHY I PICKED THAT FOR HIS GIFT.
NO WORK TOMORROW, SO LET'S DRINK UP.
SURE, I'LL HAVE SOME.
WOULD YOU LIKE SOME SALAD, TAKANE?
CAN YOU TAKE OUT THE TOMATOES?
OH WELL.
WHAT ABOUT YOU, DAD?
OKAY, JUST A LITTLE.
HE PUT IT ON HIS PHONE, SO IT'S ALL GOOD.

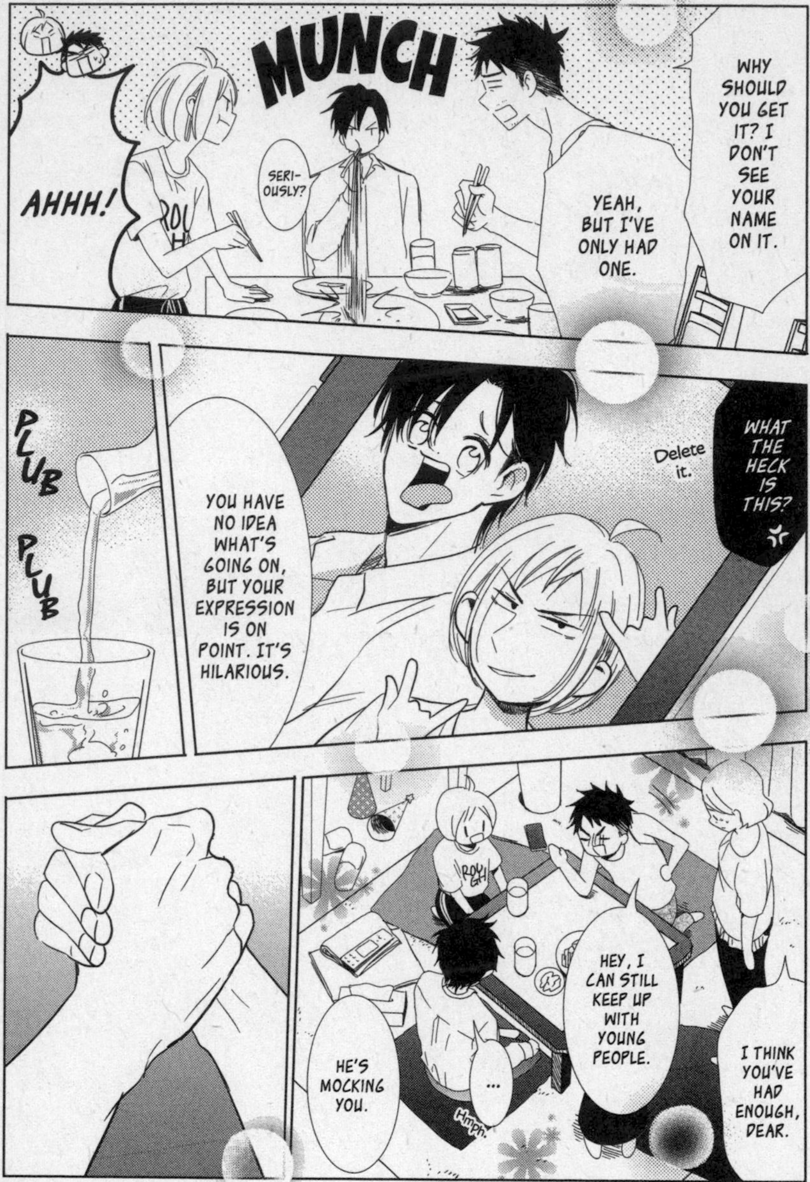
WHY SHOULD YOU GET IT? I DON'T SEE YOUR NAME ON IT.
YEAH, BUT I'VE ONLY HAD ONE.
MUNCH
SERI-OUSLY?
AHHH!
WHAT THE HECK IS THIS?
Delete it.
YOU HAVE NO IDEA WHAT'S GOING ON, BUT YOUR EXPRESSION IS ON POINT. IT'S HILARIOUS.
PLUB PLUB
I THINK YOU'VE HAD ENOUGH, DEAR.
HEY, I CAN STILL KEEP UP WITH YOUNG PEOPLE.
...
Hmph.
HE'S MOCKING YOU.

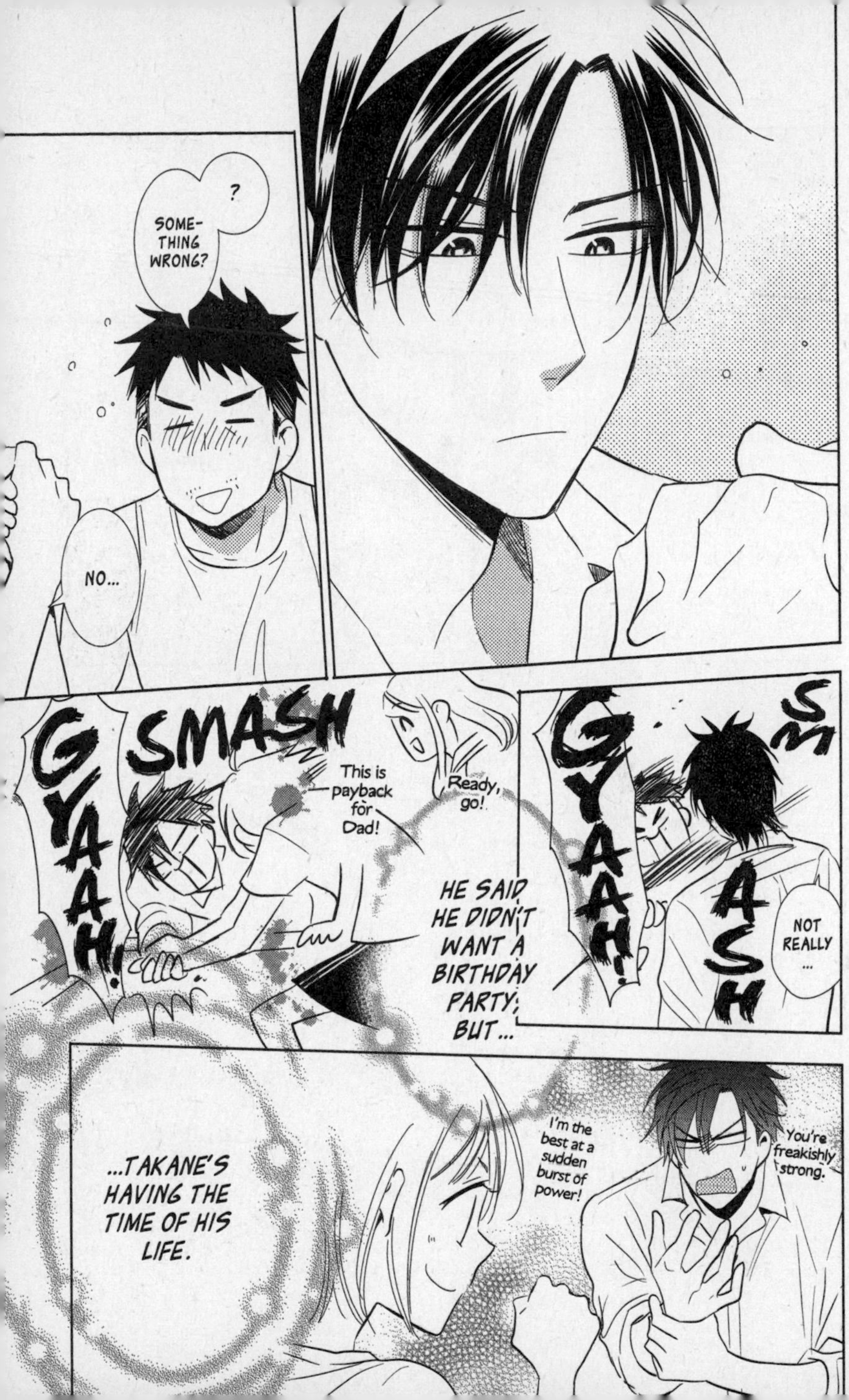
?
SOMETHING WRONG?
NO...
SMASH
NOT REALLY...
GYAAAH!
Ready, go!
SMASH
This is payback for Dad!
GYAAAH!
HE SAID HE DIDN'T WANT A BIRTHDAY PARTY, BUT...
You're freakishly strong.
I'm the best at a sudden burst of power!
...TAKANE'S HAVING THE TIME OF HIS LIFE.

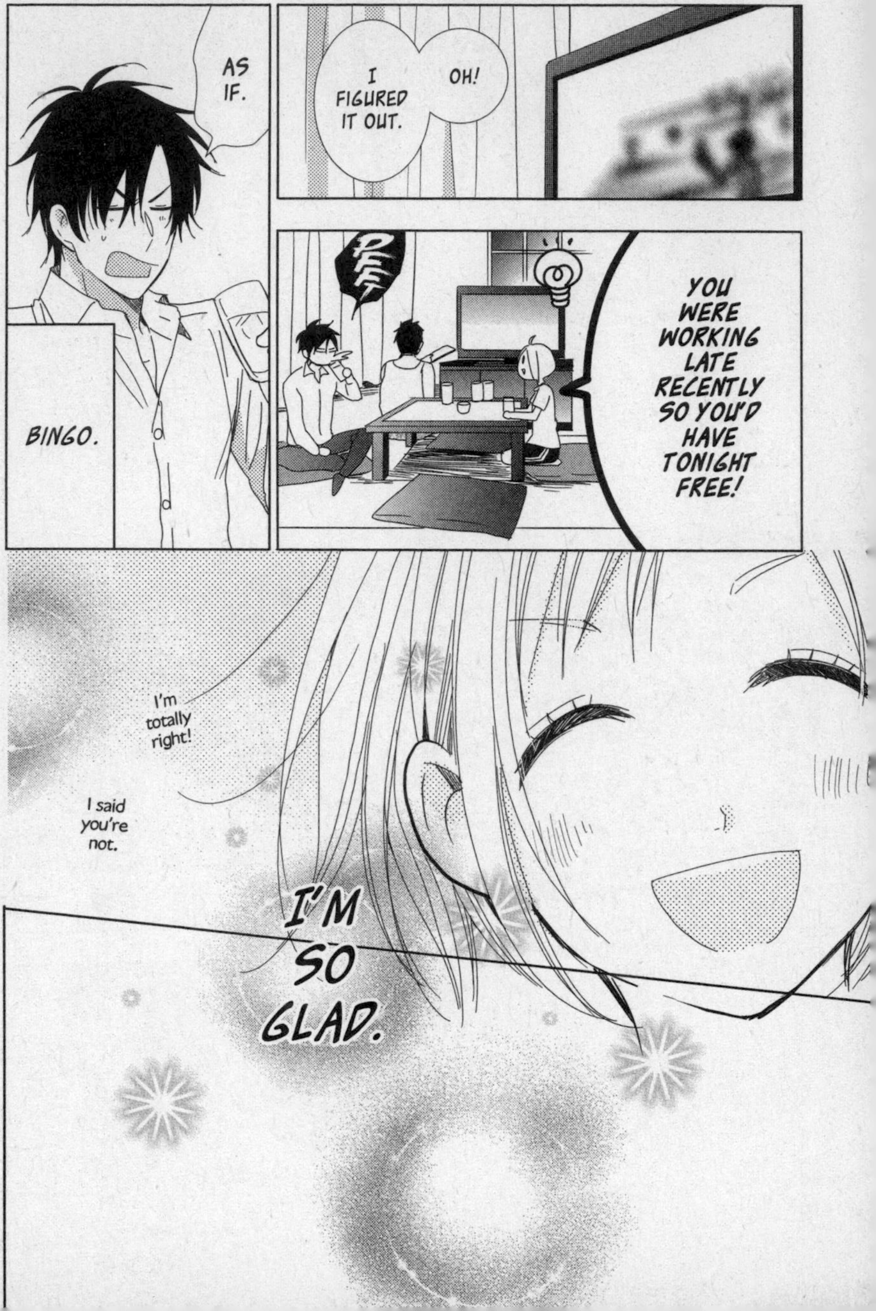
OH!
I FIGURED IT OUT.
YOU WERE WORKING LATE RECENTLY SO YOU'D HAVE TONIGHT FREE!
AS IF.
BINGO.
I'm totally right!
I said you're not.
I'M SO GLAD.

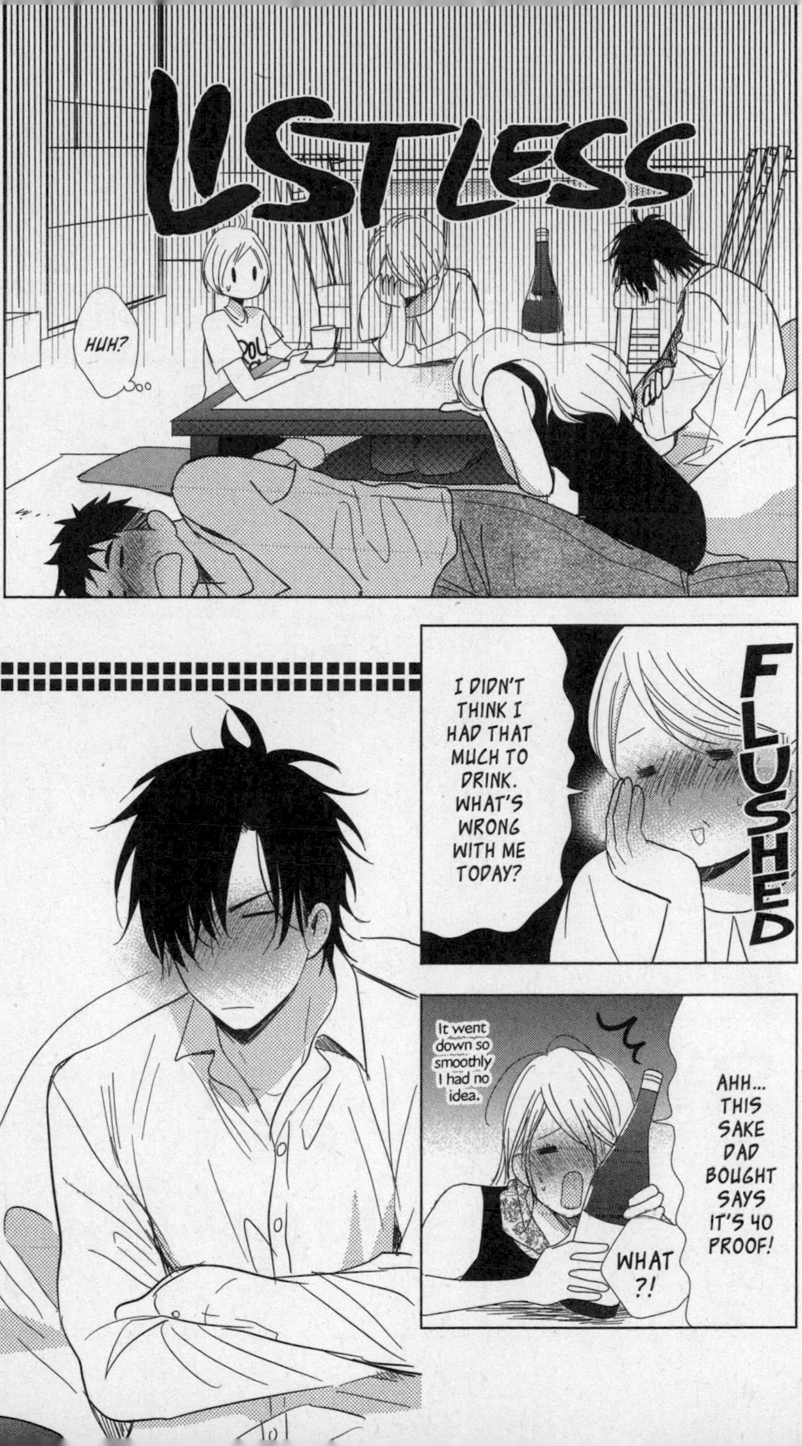
LISTLESS
HUH?
FLUSHED
I DIDN'T THINK I HAD THAT MUCH TO DRINK. WHAT'S WRONG WITH ME TODAY?
AHH... THIS SAKE DAD BOUGHT SAYS IT'S 40 PROOF!
It went down so smoothly I had no idea.
WHAT ?!

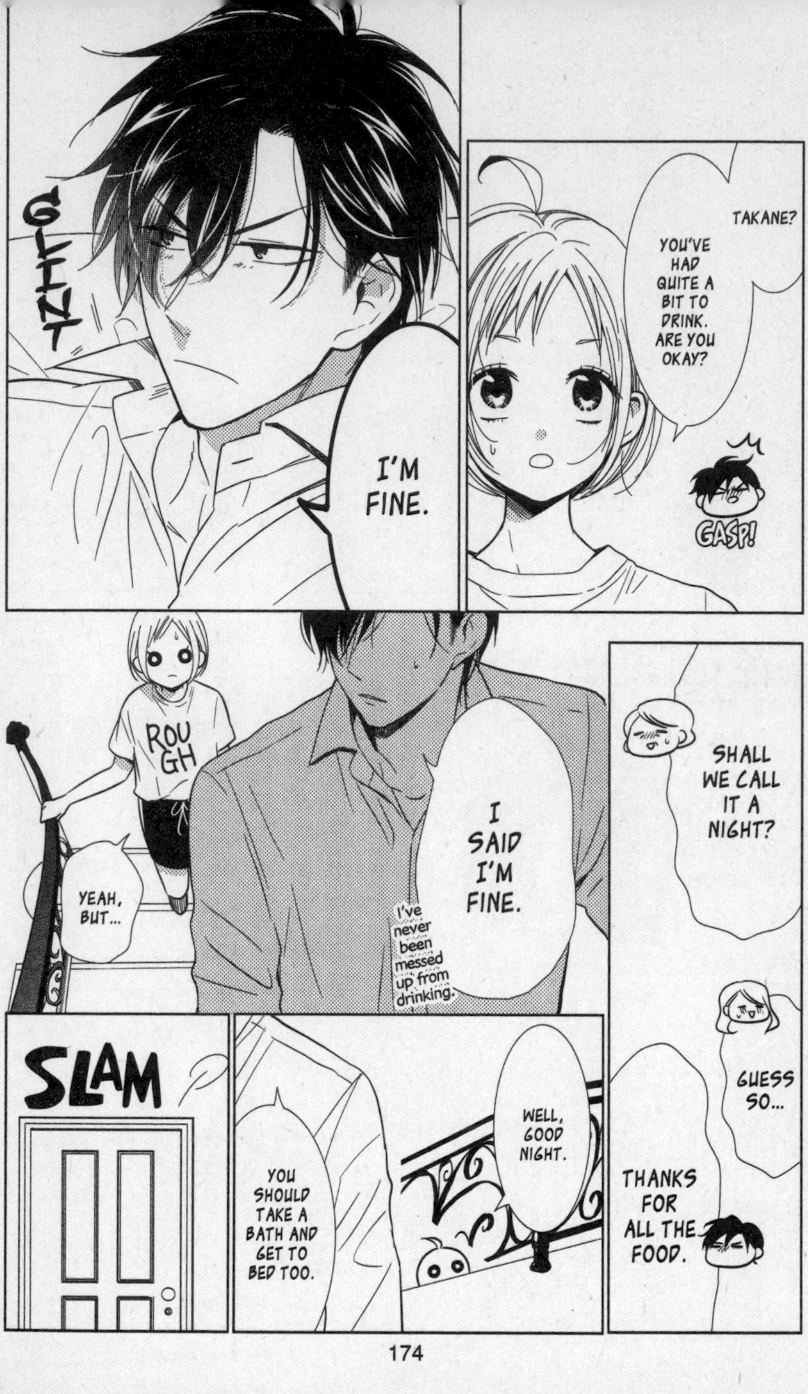
TAKANE?
YOU'VE HAD QUITE A BIT TO DRINK. ARE YOU OKAY?
GASP!
GLINT
I'M FINE.
SHALL WE CALL IT A NIGHT?
GUESS SO...
THANKS FOR ALL THE FOOD.
I SAID I'M FINE.
I've never been messed up from drinking.
ROUGH
YEAH, BUT...
WELL, GOOD NIGHT.
YOU SHOULD TAKE A BATH AND GET TO BED TOO.
SLAM

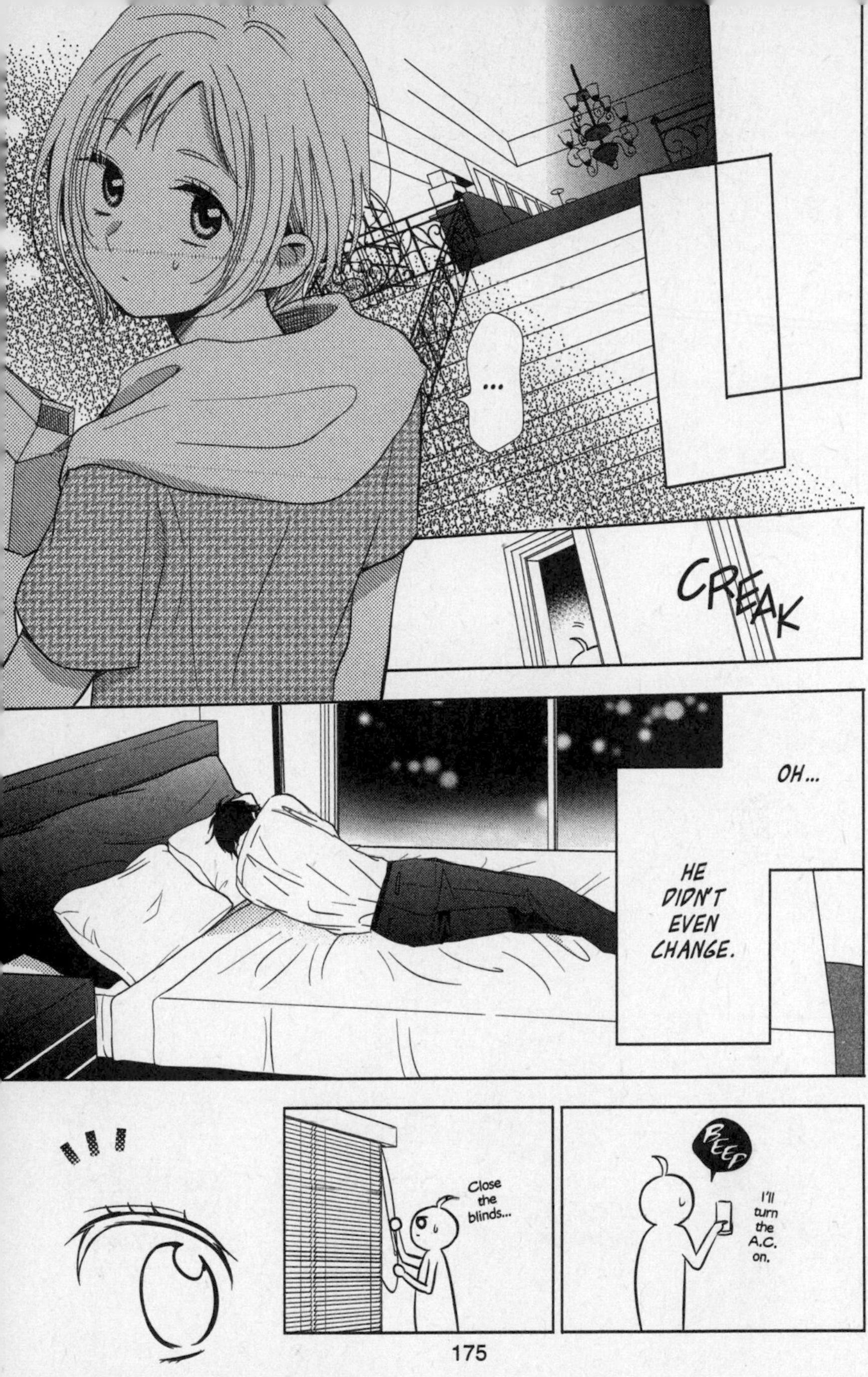
...
CREAK
OH...
HE DIDN'T EVEN CHANGE.
BEEP
I'll turn the A.C. on.
Close the blinds...
!!!

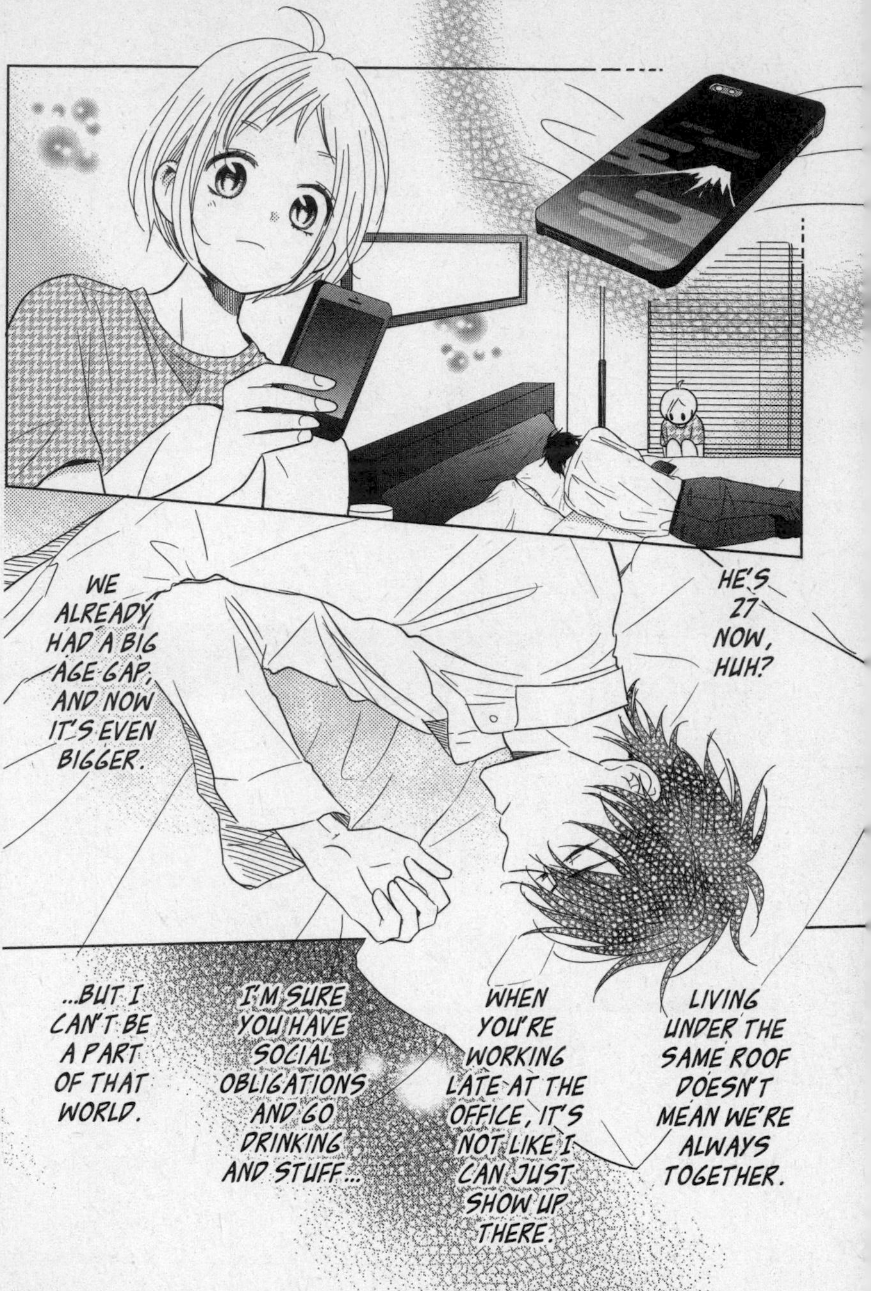
HE'S 27 NOW, HUH?
WE ALREADY HAD A BIG AGE GAP, AND NOW IT'S EVEN BIGGER.
LIVING UNDER THE SAME ROOF DOESN'T MEAN WE'RE ALWAYS TOGETHER.
WHEN YOU'RE WORKING LATE AT THE OFFICE, IT'S NOT LIKE I CAN JUST SHOW UP THERE.
I'M SURE YOU HAVE SOCIAL OBLIGATIONS AND GO DRINKING AND STUFF...
...BUT I CAN'T BE A PART OF THAT WORLD.

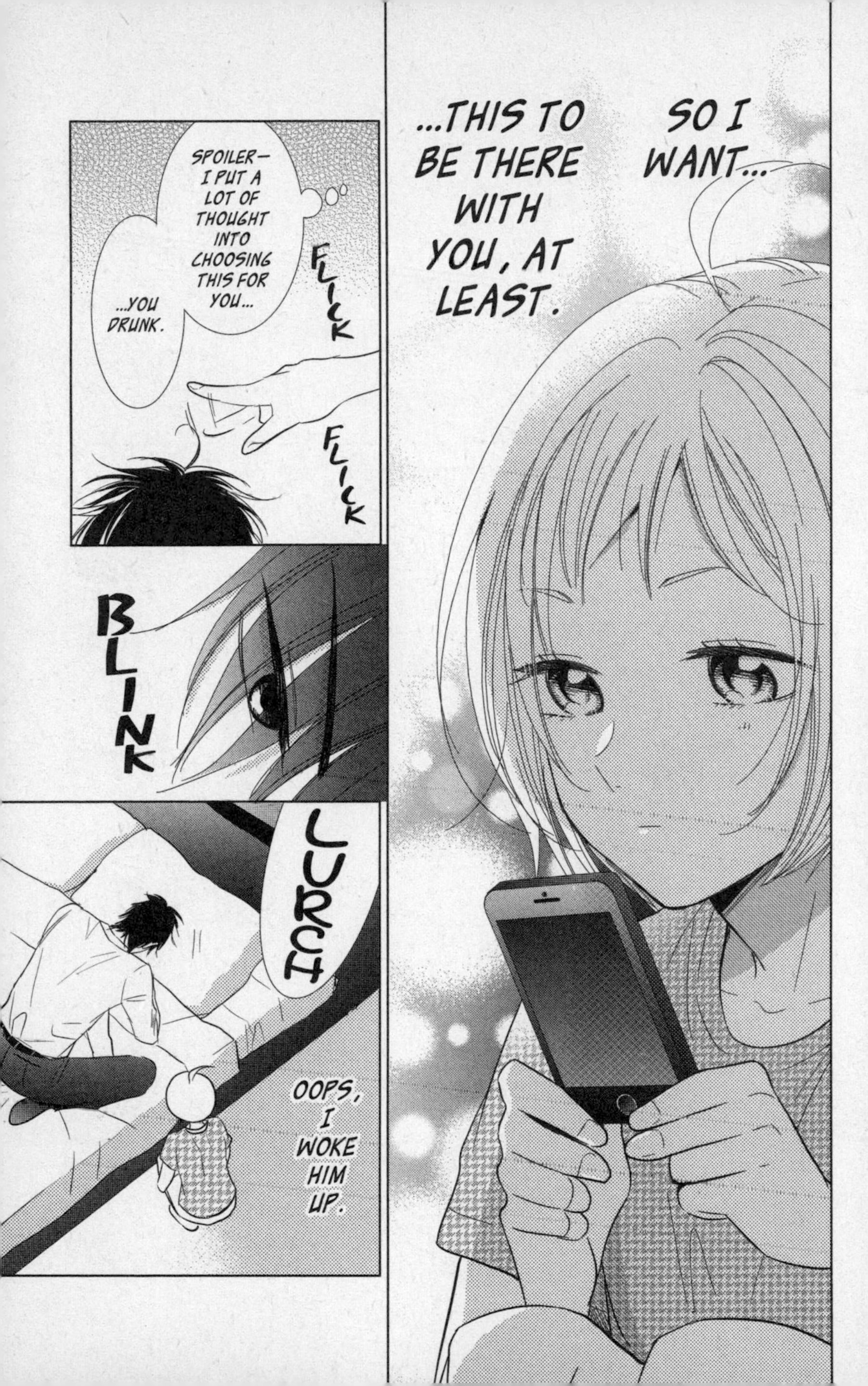
SO I WANT...
...THIS TO BE THERE WITH YOU, AT LEAST.
SPOILER— I PUT A LOT OF THOUGHT INTO CHOOSING THIS FOR YOU...
...YOU DRUNK.
FLICK
FLICK
BLINK
LURCH
OOPS, I WOKE HIM UP.

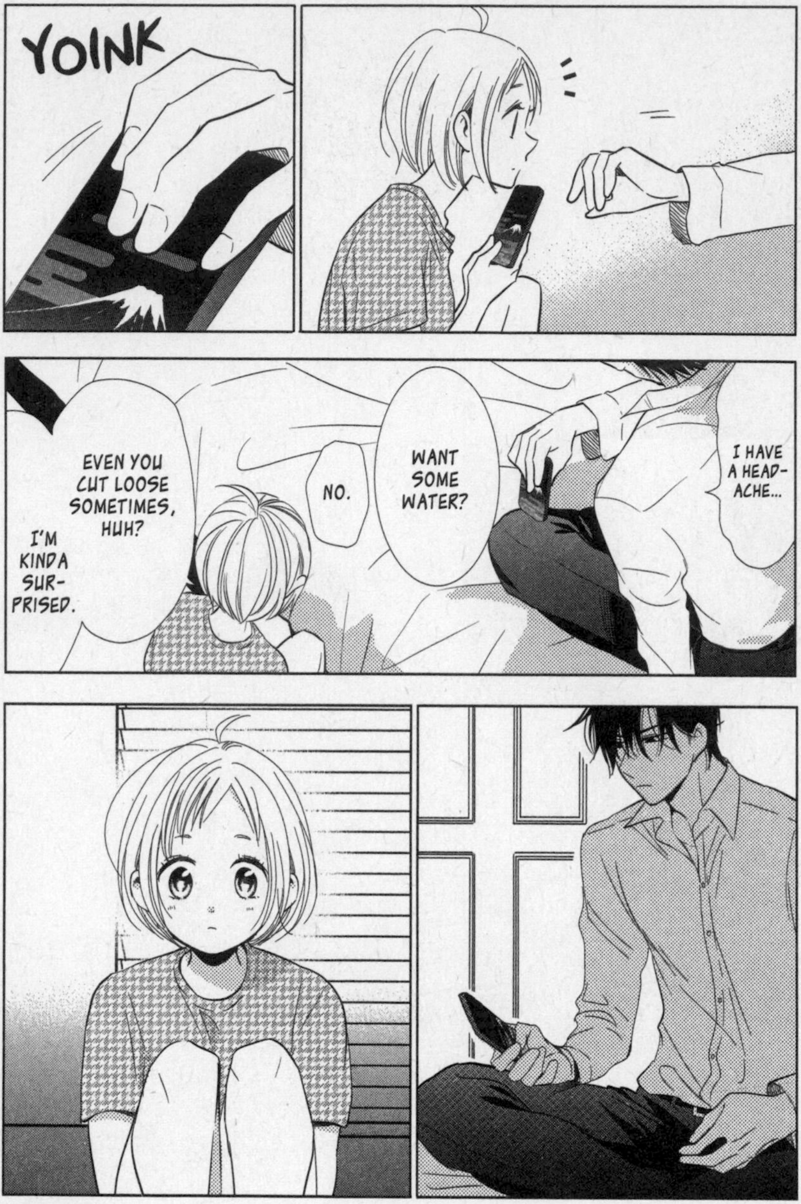
YOINK
I HAVE A HEAD-ACHE...
WANT SOME WATER?
NO.
EVEN YOU CUT LOOSE SOMETIMES, HUH?
I'M KINDA SUR-PRISED.

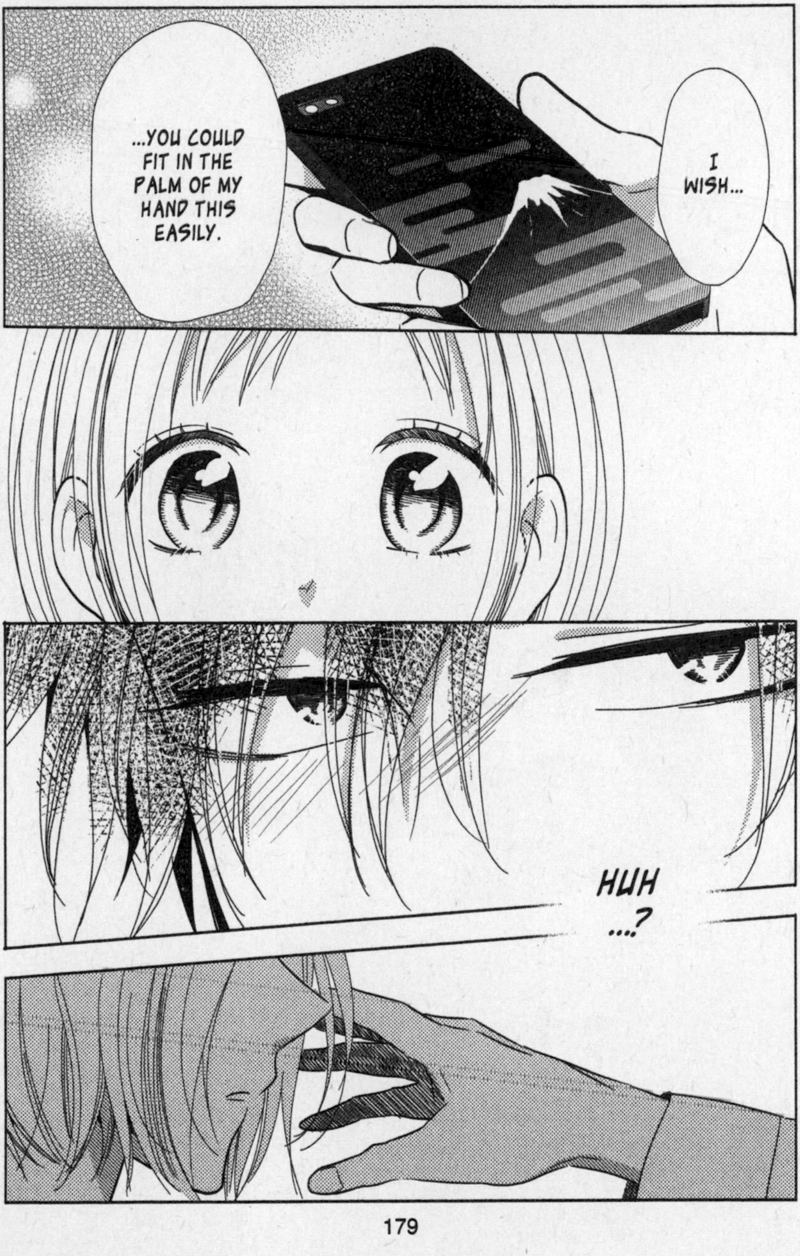
I WISH...
...YOU COULD FIT IN THE PALM OF MY HAND THIS EASILY.
HUH ...?

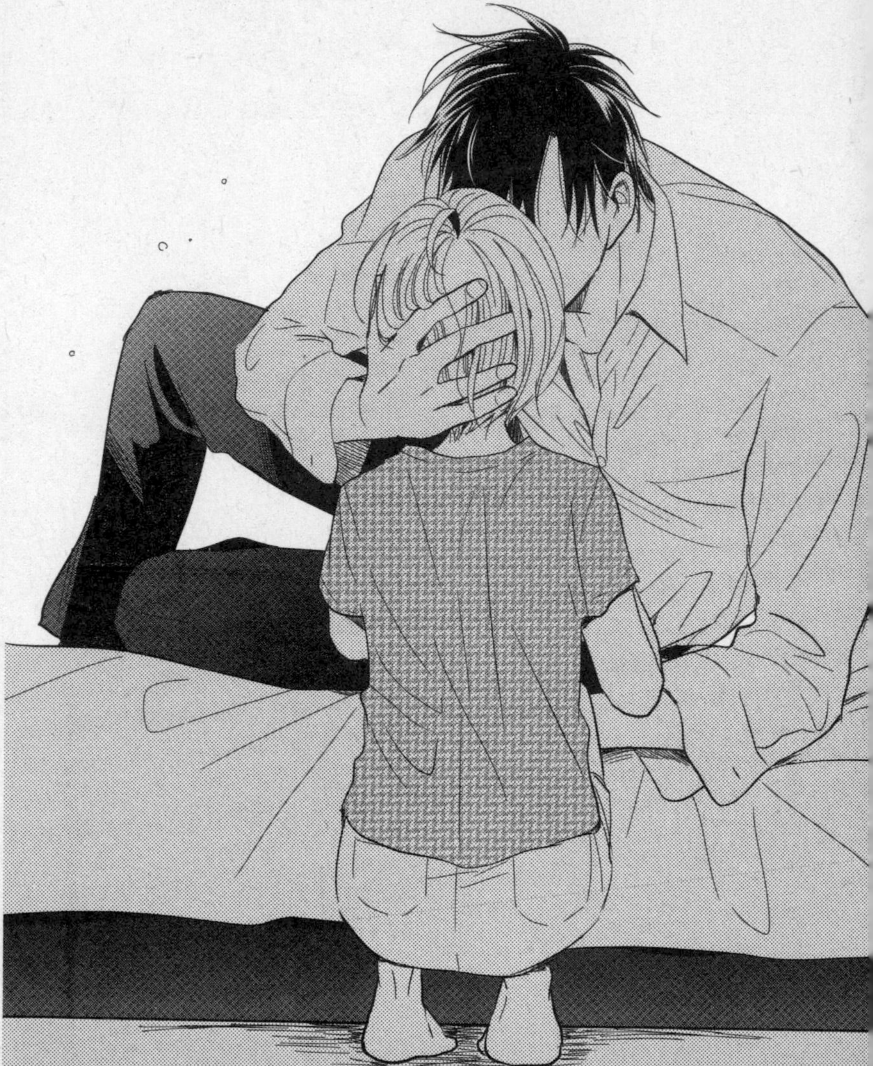

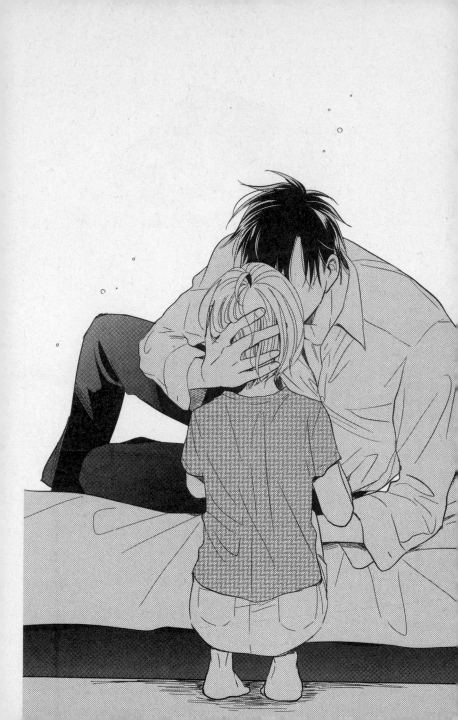

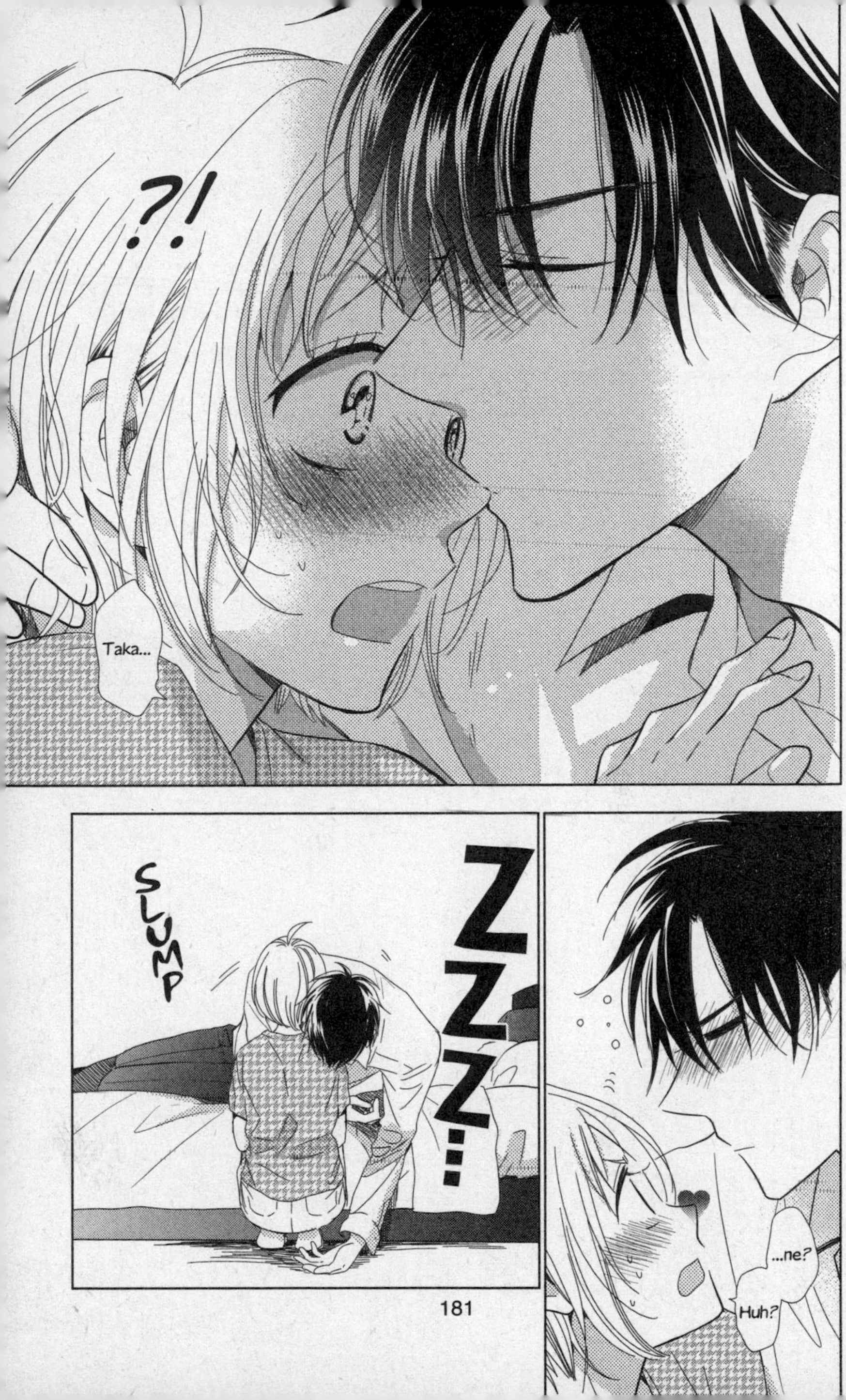
?!
Taka...
...ne?
Huh?
ZZZ...
SLUMP

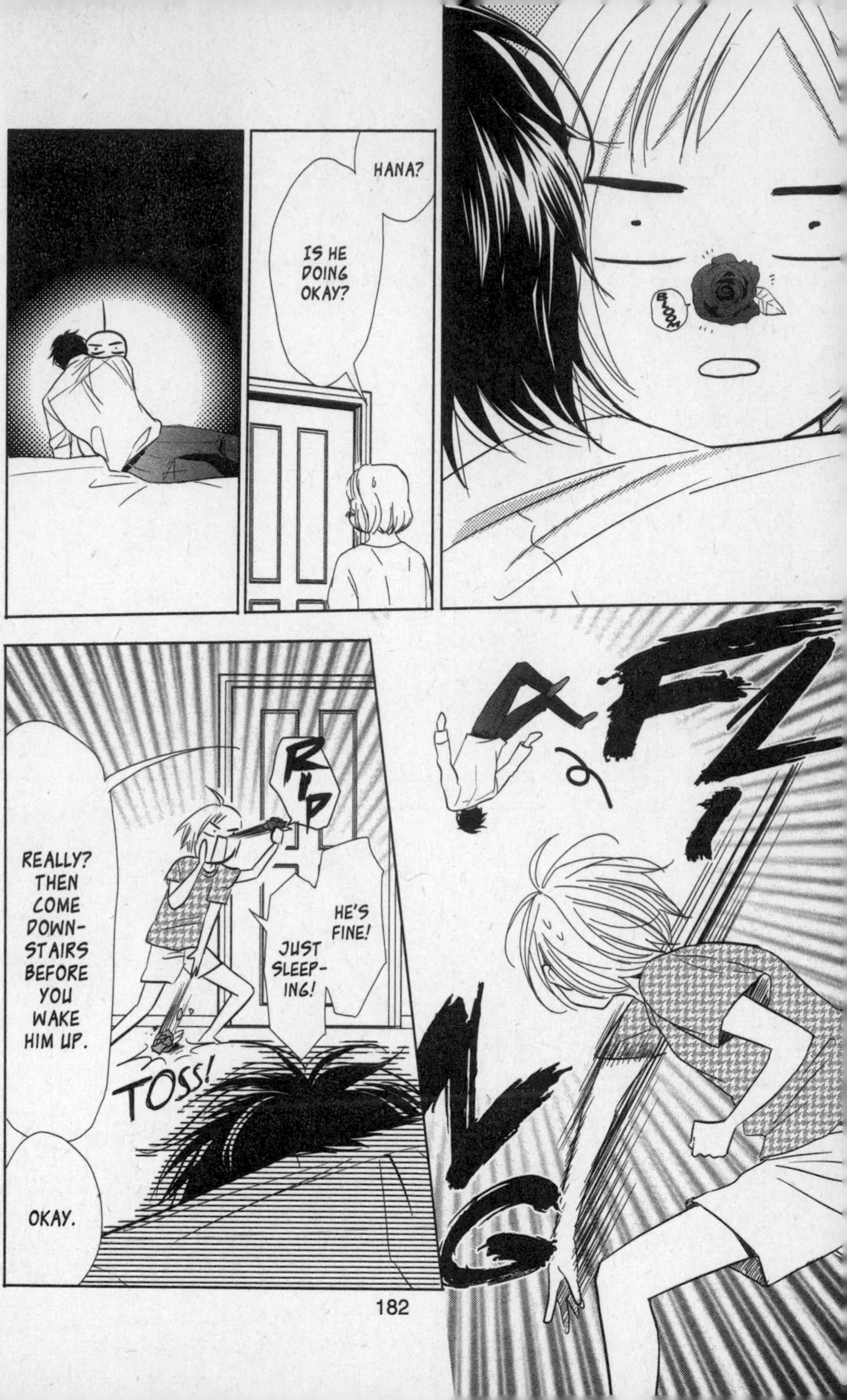
BLOOM
HANA?
IS HE DOING OKAY?
FZING
RIP
HE'S FINE!
JUST SLEEPING!
TOSS!
REALLY? THEN COME DOWN-STAIRS BEFORE YOU WAKE HIM UP.
OKAY.

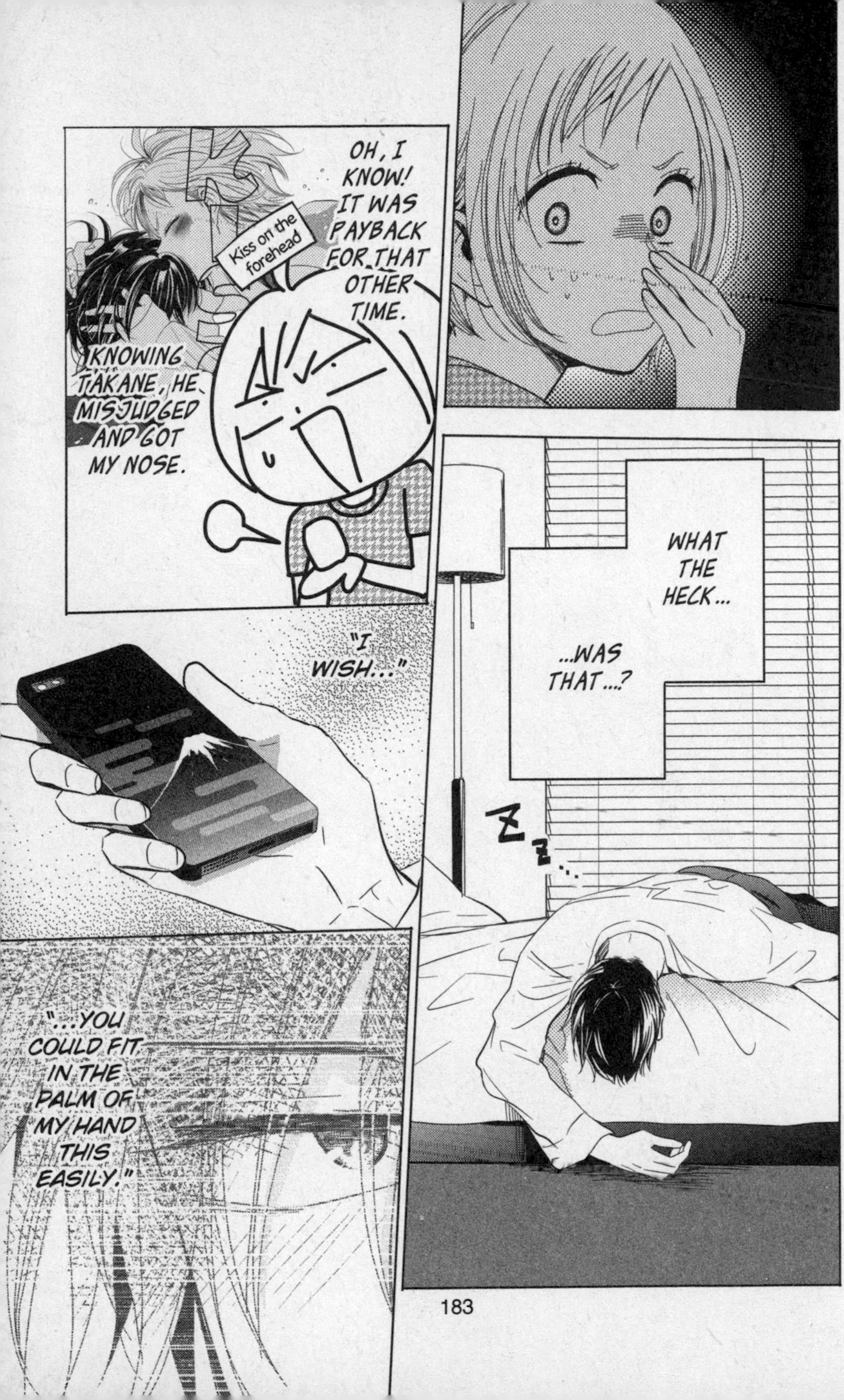
OH, I KNOW! IT WAS PAYBACK FOR THAT OTHER TIME.
Kiss on the forehead
KNOWING TAKANE, HE MISJUDGED AND GOT MY NOSE.
WHAT THE HECK...
...WAS THAT...?
ZZ...
"I WISH..."
"...YOU COULD FIT IN THE PALM OF MY HAND THIS EASILY."

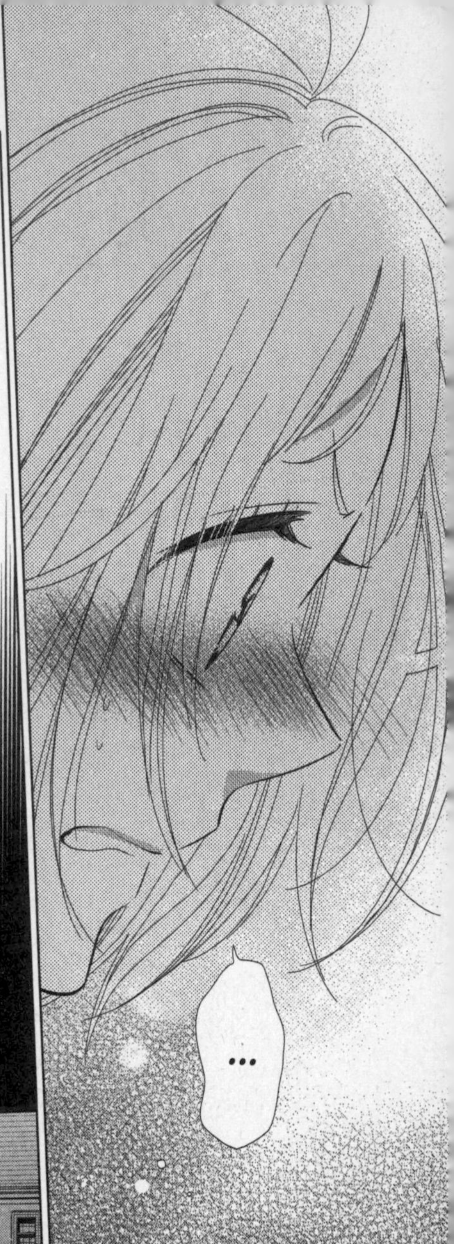
…

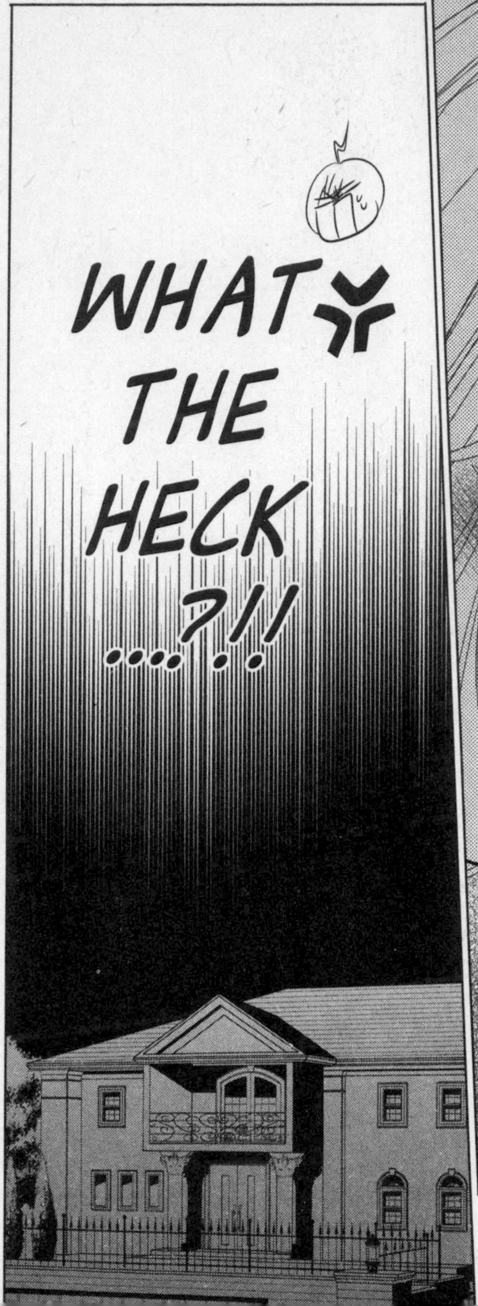
WHAT THE HECK ….?!!

Takane & Hana 10 / The End

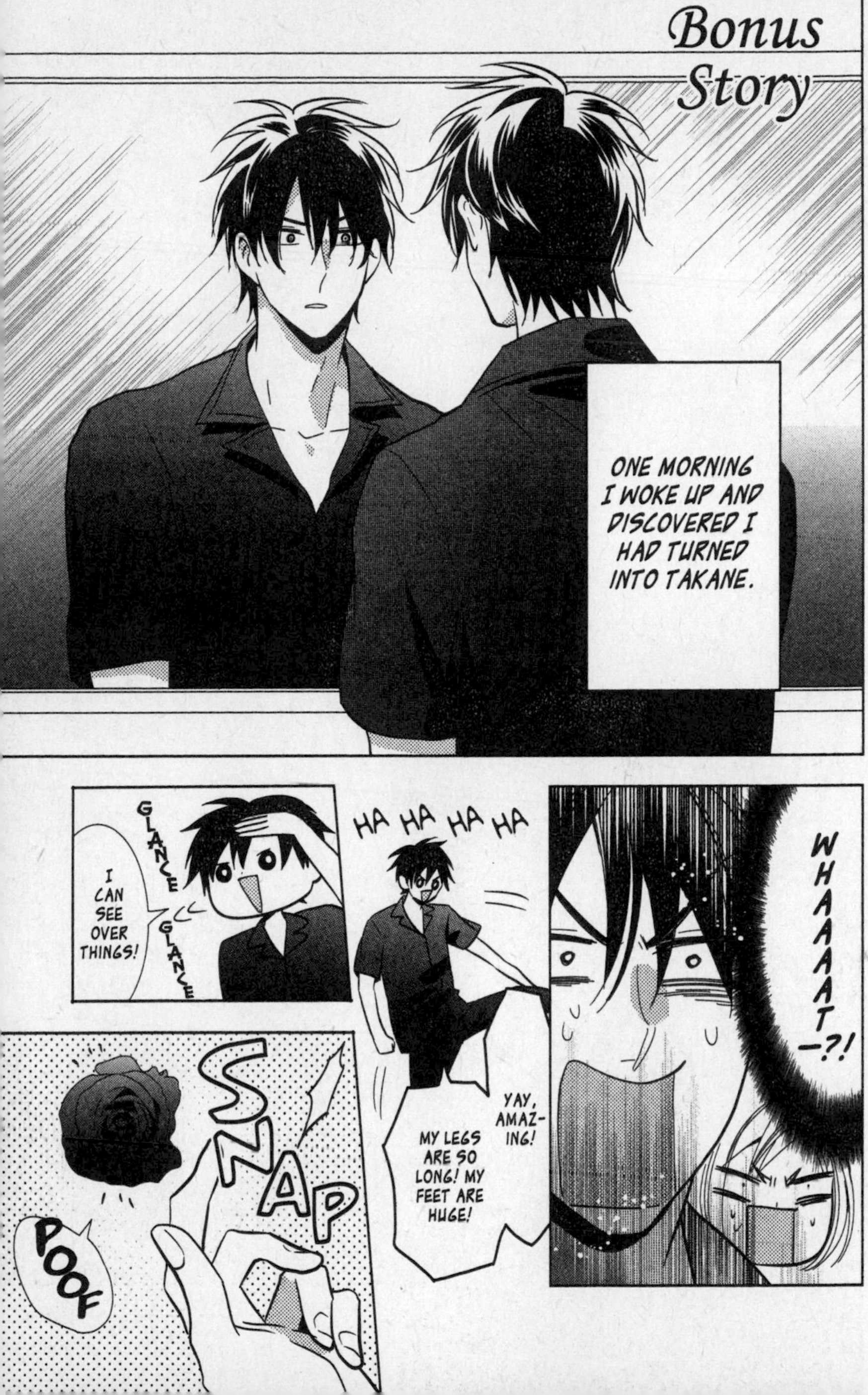
Bonus Story
ONE MORNING I WOKE UP AND DISCOVERED I HAD TURNED INTO TAKANE.
WHAAAAAT—?!
GLANCE
I CAN SEE OVER THINGS!
GLANCE
HA HA HA HA
YAY, AMAZ-ING!
MY LEGS ARE SO LONG! MY FEET ARE HUGE!
SNAP
POOF

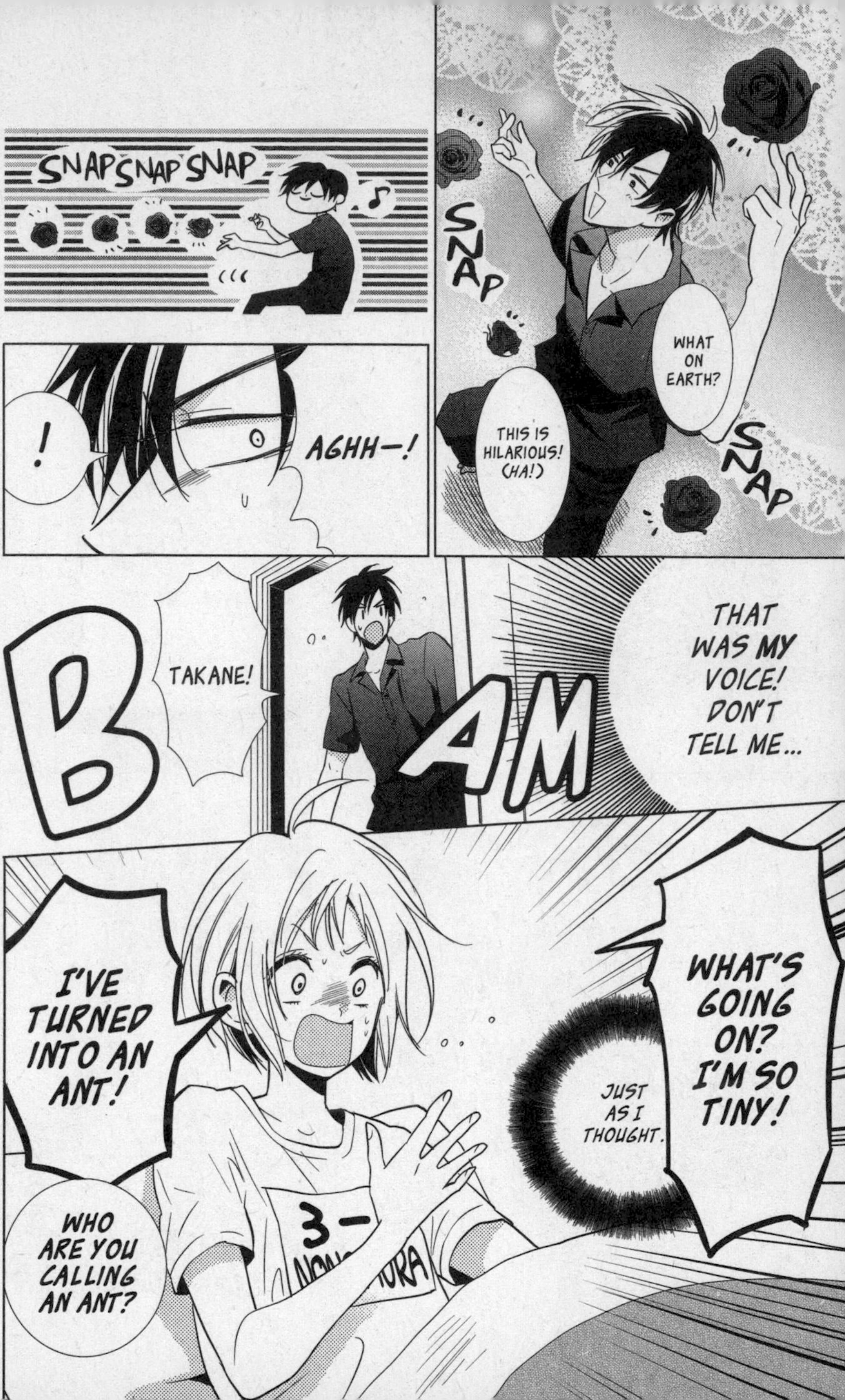
SNAP
WHAT ON EARTH?
THIS IS HILARIOUS! (HA!)
SNAP
SNAP SNAP SNAP
AGHH—!
!
THAT WAS MY VOICE! DON'T TELL ME...
BAM
TAKANE!
WHAT'S GOING ON? I'M SO TINY!
JUST AS I THOUGHT.
I'VE TURNED INTO AN ANT!
WHO ARE YOU CALLING AN ANT?
3-

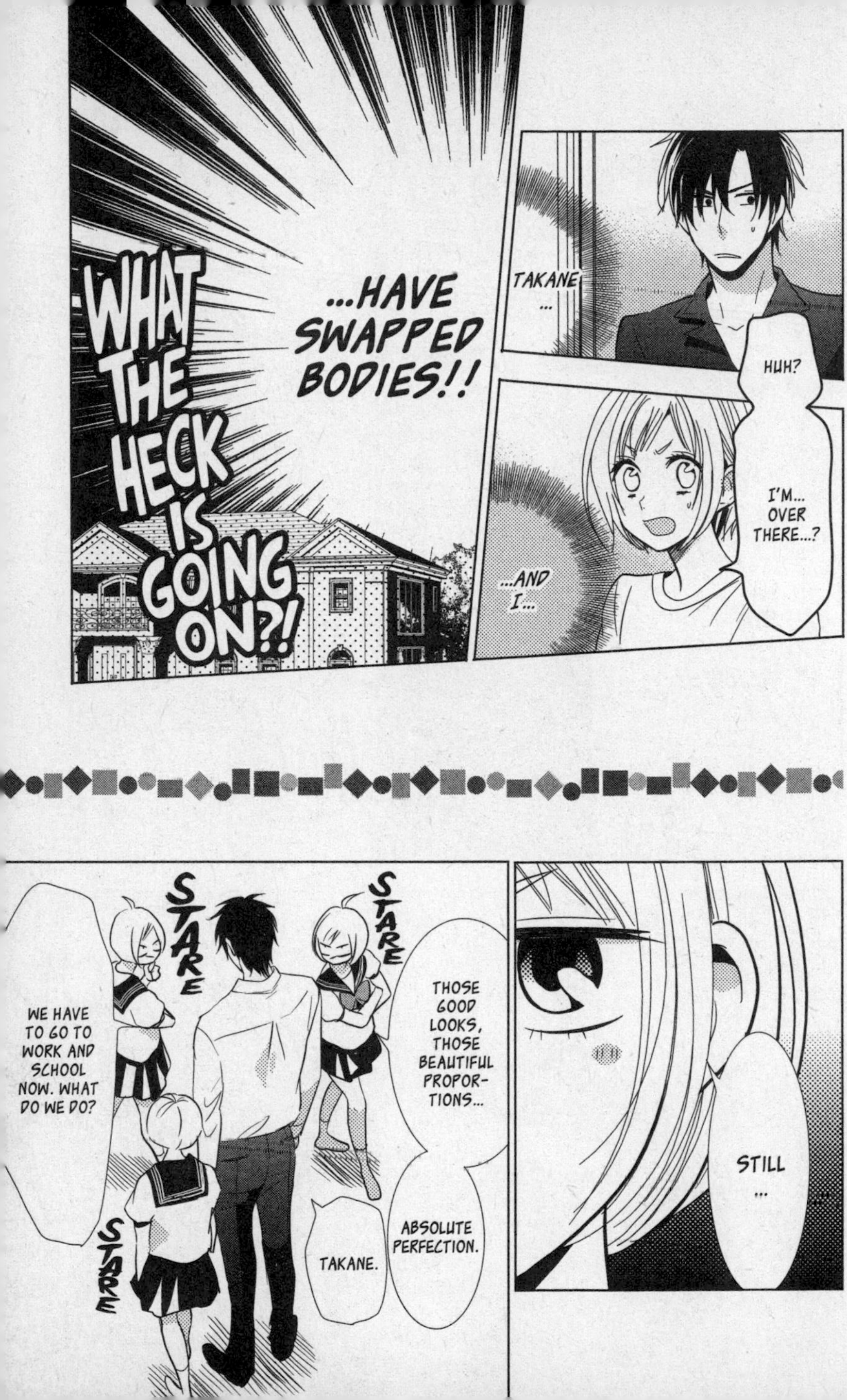
TAKANE ...
HUH?
I'M... OVER THERE...?
...AND I...
...HAVE SWAPPED BODIES!!
WHAT THE HECK IS GOING ON?!
STILL ...
STARE
THOSE GOOD LOOKS, THOSE BEAUTIFUL PROPOR-TIONS...
ABSOLUTE PERFECTION.
STARE
TAKANE.
WE HAVE TO GO TO WORK AND SCHOOL NOW. WHAT DO WE DO?
STARE

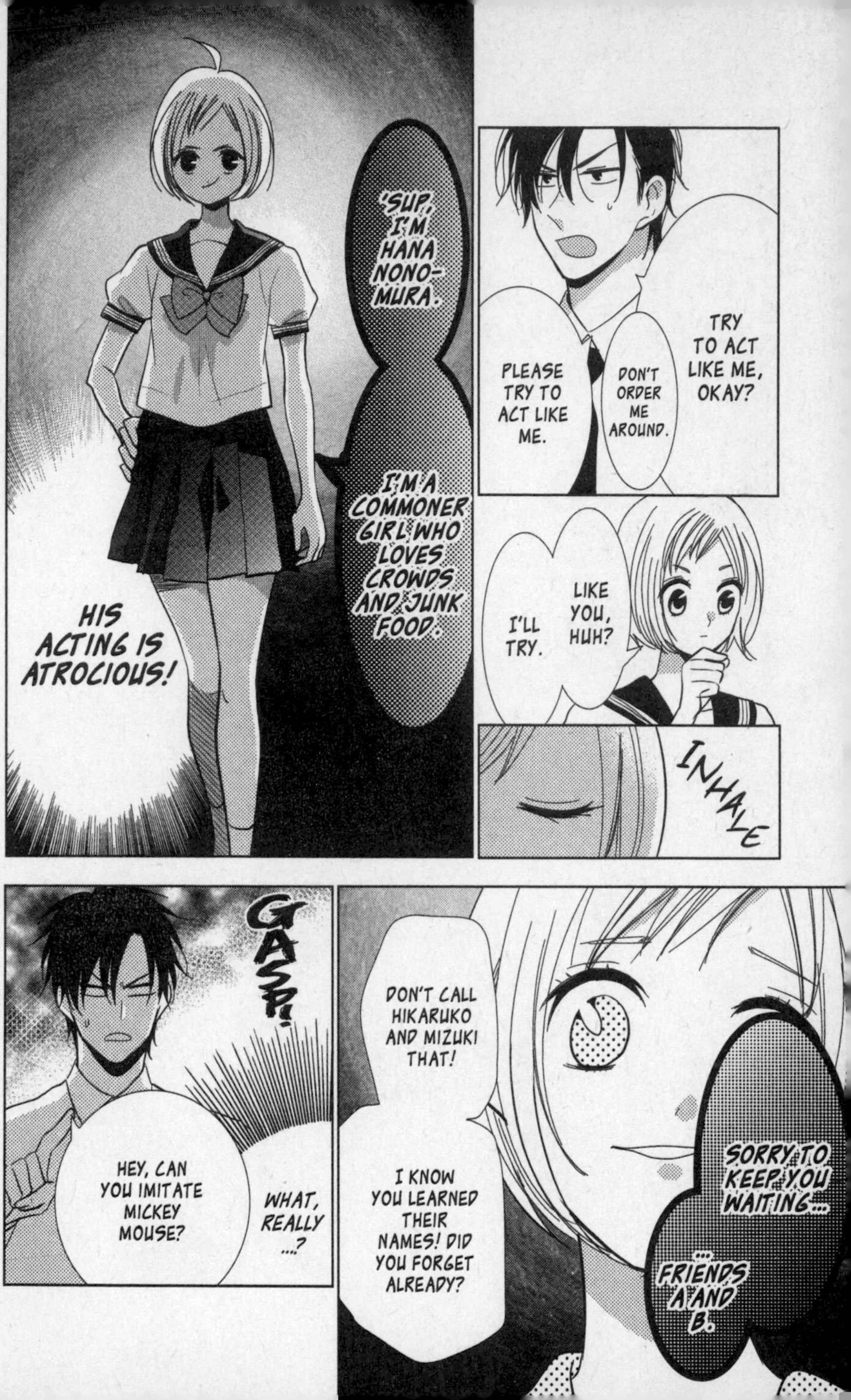
TRY TO ACT LIKE ME, OKAY?
DON'T ORDER ME AROUND.
PLEASE TRY TO ACT LIKE ME.
LIKE YOU, HUH?
I'LL TRY.
INHALE
'SUP, I'M HANA NONOMURA.
I'M A COMMONER GIRL WHO LOVES CROWDS AND JUNK FOOD.
HIS ACTING IS ATROCIOUS!
SORRY TO KEEP YOU WAITING...
...FRIENDS A AND B.
DON'T CALL HIKARUKO AND MIZUKI THAT!
I KNOW YOU LEARNED THEIR NAMES! DID YOU FORGET ALREADY?
GASP!
HEY, CAN YOU IMITATE MICKEY MOUSE?
WHAT, REALLY...?

*A character who has a very distinct voice in the manga series *GeGeGe no Kitaro*

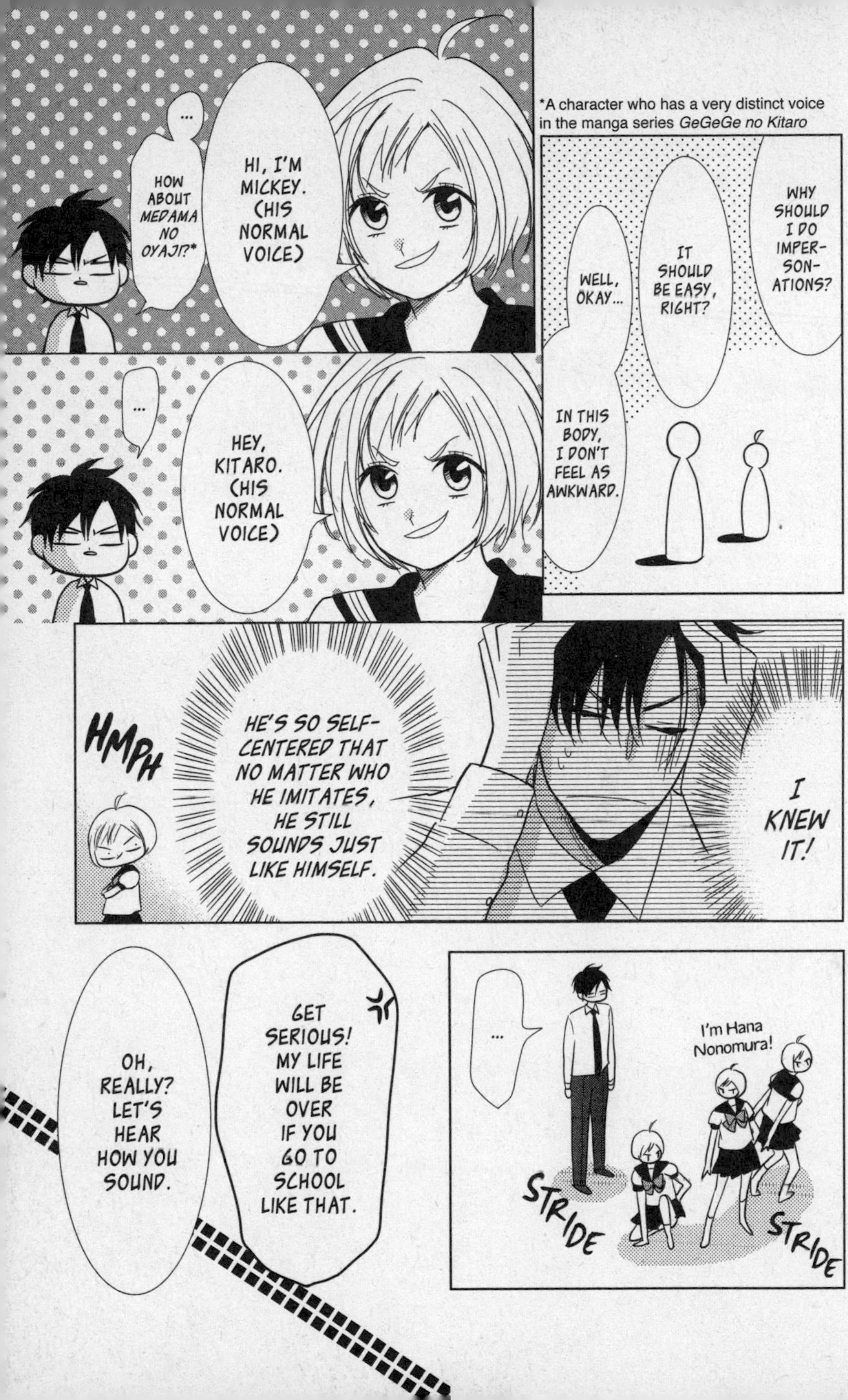
WHY SHOULD I DO IMPER-SON-ATIONS?
IT SHOULD BE EASY, RIGHT?
WELL, OKAY...
IN THIS BODY, I DON'T FEEL AS AWKWARD.
HI, I'M MICKEY. (HIS NORMAL VOICE)
...
HOW ABOUT MEDAMA NO OYAJI!?*
HEY, KITARO. (HIS NORMAL VOICE)
...
I KNEW IT!
HE'S SO SELF-CENTERED THAT NO MATTER WHO HE IMITATES, HE STILL SOUNDS JUST LIKE HIMSELF.
HMPH
...
I'm Hana Nonomura!
STRIDE
STRIDE
GET SERIOUS! MY LIFE WILL BE OVER IF YOU GO TO SCHOOL LIKE THAT.
OH, REALLY? LET'S HEAR HOW YOU SOUND.

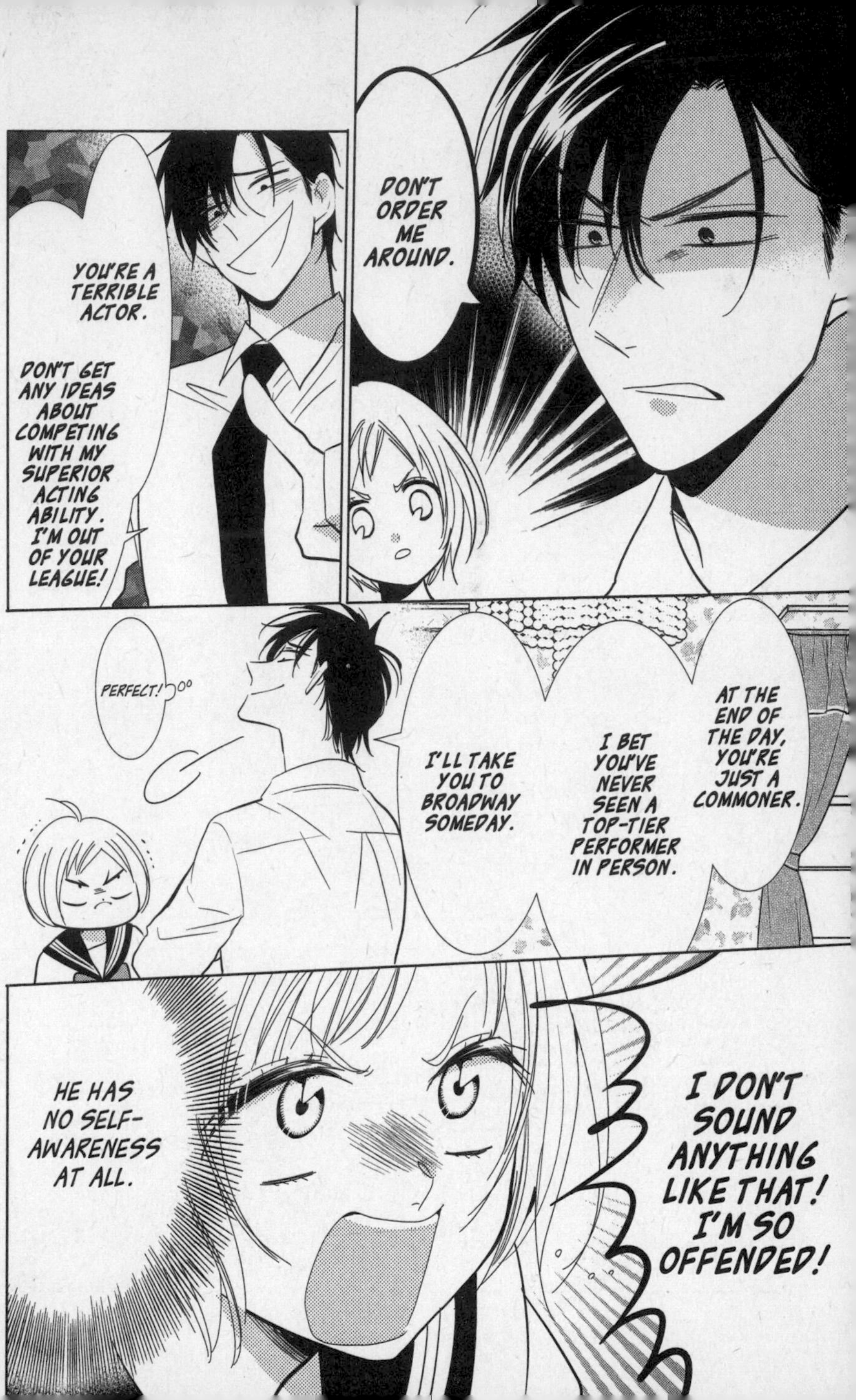
DON'T ORDER ME AROUND.
YOU'RE A TERRIBLE ACTOR.
DON'T GET ANY IDEAS ABOUT COMPETING WITH MY SUPERIOR ACTING ABILITY. I'M OUT OF YOUR LEAGUE!
AT THE END OF THE DAY, YOU'RE JUST A COMMONER.
I BET YOU'VE NEVER SEEN A TOP-TIER PERFORMER IN PERSON.
I'LL TAKE YOU TO BROADWAY SOMEDAY.
PERFECT!
I DON'T SOUND ANYTHING LIKE THAT! I'M SO OFFENDED!
HE HAS NO SELF-AWARENESS AT ALL.

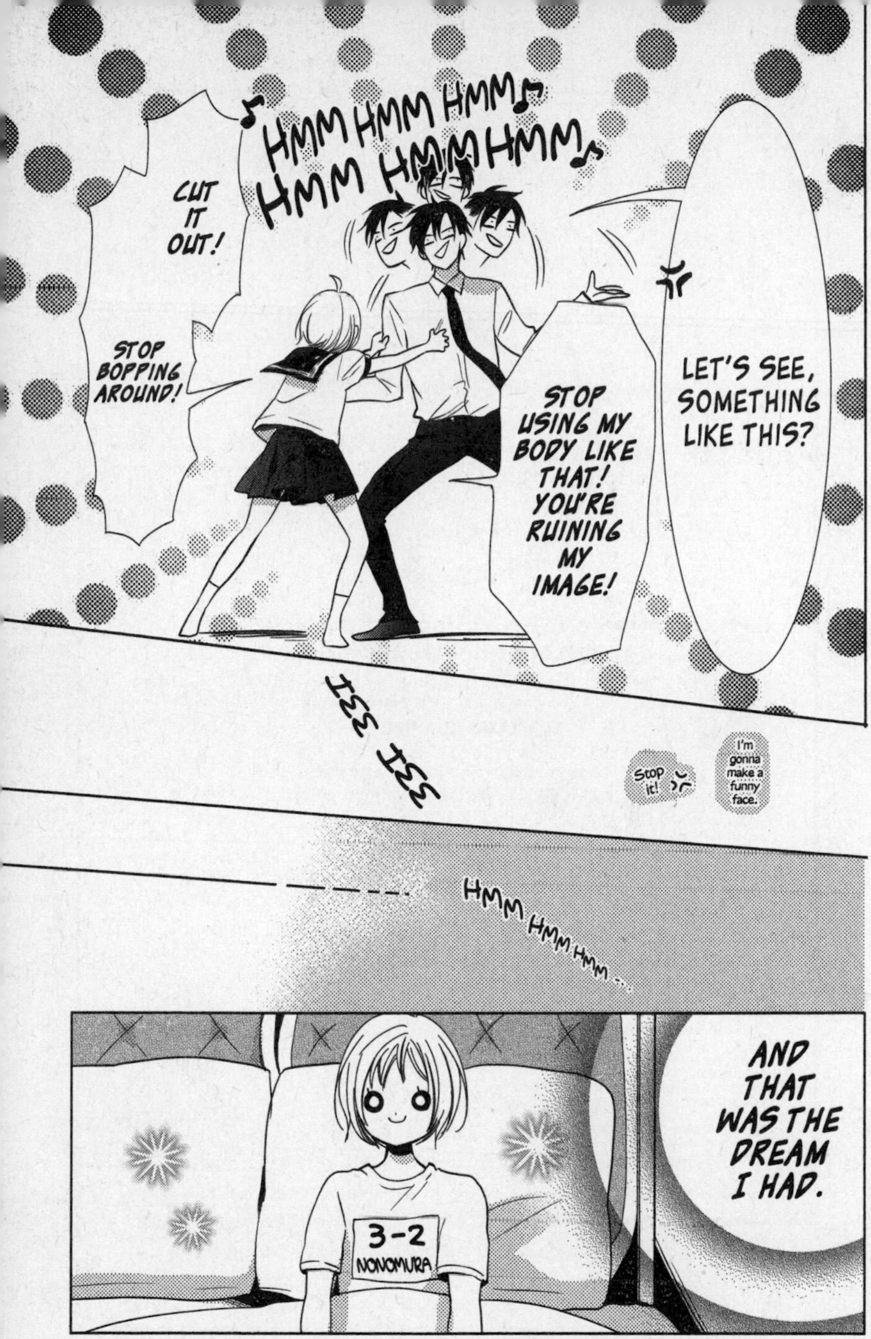
LET'S SEE, SOMETHING LIKE THIS?
STOP USING MY BODY LIKE THAT! YOU'RE RUINING MY IMAGE!
HMM HMM HMM HMM HMM HMM
CUT IT OUT!
STOP BOPPING AROUND!
TSS TSS
I'm gonna make a funny face.
Stop it!
HMM HMM HMM...
AND THAT WAS THE DREAM I HAD.
3-2
NONOMURA

Bonus Story / The End

Volume 10! We're now in the double digits! And fittingly, the theme for this cover is "Takane and Hana."*

—YUKI SHIWASU

*Takane means "high peak," as symbolized by Mt. Fuji, and Hana means "flower."

Born on March 7 in Fukuoka Prefecture, Japan, Yuki Shiwasu began her career as a manga artist after winning the top prize in the Hakusensha Athena Newcomers' Awards from *Hana to Yume* magazine. She is also the author of *Furou Kyoudai* (Immortal Siblings), which was published by Hakusensha in Japan.

Takane &Hana

VOLUME 10
SHOJO BEAT EDITION

STORY & ART BY **YUKI SHIWASU**

ENGLISH ADAPTATION **Ysabet Reinhardt MacFarlane**
TRANSLATION **JN Productions**
TOUCH-UP ART & LETTERING **Annaliese Christman**
DESIGN **Shawn Carrico**
EDITOR **Amy Yu**

Takane to Hana by Yuki Shiwasu
© Yuki Shiwasu 2018
All rights reserved.
First published in Japan in 2018 by HAKUSENSHA, Inc., Tokyo.
English language translation rights arranged with HAKUSENSHA, Inc., Tokyo.

Printed in the U.S.A.

Published by VIZ Media, LLC
P.O. Box 77010
San Francisco, CA 94107

10 9 8 7 6 5 4 3 2 1
First printing, August 2019

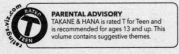

viz.com   shojobeat.com

Snow White with the Red Hair

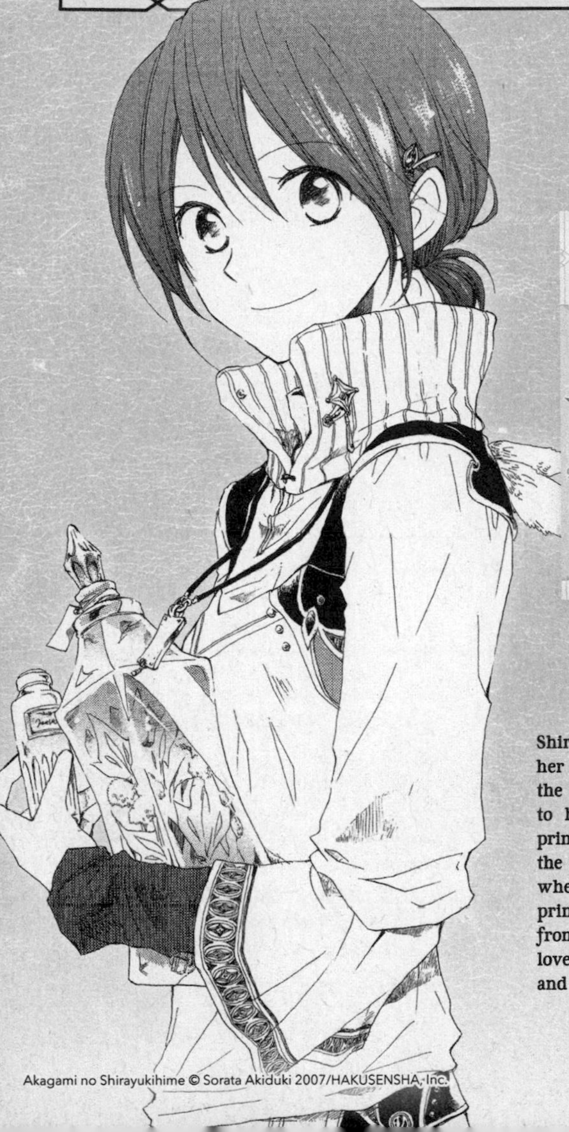

Inspired the anime!

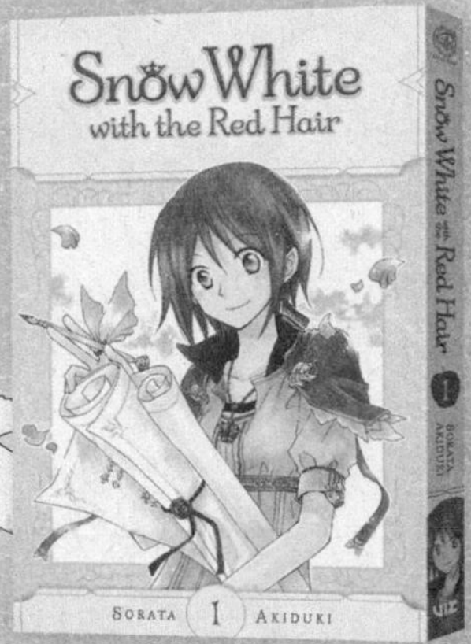
Snow White with the Red Hair
Snow White with the Red Hair
1
SORATA AKIDUKI
SORATA
1
AKIDUKI
VIZ

STORY & ART BY
SORATA AKIDUKI

Shirayuki is an herbalist famous for her naturally bright-red hair, and the prince of Tanbarun wants her all to himself! Unwilling to become the prince's possession, she seeks shelter in the woods of the neighboring kingdom, where she gains an unlikely ally—the prince of that kingdom! He rescues her from her plight, and thus begins the love story between a lovestruck prince and an unusual herbalist.

RATED T TEEN

VIZ

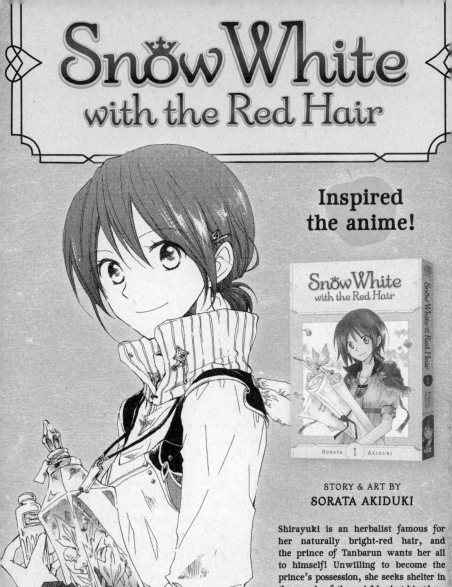

Immortal tales of the past
and present from the world
of *Vampire Knight.*

VAMPIRE KNIGHT
MEMORIES

STORY & ART BY **Matsuri Hino**

Vampire Knight returns with stories
that delve into Yuki and Zero's time
as a couple in the past and explore
the relationship between Yuki's
children and Kaname in the present.

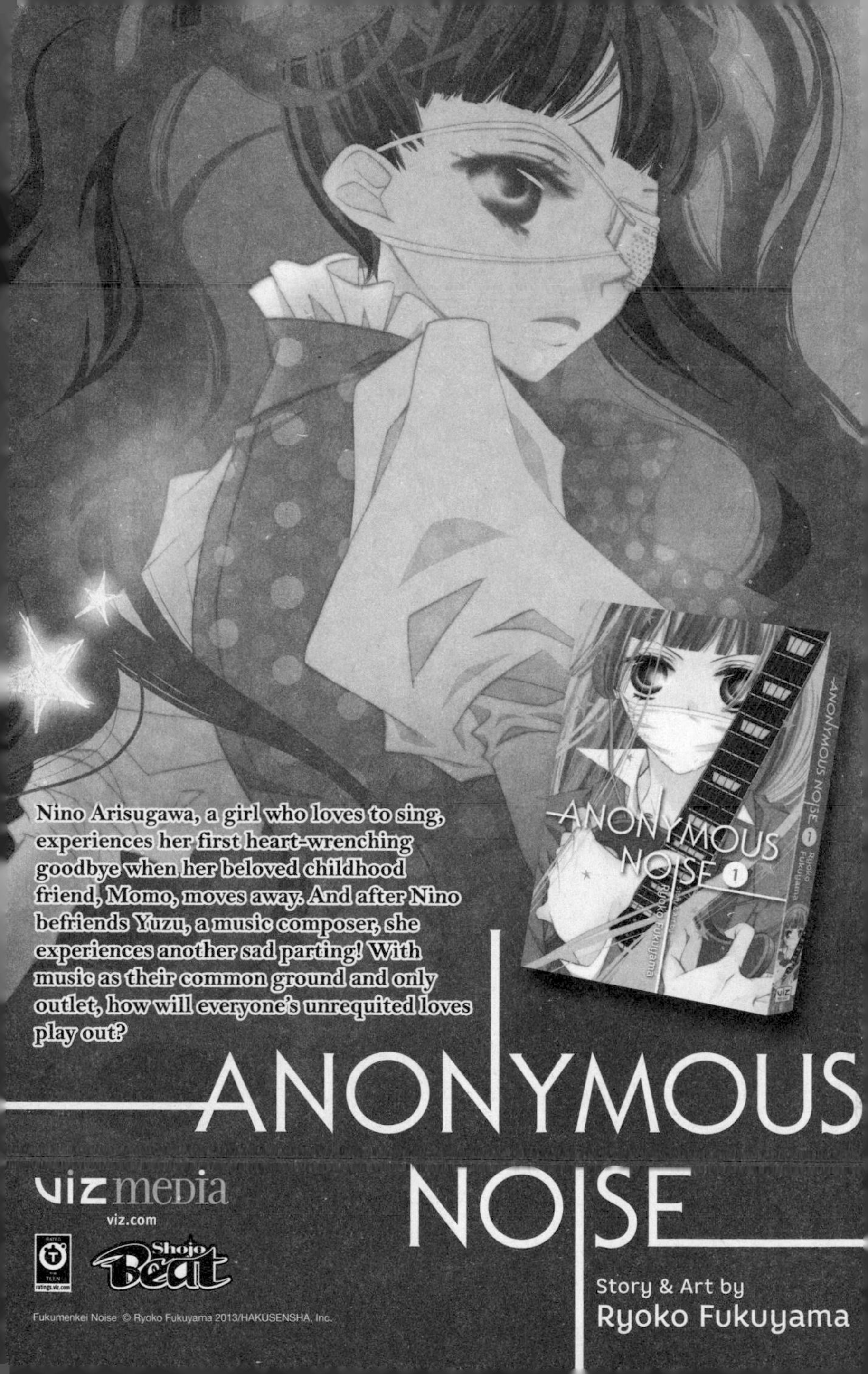
ANONYMOUS NOISE
1
Ryoko Fukuyama
VIZ
Nino Arisugawa, a girl who loves to sing, experiences her first heart-wrenching goodbye when her beloved childhood friend, Momo, moves away. And after Nino befriends Yuzu, a music composer, she experiences another sad parting! With music as their common ground and only outlet, how will everyone's unrequited loves play out?
ANONYMOUS NOISE
VIZ media
viz.com
T TEEN
ratings.viz.com
Shojo Beat
Story & Art by
Ryoko Fukuyama
Fukumenkei Noise © Ryoko Fukuyama 2013/HAKUSENSHA, Inc.

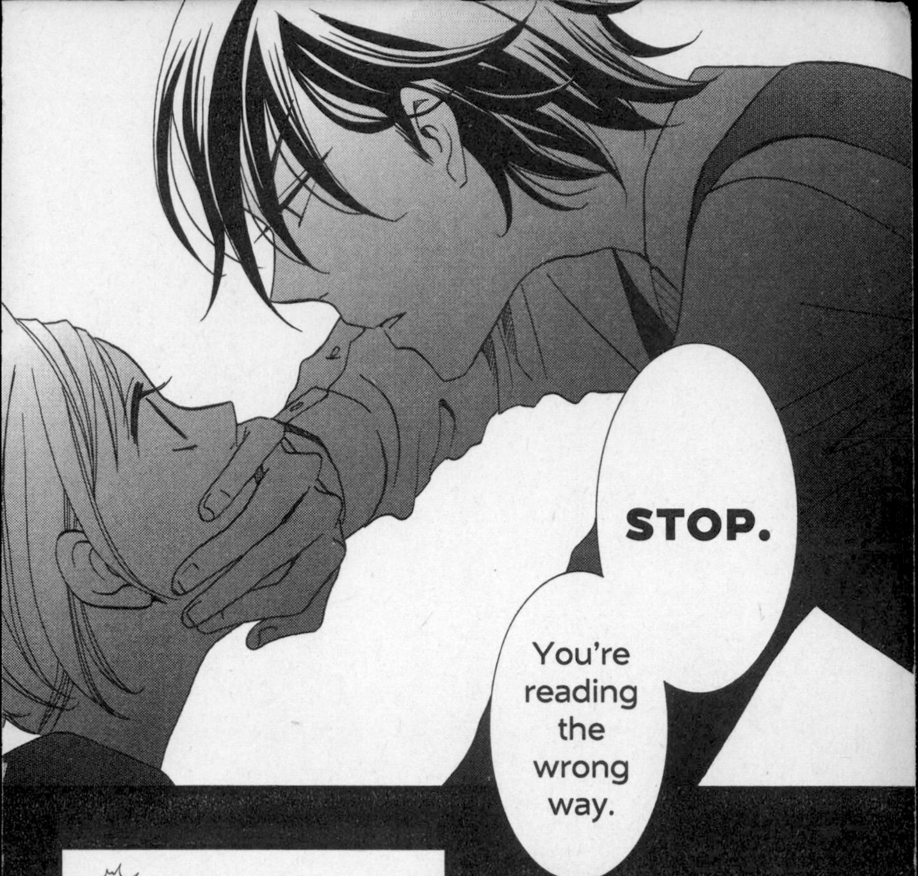
STOP.
You're reading the wrong way.

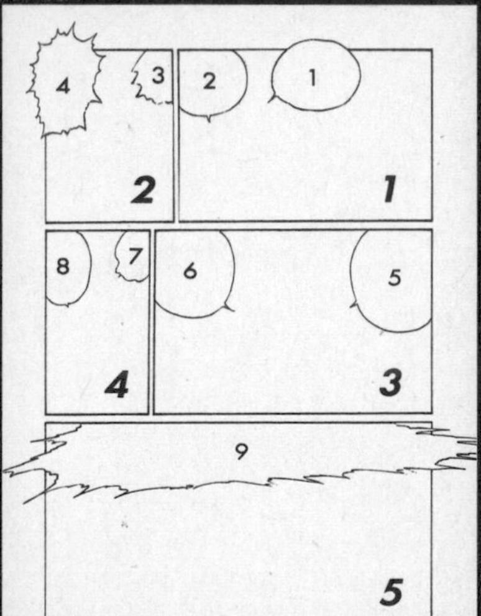
1
2
3
4
1
2
5
6
7
8
3
4
9
5
142

In keeping with the original Japanese comic format, this book reads from right to left—so action, sound effects and word balloons are completely reversed to preserve the orientation of the original artwork.

Check out the diagram shown here to get the hang of things, and then turn to the other side of the book to get started!